REDISCOVERING THE TRADITIONS OF ISRAEL

Studies in Biblical Literature

Number 16
REDISCOVERING THE TRADITIONS OF ISRAEL

REDISCOVERING THE TRADITIONS OF ISRAEL

Third Edition

by

Douglas A. Knight

Society of Biblical Literature
Atlanta

REDISCOVERING THE TRADITIONS OF ISRAEL

Copyright © 2006 Douglas A. Knight

All rights reserved. No part of this work may be reproduced or transmitted in any form or by any means, electronic or mechanical, including photocopying and recording, or by means of any information storage or retrieval system, except as may be expressly permitted by the 1976 Copyright Act or in writing from the publisher. Requests for permission should be addressed in writing to the Rights and Permissions Office, Society of Biblical Literature, 825 Houston Mill Road, Atlanta, GA 30329 USA.

Library of Congress Cataloging-in-Publication Data

Knight, Douglas A.
    Rediscovering the traditions of Israel / by Douglas A. Knight. — 3rd ed.
       p. cm. — (Society of biblical literature studies in biblical literature ; 16)
    Includes bibliographical references and index.
    ISBN-13: 978-1-58983-162-9 (paper binding : alk. paper)
    ISBN-10: 1-58983-162-4 (paper binding : alk. paper)
    1. Bible. O.T.—Criticism, interpretation, etc.—History—Modern period, 1500-
I. Title. II. Series: Studies in biblical literature (Society of Biblical Literature) ; 16.
    BS1160.K57 2006
    221.6'70903—dc22   2006013718

14 13 12 11 10 09 08 07 06   5 4 3 2 1
Printed in the United States of America on acid-free, recycled paper
conforming to ANSI/NISO Z39.48-1992 (R1997) and ISO 9706:1994
standards for paper permanence.

CONTENTS

Preface xi
Abbreviations xv
PROLEGOMENA 1

1. TRADITIO ET TRADITUM 5
   A. Aspects of *Traditio* 5
   B. Aspects of *Traditum* 9

2. WHAT IS "TRADITION HISTORY"? 17
   A. Previous Understandings 17
   B. Definition of Tradition and of Tradition History 21
   C. Methodology 24
   D. Yield 25

3. SCOPE AND METHOD OF THE PRESENT STUDY 27

   PART 1: THE RISE OF THE TRADITIO-HISTORICAL RESEARCH OF THE
   OLD TESTAMENT (EXCLUDING SCANDINAVIAN CONTRIBUTIONS)

4. RICHARD SIMON AND THE AWAKENING TO THE PROBLEM OF
   OLD TESTAMENT TRADITION 33
   A. Background 33
   B. Simon's Critical Research 37
   C. Understanding of Tradition 40
   D. Influence on Later Researchers 42

5. THE ERA OF SOURCE CRITICISM: GENERAL NEGLECT OF THE
   PRECOMPOSITIONAL STAGE 45
   A. The Beginnings of Source Criticism 45
   B. Johann Gottfried Herder: Impulses from Romanticism ... 47
   C. Johann Christoph Nachtigal: Recognition of
      Precompositional Developments 49
   D. Julius Wellhausen: The Documentary Hypothesis
      and Tradition 51

    E. August Klostermann: The Crystallization Hypothesis and Public Recital 55
6. HERMANN GUNKEL AND THE RECOGNITION OF THE IMPORTANCE OF ANCIENT TRADITIONS 57
    A. The Influence of Albert Eichhorn 57
    B. New Directions 58
    C. *Schöpfung und Chaos:* Impulses from Religionsgeschichte 60
    D. Commentary on Genesis: Impulses from Gattungsgeschichte 62
7. FROM HUGO GRESSMANN TO ALBRECHT ALT: SECURING AND EXTENDING THE FOUNDATION 67
    A. Hugo Gressmann and Tradition Criticism 67
    B. Early Understandings of Oral Tradition 69
    C. Albrecht Alt's Fundamental Contributions 73
8. GERHARD VON RAD AND MARTIN NOTH: THE FATHERS OF TRADITIO-HISTORICAL RESEARCH 77
    A. Gerhard von Rad 77
        1. The Form-Critical Problem of the Hexateuch 78
            a. Point of Departure 78
            b. The Traditio-Historical Independence of the Sinai Tradition from the Exodus–Conquest Complex 81
            c. The Fusion of the Tradition Complexes by the Jahwist 83
        2. Commentary on Genesis 87
            a. Comparison with Gunkel's Commentary on Genesis ... 88
            b. Hermeneutical Priority of the Jahwist's Composition .. 89
            c. Tradition History in the Service of Old Testament Theology 91
            d. Assessment of Israel's Sagas 92
        3. Theology of the Old Testament 94
            a. The Subject Matter: Israel's Testimonies to Jahweh's Involvement in History 95
            b. Theological Reception of the Traditio-Historical and Form-Critical Methods 96
            c. Tradition and History 98
            d. Tradition History and Heilsgeschichte 102
            e. A Traditio-Historical Relationship between Old Testament and New Testament? 105
            f. The Importance of von Rad's Use of Tradition History .. 108
    B. Martin Noth 109
        1. History of the Pentateuchal Traditions 109

CONTENTS

      a. Task and Point of Departure 110
      b. Isolating the Five Pentateuchal Themes and the
         Additional Elements of Tradition................................ 113
      c. The Merging of the Themes and the Individual
         Traditions 116
    2. Traditio-Historical Study of the Deuteronomist's and
       of the Chronicler's Compositions 120
      a. The Deuteronomistic History 120
      b. The Chronicler's History 124
    3. History of Israel 126
  C. Summary 130

9. SUBSEQUENT EXAMPLES OF TRADITIO-HISTORICAL STUDIES 135
  A. Hartmut Gese on Ezekiel 40–48 135
  B. Wolfgang Richter on Judges 3–9 139
  C. Odil Hannes Steck's History of a Notion 142

10. CRITICAL REACTION TO TRADITIO-HISTORICAL RESEARCH 147
  A. The Dependency of Traditio-Historical Analysis on Other
     Investigative Procedures 148
    1. The Issue of External Evidence 148
    2. Traditio-Historical Criteria and the Question of Historicity 151
  B. The Question of Traditio-Historical Overkill 154
    1. Overextension of the Method 154
    2. Implausibility of the Results 157
  C. The Need for a Basic Trust in the Traditional Outline
     of History 159
  D. The Necessity of Avoiding Modern Cultural Presuppositions 160
  E. Summary 161

PART 2: THE SCANDINAVIAN DEBATE ON TRADITIO-HISTORICAL PROBLEMS

PRELIMINARY REMARKS 165

11. THE BEGINNINGS 169
  A. Sigmund Mowinckel's Early Work on Prophetic Tradition 169
  B. Johannes Pedersen: Initial Opposition to Literary Criticism 171
  C. Ivar Hylander and Basic Problems of Method 174
    1. The Traditio-Critical Task 174
    2. Literary Criticism and Tradition History 175
  D. Henrik Samuel Nyberg: The Thesis of a Predominant
     Oral Tradition 177
    1. The Nature of Transmission in Israel 178

2. Tradition History of Numbers 16–17 180
   3. Contributions to the Debate 181
 E. Harris Birkeland: Establishing the Thesis and
    Demonstrating Its Consequences..182
 F. Johannes Lindblom's Research: Evidence of the Force of
    These Ideas...185
   1. The Prophetic Literature...186
   2. Tradition History of the Book of Job 188
 G. Sigmund Mowinckel's Further Studies..190
   1. The Indispensable Work of Literary Criticism 190
   2. The Rise of the Prophetic Literature...191
     a. Oral Tradition as the Foundation...192
     b. The Prophetic Word as Authoritative 193
     c. Interpretation and Actualization among the Disciples 194
     d. Creation of the Written Literature 195
   3. Summary..195

12. Ivan Engnell: The Center of the Debate..197
 A. Engnell's Traditio-Historical Introduction to the
    Old Testament 198
   1. The Importance Given Tradition History 199
   2. Oral Tradition and Its Significance for Text Criticism 200
   3. The Literary Forms..202
   4. Tradition History as an Alternative to Literary Criticism..........203
   5. Tradition History of the Pentateuch..205
 B. Prophecy and Tradition: Mowinckel versus Engnell.....................208
   1. Mowinckel 208
     a. The Need for Both Traditio-Historical and
        Literary-Critical Research 208
     b. The Critical Stratification of the Tradition...........................209
     c. Source Analysis of Oral Tradition..210
     d. General Principles of Israelite Tradition 211
   2. Engnell 212
     a. Limiting the Range of Oral Tradition...................................213
     b. *Ipsissima Verba* and Tradition...214
     c. The Analytical Task..214
     d. General Principles of Tradition History...............................215
   3. The Result of the Debate 216
 C. Engnell's Subsequent Work...217
   1. Oral Tradition 217
   2. "Primary" versus "Secondary" Elements......................................218
   3. The Traditio-Historical Method 219

CONTENTS

  4. The Primacy of Traditio-Historical Research 219
13. The "Uppsala Circle" 221
  A. Alfred Haldar: Prophetic Circles and Transmission................223
    1. Associations of Cult Prophets 224
    2. Prophetic Tradition and Transmission 225
  B. Geo Widengren's Refutation of the Thesis of a Predominant Oral Tradition 228
    1. The Importance of Writing in the Ancient Near East.........229
    2. Supportive Evidence 231
      a. Mesopotamia 232
      b. Arabic Cultures 232
      c. The Old Testament 234
    3. Conclusions 236
  C. Helmer Ringgren 238
    1. Oral Transmission as Explanation for Certain Variant Readings..238
    2. The Place of Tradition History in Old Testament Research........240
  D. Gösta W. Ahlström 241
    1. Tradition History of Psalm 89......................................241
    2. The "Oral/Written" Debate 243
  E. R. A. Carlson on Second Samuel 245
    1. Traditio-Historical Method and Scope 245
    2. A Pre-Deuteronomic Davidic Epic 248
    3. Compositional Analysis of Second Samuel 250
    4. Evaluation of His Traditio-Historical Analysis 252
14. The Influence of And Response to the Uppsala Circle 255
  A. Aage Bentzen 255
    1. Hypothesis of Hexateuchal Stratification 257
    2. Israel and Ancient Near Eastern Motifs 258
    3. The Book of Daniel..258
    4. Summary 259
  B. Arvid S. Kapelrud 260
    1. The Origin of the Ezra-Narrative 260
    2. Pentateuch Miscellanea 262
    3. Origin and Development of the Book of Joel 263
  C. Eduard Nielsen 264
    1. The Thesis of a Predominant Oral Tradition 265
    2. Tradition History of the Decalogue 268
      a. Form-Critical Reconstruction of the Original Decalogue 269

CONTENTS

       b. Traditio-Historical Analysis..272
  D. Magne Sæbø on Deutero-Zechariah 275
     1. Analytical Orientation and Procedure..................................276
     2. Text Criticism Understood Traditio-Historically......................277
     3. Form Criticism Understood Traditio-Historically....................281
     4. Preliminary Conclusions about Composition
        and Background..284
     5. Summary..286

15. CRITIQUE..287
  A. Oral Composition and Transmission..289
     1. The Question of Reliability...290
     2. Comparative Evidence..291
     3. The Critical Analysis of "Oral Literature" 291
     4. The Stage of Literary Fixation..292
     5. The Scandinavian Contributions...293
  B. The Importance of Religio-Historical Studies.............................294
     1. On the Divine-Kingship Ideology..294
     2. Constitutive Elements of the *Traditum*..................................296
  C. General Contributions and the Present State of
     the Research...297

EPILOGUE: DOES TRADITION HISTORY HAVE A FUTURE?......................301
  A. Historiography 303
  B. Social History 307
  C. Ideological Criticism 309
  D. The Tradents: Who and Who Not?..311
  E. Modern Exegetes..315
  F. Conclusion...317

Bibliography..319
Index of Authors..349
Index of Subjects..355

Preface

The present study, a doctoral dissertation submitted in October 1972 to the Theologische Fakultät der Georg-August-Universität in Göttingen, Germany, seeks to examine the rise of Old Testament traditio-historical research, to assay the investigative methods that have been employed by various tradition historians, and to probe certain historical, technical, and theological issues that bear upon this research. Because of the nature of such a history and critique of the research, it has seemed advisable to quote frequently from sources used—especially since much of the literature (e.g., Scandinavian) may not be accessible to most scholars. Usually these quotations are in the original language, even without "modernizing" older German or French orthography. Only for excerpts from originally Norwegian, Swedish, Danish, or Dutch literature have I made translations into English.

One who has just completed formal education is intensely aware of the debt owed to many people, all of whom cannot easily be mentioned. Initial appreciation for the riches of the Bible was instilled in me by my parents, Allan R. and Pearl P. Knight. Professors Robert B. Laurin and David H. Wallace of the American Baptist Seminary of the West, Covina, California, introduced me to historical-critical research. I am especially grateful to my doctoral adviser in Göttingen, Professor Hans-Joachim Kraus, for his friendly guidance during the planning and researching stages of this dissertation. I benefited also from consultations with other members of the Göttingen faculty, particularly Professors Walther Zimmerli, Rudolf Smend, Robert Hanhart, and Horst Dietrich Preuß. Drs. Werner Klatt and Hans Ulrich Boesche, also of Göttingen, were very generous with their time and help in clarifying diverse, enigmatic aspects of German research. My understanding of Scandinavian work in tradition history was enhanced through conversations with several scholars, primarily during the VIIth Congress of the International Organization for the Study of the Old Testament, in Uppsala, August 1971: Gösta W. Ahlström (Chicago), R. A. Carlson (Uppsala), Helmer Ringgren (Uppsala), Magne Sæbø (Oslo), Ilmari Soisalon-Soininen (Helsinki), and Geo Widengren (Uppsala). Of course, I myself bear responsibility for all positions taken and all representations made in this study. Dr. William W. Reader and Mr.

Desmond Gerard, fellow doctoral students and frequent conversation partners in Göttingen, assisted with some of the proofreading.

I also want to express my sincere thanks to the Deutscher Akademischer Austauschdienst, Bad Godesberg, for their stipend during 1970–1972 and for their subvention of this publication. Professors Rolf Knierim (Claremont) and Gene M. Tucker (Atlanta) very kindly read the dissertation and recommended its publication by the Society of Biblical Literature.

Finally, I want to thank my wife Evelyn, who, as a native of Norway, introduced me to Scandinavian life and languages, initiating thereby the present interest in the Scandinavian research of the Old Testament. To her also goes the credit for typing the greater part of this manuscript. I wish to dedicate this book to her and to our daughter Lisa.

Covina, California   D.A.K.
May 1973

Preface to the Revised Edition

At the urging of several readers and colleagues I have rendered into English all remaining foreign quotations, those in German, French, and Latin, which had been left in their original form in the first edition. Published translations that were available have been used, with credit given in the footnotes. For production reasons, unfortunately, it was generally not possible to include the page numbers of such English editions except where there was a direct quotation from them. It is hoped that the greater accessibility of the text to readers not fluent in the foreign languages will offset such occasional stylistic inconsistencies. While some typographical errors have been corrected, there has been no substantive revision of the text. I want to thank graduate assistant Toni Craven for her considerable assistance in the tedious work of fitting the translations into the original manuscript. Appreciation is also due the Vanderbilt University Research Council for its financial support of this revision.

Nashville, Tennessee   D.A.K.
March 1975

Preface to the Third Edition

The previous editions of this book have been out of print for a number of years, and I have frequently received requests for it to be made available again.

I am grateful to the Society of Biblical Literature, which originally published it in its Dissertation Series, for issuing this third edition, and to E. J. Brill, Leiden, for co-publishing it.

As may be expected, had I first undertaken the task of writing this book now, I would have written it quite differently than I did more than thirty years ago. Most importantly, numerous critical methods have emerged in the interim, and traditio-historical research cannot now be conducted blind to the insights and issues raised by these other approaches to the text. To address this matter I have added an epilogue to the third edition, "Does Tradition History Have a Future?" The latter is a translation, with slight modifications, of a lecture delivered in Norway and subsequently published as "Har gammeltestamentlig tradisjonshistorie en fremtid?" *Tidsskrift for Teologi og Kirke* 4 (1998): 263–77; I want to thank the journal editors for permission to include it in this context.

Second, the religious and cultural sensibilities reflected in the earlier editions would appear quite different now if it were a new publication. For example, the term "Old Testament" would be replaced virtually everywhere by "Hebrew Bible." I now conventionally limit use of "Old Testament" to cases where a Christian interpretation, presupposing a New Testament, is intended; its rough counterparts in contemporary Jewish usage are "Tanak," "Miqra'," "Jewish Bible," or other variants. As with many colleagues, I now tend to use the phrase "Hebrew Bible" as an alternative that has less of a confessional limitation, even though in itself it is not ideal for other reasons (e.g., there are also Aramaic parts of the Hebrew Bible; moreover, translations into other ancient languages, especially the Greek Septuagint, are pertinent to its interpretation and textual history). For this third edition, I have, at the suggestion of the publisher and other consultants, opted to let the phrase "Old Testament" stand as indicative of the character or orientation of much biblical scholarship in the years prior to 1972, after which new sensitivities to issues of diversity and pluralism took hold in ways not previously practiced. Changing this terminology in the third edition would have required rephrasing many sentences; in contrast, the few references to B.C. or A.D. could more easily be replaced with B.C.E. or C.E., respectively. It is worth emphasizing that traditio-historical research is by no means a function of Christian scholarship alone, even though the majority of traditio-historical researchers have operated within or emerged from Christian contexts. In its very effort to recover the pre-Christian and pre-Jewish (or, after the Babylonian exile, early Jewish) growth of those traditions that were, in the end, incorporated into canonized scripture, this method of research must necessarily attend to a variety of religious, ideological, and cultural circumstances throughout antiquity, not to a single or dominant perspective.

PREFACE

Only a few slight changes have been made of a substantive nature. Regarding stylistic matters, I should note that the first edition of the book was completed in 1972 while I was living in Germany, and it contains details of literary and formatting style typical of both that period and that place. For the most, these characteristics have been left in their original form, since bringing everything into conformity with today's stylistic norms would have required considerable effort, though without significant benefit. Instead, I have generally changed only details that may improve clarity. An exception is the abbreviations, which now conform to *The SBL Handbook of Style* (ed. Patrick H. Alexander et al.; Peabody, Mass.: Hendrickson, 1999), since the *Religion in Geschichte und Gegenwart* list, which served as the basis for the abbreviations in the earlier editions, is not commonly at hand for non-German readers.

A number of individuals contributed to the production of this third edition, some of them helping several years ago when I first contemplated preparing it. Gene Tucker and Kent Richards supported the project and offered important advice from the outset. Paul Kobelski of Scriptorium scanned the original printing and assisted in its reformatting. While graduate students at Vanderbilt University, Gordon Matties, Ken Stone, and Bobby Morris gave invaluable help in proofreading the manuscript at its various stages. Bob Buller of the Society of Biblical Literature ushered it through the final production process. To all of them I express my sincere gratitude.

As will often be described below, traditions can undergo substantial changes over time. So can individuals and groups, of course. Accordingly, I want to acknowledge, with deep appreciation, the support of my family—my wife, Catherine Snow, and our two children, Lisa and Jonathan. To the three of them I dedicate this book.

Nashville, Tennessee
April 2006

D.A.K.

Abbreviations

AAAbo	Acta Academica Aboensis
AAB	Abhandlungen der Deutschen (until 1944: Preußischen) Akademie der Wissenschaften zu Berlin
AcOr	*Acta orientalia*
ANVAO	Avhandlinger utgitt av Det Norske Videnskaps-Akademi i Oslo
ArOr	*Archiv orientální*
ASNU	Acta seminarii neotestamentici upsaliensis
ASTI	*Annual of the Swedish Theological Institute*
ATANT	Abhandlungen zur Theologie des Alten und Neuen Testaments
ATD	Das Alte Testament Deutsch
ATDan	Acta theologica danica
BAL	Berichte über die Verhandlungen der sächsischen Akademie der Wissenschaften zu Leipzig
BASOR	*Bulletin of the American Schools of Oriental Research*
BBB	Bonner biblische Beiträge
BETL	Bibliotheca ephemeridum theologicarum lovaniensium
BEvT	Beiträge zur *EvT*
BGBE	Beiträge zur Geschichte der biblischen Exegese
BGH	Beiträge zur Geschichte der biblischen Hermeneutik
BHH	B. Reicke and L. Rost, eds., *Biblisch-Historisches Handwörterbuch*
BHT	Beiträge zur historischen Theologie
BJRL	*Bulletin of the John Rylands University Library of Manchester*
BK	*Bibel und Kirche*
BKAT	Biblischer Kommentar: Altes Testament
BN	*Biblische Notizen*
BO	*Bibliotheca orientalis*
BTF	*Bangalore Theological Forum*
BWANT	Beiträge zur Wissenschaft vom Alten und Neuen Testament
BZAW	Beihefte zur Zeitschrift für die alttestamentliche Wissenschaft
CBQ	*Catholic Biblical Quarterly*
CN	Coniectanea neotestamentica

ConBOT	Coniectanea biblica: Old Testament Series
CTJ	Calvin Theological Journal
DLZ	Deutsche Literaturzeitung
DS	Danske Studier
DTT	Dansk teologisk tidsskrift
ET	English translation
EKL	E. Fahlbusch et al., eds., Evangelisches Kirchenlexikon
ETL	Ephemerides theologicae lovanienses
ETS	Erfurter theologische Studien
EvT	Evangelische Theologie
ExpTim	Expository Times
FGLP	Forschungen zur Geschichte und Lehre des Protestantismus
FPHex	G. von Rad, Das formgeschichtliche Problem des Hexateuch
FRLANT	Forschungen zur Religion und Literatur des Alten und Neuen Testaments
FSTR	Forschungen zur systematischen Theologie und Religionsphilosophie
GBSOT	Guides to Biblical Scholarship: Old Testament Series
Ges. Stud.	Gesammelte Studien
GGA	Göttingische Gelehrte Anzeigen
GT	German translation
GT-I	I. Engnell, Gamla Testamentet: En traditionshistorisk inledning, vol. I
GTMMM	S. Michelet, S. Mowinckel, and N. Messel, translators, Det Gamle Testament, vols. I–III
HAT	Handbuch zum Alten Testament
HKAT	Handkommentar zum Alten Testament
HS	Horae Soederblomianae
HTR	Harvard Theological Review
IDB	G. A. Buttrick, ed., Interpreter's Dictionary of the Bible
IEJ	Israel Exploration Journal
Int	Interpretation
JSOT	Journal for the Study of the Old Testament
JSOTSup	Journal for the Study of the Old Testament: Supplement Series
JSS	Journal of Semitic Studies
Jud	Judaica
KD	Kerygma und Dogma
Kl. Sch.	A. Alt, Kleine Schriften zur Geschichte des Volkes Israel. 3 vols. Munich: Beck, 1953–1959.
MO	Le monde oriental
MVÄG	Mitteilungen der vorderasiatischen-ägyptischen Gesellschaft

NTT	Norsk teologisk tidsskrift
OLZ	Orientalische Literaturzeitung
OrAnt	Oriens antiquus
OTMS	H. H. Rowley, ed., *The Old Testament and Modern Study*
OtSt	Oudtestamentische Studiën
PJ	Palästina-Jahrbuch
PTR	Princeton Theological Review
RB	Revue biblique
RE	Realencyklopädie für protestantische Theologie und Kirche. Gotha, 1861.
RGG³	Religion in Geschichte und Gegenwart, 3rd ed.
RHPR	Revue d'histoire et de philosophie religieuses
RHR	Revue de l'histoire des religions
RoB	Religion och Bibel
SamT	Sammlung Töpelmann
SAT	H. Gunkel et al., *Die Schriften des Alten Testaments in Auswahl*, 2nd ed.
SBS	Stuttgarter Bibelstudien
SBT	Studies in Biblical Theology
SBU¹	I. Engnell and A. Fridrichsen, eds., *Svenskt Bibliskt Uppslagverk*. Gävle: Skolförlaget, 1948–1952.
SBU²	I. Engnell and A. Fridrichsen, eds., *Svenskt Bibliskt Uppslagverk*. 2nd ed. Stockholm: Nordiska uppslagsböcker, 1962–1963.
SEÅ	Svensk exegetisk årsbok
SHANE	Studies in the History of the Ancient Near East
SHR	Studies in the History of Religions (Supplements to *Numen*)
SJOT	Scandinavian Journal of the Old Testament
SJT	Scottish Journal of Theology
SGK	Schriften der Königsberger Gelehrten Gesellschaft
SM	Scripta minora Regiae Societatis humaniorum litterarum Lundensis
SNVAO	Skrifter utgitt av Det Norske Videnskaps-Akademie i Oslo
ST	Studia theologica
SThU	Schweizerische Theologische Umschau
SymBU	Symbolae biblicae upsalienses
TB	Theologische Bücherei
TF	Theologische Forschung
ThSt	Theologische Studiën
TLZ	Theologische Literaturzeitung
TRu	Theologische Rundschau
TTK	Tidsskrift for teologi og kirke

TTZ	*Trierer theologische Zeitschrift*
TZ	*Theologische Zeitschrift*
ÜPent	M. Noth, *Überlieferungsgeschichte des Pentateuch*
ÜSt	M. Noth, *Überlieferungsgeschichtliche Studien*
UUÅ	Uppsala Universitets Årsskrift
VF	*Verkündigung und Forschung*
VT	*Vetus Testamentum*
VTSup	Vetus Testamentum, Supplements
WMANT	Wissenschaftliche Monographien zum Alten und Neuen Testament
WZ	Wissenschaftliche Zeitschrift
ZA	*Zeitschrift für Assyriologie*
ZAL	*Zeitschrift für deutsches Altertum und deutsche Literatur*
ZAW	*Zeitschrift für die alttestamentliche Wissenschaft*
ZDPV	*Zeitschrift des deutschen Palästina-Vereins*
ZKT	*Zeitschrift für katholische Theologie*
ZTK	*Zeitschrift für Theologie und Kirche*
ZWT	*Zeitschrift für wissenschaftliche Theologie*

Prolegomena

Scholarly research of the past century has come to recognize the fundamental role played by *tradition* in human history. As a ubiquitous element of culture it constitutes the link between generations, the bond between present and past, a foundational factor of the community, a means for individuals to become integrated into a whole extending beyond themselves. Tradition occupies furthermore a central position in the structure of knowledge and understanding, and thus one must reckon with it as an integral aspect of the general hermeneutical process.[1]

For convenience we can distinguish between *verbal tradition* and *practical tradition*.[2] The former refers to words and texts that are transmitted from one generation to the next by oral and/or written means. The latter encompasses practices, customs, habits, rules, experiences, social and religious institutions—in short, any part of the heritage from the past that is not necessarily fixed in a set form in word or writing. Actually, the boundary between these two types of tradition is fluid, and it must be emphasized that there can be a good deal of determinative interplay between the two. But the purpose of this distinction is to show that what is to command our attention in this study is primarily tradition in the former sense—oral and written tradition that narrates, instructs, regulates, informs, interprets, and is constitutive for faith and community life.

Biblical studies have followed the lead of other literary sciences in attributing an increased importance to the preliterary stage of the texts. This broadening of the inquiry applies above all to the realm of Old Testament

---

1. Tradition as epistemological factor has been treated thoroughly by H.-G. Gadamer, *Wahrheit und Methode: Grundzüge einer philosophischen Hermeneutik*, 2nd ed., Tübingen 1965, especially 250ff.; cf. also his article, "Tradition: I, Phänomenologisch," *RGG*, vol. 6, 3rd ed., Tübingen 1962, cols. 966–67.

2. Cf. also B. Gerhardsson, "Tradition," *SBU* II, 2nd ed., Stockholm 1962, col. 1254. S. Gandz ("The Dawn of Literature: Prolegomena to a History of Unwritten Literature," *Osiris* 7, 1939, 267–68) specifies four distinct phases of tradition in the realm of life: tradition by heredity and instinct, parental tradition, verbal tradition, and writing.

literature. The epoch dominated by Wellhausen's literary-critical program, which postulated the writing of the texts and sources as the creative stage, was gradually succeeded by an era in which *form-critical* questions and later also the *traditio-historical* approach prevailed. These methods of investigation address themselves to the problem of discovering the details of the prehistory of our present texts—their origins, development, and formal characteristics. The basic assumption of such studies—in contrast to the presupposition of the "classical" literary-critical work—is that *the majority of our Old Testament underwent an often lengthy and complex process of growth in real life situations, the result being a body of cumulative, multiplex traditions that reflect the life and religion of the community in various periods of its history.* It is further assumed that by probing the depths of these traditions we not only will gain data of historical importance but also will enhance our understanding of the texts in their present form.

Whereas the critical studies of Richard Simon in 1678 indicate a beginning awareness of the problem of Old Testament tradition, Gunkel at the turn of this century was the first to devote himself to uncovering this prehistory of our present texts. With the aid of his Gattungsgeschichte and Religionsgeschichte,[3] his pioneering commentary on Genesis demonstrated the feasibility and importance of penetrating back to the origins of the first small units of the tradition. Noth and von Rad, three and four decades later, directed attention to the tradition process as such, seeking through analytic and synthetic examinations to explain the way in which the historical narratives in the Old Testament came to be. Concurrent with this research in Germany, Old Testament scholars in Scandinavia were developing interests along similar lines, emphasizing above all the central role of oral means in the formation and transmission of the Israelite traditions. The latter group of scholars was also responsible for introducing traditio-historical considerations to the prophetic literature. Since the initial awakening to the need for reckoning seriously with this aspect of tradition, subsequent research has made great gains in understanding the prehistory of our texts. Numerous studies are devoted to this area, and there is hardly a commentary produced in recent decades that has not in some manner incorporated this perspective on the text. Whereas general agreement has been reached regarding the important part played by tradition in the formation and continuation of the Israelite community, the fact that a tradition existed raises crucial, still-unresolved problems in the

---

3. At this point it may be noted that certain German words, having found their way into the English language as *termini technici* of the biblical sciences, will always occur in this study without italics or quotation marks: Gattungsgeschichte, Formgeschichte, Religionsgeschichte, Sitz im Leben, Gattung, Heilsgeschichte, Redaktionsgeschichte, Literaturgeschichte.

historical and theological fields. Prominent among these are the implications that tradition has for our understanding of revelation, of canon, of Heilsgeschichte, of history as such, and of the relation between the Old and the New Testaments. Among other problems with which we are faced, we hope to cast some light on these issues in the discussions below.

1
TRADITIO ET TRADITUM

The phenomenon of verbal tradition can be formally divided into two aspects. On the one hand, there is the *traditio:* the process (in its totality and in its details) whereby traditional material is passed from one generation to the next; this process is variable, at times being a rigid and faithful transmission and at other times including intentional or unintentional alterations, additions, or deletions due to a number of different factors. On the other hand, there is the aspect of the *traditum:* the traditional material itself that is being transmitted. These two aspects are obviously integrally related with each other so that the interplay between them, the effect of the one on the other, must not be underestimated. For our purposes we choose to use them as general rubrics under which the many particulars and facets of tradition can be grouped. "Tradition" itself is such an extensive, complex entity that it seems advisable now at the outset to list and describe its major aspects and characteristics, paying special attention to the situation in ancient Israel.

A. Aspects of Traditio

(1) *Interpretation and actualization.* The central characteristic of the Israelite transmittal process from its very beginning is not a rigid, passive handing down of static traditions but rather the recurring need felt by each generation to interpret and apply—to "reactualize" (= "vergegenwärtigen")—the old traditions for the present age.[1] Indeed, "tradition" and "actualization" can indicate two aspects of the total process—on the one hand the conservative or reverential attempt to transmit further the account of what once happened under past historical conditions, and on the other hand the need felt to apply

---

1. Cf. also M. Noth, "Die Vergegenwärtigung des Alten Testaments in der Verkündigung" (1952/53), *Probleme alttestamentlicher Hermeneutik,* ed. C. Westermann, TB 11, 3rd ed., Munich 1960, 54–68; and G. Fohrer, "Tradition und Interpretation im Alten Testament," *ZAW* 73 (1961), 1–30.

"existentially" these truths for the particular situation of each age.[2] That these new interpretations were often integrated into the traditions themselves was perhaps inevitable—but from a theological and historical point of view hardly regrettable. Some of the best examples of this process can be seen in the Deuteronomistic History and in the prophetic literature. We will see below how this principle of active tradition reception—which was also prevalent in the early Jewish and Christian periods—achieves fundamental importance in von Rad's theology of the Old Testament and in Noth's history of Israel.

(2) *Agglomeration and fusion.* The typical pattern of tradition growth is from simple to complex. This pattern can apply to the isolated tradition in its own development through accumulation and embellishment. It is an especially important factor for the process in which the original units, generally limited in size and purpose, became gathered together with other units, thereby forming a larger whole. The cementing factor could be commonly shared motifs, participating characters, historical subject matter, key words of association, etc. Resultant complexes of tradition could similarly be connected or even interwoven with other complexes, this process continuing until entire compositions, sources, or books were reached. That this agglomerating and fusing of traditions, which very often began already at the oral stage, implies an act of interpretation on the part of the traditionist(s) is obvious, just as is the fact that merged traditions could come to mean something quite different than what they intended separately; this is a problem of *traditum*. This process can be seen in cycles of sagas (e.g., about Abraham), for the pentateuchal themes (cf. Noth), in the grouping together of prophetic utterances, and at numerous other points.

(3) *Traditionists, circles, schools.* One of the more crucial problems is to determine which group or groups were responsible for forming, cultivating, and preserving a given tradition during its history and at what points a specific individual may have been determinative or influential in this process (e.g., for the prophetic traditions). Assuming that a tradition would not have survived unless some traditionist(s) vested interest in it, the tradition historian should seek to establish the importance that the tradition had for its transmitters. It follows that these persons could easily have left their imprint on the tradition, whether internally, formally, or linguistically. And not least, these circles or later ones were instrumental in collecting and joining individual traditions into larger complexes. Some of the groups of traditionists discovered include priestly circles, Levites, storytellers, court officials, profes-

---

2. Cf. also J. M. Schmidt, "Vergegenwärtigung und Überlieferung: Bemerkungen zu ihrem Verständnis im dtn.-dtr. Überlieferungsbereich," *EvT* 30 (1970), 169–200.

sional mourners, sages, elders, the family, and schools of disciples gathered around significant prophets.

(4) *Geographical location.* Traditions often have a tendency not only to be connected with certain groups but also to remain attached to specific locations, sites, or regions. This aspect, known as "Ortsgebundenheit," has been argued forcefully by Alt and Noth, as we will see below. These locations vary from smaller towns and singularly shaped phenomena (e.g., a tell) with their popular traditions (often etiologies), to cultic centers and sanctuaries (e.g., Shechem, Bethel, Gilgal), and even to larger regions (e.g., Israel in the north, Judah in the south, Jerusalem). One must also reckon with the transfer of traditions from one location to another, as when the northern traditions were removed to the south at the fall of the northern kingdom in 722/1 B.C.E.

(5) *Political, social, psychological, religious/cultic factors.* What is meant here is not the Sitz im Leben of a tradition, but rather the forces from outside that influenced both the transmission and the contents of the tradition. Thus the fall of the northern kingdom caused the traditions to be transferred to Jerusalem and subsequently reworked in part, and the exile brought the need to stabilize and organize the traditions of the past. Knowledge of the history of the cult,[3] of the sociology of ancient Israel, and of the psychology of the Israelites (cf., e.g., Pedersen) can similarly elucidate elements in the development of certain traditions.

(6) *Transmittal means: oral or written?* It is now widely assumed that people in the ancient Near East depended largely on oral means for passing on traditions to later generations, but the exact extent of orality with respect to the Old Testament is still debated.[4] Gunkel posited orality for sagas, songs, fables, and other narrative types; and the Scandinavians have emphasized that the prophets were predominantly speakers and that their traditions were transmitted long at the oral level among their disciples. Legal materials, on the other hand, were conceivably recorded quite early. "Oral tradition" includes not only the stage of transmission but also the periods of formation and development. It seems clear that individual traditions could be combined and merged orally into complexes, so there may be some justification in Engnell's use of the term "oral literature."[5] In some cases a tradition could have existed simultaneously in oral and written forms, the latter controlling the former or the former supplementing and perhaps subsequently worked into

---

3. Cf., e.g., H.-J. Kraus, *Gottesdienst in Israel: Grundriß einer Geschichte des alttestamentlichen Gottesdienstes*, 2nd ed., Munich 1962.

4. See the discussions below, pp. 69-72; and part 2, passim, especially pp. 289-94.

5. Cf. below, p. 202.

the latter.⁶ The problem for the tradition historian is to attempt to determine at what points a tradition existed at the oral level and at what points at the written level. Such information can be important for explaining linguistic and formal characteristics, repetitions and internal tensions, and also the function of a tradition in its environment.

(7) *Memory*. Since the tradition historian has primarily to do with oral tradition, and since reinterpretation and reactualization are central elements of the tradition process, the question arises as to the reliability or "faithfulness" of the transmission. For this reason the problem of memory in ancient Israel has gained in importance and is treated now in several thorough studies.⁷ Relevant issues include: the existence of some common "genuine historical recollection" or "Urerinnerung,"⁸ whereby at least the basic fact or essence or kernel of a tradition was allegedly remembered and guarded, in contrast to the details and embellishments; the practiced ability of the Semitic memory—both ancient and modern—to retain accurately a great mass of literature;⁹ and the devices (mnemonic, poetic, associative) employed to aid the memory.

(8) *The transition from oral to written form*. Engnell and others¹⁰ have argued that traditions attained a high degree of complexity and fixity still at the oral stage and that their recording in writing in some later (probably postexilic) period signifies in itself nothing particularly new or revolutionary. This thesis may hold true for some cases, but as a rule the transition from oral to written form is not to be underrated. For one thing, taking the step to fix an oral tradition in writing is itself an act of interpretation. Secondly, traditions undergo a change when they are removed from their Sitz im Leben and made a part of a written composition.¹¹ Moreover, written texts are more suitable for later redactional work. Thus the recording process, whether of smaller units or of larger complexes, is an important traditio-historical stage. Forces from outside (e.g., the fall of Judah and the deportation in 587 B.C.E.)

---

6. For example, Mowinckel ("Tradition, Oral," *IDB* 4, New York 1962, 685) suggests that the pentateuchal source E was primarily oral until worked into J.

7. Especially: B. S. Childs, *Memory and Tradition in Israel*, SBT 37, London 1962; P. A. H. de Boer, *Gedenken und Gedächtnis in der Welt des Alten Testaments*, Stuttgart 1962; W. Schottroff, *'Gedenken' im Alten Orient und im Alten Testament: Die Wurzel zākar im semitischen Sprachkreis*, WMANT 15, 2nd ed., Neukirchen-Vluyn 1967.

8. Cf. below, pp. 159–60.

9. This thesis has also been argued by several Scandinavian scholars, especially Nyberg, Birkeland, Engnell, and Nielsen.

10. Cf. below, pp. 200–201.

11. Cf., e.g., A. B. Lord, *The Singer of Tales*, Cambridge, Massachusetts, 1960, 124ff. Cf. also below, pp. 118–19, 192–93, 292–93.

often instigated the formation of written literature. The canonization process starts when the written text becomes regarded as absolute and unchangeable.

(9) *Compositional and redactional techniques*. The later redaction of primarily written materials is best considered as the domain of Redaktionsgeschichte and not a part of tradition history as such. However, compositional and even redactional techniques are in play also at the oral stage of combining traditions. Carlson has made this point well with regard to 2 Samuel.[12] Thus the tradition historian must pay attention to such techniques as word-play, the principle of association, "ring" composition, sevenfold and threefold patterns, and perhaps even more complicated structural and liturgical patterns. Also important are basic organizational principles employed by initial compilers, such as the "kleines geschichtliches Credo" used by the Jahwist (according to von Rad). These are relevant aspects of preliterary tradition growth and of initial literary compositions.

B. Aspects of *Traditum*

(1) *Expressions of faith and community life*. The basic aspect of Israelite tradition (though by no means restricted to this people alone) is closely related to *traditio* factors 1, 3, and 5 above: The contents of the traditions reflect the life of the people—their interests, beliefs, needs for historical rootage, religious proclamations, instructions for family and for worship, juridical directives, laments, reproaches, hopes. This fundamental relation to the concreteness of life has been recognized since Gunkel and is implied in Nyberg and Engnell's phrase "living tradition."[13] It necessitates a careful consideration of the religious, sociological, or psychological function of the tradition at each of its developmental stages.

(2) *Changes in size*. The expression "growth of tradition" indicates that a given tradition went through historically successive stages of development, usually increasing in magnitude through accumulation and agglomeration but at times becoming trimmed for specific pragmatic, aesthetic, theological, or historical reasons. Beginning with the tradition unit isolated literary-critically and form-critically in the text, the tradition critic will want to determine and describe each of the successive stages and strata in this process, striving to follow the tradition back to its original element(s)—although a complete, detailed picture of this developmental course is scarcely possible and remains at any rate hypothetical.

---

12. Cf. below, pp. 250–52.
13. Cf. below, pp. 178–80, 200–201; cf. also J. Hempel, "The Contents of the Literature," *Record and Revelation*, ed. Robinson, Oxford 1938, 45–73.

(3) *Changes in meaning.* At the various stages in the development of the content of a tradition a shift in meaning and thus also in function can occur. Such changes can be observed in individual traditions (e.g., the heightened, embellished account of Elijah on Mount Carmel) as well as in the inclusion of separate traditions into a complex (e.g., the Jacob-Esau-Laban cycle). And quite obviously the meaning of a pericope in its present context in the Old Testament can be quite contrary to its early traditional content and intention.[14]

One vital consequence of these first three points is that the classical literary-critical categories of "genuine/nongenuine" have become relativized, rendered less meaningful. For the tradition historian, the process of tradition growth and agglomeration is an aspect to be affirmed. It is unacceptable to devaluate later additions, for they can contain not only historical information but also new interpretations of theological importance. Good examples can be seen in the disciples' reactualization and reworking of the *ipsissima verba* of their prophet master.[15]

(4) *Changes in language.* The textual history of the Old Testament indicates numerous alterations of individual words in the transmitted texts (cf. Kethib/Qere, Tiqqune sopherim, Itture sopherim). Similar shifts in the set linguistic structure of a fixed oral tradition are also possible. Verbal changes may have occurred especially when early words or word meanings were misunderstood or unknown in later times; consequent modifications can thus also be categorized as interpretative incursions in the course of the tradition. Research into the history of the Hebrew language, especially with regard to other Semitic languages, can provide the tradition historian with insights into such possible transpositions in the transmitted vocabulary of a tradition.[16]

(5) *Form and Gattung.* Since a tradition per se can be historically retraced only as long as it remains tangible in form ("formal greifbar"),[17] the aspects of form and of Gattung are also relevant for tradition history. "Form" applies to the structure or artistic character of an *individual text*; "Gattung," on the other hand, is a *text type*, derived inductively from independent units similar in form. The Gattung can thus be conceived as existent "behind" and

---

14. For a list of five ways in which a tradition could change in meaning and intent, cf. H. Barth and O. H. Steck, *Exegese des Alten Testaments: Leitfaden der Methodik*, 2nd ed., Neukirchen-Vluyn 1971, 40–41.

15. Cf., e.g., W. Zimmerli, *Ezechiel* I, BKAT 13/1, Neukirchen-Vluyn 1969, 111; G. von Rad, *Theologie des Alten Testaments* II, 5th ed., Munich 1968, 54–57 (ET: *Old Testament Theology* II, trans. Stalker, New York 1965, 46–49); also E. Nielsen, *Oral Tradition: A Modern Problem in Old Testament Introduction*, SBT 11, London 1954, 81.

16. Cf. the basic work executed by J. Barr, *Comparative Philology and the Text of the Old Testament*, Oxford 1968.

17. W. Richter, *Exegese als Literaturwissenschaft*, Göttingen 1971, 156.

determinative for the individual units.[18] Primary Gattungen, formulas,[19] and premolded schemata—each one of these must by definition be present in two or more literarily independent contexts—indicate that our text may contain traditions with their own history.[20] Another factor is that the form of a specific unit can change in the course of its history, so that the unit at the end of its development may be structured quite differently than it was at the outset. Both form and Gattung are thus aspects of *traditum*; it is wiser however to restrict their examination to the methodological steps of Formgeschichte and Gattungsgeschichte and to consider the results and insights of these studies when drawing up the history of the tradition.

The following six special facets of *traditum* can all be component parts of a tradition, factors abstracted from its contents. Three have to do with its substance ("Inhalt"): plot, motif, and theme; the remaining ones concern its philosophical, religious, and ethical import ("Gehalt"): concept, problem, and notion. Two essential conditions must be stressed for all of these: First, each is an *abstraction*, derived indeed from the contents of a tradition or text but not transmitted by and for itself in isolation from a context.[21] Secondly, each of these six items *can be preexistent* to the given individual unit in which it appears, and the extent to which its prehistory colors its use in the tradition in question must always be examined—not simply assumed. A critical attempt to trace the history of, e.g., a motif, plot, or notion is possible—though it must *not* be pursued *in abstracto*, isolated from its concrete appearances. A history of a motif or conception is no more than just that; it is not to be confused with the history of a structured tradition unit. At most it can provide information about certain of the building blocks in the tradition. Furthermore, one must avoid the danger of giving a motif or a plot an independent existence, thus bringing materially diverse and historically separate traditions containing them into apparent connection with each other.[22]

(6) *Plot* (German: "Stoff"). Not the unstructured raw material but the dramatic plan or skeleton of happenings constitutes the basis of sagas, epics,

---

18. Ibid., 72ff.

19. Cf., e.g., I. Lande, *Formelhafte Wendungen der Umgangssprache im Alten Testament*, Leiden 1949.

20. Richter, *Exegese als Literaturwissenschaft*, 99ff., 159ff.

21. Cf. C. Westermann, "Zur Auslegung des Alten Testaments," *Die hermeneutische Frage in der Theologie*, ed. O. Loretz and W. Strolz, Schriften zum Weltgespräch 3, Freiburg 1968, 218: "That which is transmitted must have a form in some sense. Thus it is not thoughts, notions, theories, even free-floating motifs that are transmitted, but only linguistic structures, which are transmittable because they have a stable form in which they can be handed on."

22. Cf. Barth/Steck, *Exegese des Alten Testaments*, 75–76; and E. Frenzel, *Stoff-, Motiv- und Symbolforschung*, 3rd ed., Stuttgart 1970, 47–48; also Bentzen, below, pp. 257–58.

narratives, novelle (lyrical Gattungen are thus excluded). This dramatic plot often precedes a tradition in which it occurs, and a literary history of its treatment and variations, in other ancient Near Eastern texts as well, can be profitable. The plot is not necessarily an invented series of happenings but can also be founded on a personal experience, a historical or contemporary event, a mythical or religious account, or an already existent piece of literature. This "Stoff" can contain several motifs and is not to be confused with the import or spiritual problem of the tradition. The originality and fantasy of the traditionists or the author come at the point of artistically forming and filling out the pregiven plot.[23]

(7) *Motif.* The word "motif" is best understood as "a smaller substantive unit which, while not yet comprising a whole plot, nonetheless presents a material, situational element."[24] This element may be an item or a person, portrayed not in isolation but in a context or situation. It is preformed, not bound to a single text, and can therefore be examined in its historical development, significance, and use in various traditions.[25] Motifs, which occur in almost all Gattungen including lyrical pieces, may be classified according to their contents[26] or according to their function in the tradition unit (e.g., main motif, auxiliary motif, "Leitmotif," "blind" motif).[27]

(8) *Theme.* The third component abstracted from the subject matter of the tradition is the theme, the basic idea from which a narrative springs and which holds it together. Since the theme is realized through the plot, the former is derived by disregarding the latter and formulating briefly the sub-

---

23. The specification of "Stoff" in this sense has become established in the nonbiblical literary sciences; cf. Frenzel, *Stoff-, Motiv- und Symbolforschung*, 23ff.; Frenzel, *Stoff- und Motivgeschichte*, Grundlagen der Germanistik 3, Berlin 1966, 24ff.; G. von Wilpert, *Sachwörterbuch der Literatur*, 5th ed., Stuttgart 1969, 742–43; and Richter, *Exegese als Literaturwissenschaft*, 136–37, 153ff., 182–83.

24. Frenzel, *Stoff-, Motiv- und Symbolforschung*, 28; cf. also Frenzel, *Stoff- und Motivgeschichte*, 11ff.

25. "Motif transposition" or "motif mutation," filling an old motif with new meaning, is an aspect of Motivgeschichte; cf. H. Gross, "'Motivtransposition' als überlieferungsgeschichtliches Prinzip im Alten Testament," *Sacra Pagina* I, BETL 12, Gembloux 1959, 324–34; and Frenzel, *Stoff- und Motivgeschichte*, 80ff.

26. So Gunkel, *Genesis*, 7th ed., Göttingen 1966, xx ff.

27. A good example of a Motivgeschichte is U. Steffen, *Das Mysterium von Tod und Auferstehung: Formen und Wandlungen des Jona-Motivs*, Göttingen 1963; cf. also various articles in *Biblical Motifs: Origins and Transformations*, ed. A. Altmann, Cambridge, Massachusetts, 1966. Old Testament scholarship has often operated with an imprecise and vague understanding of "motif" and has not seldom identified Motivgeschichte with Traditionsgeschichte; cf. also Richter, *Exegese als Literaturwissenschaft*, 75–76, 89, 182–83; and K. Koch, *Was ist Formgeschichte?*, 2nd ed., Neukirchen-Vluyn 1967, 70–71.

ject and intent of the unit.[28] In Noth's tradition history of the Pentateuch the five basic themes gain the function of crystallization centers for the individual, related traditions.[29] Wolff has demonstrated the feasibility and usefulness of tracing the history of a theme in various contexts and times.[30]

(9) *Concept* (German: "Begriff"). Part of the import of the transmitted unit, a "concept" is the mental image of a thing and has its formal basis in lexemes. The danger, however, of identifying a concept too closely with a word used to express it has been exposed fully in Barr's criticism of Kittel's *Theologisches Wörterbuch zum Neuen Testament*.[31] Because of its basic nature as an abstraction (e.g., love, sin, goodness), a concept must never be traditio-historically examined without giving its context full consideration.[32]

(10) *Problem*. Many traditions were apparently developed to deal with or to try to solve some distressing human problem. For other traditions such a problem may lie in the background and therefore may be only indirectly treated. Inasmuch as these problems are often of a rather general nature and can perturb persons in different ages and situations, their treatment and even their urgency in each time can be compared historically. As is true for both "concept" and "notion," considerations of contemporary history, religion, intellectual atmosphere, psychological stress situations, and so forth are essential in our examining a specific problem. The analysis must begin with the individual text and proceed then to ever greater and temporal groupings.[33] A well-known problem in the Old Testament is that of theodicy; others concern fate, nature, love, upbringing of children, and community.[34]

(11) *Notion* (German: "Vorstellung"). One final aspect of the subject matter of a tradition needs to be mentioned. A specific notion of historical, theological, or intellectual nature can often be found in a transmitted unit under examination. It usually tends to be concretely oriented and is therefore not to be confused with abstract ideas or isolated motifs. The tradition histo-

---

28. Cf. Richter, *Exegese als Literaturwissenschaft*, 182.

29. Cf. below, pp. 113–20.

30. H. W. Wolff, "Das Thema 'Umkehr' in der alttestamentlichen Prophetie" (1951), *Gesammelte Studien zum Alten Testament*, TB 22, Munich 1964, 130–50. Cf. also H. H. Guthrie, Jr., *Israel's Sacred Songs: A Study of Dominant Themes*, New York 1966.

31. J. Barr, *The Semantics of Biblical Language*, Oxford 1961, 206ff.

32. Cf. also Barth/Steck, *Exegese des Alten Testaments*, 83. For an example, cf. R. Knierim, *Die Hauptbegriffe für Sünde im Alten Testament*, 2nd ed., Gütersloh 1967.

33. Cf. Richter, *Exegese als Literaturwissenschaft*, 184.

34. Cf. also J. Hempel, "The Contents of the Literature," *Record and Revelation*, ed. Robinson, 68–73. For a discussion of the importance that such fundamental human problems have for the writer and poet, cf. R. Unger, *Literaturgeschichte als Problemgeschichte*, SGK, Geisteswiss. Klasse, 1, Berlin 1924.

rian will want to identify the presence of such a notion in its specific context and then try to establish whether this notion was current in other times and in other literarily independent texts. Formalistically, a notion betrays a "fixed linguistic field, characteristic formulatory structure, specific notional contour ... and typical line of assertion (logic of material),"[35] all of which remain basically constant and recognizable as the notion continues to appear in later times, even if in a somewhat modified form. A notion is not restricted to a single Gattung but seems to be handed down more or less as a part of the intellectual heritage of a people.[36] Writing the history of a specific notion necessitates consideration of the origin, developmental path, modifications, traditionists, localization, and the contexts in which it appears in biblical and extrabiblical texts. A good example of such a history is Steck's study of the notion of the violent fate of the prophets.[37]

(12) *Streams of tradition* (German: "theologische Strömungen"). We have just described six primary elements of *traditum*, all of which can be components of a given tradition and, to the extent that they are discovered in independent texts, can have a "history" of their own (though, as we emphasized, not detached from each of their contexts). However, traditio-historical investigations do not stop when these elements have been identified and traced historically, nor when the individual tradition unit has been described from its origin on through its developmental stages until its final form and context have been reached. How are we to explain why a tradition complex contains specifically its own elements, motifs, themes, and so forth—and not different or additional ones? Scholars have become aware of the need to consider this wider horizon—the particular heritage and intellectual background of the various tradition initiators, authors, and traditionists. One assumes that there existed in Israel a number of traditional lines or "streams," each consisting of its own bundle of thought-patterns, viewpoints, theological orientation, and traditional materials. To determine such a stream requires the work of *synthesis*, drawing together the traditio-historical insights gained from the examination of a wide range of texts and *traditum* elements. Two characterizing features of a stream will be its geographical localization (e.g., the northern kingdom, Judah, Jerusalem) and its special circle of traditionists (e.g., priests, Levites, prophets, court officials). The difficult task facing the historian of a tradition stream includes trying to determine how it originated and gained its distinct existence, what specific ideas came to constitute

---

35. Barth/Steck, *Exegese des Alten Testaments*, 74.
36. Cf. also ibid., 70ff., 83; and O. H. Steck, *Überlieferung und Zeitgeschichte in den Elia-Erzählungen*, WMANT 26, Neukirchen-Vluyn 1968, 103, n. 3.
37. Cf. below, pp. 142–46. Another is P. Diepold, *Israels Land*, BWANT 95, Stuttgart 1972.

it, how traditional materials and ideas of diverse origin could have come together in this manner, what historical impulses from outside could have been determinative—in short, how this specific theological and historical position developed.[38] Attendant to these issues is the problem of *continuity*, primarily that of faith, traditions, and religious practices.[39] So far, great attention has been given to the streams of tradition in which the various prophets stood,[40] although there has also been some opposition to this approach as a sacrifice of the originality and singularity of the prophets as special messengers of Jahweh.[41] We thus do well to remember the danger of glossing over diversity in our search for continuity;[42] especially the occasions of reactualization and reinterpretation, while based on the traditions of the past, often have the effect of upsetting or altering the traditional line. Another area in which exemplary investigations have been made is the history of postexilic theology.[43] It remains for us to emphasize again that a stream of tradition is a *composite* of numerous different themes, motifs, concepts, notions, etc. Therefore, a history of an individual theme or motif[44] may contribute to, but is not to be identified with, the investigation of the larger stream of tradition.

(13) *Post-history* (German: "Nachgeschichte," "Nachinterpretation," "Auslegungsgeschichte," "Wirkungsgeschichte"). When a tradition becomes firmly fixed and stabilized, it can assume the character of scripture, practically though not necessarily officially canonized. Such a development usually

---

38. For more details on the special importance of studying streams of tradition, cf. Barth/Steck, *Exegese des Alten Testaments*, 72–73, 78; and Steck, "Das Problem theologischer Strömungen in nachexilischer Zeit," *EvT* 28 (1968), 445–58.

39. Cf. P. R. Ackroyd, *Continuity: A Contribution to the Study of the Old Testament Religious Tradition*, Oxford 1962; Ackroyd, "The Temple Vessels—A Continuity Theme," VTSup 23 (1972), 166–81; and N. W. Porteous, "The Prophets and the Problem of Continuity," *Israel's Prophetic Heritage: Essays in Honor of James Muilenburg*, ed. B. W. Anderson and W. Harrelson, New York 1962, 11–25.

40. Cf. especially von Rad, *Theologie* II; H. W. Wolff, "Hoseas geistige Heimat" (1956), *Ges. Stud.*, 232–50; Wolff, *Amos' geistige Heimat*, WMANT 18, Neukirchen-Vluyn 1964.

41. Cf. especially J. Vollmer, *Geschichtliche Rückblicke und Motive in der Prophetie des Amos, Hosea und Jesaja*, BZAW 119, Berlin 1971; and M.-L. Henry, *Prophet und Tradition: Versuch einer Problemstellung*, BZAW 116, Berlin 1969.

42. This point is developed in an article not available to this writer: Ackroyd, "The Theology of Tradition: An Approach to Old Testament Theological Problems," *BTF* 3 (1971), 49–64.

43. Cf. Steck, *EvT* 28 (1968), 448ff., and the literature referred to there, especially O. Plöger, *Theokratie und Eschatologie*, WMANT 2, 2nd ed. Neukirchen Kreis Moers, 1962.

44. As carried out by, for example, E. Rohland, *Die Bedeutung der Erwählungstraditionen Israels für die Eschatologie der alttestamentlichen Propheten*, Diss. Heidelberg 1956; or G. F. Hasel, *The Remnant: The History and Theology of the Remnant Idea from Genesis to Isaiah*, Andrews University Monographs 5, Berrien Springs, Michigan, 1972.

takes place only after the tradition has attained written form in its final (present) context. As the entire tradition is transmitted on to later generations, two important things can occur: For one thing, minor additions, alterations, or glosses may appear as the text is passed through the filter of the later transmitters, interpreters, and editors.[45] Secondly, the text, as a total piece of *traditum*, may have an effect (thus "Wirkungsgeschichte") on other traditions, both within and without the Old Testament and either as a stimulant or as an object to be interpreted and exegeted (thus "Nachinterpretation," "Auslegungsgeschichte"). In this way we can see that, just as a tradition may have a "prehistory," it also may experience a vivid "post-history" as a fully developed and finalized entity.[46]

---

45. Cf., e.g., A. Gelin, "La question des 'relectures' bibliques à l'intérieur d'une tradition vivante," *Sacra Pagina*, vol. 1, Gembloux 1959, 303–15; and J. Becker, *Israel deutet seine Psalmen: Urform und Neuinterpretation in den Psalmen*, SBS 18, Stuttgart 1966.

46. For further discussion and literature references, cf. below pp. 107–8.

2
WHAT IS "TRADITION HISTORY"?

Having described briefly some of the most important aspects of tradition and of the transmittal process, we turn now to the means devised to investigate these phenomena. Although the general ideas of an oral tradition and of a gradual growth of the Old Testament literature are several centuries old, Hermann Gunkel was the first Old Testament scholar to employ the term "tradition history" ("Überlieferungsgeschichte") in approximately its present sense.[1] The term "Geschichte der Tradition" can be found earlier in Wellhausen's writings,[2] although not with reference to the formation and transmission of literature at the oral stage. Despite these occasional appearances of "tradition history" in the work of Gunkel and others, the first real attempt to develop a traditio-historical approach and program for the Old Testament was made by Martin Noth.[3]

A. Previous Understandings

In the four decades after 1930, tradition historians were unable to reach unanimity on what "tradition history" really is.[4] Terminological imprecision and confusion have plagued the research since its very beginning, and one finds little uniformity in method and scope. One of the main reasons for this regret-

---

1. Gunkel, *Schöpfung und Chaos in Urzeit und Endzeit*, Göttingen 1895, 3, 209, also 256. Cf. also W. Klatt, *Hermann Gunkel: Zu seiner Theologie der Religionsgeschichte und zur Entstehung der formgeschichtlichen Methode*, FRLANT 100, Göttingen 1969, 56 n. 16; see also below, p. 58.
2. For example, as the title of the second section of his *Prolegomena zur Geschichte Israels*, Berlin/Leipzig, 6th ed. 1927 (1st ed. as *Geschichte Israels*, 1878).
3. The beginnings in his book, *Das System der zwölf Stämme Israels*, BWANT IV/1, Stuttgart 1930; further developed later in *ÜSt* (1943) and in *ÜPent* (1948).
4. Compare, e.g., the descriptions and the methodologies in: K. Koch, *Was ist Formgeschichte?*; Richter, *Exegese als Literaturwissenschaft*; and Barth/Steck, *Exegese des Alten Testament*.

table situation is the existence of several "schools," or more properly stated: basic approaches, each with its adherents and subsequent modifications. It does not do to delineate these approaches geographically (e.g., Scandinavian, German, American), for some of the most profound differences exist *within* each of these regions. The absence of a consensus or of a normative approach permits each researcher to develop his or her own methodological conception. The situation becomes further complicated when an individual scholar varies the approach from one study to another. The resultant abundance of definitions of "tradition history" may be grouped according to their two parts: scope (the subject matter to be studied) and method. Obviously, such a delineation should not imply that these two categories do not go hand in hand (a method needs an object to be analyzed, and vice versa), although the fact is that some of the definitions emphasize only one of these sides. Furthermore, these numerous understandings are not always mutually exclusive since several of them lay special weight on only one or just a few of the factors of *traditio* and *traditum* discussed above.

According to the following understandings of the *scope*, "tradition history" consists of the study of:

(1) The history and nature of primarily oral materials, whereby the emphasis is put on this corpus in itself rather than on the oral materials as a prelude to further development at the written level.[5]
(2) Only the oral prehistory of a literary work (= "Überlieferungsgeschichte" according to Sellin/Fohrer and Barth/Steck).[6]
(3) The development of oral as well as written tradition units but not including the literary stages of composition and redaction.[7]
(4) The whole history of a literary piece—from its earliest beginnings as independent units of oral tradition, through its development, growth, and composition at the oral and written levels, and on to its redaction and finalization in its present form.[8]

---

5. Nyberg, Birkeland, Engnell, Nielsen; cf. below, part 2.

6. Mowinckel, *Prophecy and Tradition*, Oslo 1946; J. Scharbert, "Das Traditionsproblem im Alten Testament," *TTZ* 66 (1957), 321; Sellin/Fohrer, *Einleitung in das Alte Testament*, 11th ed., Heidelberg 1969, 28–30; Barth/Steck, *Exegese des Alten Testaments*, 1, 3, 37ff.; H. W. Wolff, *Bibel: Das Alte Testament*, Berlin 1970, 29ff.

7. Richter, *Exegese als Literaturwissenschaft*, 152ff.

8. Noth, *ÜPent*, 1; A. Jepsen, "Zur Überlieferungsgeschichte der Vätergestalten," *WZ Leipzig* 3, Gesellschafts- und sprachwiss. Reihe (1953/54), 139; von Rad, *Theologie* I, e.g., 17–19 (ET: I, 3–5); Richter, cf. below, p. 139; Carlson, cf. below, pp. 245–46; A. H. J. Gunneweg, "Traditionsgeschichtliche Forschung," *BHH*, vol. 3, Göttingen 1966, cols. 2018–19; Koch, *Was ist Formgeschichte?*, 49ff., 64ff.; H. Ringgren, "Literarkritik, Formgeschichte, Überlieferungsge-

(5) The compositional stage, virtually omitting its prehistory.[9]
(6) The history of the occurrences of specific notions, motifs, themes, "Stoffe"(= "Traditionsgeschichte" according to Sellin/Fohrer and Barth/Steck).[10]
(7) The tradition streams—the milieu, background, heritage, or roots of the specific traditionists (especially with respect to the prophets).[11]
(8) The history of the people's reflection and rumination on the basically reliable historical account of past events.[12]

According to the various understandings of its *method*, "tradition history" is seen to be:

(1) The totality of all methods used to examine the text, including thereby text criticism, literary criticism, form criticism, motif criticism.[13]
(2) A branch of Formgeschichte.[14]
(3) Essentially Formgeschichte.[15]
(4) An alternative to and replacement for the literary-critical method.[16]
(5) An investigative step clearly delineated (in subject matter and criteria) from all the other methods of text criticism, literary criticism, form criticism, Gattung criticism, and redaction criticism.[17]
(6) Tradition criticism alone.[18]

---

schichte," *TLZ* 91 (1966), col. 644; R. Rendtorff, "Literarkritik und Traditionsgeschichte," *EvT* 27 (1967), 148–53; Westermann, "Zur Auslegung des Alten Testaments," 216; O. Kaiser (/W. Kümmel/G. Adam), *Einführung in die exegetischen Methoden*, 4th ed., Munich 1969, 24; Kaiser, *Einleitung in das Alte Testament*, Gütersloh 1969, 46; Sæbø, cf. below, p. 276; Steck, *Elia-Erzählungen*, 6–8; W. Rast, *Tradition History and the Old Testament*, Philadelphia 1972, 16–18.

9. Noth, *ÜSt*; Carlson, cf. below, p. 248.

10. Sellin/Fohrer, *Einleitung*, 27–28; Barth/Steck, *Exegese des Alten Testaments*, 4–5, 70ff.; cf. also the discussion in Richter, *Exegese als Literaturwissenschaft*, 153–56.

11. von Rad, "Literarkritische und überlieferungsgeschichtliche Forschung im Alten Testament," *VF* 1947/48 (1949/50), 177; Ringgren, *TLZ* 91 (1966), col. 645.

12. S. Herrmann, cf. below, pp. 155–56.

13. Engnell and Sæbø, cf. below, pp. 214–15, 219, 277.

14. Koch, *Was ist Formgeschichte?*, 66; H. Zimmermann, *Neutestamentliche Methodenlehre: Darstellung der historisch-kritischen Methode*, 2nd ed., Stuttgart 1968, e.g., 175, 200.

15. von Rad, *FPHex* (1938); on von Rad in this respect, cf. also Richter, *Exegese als Literaturwissenschaft*, 73 n. 2.

16. Engnell, Nielsen, Carlson, cf. below, pp. 203–5, 219–20, 247, 265.

17. Richter, *Exegese als Literaturwissenschaft*; and Barth/Steck, *Exegese des Alten Testaments*.

18. Gressmann, cf. below, pp. 67–69.

(7) First an analytic, synchronic examination of a tradition, followed by a synthetic, diachronic step.[19]

(8) An examination of a tradition primarily according to its formal aspects, taking the contents into consideration at a later phase of the exegesis.[20]

(9) The type of investigative approach and presuppositions identified with the "Uppsala School," characterized by a "respect for tradition"[21] and not just for documents, the assumption of a reliable and predominant oral tradition, and an antipathy toward the literary-critical method.[22]

To be sure, several of these conceptions can be combined into a more broadly based definition by individual tradition historians. But such a move does not detract from the general problem: The researchers themselves—to say nothing of the beginning students of the exegetical methods—cannot be blamed for being bewildered, even frustrated, at the pluralistic, diverse, often contrary ways in which traditio-historical research presents itself. The problem, of course, is rooted in the extensive meaning that "tradition" can have. In its larger sense of being everything and anything that is transmitted on to a later generation, tradition requires a methodological scope that can embrace as much as possible. Furthermore, the literature types in the Old Testament vary considerably among themselves, so each of these options can have certain texts for which it is most suited. Thus in a real sense almost all of the above methods can be granted their respective, though qualified right.[23] There is indeed good reason for arguing that tradition history should be all-inclusive. The basic *traditio* principle of interpretation and actualization was in play at all periods of Israel's history, also in Jewish and early Christian times, and in fact still today. The recognition of these facts seems to require methodological flexibility on our part.

---

19. Engnell, cf. below, p. 219; also Richter, *Exegese als Literaturwissenschaft*, 158ff.; and Barth/Steck, *Exegese des Alten Testaments*, 1, 3, 37ff.

20. Richter, *Exegese als Literaturwissenschaft*, 156ff.

21. Nielsen, cf. below, p. 265.

22. Ringgren, *TLZ* 91 (1966), cols. 644ff.; Rendtorff, *EvT* 27 (1967), 138–40, 147ff.; Koch, *Was ist Formgeschichte?*, 98ff.

23. Cf. an analogous conclusion regarding the critical hypotheses in pentateuchal research, Kaiser, *Einleitung*, 47–48.

B. Definition of Tradition and Tradition History

But is this "Methodenstrudel" nonetheless desirable or necessary? For pragmatic reasons, it seems wiser to have a more defined, limited conception of tradition history than the comprehensive definition of tradition would require. A focused understanding of the field should permit us to develop a method that is controllable, operational, and productive. However, there should be no illusions about the arbitrariness of this delimitation. Its justification is clarity, precision, economy, and practicality. One final preliminary remark: The following description of tradition history is an "ideal type"; the investigation of specific Old Testament texts will at times require slight modifications and adjustments of this theoretical structure.

According to our understanding, a *tradition* has the following characteristics:

(1) It is received from others and transmitted further, especially from one generation to the next.
(2) It has both form and content. The history of a tradition can only be retraced as long as it remains "formal greifbar";[24] beyond this point the elements of content must be examined under the rubrics of Motivgeschichte, Stoffgeschichte, Themengeschichte, Begriffsgeschichte, Vorstellungsgeschichte, or Problemgeschichte.
(3) A tradition is the immediate property of a group or a community, i.e. it has a direct function for the people who transmit it.
(4) A tradition is "living," developing, malleable, and only relatively stable; it can become changed and reinterpreted to meet the needs of its transmitters.
(5) A tradition is usually oral but can also be in written form as long as it fulfills the other criteria mentioned here, especially that of being able to develop and adapt.[25]
(6) Tradition tends to be cumulative and agglomerative.

This definition of tradition would usually exclude the Gattungen composed at the written stage: novelle, annals, lists of officials and of geographical places (though not the total genre of lists).[26] Traditions are not limited to narrative Gattungen but include also poetry, proverbs, laws and regulations,

---

24. Cf. above, p. 10.
25. *Oral* transmission is therefore not the determinative criterion for a tradition—contrary to the position of many; cf., e.g., above, p. 18 n. 6.
26. Cf. also Richter, *Exegese als Literaturwissenschaft*, 165.

prophetic sayings, psalms. If traditions are joined by their traditionists into a cycle or complex, this complex may continue to exist as a tradition. *However, a tradition ceases to be such at that point at which it is removed* (by an individual or by a subgroup of its usual traditionists) *from its normal context in life and is entered into a written composition*, thereby virtually losing its ability to develop and adapt. This juncture also marks the *terminus ad quem* for the tradition history. The chief criterion is not that an oral tradition becomes recorded in writing; note that we stated under (5) that a tradition can also be in written form. Rather, the criterion is that the tradition is separated from its life context and has been made a part of a relatively static written composition. From this point onwards, the researcher is not dealing with tradition history but with the compositional stage (the techniques and personal involvement of the composer, the historical impetus for the writing, the writer's reception of traditional materials), then with the history of this composition as a piece of literature and as a source document, and finally its later redaction(s) and finalization into its present form.[27] Thus tradition history should be distinguished from compositional analysis and from Redaktionsgeschichte, rather than regarded as embracing the two.[28]

To take the place of "tradition history" as the all-inclusive term,[29] there is another concept which has been at our disposal since early in this century: "*Literaturgeschichte.*" According to Gunkel, literature is to be seen as a life expression of the people producing it, and writing a history of it requires taking into consideration all the factors which contributed to its coming into being and all the levels of meanings which it contains. In this same sense "Lit-

---

27. This means then that von Rad's treatment of the Jahwistic composition (in *FPHex*, 1938) falls outside the realm of tradition history, whereas Noth's G is very much a part of it inasmuch as he argues that G is a product of the amphictyonic community. However, Noth's study of the Deuteronomistic composer is not to be included in tradition history in this sense, despite his title *Überlieferungsgeschichtliche Studien* (1943). We can also avoid creating a new entity, a "documentary-literary method" (so Engnell and Carlson, cf. below, p. 247), to deal with, e.g., Dtr and Chr.

28. The extent to which this definition and delimitation of tradition and tradition history may be applicable also for New Testament conditions would require special investigation alone. One may suspect that tradition could still be defined according to its growth and life among its traditionists (the disciples, the primitive church), but the difference in the time span (a few decades in New Testament times compared with a matter of centuries in ancient Israel) raises new problems and considerations. It is interesting to note that a position quite similar to ours is taken by G. Schille, who argues that New Testament *written* sources are no longer internally malleable and therefore not the subject matter of Überlieferungsgeschichte; "Literarische Quellenhypothesen im Licht der Wahrscheinlichkeitsfrage," *TLZ* 97 (1972), cols. 336–338.

29. That many scholars conceive of tradition history as such can be seen above, pp. 18–19.

eraturgeschichte" is understood in our contemporary literary sciences.[30] For the Old Testament, the history of literature will therefore not be restricted to the level of written documents but will cover the whole span stretching from the earliest oral traditions and tradition complexes on to the subsequent stages of composition, redaction, and finalization, including thereby all matters of content (motifs, themes, concepts, etc.), relevant historical aspects, and theological import.[31]

In conclusion, a word should be said regarding terminology. The German language has two different words at its disposal for "tradition history": "Traditionsgeschichte" and "Überlieferungsgeschichte."[32] For decades these words have been used interchangeably with no apparent difference in meaning between them. A few German scholars have tried to distinguish—artificially and arbitrarily, it would seem—between them, applying "Überlieferungsgeschichte" to the prehistory of a text unit and "Traditionsgeschichte" to the history of elements of content (notions, motifs, streams, etc.) not limited to a specific tradition unit.[33] This distinction has not become established,[34] and the confusion continues. The best solution may be to avoid differentiating in meaning between these two terms and to prefer the Latinized form "Traditionsgeschichte" for the prehistory of the text unit.[35] Such a move will facilitate understanding in other languages where only the derivative from the Latin is available. If one is referring to the history of any other object (a notion, motif, theme, concept, tradition stream, the ideological background), then it should go under these respective names rather than simply and imprecisely being called "tradition history." It should also be obvious that this term must include all methodological directions taken and not be restricted to one specific approach (e.g., that of the Scandinavians, notably Engnell).

---

30. Cf., e.g., the articles "Literatur" and "Literaturgeschichte" in Von Wilpert, *Sachwörterbuch der Literatur*, 440–45.

31. Cf. also Richter, *Exegese als Literaturwissenschaft*, 36–37, 72 n. 91, 166, 190 n. 63; and Koch, *Was ist Formgeschichte?*, 125–30.

32. A similar distinction can be made also in Norwegian, Danish, and Dutch.

33. Cf. especially Sellin/Fohrer, *Einleitung*, 27–30; Ringgren, *TLZ* 91 (1966), col. 644; and Barth/Steck, *Exegese des Alten Testaments*, 37–38, 70–71.

34. Cf., e.g., Westermann, "Zur Auslegung des Alten Testaments," 216–19, where the terms are used synonymously; and Richter, *Exegese als Literaturwissenschaft*, 152–65, where "Überlieferungsgeschichte" is not used and "Traditionsgeschichte" is identical to the "Überlieferungsgeschichte" of Fohrer and Barth/Steck.

35. The Germanic word "Überlieferungsgeschichte," if it is to be used, should be synonymous to "Traditionsgeschichte," as it was originally.

C. Methodology

A brief description of the traditio-historical method of investigation may be helpful.[36] Since according to our definition tradition history is concerned with illuminating the precompositional[37] history of the text, the point of departure for the examination must be the text (whether smaller unit or larger section) as we have it. The traditio-historical examination must be preceded by the text-critical, literary-critical, form-critical, and Gattung-critical analyses of the unit in question. These preliminary steps can provide information about the original text, its unity or disunity, its structure, pregiven elements, and pregiven units.[38] On the basis of these insights, the tradition historian begins with a *critical analysis* of the tradition, trying to determine and describe each of the stages through which it passed in its process of development. The effort should be made to trace the tradition back as far as possible, although it will seldom be possible to reach its origins. The second step consists of *historical synthesis*, the diachronic consideration of the analytical findings in an attempt to present a relative chronology of the growth of the tradition up to the point of its inclusion in a written composition. The first step is called "tradition criticism"; the second is "tradition history."[39] For both, attention is directed to all the aspects of *traditio* and *traditum* listed above in chapter 1. Despite all our efforts to carry out this examination with as objective, thorough, and sophisticated means as are at our disposal, we must have no illusions about the fact that we are working in a domain of hypotheses and conjectures. Certainty is elusive, if not even unattainable; the great variations among suggested solutions to certain problems give silent witness to this fact. This hypothetical character of traditio-historical work makes caution essential also in our attempts to draw historical and theological consequences from our results.

---

36. A detailed discussion is superfluous here in light of several methodological presentations (with examples) published: Richter, *Exegese als Literaturwissenschaft*, 152–65; Barth/Steck, *Exegese des Alten Testaments*, 37–47; Rast, *Tradition History*; and Koch, *Was ist Formgeschichte?*, 49–71 and 97–112.

37. In the present study the term "precompositional" refers to the period *prior to the initial written composition* of traditions. When reference is made to a composition executed at the oral stage, this will be referred to explicitly as *oral composition*.

38. Cf. also Richter, *Exegese als Literaturwissenschaft*, 156–57.

39. While this terminological distinction is important, "tradition history" is usually used—also in the present study—to designate the total methodological process. It should nonetheless not be forgotten that the critical analysis must always precede the synthesis. For a different distinction between "tradition criticism" (or "analysis") and "tradition history," cf. B. Otzen, *Studien über Deuterosacharja*, ATDan 6, Copenhagen 1964, 213–14, 225; and J. B. Grønbæk, *Die Geschichte vom Aufstieg Davids (1. Sam. 15–2. Sam. 5)*, ATDan 10, Copenhagen 1971, 17.

D. Yield

How can traditio-historical research benefit the scholar and the layperson? What are its yield and gains? Quite generally, these include:[40]

(1) Awareness that the Old Testament on the whole is much more than a scribal compilation or creation; it incorporates the experiences, interpretations, and reflections of a worshiping community.
(2) Appreciation for the depth dimension of a textual unit, complex, or book—its origin and development with respect to location, time, participants, intentions, function; this information is indispensable for exegesis.
(3) Recognition of the importance of the reactualization and reinterpretation process and its relevance for later ages, even for today.[41]
(4) Insight into the relation of a text and its message to overriding theological streams and historical continuities, especially when a concept or idea is critically received and altered.
(5) Knowledge of the history of Israel's faith, cult, and religion.
(6) Information about historical and religio-historical conditions in Israel and often in other ancient Near Eastern cultures as well.

---

40. Cf. also Zimmerli, "Form- und Traditionsgeschichte im Dienst der Verkündigung," *ZKT* 92 (1970), 72–81; Barth/Steck, *Exegese des Alten Testaments*, 43–45, 77–78; Koch, *Was ist Formgeschichte?*, 67–70, 123ff.; and Rast, *Tradition History*, 72ff.

41. Cf. also Noth, "Die Vergegenwärtigung des Alten Testaments in der Verkündigung" (1952/53), *Probleme alttestamentlicher Hermeneutik*, ed. Westermann, 54–68.

3
Scope and Method of the Present Study

Is it possible to write a history of a specific investigative method that has been employed—and so differently—on all sections of the Old Testament? If so, how can such an account best be executed? Breadth of subject matter and diversity of treatment within traditio-historical research counsel against simple answers to these questions. Unifying elements for our study seem elusive, for we are not dealing with a single scholar, a specific tradition complex, a problem, a motif, or a period of past history—but with a type of research, a series of questions which scholars try to answer.

The purpose of the present study is to provide a critical history of the rise of Old Testament traditio-historical research and of the treatment of basic traditio-historical problems. It will not do to give a strict definition of "tradition history" (as we have done above) and then to restrict our history of the research to only this limited area of concern. Rather, we must try to understand everything that has gone under the name of "tradition history" or that has contributed to its rise and research. Such an approach means that we will be touching on many varied topics, but then diversity has been the central characteristic of traditio-historical work since its very outset. A negative goal of our study is thus to demonstrate these contrasts in methods as well as the lack of unanimity regarding questions of substance. But more than this, we are interested in determining the positive contributions and advances made by each scholar along the way. All of the aspects of *traditio* and *traditum* described in chapter 1 will be our points of orientation. We do not pretend to plumb the depths of each problem or topic—although an intensive scrutiny is needed at many points—but rather to indicate the problems and to discuss some of the solutions already suggested. Chief attention is directed to foundational studies, with only cursory reference to subsequent developments in the discussion.

Although other organizational options are available, it seems best to structure this history of the research according to the main participants and their contributions.¹ The other prime alternative would be to examine the advances made in the study of each individual Old Testament book and tradition complex, but there is no lack of critical surveys organized in this way.² Contemporary research tends, perhaps unfortunately, to be very much person- or school-oriented, a circumstance that in itself may justify structuring a critical history of the research in the same way. However, by approaching the problem from this angle, we will try also by means of cross-references to afford a broader picture of each problem or Old Testament tradition and its treatment. Selectivity is unavoidable, and certain key figures (especially Simon, Gunkel, von Rad, Noth, Mowinckel, Engnell, Widengren, Carlson, Nielsen, Sæbø) receive proportionately much more attention either because of their importance in the debate or because of their especially exemplary traditio-historical studies of some tradition complex. For each researcher we will want to give an adequate picture of work in this direction and to distill from it the understanding of the traditio-historical task. In the course of our study examples are offered from all of the major literary genres—historical, legal, prophetic, psalmic—as well as the history of a notion. A critique of basic methodological matters concludes each of the two major parts.

For pragmatic reasons, Scandinavian scholars are treated separately in part 2. The existence of an "Uppsala School" or "Scandinavian School" is generally assumed—though without full justification, as we hope to show. Admittedly, a few of these scholars tended often to work in isolation from, e.g., German scholarship, but then several others were from the outset greatly attached to and influenced by non-Scandinavian work. By discussing the Scandinavian debate separately, we hope to clarify the exact extent of unity and disunity among these researchers and to emphasize their contributions to the total traditio-historical enterprise. The purpose of part 2 thus varies somewhat from that of part 1, which is designed to trace the growing awareness of traditio-historical problems and the development of an investigative method. Scandinavian research is still often misunderstood, caricatured, and unknown in its details. The great attention paid here to some of its basic features and to its diversity strives to close this gap.

Finally, this history of the research aspires to a sober appraisal of traditio-historical directions taken by various exegetes. The precision encouraged and promoted in various methodological studies (especially by Richter, Barth/

---

1. For a basic, brief study done already in this direction, cf. H.-J. Kraus, "Zur Geschichte des Überlieferungsbegriffs in der alttestamentlichen Wissenschaft," *EvT* 16 (1956), 371–87.

2. Cf. especially the various introductions to the Old Testament books, the pertinent articles in *VF* and *TRu*, and such publications as H. H. Rowley, ed., *The Old Testament and Modern Study: A Generation of Discovery and Research*, Oxford 1951.

Steck, Koch, Rast—for all of their differences) gives new hope for more purposeful research and controllable results. A history of the research can be of benefit as a means for establishing which techniques and results have proved worthwhile and which have not. The basic conviction underlying this present study is that scientific research—also in the area of religion and the humanities—is self-scrutinizing and self-correcting: Investigative paths that are not promising or that are suspect in method or presuppositions will eventually be abandoned in favor of those which are more effective, controllable, and productive.[3] The same applies analogously to the results attained, for the conclusions reached at the end of the analytical process need to be exposed to the consideration and critique of other researchers. Those results which prove to be most plausible and which can explain most adequately and fully the past historical conditions under examination can be considered provisionally valid and true—until they can be replaced by superior solutions.[4] Our present study aims to assess basic traditio-historical methods and results and thereby to contribute to the charting of the paths which continuing research can take.

---

3. Cf. also Engnell, "Methodological Aspects of Old Testament Study," VTSup 7 (1960), 28; and Rendtorff, *EvT* 27 (1967), 149.

4. For example, a few traditio-historical theses that have been able to stand firm under attack are: the central role of the Israelite cult in the growth and preservation of traditions, the importance of oral transmission and oral composition, the presence of clear streams of tradition, and the idea of reactualization and reinterpretation.

PART 1

THE RISE OF THE TRADITIO-HISTORICAL RESEARCH OF THE OLD TESTAMENT

(Excluding Scandinavian Contributions)

4
RICHARD SIMON AND THE AWAKENING TO THE PROBLEM OF OLD TESTAMENT TRADITION

A. Background

The period of the Reformation witnessed the establishment of a new understanding of Scripture. In opposition to the Roman Catholic investment of prime authority in the on-going tradition of the Church (the Fathers, the popes, the Councils), the Protestant Reformers confessed *sola scriptura*. Luther saw in the Bible the incarnation of the Word of God; for Calvin it was inspired at all points by the Holy Spirit. Despite their occasional references to the possibility of some active human participation in the production of the Bible, the concept of *scriptura sacra* dominated all questions of biblical origins. The epoch of Protestant orthodoxy (e.g., Johann Gerhard and Martin Chemnitz) sought to secure this position—especially the doctrine of inspiration, the concept of pure truth contained in the Bible, and the anti-Catholic denunciation of the authority of tradition. Yet beginning already among the Reformers and gaining ever more ground in the seventeenth century, historical criticism of the Old Testament found expression—usually carefully and without the intent of shaking Christian belief in the Bible as God's Word. These scattered critical remarks were spurred on also by influences from without—especially humanism with its emphasis on humanity and English deism with its attention to forces and materials not limited to Israel. On the whole, the seventeenth century experienced "an intellectual process, at the end of which came the dethronement of the Bible as the authoritative source of all human knowledge and understanding"[1] and of which process the individual critical expressions are perhaps more symptoms than causes.[2]

---

1. K. Scholder, *Ursprünge und Probleme der Bibelkritik im 17. Jahrhundert: Ein Beitrag zur Entstehung der historisch-kritischen Theologie*, FGLP X/33, Munich 1966, 14.

2. For more details on the various aspects of early biblical criticism, cf. especially L. Diestel, *Geschichte des Alten Testamentes in der christlichen Kirche*, Jena 1869; F. Stummer, *Die*

During most periods of historical-critical work on the Old Testament, the historical books (usually the Pentateuch) seem to occupy a keystone position in the debate. The situation is no different with regard to the initial considerations of the traditions of Israel. The beginnings stem from *the question concerning the Mosaic authorship of the five books traditionally attributed to him.* As early as 1152–1153 in his commentary on the Pentateuch, Abraham ben Meir Ibn Ezra raised doubts about Moses' immediate responsibility for the entirety of these books. Similar positions were taken more decidedly by Carlstadt and the Roman Catholics Andreas Masius and Bento Pereira in the sixteenth century;[3] and in the following century Cornelius a Lapide (van der Steen), the Jesuit Jacques Bonfrère, the English philosopher Thomas Hobbes, Isaak de la Peyrère, the Jewish philosopher Benedict de Spinoza, and Richard Simon endeavored to deliver the proof that Moses could not have written the Pentateuch in its present form.[4] To take the place of Mosaic authorship another explanation for the origin of the Pentateuch had to be found, providing the occasion for the first serious consideration of the principles of tradition and transmission.

Two essentially different theories were proposed, one for the pre-Mosaic period and one for the Mosaic and post-Mosaic period. (1) For the book of Genesis several of these pioneers of biblical criticism postulated an *oral tradition* passed down from Adam via Noah and the patriarchs and finally to Moses, who then recorded it (with the assistance of the Holy Spirit, it was held). Calvin (in 1554) was among the first to offer such a suggestion, implying that the tradition was faithfully preserved until Moses' time but that it needed to be recorded in order to preserve it from likely corruption in later periods.[5]

Bedeutung Richard Simons für die Pentateuchkritik, Alttestamentliche Abhandlungen III/4, Münster 1912; E. McQ. Gray, *Old Testament Criticism, its Rise and Progress from the Second Century to the End of the Eighteenth: A Historical Sketch,* New York/London 1923; Kraus, *Geschichte der historisch-kritischen Erforschung des Alten Testaments,* 2nd ed., Neukirchen-Vluyn 1969, 6ff.; and Kraus, *EvT* 16 (1956), 371ff.

3. Carlstadt, *De canonicis Scripturis libellus,* Wittenberg 1520; Masius, *Josuae imperatoris historia illustrata atque explicata,* Antwerp 1574; and Pereira, *Tomus I–IV commentariorum et disputationum in Genesim,* Lyon 1594–1600.

4. A Lapide, *Commentaria in Pentateuchum Mosis,* 1616; Bonfrère, *Pentateuchus Moysis commentario illustratus,* Antwerp 1625; Hobbes, *Leviathan, or the Matter, Forme, and Power of a Commonwealth Ecclesiastical and Civil,* London 1651, part 3, Chap. 33; Peyrère, *Systema Theologicum, ex Praeadamitarum Hypothesi,* pars prima, 1655; Spinoza, *Tractatus theologico-politicus,* Hamburg 1670, Chap. 7 and 8; and Simon, cf. below, pp. 38–39.

5. Because Kraus (*EvT* 16, 1956, 371–73; and *Geschichte,* 6–8) emphasizes that a Roman Catholic-like concept of human *traditio oralis* was basically incompatible with the Reformers' understanding of the divine origin of the Bible, it seems best to quote the entire passage from Calvin's introduction to his *Commentaries on the First Book of Moses, called Genesis* (trans.

Similar ideas can be found in the writings of Martin Chemnitz[6] and even Blaise Pascal.[7] (2) However, for the books of Exodus–Joshua these early critics envi-

---

J. King, Edinburgh 1847, vol. 1, 58–59, emphases added), regarding Moses' writing of Genesis: Moses "does not here put forward divinations of his own, but is the instrument of the Holy Spirit for the publication of those things which it was of importance for all men to know. They greatly err in deeming it absurd that the order of the creation, which had been previously unknown, should at length have been described and explained by him. *For he does not transmit to memory things before unheard of, but for the first time consigns to writing facts which the fathers had delivered as from hand to hand, through a long succession of years, to their children.* Can we conceive that man was so placed in the earth as to be ignorant of his own origin, and of the origin of those things which he enjoyed? No sane person doubts that Adam was well instructed respecting them all. Was he indeed afterwards dumb? Were the holy Patriarchs so ungrateful as to suppress in silence such necessary instruction? Did Noah, warned by a divine judgment so memorable, neglect to transmit it to posterity? Abraham is expressly honoured with this eulogy, that he was the teacher and the master of his family, (Gen. xviii. 19). And we know that, long before the time of Moses, an acquaintance with the covenant into which God had entered with their fathers was common to the whole people. When he says that the Israelites were sprung from a holy race, which God had chosen for himself, he does not propound it as something new, but only commemorates what all held, what the old men themselves had received from their ancestors, and what, in short, was entirely uncontroverted among them. Therefore, we ought not to doubt that The Creation of the World, as here described, was already known through the ancient and perpetual tradition of the Fathers. *Yet, since nothing is more easy than that the truth of God should be corrupted by men, that, in a long succession of time, it should, as it were, degenerate from itself, it pleased the Lord to commit the history to writing, for the purpose of preserving its purity. Moses, therefore, has established the credibility of that doctrine which is contained in his writings, and which, by the carelessness of men, might otherwise have been lost.*" It is not fully clear in this text whether Calvin assumed that Moses wrote Genesis more on the basis of the tradition from the ancestors or on the basis of divine inspiration. Presumably he believed that the Spiritus sanctus guided Moses to keep the Scripture free from error, yet Calvin's reference to the corruptibility of tradition seems to apply more to the post-Mosaic than to the pre-Mosaic period. If so, Calvin's usual view (as emphasized by Kraus) of the origin of the Bible is here modified: *for Genesis, Calvin attributes a major role to human transmission and participation.* —Appreciation is due to Prof. Martin Metzger of Hamburg for the private reference (in August 1971) to this passage in Calvin's commentary on Genesis.

6. *Examen Consilii Tridentini*, Frankfurt 1578, prima pars, 8–12. Kraus (*EvT* 16, 1956, 373; and *Geschichte*, 33) points out that for Chemnitz (applicable also for Calvin) the essential aspect of this pre-Mosaic oral tradition was that the line of transmitters could be traced, thereby insuring through testimony the *pura doctrina*. One is reminded of the Arabic habit of requiring transmitters to legitimize themselves by recounting the line of their predecessors in transmission.

7. In his *Pensées* (article 11 in the Port-Royal edition, 1670; Paragraph No. 870 in Michaut's edition, 1896; paragraph 625 in the Brunschvicg edition; paragraph 573 in the Lafuma edition): "Shem, who saw Lamech, who saw Adam, also saw Jacob, who saw those who saw Moses. Therefore the Flood and the Creation are true. That is conclusive for certain people who understand it properly." Jean Astruc, in his *Conjectures*, Bruxelles 1753, 6, quotes this passage in a slightly different form, with the following interesting comment: "'Shem, who saw Lamech, who

sioned a type of *written transmission*. According to the various hypotheses, Moses and Joshua (or the high priest Eleazar) kept detailed records of all laws and events during their lifetime, and these *diaries and annals* were passed on throughout Israelite history until some later individual (Ezra is usually suggested) compiled them and produced the historical books as we have them. Calvin (in 1563) and Chemnitz (in 1578) were among the first to propose this theory, though they were careful to include a security factor: These diaries and annals were deposited in the ark of the covenant and thereby preserved from corruption and tampering.[8] This idea of a written transmission was adopted also by Masius (in 1574),[9] a Lapide (in 1616), Peyrère (in 1655),[10] and Spinoza (in 1670)—several of these individuals being willing (in contrast to Calvin) to allow for some amount of alterations and additions at the hands of later transmitters and compilers.

This then is the situation prior to Simon's critical study of the Old Testament. Certain Roman Catholic, Protestant, and Jewish scholars recognized the working of some *traditio* principle in the origin of specific sections of

---

saw Adam, saw at least Abraham, and Abraham saw Jacob, who saw those who saw Moses.' This reflection, which is correct, was proposed long ago, and it has been adopted by all who have written on this subject. They attempt to render the tradition more simple and certain by avoiding a transmission by too great a number of hands, where it could have become obscured, weakened, or altered."

8. Cf. Kraus, *EvT* 16 (1956), 372–73; *Geschichte*, 33. Interestingly enough, this same idea (that diaries and records from Moses' time onward were deposited in the "Ark library") has been revived in our century: E. C. Richardson, "Oral Tradition, Libraries and the Hexateuch," *PTR* 3 (1905), 211ff.

9. In the preface to his *Josuae imperatoris historia*, Masius asserted that the book of Joshua, though bearing Joshua's name, was not necessarily authored by him but more likely by Ezra: "In my opinion it is certain that Ezra, a man who was divinely inspired with a unique piety and depth of learning, either alone or with the help of others of equal ability, edited and put in proper order not only the book of Joshua, but also the books of Judges and Kings. He did the same with the other books which we read in those writings called the Bible, and *he compiled them from different annals which were preserved within the community of God*" (2, emphasis added). Among the diaries and annals were such sources as the "Book of the Wars of the Lord." In the process of compilation the accounts were mended or improved ("sarcitum") by the introduction of words and sentences for the purpose of clarification (2).

10. *Systema theologicum*, 174 (emphasis added): "I would be willing to claim as certain the view that *Moses composed diaries* of all the wondrous deeds which God, under the leadership of Moses, performed for the benefit of the Jews. From these diaries, a long time after Moses, that book called 'The Wars of the Lord' could have been put together. The book of Numbers was excerpted from this latter work, but Numbers should not be considered an autograph, nor as a copy made from an autograph, but actually as a *copy made from a copy*." Peyere postulated the long literary development ("excerpted and translated from different authors," 178) not only of Numbers but of the rest of the Pentateuch as well.

the Bible. The newly formulated position regarding the *traditio oralis* of the Church as issued by the Council of Trent (1545–48) stood in the background but had no positive influence on the understanding of how Scripture came to be. It remained for Simon to draw the strings together and to develop a precise concept of the importance and nature of *traditio* in ancient Israel.

B. Simon's Critical Research

There are inherent difficulties in trying to locate the inception of an idea. Critical sciences tend to be progressive in nature, "novel" hypotheses and analytical approaches being so often a matter of combining, building on, or establishing already existent theories and techniques. The "totally new" is a rare phenomenon—and not the defining characteristic of epoch-making works.[11] Richard Simon (1638–1712) can rightly be identified as the pioneer of historical-critical biblical research and as *the precursor of the traditio-historical investigation of the Old Testament*[12]—and this despite the fact that many of his ideas and theories had already been propounded prior to him. His work deserves closer attention at this point if we are to assess properly his contributions to the research.[13]

Simon, French Catholic priest of the Congregation of the Oratory, published in 1678 his chief and most significant work: *Histoire critique du Vieux Testament*.[14] Despite his frequent statements of allegiance to Roman Catholicism and his heated attacks on Spinoza and the Protestants, the book aroused the anger of other priests in France to the extent that Simon was expelled from the Oratory and his book was suppressed and in 1683 officially listed in the Roman Catholic *Index librorum prohibitorum*. Nevertheless, a copy of

---

11. Cf. also Diestel, *Geschichte*, 353 n. 19; and Kraus, *Geschichte*, 70.

12. Kraus was the first to have grasped this importance of Simon's idea of tradition; *EvT* 16 (1956), 375–76; and *Geschichte*, 65–70. Kraus has privately referred to a much earlier study by J. H. Majus (1653–1719) on Simon and his view of tradition; Majus's book was not available to this writer.

13. For further critical and biographical information on Simon, cf. the following: K. H. Graf, "Richard Simon," *Beiträge zu den theologischen Wissenschaften*, vol. 1 (Jena 1847), 158–242; A. Bernus, *Richard Simon et son Histoire critique du Vieux Testament: La critique biblique au siècle de Louis XIV*, Lausanne 1869; Diestel, *Geschichte*, 352–57; A. Westphal, *Les Sources du Pentateuque, étude de critique et d'histoire: I, Le problème littéraire*, Paris 1888, 67ff., passim; H. Margival, *Essai sur Richard Simon et la critique biblique au XVIIe siècle*, 1st ed., Paris 1896–1900, reprinted Genève 1970; Stummer, *Die Bedeutung Richard Simons*; Gray, *Old Testament Criticism*, 101–15; J. Steinmann, *Richard Simon et les origines de l'exégèse biblique*, Paris 1960; and the two above-mentioned publications of Kraus.

14. Paris 1678; 5th ed., Rotterdam 1685; reprinted Frankfurt 1967. References here are to the 5th edition.

the book got to Rotterdam where several defective and pirated editions were issued until 1685, when Simon himself apparently supervised the publication of the fifth edition. The book then received fairly wide distribution and prompted numerous polemical publications, but its positive effect on biblical studies was minimal and its real value unappreciated for almost a century. Yet the its significance must not be underestimated: "It was, in a word, the first serious and, to a certain degree, scholarly attempt to write a history of the Bible as a literary work."[15]

Histoire critique du Vieux Testament is divided into three parts, treating respectively the history of the text, the versions, and Old Testament interpretation. It is primarily the first of these which holds our attention in this discussion,[16] although we must not overlook the fact that Simon made significant contributions in the other areas as well. *The primary problem which he sought to solve was that of dissociating the idea of the divine inspiration of biblical books from the question of their authenticity.*[17] The book of Genesis, for example, can be Holy Scripture without being the literary product of Moses. And having freed himself from the need to perpetuate uncritically the traditional beliefs regarding authorship, he could develop his own alternative: the historical, human process of transmission and the subsequent compilation of the materials into our present books. Simon is clear about the importance of understanding this process: "it is impossible to understand the sacred books perfectly unless one has prior knowledge of the different states in which the text of the books is formed according to the different times and different places and unless one is instructed exactly in all the changes that happened to it."[18] The awareness of this need to differentiate between the developmental stages is the crucial characteristic of Simon's work.

Simon posited a plurality of sources and a long period of transmission for much of the Old Testament. For example, he maintained that the entire Pentateuch could not be the work of only Moses.[19] We have seen in the above section that this idea was not original to Simon but had been proposed by a

---

15. E. Reuss, "Richard Simon," *RE*, vol. 14, 1st ed. 1861, 401; 3rd ed., vol. 18, 1906, 363.

16. Specifically: book 1, chs. 2–5 and 7; also chs. 4, 6, 8, 10, and 11 of his *Réponse au Livre intitulé Sentimens de quelques Theologiens de Hollande sur l'Histoire Critique du Vieux Testament*, Rotterdam 1686.

17. Cf. also Steinmann, *Richard Simon*, 100–102.

18. *Histoire critique du Vieux Testament*, Préface.

19. The title of the fifth chapter of the first section was precisely to this point: "Moses cannot be the author of everything in the books that are attributed to him." When the prospectus of the book was circulated prior to publication in 1678, it was apparently this statement that aroused the attention, and the anger, of his French colleagues (especially Bossuet), resulting in the condemnation and suppression of the book. Cf. also Steinmann, *Richard Simon*, 124–30.

number of scholars prior to him.[20] His contribution was in gathering the criticisms of others and, supported by his own research and ideas, constructing the argument into a reasonable whole. He found four general groups of facts to disprove the Mosaic authorship of the entire Pentateuch: (1) those passages that have a different historical background than the time of Moses, e.g., Deut 34; Gen 12:6; Num 21:14;[21] (2) repetitions "of an identical thing in the Pentateuch—repetitions that apparently are not at all from Moses but rather from those who made the collection of the sacred books and who joined together several readings or explications of the same words, without considering it necessary to remove anything from their copies that would clarify the text,"[22] as, e.g., in Gen 7:17–24; Exod 31:14–16; Lev 3:9; (3) the many minor cases of poor order (e.g., the mention of woman in Gen 1:27 before her creation is described in the following chapter), which Simon attributed to the fact that the books in ancient times were written on small scrolls or separate sheets, the order of which could easily have been changed;[23] and (4) the variety of literary styles throughout the Pentateuch, which seems to indicate that the same author could not have written all of it.[24] Simon also observed the same additions and changes in the book of Joshua as in the Pentateuch, from which he concluded that Joshua could not have been the author of the book that bears his name.[25] Similarly, the other historical books are to be dated at a much later time than the period with which they deal. There exists no conflict between the question of historicity and the belief in inspiration with regard to the poetical literature (especially Job) either: "Moreover, whether a book or a history or a simple parable or a history mixed with parables, it is at any rate no less true or no less divine."[26] *Simon's awareness of these distinctions marks the onset of biblical criticism.*

---

20. E.g., Ibn Ezra, Carlstadt, Masius, Pereira, a Lapide, Bonfrère, Hobbes, Peyrère, Spinoza. The direct line of development from Masius to Pereira to Simon has been emphasized by Kraus, *Geschichte*, 40–41.

21. *Histoire critique*, 21–32. Ibn Ezra, Hobbes, and Spinoza had preceded Simon with this argument.

22. *Histoire critique*, 33.

23. Ibid., 35. Simon was probably building on Peyrère's criticism here.

24. Ibid., 39: "One sees in it sometimes a very terse style and sometimes a very expansive style, although diversity of material does not require it."

25. Ibid., 53.

26. Ibid., 58.

C. Understanding of Tradition

Simon thus posited that the historical books of the Old Testament were compiled at a relatively late date. Prior to him, Spinoza had set the *terminus a quo* of the development of the Pentateuch with Moses, and the *terminus ad quem* with Ezra.[27] But whereas Spinoza failed to elaborate on the transmission and collection of materials in this interim period, Simon's attention was directed precisely to this process. To solve the problem of transmittal agents he developed the hypothesis of *public scribes* ("écrivains publics").[28] These scribes, under Moses' direction, recorded the significant facts and events of Israel's history, and the records were kept in *public registries or archives* (which Simon identified as "the book" in Exod 17:14; cf. also Deut 31:19) for subsequent generations. The scribes were filled with the prophetic spirit (Num 11:16, 25) and were divinely inspired in their writing tasks.[29] This institution of scribes—Simon also called them prophets—continued to function long after the time of Moses, and their annals included also prophetic speeches and many songs. These public registries were the sources that the later writers used for composing collections ("recueils") or résumés ("abrégés") of the historical facts for popular consumption. It was finally *Ezra who was responsible for the "dernier recueil"*[30]—gathering, organizing, and editing the earlier collections and traditions into the present form, though some textual changes were also made to it after his time. The book of Genesis, however, was not recorded by the public scribes in this way, but rather by Moses himself since it dealt with very early history. There is no mention in Genesis of God's dictating to Moses, so Simon concluded that all of the historical accounts and the genealogies in the book are simply related "as if Moses took them from some authentic books or as if he had a constant tradition."[31] Moses also took the responsibility for writing down the laws, but the rest of the Pentateuch was the product of the public scribes. According to Simon, however, it is not pos-

---

27. *Tractatus theologico-politicus*, 1670; cf. Kraus, *Geschichte*, 62, 67.

28. Simon, *Histoire critique*, 3-4, 15-40, passim. As we have seen above (pp. 35-36), the idea of diaries and annals handed down to later generations had been previously suggested by Calvin, Chemnitz, Masius, a Lapide, Peyrère, and Spinoza.

29. The factor of inspiration is therefore no longer dependent upon a single individual (e.g., Moses or Joshua); according to Simon, God can divinely inspire a group just as well. *Histoire critique*, 50.

30. Ibid., 47. Cf. above, pp. 34-35, for the idea of a traditional line from Adam to Moses, already suggested by Calvin, Chemnitz, and Pascal. Simon's opponent Jacque Bossuet also subscribed to this idea; *Discours sur l'Histoire universelle*, Paris 1681, 2ᵉ Partie, ch. 3, 194-95.

sible for us today to determine precisely which materials stem from Moses himself and which come from the pens of his successors.[32]

Here then with Simon the basic idea of tradition and transmission gains central significance. He emphasized that numerous writers were involved in the various stages of the composition of the Old Testament (particularly the Pentateuch) and that there was *a continuous chain from Moses to Ezra* through which the traditional materials were passed. To be sure, Simon was concerned with only the general fact of *traditio*; he did not stratify it into specific, historically conditioned stages, nor did he try to trace the development of the *traditum* itself. However, it is to his credit that he attempted to present as plausible an explanation as possible for the factual situation; hence his allusions to the existence of public or religious scribes in Egypt, Babylonia, and Phoenicia.[33] He also realistically recognized that additions, alterations, and mistakes occurred during this transmittal process, the result being a corrupt and not always reliable text.

What caused Simon to propound this idea of tradition with such conviction—and at such great personal expense? Presumably it was the realization that the Roman Catholic position regarding Church tradition had relevance also for the biblical period.[34] The Council of Trent, more than a century prior to him, had reestablished the Church's principle of the authority of its cumulative tradition. Simon made frequent reference to this Council and especially to the church fathers for support for his interpretation of biblical tradition. No wonder then that Simon—mistakenly, as it turned out—expected Roman Catholics to accept his proposal of a biblical tradition that was analogous to Church tradition.[35] He even went to the extent of asserting that tradition should be preferred to the text of the Bible[36] and that the doctrine of the Church has priority over Scripture.[37] But Simon's book was banned and attacked (by

---

32. *Histoire critique*, 50.
33. Ibid., 15–16; and his *Réponse*, 58, 66.
34. This connection is emphasized also by Kraus, *EvT* 16 (1956), 376; *Geschichte*, 68–69.
35. *Histoire critique*, 8: "The Catholics, who are persuaded that their religion does not depend solely on the text of Scripture but also on the tradition of the Church, are not at all scandalized in seeing that the misfortunes of the times and the negligence of the copyists would have brought changes to the sacred books, as also to profane books. Only prejudiced and ignorant Protestants could be scandalized by this."
36. Ibid., 372: "If Scripture and tradition come equally from God, as the Jews claim, one must undoubtedly prefer tradition which explains mysteries clearly, to a text which is filled with obscurities and ambiguities."
37. Ibid., 494–95: "But Scripture, whether it be corrupted or not corrupted at all, can be cited as an authentic act when it is confined within the limits that we have set above, i.e. when it is found to conform to the doctrine of the Church." This assertion approaches our prime

Roman Catholics and Protestants alike) not directly because of his use of the idea of tradition but because the age-long beliefs in the divinely inspired authorship of the biblical books seemed to be threatened.

Simon's greatest contribution to the beginnings of *traditio*-historical research consists in his emphasis on the long human process of biblical transmission. The details of this process—viz., the postulated existence of an established body of public scribes throughout the history of the Israelites beginning with Moses— amount to a conjecture unacceptable to us today.[38] Noteworthy, however, is his stipulation that the scribes were *public* figures, not private persons writing and creating according to their own desires.[39] Nonetheless he conceived of the origins of the biblical books primarily as a *literary process* and failed to consider sufficiently the role of the community, the religious life, and the spoken word. But Simon cannot be brought to task for failing to envision all the traditio-historical advancements following his work. He deserves tribute for making it clear that biblical research must be concerned with the history of the Old Testament as literature and with the methods by which the materials were handed down from one generation to the next.

D. Influence on Later Researchers

Simon's *Histoire critique du Vieux Testament* was translated immediately— though quite defectively—into Latin (1681) and English (1682).[40] Especially the fifth French edition (1685) became well distributed, and with time the work gained a fairly wide hearing in the European countries. Biblical scholars in the nineteenth and twentieth centuries recognized Simon's decisive contributions to the research; they devoted numerous monographs to his work

---

traditio aspect of interpretation and actualization (cf. above, p. 5), according to which tradition does not remain statically normative but should be interpreted anew for each age, even for the present one.

38. Note the comment of Gray, *Old Testament Criticism*, 113: "Simon is responsible for the extension of the idea of diaries or annals into nothing less than an official chancery; and such a digression into theory unsupported by facts was one he would have been the first to censure in another."

39. This assertion thus coincides with one of our characteristics of "tradition"—that tradition is the immediate property and expression of a group or community; cf. above, p. 21.

40. Cf. Bernus, *Richard Simon*, 137–40. Semler promoted the German translation (in 1776–1781) of Simon's critical history of the *New* Testament—not of the *Old* Testament, as Kraus erroneously states, *Geschichte*, 66, 107; cf. also G. Hornig, *Die Anfänge der historisch-kritischen Theologie: Johann Salomo Semlers Schriftverständnis und seine Stellung zu Luther*, FSTR 8, Göttingen 1961, 185, 273.

and acclaimed him as the father of biblical criticism.[41] Aside from this later attention paid to him, what was Simon's influence on his contemporaries and successors? In particular, what effect did his idea of Old Testament transmission have on subsequent research?

Interestingly enough, the immediate positive effect was minimal, and especially his emphasis on *traditio* went unheeded for more than two centuries. To be sure, the book prompted numerous polemical replies,[42] but as a rule these were characterized by a dogmatic defense of traditional beliefs. One important exception was the review and critique offered by Jean Le Clerc (Johannes Clericus, 1657–1736), Protestant professor of Hebrew in Amsterdam.[43] It is quite obvious that Le Clerc learned considerably from Simon, especially with regard to his view of the origin of the Pentateuch. Like Simon and others, Le Clerc chose to distinguish between pre-Mosaic, Mosaic, and post-Mosaic portions of these five books, admitting that there was much here which Moses could not have written. However he rejected Simon's hypothesis that public scribes (also identified as prophets) were responsible for the recording and transmission. Prophets, Le Clerc declared simply, could not have been annalists because they were engaged solely in predicting the future.[44] But Le Clerc conceived also of a transmission process—though not of *public* documents but of *private* ones. On the one hand this position represents a retrogression following Simon's advance, for with Le Clerc's idea the documents are no longer seen as group property with a public rather than merely private function. On the other hand, however, Le Clerc directed increased attention to the *particular historical situations* that instigated literary fixation and to the *purposes* that the authors had in writing the documents.[45] With respect to his view of the other end of the transmission, Ezra could not have

---

41. Cf. especially the studies by Graf, Bernus, Margival, Stummer, and Steinmann (above, p. 37 n. 13).

42. Cf. Stummer, *Die Bedeutung Richard Simons*, 54–105.

43. His anonymous publication: *Sentimens de quelques théologiens de Hollande sur l'Histoire critique du Vieux Testament, composée par le P. Richard Simon de l'Oratoire*, Amsterdam 1685. For more details on Le Clerc, cf. Westphal, *Sources du Pentateuque* I, 78–100; Stummer, *Die Bedeutung Richard Simons*, 69–85; Gray, *Old Testament Criticism*, 116–20; and Kraus, *Geschichte*, 70–73.

44. Cf. Diestel, *Geschichte*, 356.

45. Le Clerc's words (*Sentimens*, 1^e lettre, 6) are noteworthy: "Writing the history of a book is not simply a matter of saying when and by whom it was done, which copyists transcribed it, and which mistakes they committed in the transcription. It does not suffice for us to say who transmitted it and to make note of the defects of its version.... It is more incumbent on us to discover, if possible, with which purpose the author composed it, what gave him occasion to take up the pen, and to which opinions or to which events allusion is made in this work."

served as final author or editor of the whole Pentateuch since the Samaritans also possessed these books; Le Clerc suggested instead that it was the unspecified priest mentioned in 2 Kgs 17:27–28.[46] It can thus be seen that at these points Le Clerc differed only slightly from Simon. The ideas of transmission and of human participation in the productive stages of the Pentateuch are not rejected; it constitutes in fact a step forward that Le Clerc challenged Simon's schematic and institutionalized means of transmission. In light of his critical approach here in 1685, Le Clerc's later return to the orthodox view of Mosaic authorship is indeed perplexing.[47]

With the exception of Le Clerc, Simon's positive influence remained negligible for several generations. No one sought to take up his hypotheses or his emphasis on transmission and to pursue the problems further. During the rest of his century and most of the next, Old Testament scholars were occupied with the debate over Mosaic authorship of the Pentateuch, the doctrine of divine inspiration, canon criticism, and finally the beginnings of source criticism. The understanding of tradition by the source critics will receive special attention in the following section. But at this point we can concur fully with Margival's statement, referring indeed to Simon's general effect on the research but being especially applicable as well to his idea of tradition: "While R. Simon founded biblical criticism, he did not—properly speaking—create a school."[48]

---

46. Ibid., 6ᵉ lettre, 129.
47. *Genesis sive Mosis prophetae liber primus*, Amsterdam 1693.
48. Margival, *Essai sur Richard Simon*, 311.

5
THE ERA OF SOURCE CRITICISM: GENERAL NEGLECT OF THE PRECOMPOSITIONAL STAGE

A. THE BEGINNINGS OF SOURCE CRITICISM

With the initiation of the Documentary Hypothesis in Old Testament research, the attention of the critics became confined to essentially only two stages in the development of our text—the composition of the initial documents and the subsequent combination and redaction of these sources into the present form of the text. Preoccupation with literary-critical analysis along such lines was accompanied by a general disregard for the complicated process of tradition formation that may have preceded the compositional stage. Whereas it was recognized that the authors of the documents drew on written and oral sources from community and cult, little effort was made to investigate this prehistory.

The views of the two founders of source criticism deserve particular attention here, for they were closest to the time of Simon's work and had the best opportunity for immediate influence. That the German pastor Henning Bernhard Witter (1683–1715) was able to develop the earliest Documentary Hypothesis was due above all to his historical approach to the Pentateuch as a body of literature with concrete origins and purposes.[1] Confining his attention especially to the book of Genesis, Witter made the following basic statement: "From these sources which were handed on by the traditions of the Fathers [πατραπαραδοτοις] and by the oral tradition, with the support of God, Moses put together the Pentateuch."[2] There was nothing unusual about this opinion

---

1. A. Lods receives credit for having recognized that Witter preceded Astruc with a method of source criticism; cf. *Jean Astruc et la critique biblique au XVIIIe siècle*, Strasbourg/Paris 1924, 54–55; and "Un précurseur allemand de Jean Astruc: Henning Bernhard Witter," *ZAW* 43 (1925), 134–35. Cf. the detailed study by H. Bardtke, "Henning Bernhard Witter," *ZAW* 66 (1954), 153–81, especially 165ff.

2. Witter, *Jura Israelitarum in Palaestinam*, Hildesheim 1711, 22.

since the same position was held by Simon, Calvin, Le Clerc, and others prior to him. He did not even vary from the traditional view of the Mosaic authorship of Genesis. The significant difference, however, was that *Witter not only posited pre-Mosaic sources but also sought to identify them in our present text.* For example, he was the first[3] to recognize that Gen 1 was such an independent source, specifically: an ancient, orally transmitted creation poem. According to him Moses began his own narrative in Gen 2:5ff.[4] Witter's criteria for distinguishing between sources consisted of differences of style, repetitions of content, and alternation between divine names. Did Witter initiate a new understanding of tradition or transmission? This question must be answered in the negative, for in essence his view was a continuation of the vague, undeveloped notion that Moses received some traditional materials from his ancestors. Witter's contribution was that he simply *designated* certain specific portions of Genesis as having been preexistent to Moses.

The situation was not changed greatly with the extensive source-critical work of the French physician Jean Astruc (1684–1766). Like his predecessors, Astruc recognized the existence of oral tradition in the pre-Mosaic period but was very skeptical that it was capable of retaining accurately all the details (especially names, ages, topographical descriptions) included in Genesis.[5] Consequently, Astruc suggested that Moses had old literary memoirs at his disposal[6]—two of these sources being major and ten being fragmentary.[7] Moses assembled the memoirs into four parallel columns, and a later editor combined these strands into our present Genesis. In contrast to Simon who found post-Mosaic portions in this book, Astruc attributed everything to Moses.[8] Like Witter's, Astruc's work represented an advance inasmuch as the pre-Mosaic material—simply identified as such, without specification, by previous

---

3. Cf. M. Metzger, *Die Paradieseserzählung: Die Geschichte ihrer Auslegung von J. Clericus bis W. M. L. de Wette*, Abhandlungen zur Philosophie, Psychologie und Pädagogik 16, Bonn 1959, 10, 14.

4. For Witter's text, cf. Lods, *ZAW* 43 (1925), 134–35.

5. Astruc, *Conjectures sur les mémoires originaux dont il paroit que Moyse s'est servi pour composer le Livre de la Genèse*, Bruxelles 1753, 6–7. It is interesting that this mistrust of the reliability of oral tradition—against which Gunkel and especially most Scandinavian scholars fought—was associated with literary-critical work as early as 1753.

6. Astruc, *Conjectures*, 9: "I maintain therefore that Moses had in his possession ancient memoirs containing the history of his ancestors since the creation of the world, that in order that nothing be lost from these memoirs he divided them into pieces according to the events described in them, that he inserted these pieces intact and in sequence, and that from this assemblage the book of Genesis was formed."

7. Ibid., 13ff., 308ff.

8. Cf. also Stummer, *Die Bedeutung Richard Simons*, 109.

critics—was assorted into distinct groupings and classified as ancient sources. But aside from this step, *he did not attempt to investigate this prehistory,* nor did be regard these sources as changing, growing traditions produced by the community.

In the critical work done after Witter and Astruc, little appreciable change in the understanding of tradition or in the analysis of the transmittal process can be observed. Even Johann Salomo Semler (1725–1791), who acknowledged his own dependency on Simon and referred to him often, did not take up and develop the problem of transmission that Simon had emphasized so strongly.[9] The same can be said for Johann Gottfried Eichhorn (1751–1827) and Karl David Ilgen (1763–1834),[10] and the situation did not change significantly with the subsequent development of the fragment hypothesis, the supplementary hypothesis, or the new Documentary Hypothesis. The adherents of each of these approaches relied primarily on source criticism alone to solve the basic problems of Genesis or of the whole Pentateuch, and the prehistory of the sources and the problem of tradition on the whole received no appreciable new attention.[11] The two main exceptions to this very general statement deserve separate review.

B. Johann Gottfried Herder: Impulses from Romanticism

Johann Gottfried Herder's (1744–1803) romantic, antirationalistic understanding of humanity and the world led him to elevate in importance the aesthetic character of the archaic expressions of Hebrew life. He sought to shift the emphasis from a critical undermining of the Bible on the one side and from an unquestioning orthodoxy on the other side—to a full, intuitive

---

9. Cf. ibid., 110–13; Kraus, *Geschichte,* 103–13; and Hornig, *Die Anfänge der historisch-kritischen Theologie,* 176–90.

10. Both Eichhorn and Ilgen were concerned about the means by which the documents could have been transmitted down to later times, arguing that these sources must have been preserved in the temple archives as well as in private possession. Noteworthy is Ilgen's attempt to put his source criticism at the service of historiography. He bewailed the fact "that we yet are unable to produce a true history of the Jewish nation. One still fails to differentiate enough the documented fact from the uncertain tradition—and cannot do it yet due to the circumstances mentioned; one still does not know how to determine the point where saga ceases and history commences" (*Die Urkunden des Jerusalemischen Tempelarchivs in ihrer Urgestalt: Erster Theil: Die Urkunden des ersten Buchs von Moses,* Halle 1798, Vorrede, xii–xiii). This pronounced preference for written sources rather than tradition is of course in accord with Astruc's position.

11. Details on the history of this early pentateuchal criticism can be found in Kraus, *Geschichte,* 133ff.; Gray, *Old Testament Criticism,* 148ff.; Stummer, *Die Bedeutung Richard Simons,* 110ff.; and O. Eissfeldt, *Einleitung in das Alte Testament,* 3rd ed., Tübingen 1964, 212ff. (ET: 160ff.).

appreciation of the human elements permeating the Scripture.[12] This move occasioned some profound advances in the ongoing understanding of tradition and transmission:[13]

(1) According to Herder's conception, the document (the *Urkunde*) constitutes "the bridge from timeless poetry to time-bound history, the intermediary concept between poetical invention (= Dichtung) and history."[14] This assertion is the fruit of Herder's awareness that poetry is not to be compared with the fine arts but with history, from which it also springs. The document assumes the character of life congealed in writing. Thus a genealogy, as a document of a family succession, has a historical as well as a poetical dimension: "Genealogies are the archive of the Orientals, and historical sagas are their commentary."[15] Similarly the entire Old Testament is to be understood as a document in the same sense, i.e. as the witness to the poetical expression of the Hebrew people. Herder thus accomplished the step prerequisite to drawing up the history of tradition: He considered *the Old Testament embedded in the life of the people.* We will see below that Gunkel responded to this challenge of Herder to write a Literaturgeschichte of the Old Testament from this viewpoint.

(2) As is evident at several points, Herder conceived of *an organic growth of tradition out of poetry.*[16] (a) He attributed doublets (as, e.g., in Abraham's trip to Egypt) to the existence of double traditions and posited that later traditions are more comprehensive than earlier ones since the narrators in later times had more traditions at their disposal. (b) Individual elements were added to traditions in the course of time in order to "establish, explain, embellish." We are therefore advised to consider always the context. (c) Herder conceived of a process of "sedimentation" which resulted not only in the individual sections but finally even in the Pentateuch as a whole. (d) At the very beginning of the process Herder perceived oral traditions as well as written annals. (e) The transition from oral to written marked indeed a break or change in the material itself; at this point the saga was altered to history. However, this written form is more of a surrogate for than an objectification of the "Volkspoesie."[17]

---

12. The literature on Herder is vast. Cf. the discussion in Kraus, *Geschichte*, 114–32; and T. Willi, *Herders Beitrag zum Verstehen des Alten Testaments*, BGH 8, Tübingen 1971.

13. Kraus (*EvT* 16, 1956, 377–78) summarily discounts any significant change in this regard, but Willi's findings (*Herders Beitrag*, especially 57–67) indicate that Herder is not to be underestimated at this point. Our brief discussion here relies primarily on Willi's exposition.

14. Willi, *Herders Beitrag*, 60.

15. Herder, *Vom Geist der Ebräischen Poesie*; quoted from Willi, *Herders Beitrag*, 61.

16. Cf. Willi, *Herders Beitrag*, 64.

17. On this final point, cf. also E. Güttgemanns, *Offene Fragen zur Formgeschichte des Evangeliums*, BEvT 54, Munich 1970, 120–23.

(3) A clear understanding of our prime *traditio* principle of *interpretation by subsequent generations* can also be observed in Herder's writing. This process is seen to be the result of the character of the epic itself—a "certain progressing, historical tone, whereby that which follows always elucidates, carries on, fulfills, specifies, interprets that which precedes."[18] Herder referred to the story of the exodus and to the messianic or royal psalms as examples. Thus here in the writings of Herder we can ascertain *the first serious consideration of this element of the traditio-historical process* to which von Rad and Noth attribute such central importance.

(4) Also at *the literary stage* this process continued by means of subsequent *redactions*. These interpretive treatments of the Pentateuch are implied in Herder's formula: "The weaving of the book according to later disposition; the materials for it, however, Mosaic."[19]

In a word: *Herder's conception of the Old Testament as the living product of the Hebrew people* (and not just as the creation of individual authors) *and his view of its organic growth through the process of interpretation mark important progress in the growing awareness of traditio-historical problems.*

C. Johann Christoph Nachtigal: Recognition of Precompositional Developments

Another noteworthy advance occurred in this same period—a contribution that has been almost totally overlooked and forgotten. Johann Christoph Nachtigal (1753–1819) published under the pseudonym Otmar a series of articles in 1794–95 dealing with the gradual formation of the Old Testament.[20] Varying from other critics during the period immediately after the source-critical ground had been broken by Witter and Astruc, Nachtigal conceived of this formation as a complex process in which both oral and written traditions were transmitted down to later generations and in the course of time were put into first smaller compilations and then ever larger ones until the entire corpus of the historical books was finally reached.

For a number of reasons which he presented and documented,[21] Nachtigal maintained that most of the pentateuchal materials were post-Mosaic

---

18. Quoted from Willi, *Herders Beitrag*, 65.
19. Quoted from ibid., 66.
20. "Fragmente über die allmähligte Bildung der den Israeliten heiligen Schriften, besonders der sogenannten historischen," *Magazin für Religionsphilosophie, Exegese und Kirchengeschichte*, ed. Henke, vol. 2 (Helmstädt 1794), 433–523, and vol. 4 (1795), 1–36, 329–370.
21. Cf. ibid., vol. 2 (1794), especially 442ff. Most of his reasons were not new but had been presented in one form or another by previous scholars. An amusing "proof" for why very

and the result of "mündliche Ueberlieferungen."[22] Dating back to Moses' time were a few written records (a shortened version of the Ten Commandments and possibly also some tribal lists and records of the names of places that the Israelites visited during their wilderness wanderings), some "bildliche Darstellungen" (e.g., Cherubim), and many orally transmitted items (ritualistic regulations, marital laws, some shorter songs, and many "Wortforschungen"). In the period from Joshua to Samuel there arose some additional written pieces (tribal and family registers, troop listings, records of Israelite battles, and a copy of the oldest book of laws), some "bildliche Denkmahle" (sculpture, embroidery, the map of Palestine mentioned in Josh 18:4, 8–9), and many orally transmitted songs and sagas.[23] It was in the Davidic period that Israel's literature as such began to appear when schools of prophets gathered together and recorded in small collections the materials that had been transmitted separately by oral and written means prior to their time.[24] The prophetic literature itself, however, was not immediately recorded: "It is evident from several places, especially Jeremiah 36:1ff., that the prophets did not write down all their speeches immediately but that they were often retained for a long time by means of oral tradition alone."[25] As Nachtigal pictured it, the Pentateuch reached its final form about the time of the exile,[26] and the rest of the Old Testament was finished in the postexilic period.

What traditio-historical advances can be seen here in Nachtigal's presentation? Five are especially noteworthy: (1) Nachtigal presented a plastic picture of the gradual process of growth that resulted in our present Old Testament. He did not conceive of Moses as the initiator of the majority of the traditional materials, nor did he reckon with the rigid transmission of static (oral or written) sources. He recognized that the process was complex and variegated. (2) He did not suppose that only the literary stage could be the effectively creative one. At the oral level much of the historical as well as prophetical traditions were developed and transmitted; their recording brought presumably little internal change to them. Nachtigal was therefore the first to propose in detail a *post*-Mosaic oral tradition. (3) The tradition process was

---

little of the Pentateuch should actually be ascribed to Moses: According to Nachtigal, the only writing material that Moses had was stone, and it is highly improbable that the Israelites would have transported, preserved, and recopied as many stone tablets as would have been necessary to contain the entire Pentateuch.

22. Ibid., vol. 2, 460–61; vol. 4, 12–13.
23. Ibid., vol. 4, 10–13.
24. Ibid., vol. 4, 14ff.
25. Ibid., vol. 4, 27.
26. Nachtigal (ibid., vol. 4, 28–30) conjectured that Jeremiah and his school of prophets were responsible for the final redaction of the Pentateuch.

postulated as well for other parts of the Old Testament and not just for the Pentateuch, which up to his time had occupied the central position in the critical research. Especially his clear understanding of the role of the spoken word among the prophets and their disciples anticipated by more than a century the work of Gunkel and the Scandinavian scholars. (4) Groups of traditionists (the schools of the prophets) took the place of lone individuals, of single authors of the sources. (5) Nachtigal attempted to delineate—in general terms though with many examples—the history of the tradition. He did not seem to be explicitly aware, as was Herder, of the factor of interpretation in the development of tradition, although he paid prime attention to the growth of the *traditum* and to the process of agglomeration and compilation. He had a firmer grasp on the problem of the gradual formation of the Old Testament than had Simon, and his description of this process was also more realistic than the latter's "écrivains publics." In contrast to the usual positions of the source critics of the eighteenth and nineteenth centuries, *both Nachtigal and Herder thus demonstrated a sensitivity for the complexities of Israelite tradition.* This awareness, though, was doomed to virtual dormancy until 1895, the year of Gunkel's pioneering religio-historical study.

D. Julius Wellhausen: The Documentary Hypothesis and Tradition

The tremendous effort of nineteenth-century scholars to explain the literary origin of the Old Testament (especially the Pentateuch) and then from this basis to draw up a history of Israel and its religion puts us before a set of difficult questions: To what extent did their preoccupation with documents result in a de-emphasis of tradition? Was the interest awakened by their predecessors in the *traditio* and *traditum* appropriated and developed further? Does the history of documents, or even literary criticism itself, necessarily preclude the history of tradition? What precisely was the source critics' conception of the precompositional stage? We hesitate to answer these questions too lightly or to align ourselves with the easy denunciations of this research by many (notably by several Scandinavian scholars). In order to assess the role attributed during this period to tradition, we need to consider three general items: the picture of the documents and of their composition; the postulated inclusion in them of older, traditional materials; and the view thereby afforded of the history of Israel. Special attention must be given to Julius Wellhausen (1844–1918), who, drawing on the results of others and on his own investigations, succeeded in constructing the classical picture of these documents and of the history of Israel.

(1) By means of a refined literary criticism, the four documents J, E, D, and P were isolated in the historical books, given relative dates, and described

according to their historical and theological backgrounds. From all that we can discern, the opinion was that the composition of these respective documents constituted the creative stage and that any pregiven elements were in such disarray and of such scattered, fragmentary nature as not to qualify as "literature." It was thus held to be fruitless to devote oneself to this precompositional period, and instead one became engrossed in source criticism as a means for solving the inherent problems of the Pentateuch. The various solutions came in the form of the fragment hypothesis (Geddes, Vater), the supplementary hypothesis (de Wette, Ewald, Bleek), and the newer Documentary Hypothesis (Hupfeld, Graf, Kuenen, Wellhausen). To be sure, the four-source theory as presented by Wellhausen has continued even throughout our present century as the *opinio communis* regarding the composition of the Pentateuch, despite modification at individual points. Not to be forgotten is the fact that Gunkel, von Rad, and Noth took this hypothesis as their point of departure. But the issue is that the nineteenth-century scholars concentrated almost exclusively on the developments at the literary level and thus *as a rule neglected the precompositional stage of tradition growth and agglomeration as well as the various factors operative during this prehistory of the documents.*

(2) What was held to be the precise state of the precompositional traditions, and to what extent were they included in the documents? That Wellhausen and his predecessors assumed the existence of preliterary materials cannot be doubted; they knew that the origin of the documents was not necessarily identical with the origin of their contents.[27] However, Wellhausen was not willing to suppose that these materials could have been greatly developed, connected with each other, and inserted into JE or P in the form of already advanced oral compositions. The authors of the documents were responsible for all work of a compositional nature;[28] the gradual, complex

---

27. Wellhausen's understanding here is recognized and admitted also by Mowinckel, *NTT* 38 (1937), 69; and Nielsen, *Oral Tradition*, 12.

28. Two quotes must suffice as evidence: Wellhausen, *Prolegomena zur Geschichte Israels*, 6th ed., Berlin 1927, 294 (3rd ed. 1886, 309) [ET: *Prolegomena to the History of Ancient Israel*, Cleveland and New York 1957, 296]: "When the subject treated is not history but legends about pre-historic times, the arrangement of the materials does not come with the materials themselves, but must arise out of the plan of a narrator.... From the mouth of the people there comes nothing but the detached narratives, which may or may not happen to have some bearing on each other: to weave them together in a connected whole is the work of the poetical or literary artist. Thus the arrangement of the sources in the plan of the narrative is not a matter of course but is a matter requiring explanation, and is only to be explained on the ground of the literary dependence of one source on the other." And similarly in his *Die Composition des Hexateuchs und der historischen Bücher des Alten Testaments*, 3rd ed., Berlin 1889 (= 4th ed. 1963), 8: "Oral

development of tradition is not offered as the explanation. Here we observe the dissatisfying status quo to which Gunkel objected by asserting that the authors J and E did not invent their materials but only collected and perhaps lightly reworked them; Gunkel then notes: "In principle this statement will be contested by no one; in practice, however, it is disregarded not infrequently."[29] And there is a further point: Not only did Wellhausen underestimate the extent to which the tradition could develop at the precompositional stage, but he also devaluated the worth of these earlier forms for the exegete. His position in this regard becomes clear especially in his rebuttal of Gunkel's religio-historical investigations: Such search for the origins "is perhaps of antiquarian interest but is not the task of the theologian and the exegete,"[30] who must evaluate the materials in their present context. On this basis we must conclude that *Wellhausen (similarly the other source critics of his century) obscured the important difference between the composition of a document and the fact of its prehistory and that he devalued the importance of the latter for exegesis.* Against this background the innovations of Gunkel, von Rad, and Noth stand out in striking relief.

(3) Wellhausen's efforts to draw up the history of Israel and of its religion were based—and rightly so—on the assumption that history writing is possible only after the pentateuchal documents have been analyzed and historically classified, especially concerning their origins, compositional principles, theological orientations, and authenticity. According to him, though, this source analysis of the Pentateuch provides definitely more direct information about the era in which the document was composed than about the period which it describes. Only the basic skeletal course of events in the pre-Mosaic and Mosaic times can be regarded as reliable, while the details as reported in the Pentateuch are hardly to be believed.[31] Wellhausen, like Ewald, attributed this circumstance to the fundamental distinction between saga and history, as well as to the decisive work carried out at the compositional stage.[32] But for us the important point is that Wellhausen found no reason to question

---

tradition among the people includes only individual stories which surely come from the same circle of thought yet which are not organized into a planned totality. The recorder of the individual narratives is the one who initiates the plan and the connections."

29. Gunkel, *Schöpfung und Chaos*, 143 n. 3; cf. also 144–45 n. 2.

30. Wellhausen, "Zur apokalyptischen Literatur," *Skizzen und Vorarbeiten* 6 (1899), 233.

31. Wellhausen, *Israelitische und jüdische Geschichte*, 7th ed., Berlin 1914, 10 (3rd ed. 1897, 11): "The specific and colorful details, which the saga relates about the wondrous dawn of Israel's history, can certainly not be reckoned as credible. Only the main features, the most general presuppositions of all individual narratives about this period, can be understood as not being fictitious."

32. Cf. also L. Perlitt, *Vatke und Wellhausen*, BZAW 94, Berlin 1964, 171–72.

also the linear course of successive historical events—the slavery in Egypt, Sinai, wilderness wanderings, conquest—and the central role of Moses as leader in this period. Not until von Rad and then especially Noth did this historical framework of the Pentateuch become destroyed. Whereas Wellhausen sought to explain *historically or source-critically* the "Digression" to Sinai and the zigzag itinerary through the wilderness,[33] von Rad and Noth suggested a traditio-historical solution: independent groups existing prior to the conquest, with their respective traditions being joined and "Israelitized" at a later date.[34] *The source critics and the historians during the nineteenth century did not grasp this traditio-historical possibility: that the picture of history arose with the development of tradition and was based on a theological conception of the Heilsgeschichte.*[35]

This source criticism and especially the Documentary Hypothesis presented by Wellhausen constitute the immediate background for the rise of traditio-historical research in our present century. One must by all means avoid picturing the nineteenth century as a dark and misguided age in biblical criticism—the impression one often receives from certain statements by Pedersen, Engnell, Nielsen, and others.[36] It is similarly amiss to identify literary criticism with source criticism or with the Documentary Hypothesis, for literary criticism is no more and no less than a critical method for determining the unity or disunity of a text.[37] The basic results of source criticism have remained, and the importance of literary criticism as the initial exegetical step is established. Yet in light of the fact that the precompositional growth of Old Testament traditions was virtually neglected by Wellhausen and his colleagues, the general observation made by Smend is particularly appropriate

---

33. Wellhausen, *Israelitische und jüdische Geschichte*, 7th ed. 1914, 10ff.; *Prolegomena*, 6th ed. 1927, 341ff.

34. Cf. von Rad, *VF* 1953/55 (1956), 131–32; and the detailed discussions of von Rad and Noth below.

35. It seems that S. Herrmann ("Mose," *EvT* 28, 1968, 301–28; cf. also below, pp. 155–57), in his critique of the traditio-historical method of von Rad and Noth, actually has more in common with Wellhausen at this point due to his acceptance of the pentateuchal course of events and his interest in examining essentially only Israel's reflection and rumination on these happenings.

36. Their criticisms are directed at the alleged modern European bookish view of the Orient, the wooden and subjective verse-chopping, the evolutionary concept of religion, and the like; cf. part 2 below, passim.

37. The frequent failure to make this distinction is also pointed out by Richter, *Exegese als Literaturwissenschaft*, 50. Engnell, Carlson, and others are mistaken in supposing that the tradition historian can dispense with literary criticism; cf. below, p. 247.

with regard to our history of traditio-historical research: "In many respects Wellhausen was an end and Gunkel a beginning."[38]

E. August Klostermann: Crystallization Hypothesis and Public Recital

Yet before the actual traditio-historical investigation of the Old Testament was initiated in full, an interesting idea regarding the origin of the Pentateuch was suggested—a macroscopic parallel to what was later to be recognized as a principle in the growth of individual traditions and complexes of these. We are referring to the *crystallization hypothesis* with which August Klostermann[39] (1837–1915) sought to counter Wellhausen's Documentary Hypothesis. According to Klostermann, the Pentateuch is not so much the end result of a process of compositional and redactional work by individual personalities (as are implied in the designations "Jahwist," "Elohist," "Priestly writer"). Rather, it more probably grew out of the cultic life of the people. The Sinaitic law constituted its center, and around this kernel the rest of the Pentateuch was gradually deposited or crystallized. To be sure, Klostermann reckoned with primarily literary activity, though he emphasized that the gathering together of diverse materials and the drawing up of the earliest forms of the Pentateuch were always done for the purpose of *oral address and public recital before the community*. This oral presentation occasioned also the recurring attempts to "modernize" his postulated pre-Josianic Pentateuch.[40] Similarly the Deuteronomic law in Deut 5–28, inserted later into its present place in the Pentateuch, is to be understood not as a merely privately kept law book but as "the developed result of the living practice of publicly reciting the law."[41]

That Klostermann did not abandon the idea of literary sources and that he in fact developed a type of supplementary hypothesis to explain how the text was kept current for public recital—these were the marks left on him by the documentary criticism which he fought. But his awareness of the process

---

38. R. Smend, Jr., "Vorwort," in J. Wellhausen, *Grundrisse zum Alten Testament*, ed. Smend, TB 27, Munich 1965, 5.

39. *Der Pentateuch: Beiträge zu seinem Verständnis und seiner Entstehungsgeschichte*, Leipzig 1893; and ibid., Neue Folge, Leipzig 1907.

40. *Der Pentateuch*, 1893, 23ff.

41. *Der Pentateuch*, Neue Folge 1907, 347; also *Der Pentateuch*, 1893, 85ff. This thesis that the law was orally recited in the cult was later taken up by von Rad, *FPHex* (1938), *Ges. Stud.*, 37ff. Klostermann was also the first to draw the analogy between Deuteronomy and Icelandic legal tradition; cf. Nielsen, *Oral Tradition*, 47–48. A crystallization hypothesis somewhat similar to Klostermann's has been forwarded by E. Robertson, *The Old Testament Problem: A Re-Investigation*, Manchester 1950, 137–58.

of gradual agglomeration and of the key importance of cultic and community life anticipated two principles central to subsequent traditio-historical work.

6
HERMANN GUNKEL AND THE RECOGNITION OF THE IMPORTANCE OF ANCIENT TRADITIONS

A. The Influence of Albert Eichhorn

With Albert Eichhorn (1856–1926) the attention of modern scholarship became directed to the period of tradition development. Eichhorn had the misfortune of poor health, and his writings were consequently limited to only a few articles. Most of his influence occurred through his personal friendship with such individuals as Wrede, Gunkel, Bousset, Gressmann, and Troeltsch. Eichhorn is generally accepted as one of the founders of the "Religionsgeschichtliche Schule," but his exact role in determining its method and direction is quite nebulous due to the paucity of his publications. Gressmann provides perhaps the best description of him as a scholar.[1] Eichhorn was motivated partially by his distaste for a one-sided literary criticism that left unanswered the question of preliterary origins. He had a strong predilection for history and historical development, as was evident even in the thesis that he defended in 1886 at Halle: "Any interpretation of a myth that does not consider the origin and development of the myth is false."[2] And in an article written in 1898 on communion in the New Testament, he made it clear that he rejected any historical-critical method that was content with simply comparing the different texts in order to determine the oldest form of the tradition. Eichhorn wanted to penetrate beyond the history of the text and study the history of its substance and ideas, in this way trying to grasp the inner "sense" of the tradition.[3] In his opinion, the development of the religious elements would explain most of the different variants and alterations of the text. Espe-

---

1. In his book: *Albert Eichhorn und die Religionsgeschichtliche Schule*, Göttingen 1914. Cf. also W. Klatt, ed., "Ein Brief von Hermann Gunkel über Albert Eichhorn an Hugo Greßmann," *ZTK* 66 (1969), 1–6; Klatt, *Hermann Gunkel*, passim; and Kraus, *Geschichte*, 328ff.

2. The eleventh of twenty-four theses; cited from Gressmann, *Albert Eichhorn*, 8.

3. Ibid., 14–17.

cially the history of the Israelite religion as it came in contact with various environmental factors could provide important insights.

Thus Eichhorn's decisive contribution was that he drew attention to the central elements of the *traditum*. No longer would it suffice to execute solely a literary-critical analysis of the text. The prehistory of the contents must of necessity also be investigated. These impulses from the field of Religionsgeschichte had an immediate effect on Gunkel and occasioned the first actual attempt to probe the depths of an Old Testament tradition.

B. New Directions

The significance of Hermann Gunkel (1862–1932) as perhaps the greatest Old Testament scholar of the twentieth century has become increasingly recognized with the appearance of several appraisals of his work.[4] These assessments, however, concentrate primarily on Gunkel's foundational contributions to the fields of Religionsgeschichte and Gattungsgeschichte and do not adequately consider that his work in these areas also prompted the modern study of the history of Old Testament traditions. *Gunkel is to be regarded as the chief pioneer of traditio-historical research*. Even more so than A. Eichhorn, Gunkel has the distinction of being the one to thrust permanently the question of transmission and tradition onto the scene of discussion after it had been lying relatively dormant for the two centuries of source-critical work. Gunkel himself realized the importance of the undertaking: "Until now Old Testament research has occupied itself primarily with literary problems; similarly, literary criticism has provided the main context for treating religio-historical questions. Thus past study of Genesis has concentrated on analyzing and dating the sources, while the origin and tradition history of the narratives of Genesis have received less attention."[5] The latter became the prime task which Gunkel set for himself—although it is not entirely clear what induced him to turn his sights in this direction. Surely Eichhorn wielded some influence in his personal contacts with Gunkel, and Herder's emphasis on aesthetics did not occur without effect. Direct dependence on the considerable form-critical investigations already conducted in the fields of

---

4. Cf. above all the perceptive and thorough work of W. Klatt, *Hermann Gunkel: Zu seiner Theologie der Religionsgeschichte und zur Entstehung der formgeschichtlichen Methode*, FRLANT 100, Göttingen 1969.

5. Gunkel, *Schöpfung und Chaos in Urzeit und Endzeit: Eine religionsgeschichtliche Untersuchung über Gen 1 und Ap Joh 12*, Göttingen 1895, 1; see also 209. As we have noted above (see p. 17), this seems to be the earliest appearance of the term "Überlieferungsgeschichte" in approximately its modern sense.

Germanic and classical literature and folklore is less likely for his earlier than for his later publications.[6] Gunkel himself seems to have been the one who recognized clearly the need to go beyond the literary-critical work of his era and develop the method for researching the precompositional period of traditions and motifs. It is to his genius that tradition historians are in debt.

Before examining the impulses which Gunkel gave to the study of traditions, a further word is necessary regarding his point of orientation and his relationship to the ruling source criticism of his predecessors. Gunkel did not intend to oppose or overthrow the tasks and methods of literary criticism; rather, he was interested in taking up *new tasks*. Only a superficial glance at his commentary on Genesis is necessary to see that he presupposes, even builds on the usual literary-critical division of the text: The primitive history is first treated in its Jahwistic form and then according to the Priestly account, and the ancestral traditions are similarly divided. Source criticism thus constitutes the point of departure for his further religio-historical and Gattung-historical work.[7] But Gunkel's dissatisfaction with source criticism alone resulted eventually in his parting paths with the approach typified by Wellhausen. Gunkel's research into the ancient traditions of Israel greatly reduced the importance that the Old Testament authors and their documents had enjoyed in the work of "classical" literary criticism, and it is perhaps small wonder that Wellhausen responded in protest.[8] Inasmuch as this only hardened Gunkel's will,[9] he and Gressmann[10] became aware that they were creating a new, distinct research method and field. In the following, we propose to specify the precise contri-

---

6. Cf. Klatt, *Hermann Gunkel*, 52–53, 106–25; and Klatt, *ZTK* 66 (1969), 1–6.

7. Despite his considerable interest in the preliterary period, Gunkel was not forgiven by several Scandinavian scholars for his unwillingness to free himself completely from the literary-critical dissection of the Pentateuch; cf., e.g., Nielsen, *Oral Tradition*, 11–12; however, see also Mowinckel, *Prophecy and Tradition*, 7ff.

8. "Zur apokalyptischen Literatur," *Skizzen und Vorarbeiten* 6 (1899), 215–49. Cf. also the description of this conflict in Klatt, *Hermann Gunkel*, 70–74.

9. Gunkel's rejoinder to Wellhausen is interesting ("Aus Wellhausens neuesten apokalyptischen Forschungen: Einige principielle Erörterungen," *ZWT* 42 (1899), 620–21): "We recognize very well this voice of an older school which in the final analysis seeks to examine the religion of the Israelite people *alone* and which maintains that treating Israel's contacts with other civilizations is of no theological, though 'perhaps' of antiquarian interest.... [That school] has no concern for the mighty picture of the history of the peoples and religions constituting the background of such compilations; to be sure, there is occasional talk of 'tradition,' but in the exegesis consideration is almost always given to the *author* alone. We recognize very well this voice, but we are astonished to hear it coming from so far-sighted a man whom we have honored as our pioneer and leader."

10. Cf., e.g., Gressmann's declaration published for the first time in Klatt, *Hermann Gunkel*, 73–74.

butions that Gunkel's Religionsgeschichte and Gattungsgeschichte have made to the rise of the traditio-historical research of the Old Testament.

C. Schöpfung und Chaos: Impulses from Religionsgeschichte

In pointed opposition to the prevalent literary-critical opinion, Gunkel entitled the second chapter of his *Schöpfung und Chaos*: "Gen 1 is not a free construction of the author." For Gunkel, the opening chapter of P's primitive history is not a cosmic theory which the Priestly writer systematically constructed and upon which he then reflected. Rather, it is a recorded tradition containing elements of apparently very old age. In his religio-historical analysis of these elements in both Gen 1 and Rev 12, Gunkel arrives at the conclusion that we have here traces of *the ancient creation myth in which the chaos dragon and the primordial ocean play the key roles*. The Israelites received these notions from Babylonia—not by means of written documents but through an oral tradition stretching over centuries. Inasmuch as Gunkel attempts to establish this historical connection between the Israelite and the Babylonian renditions of this myth, he becomes involved also with traditio-historical considerations. But these latter become theologically and historically important for him in *Schöpfung und Chaos* only in the context of establishing religio-historical dependency. Gunkel is more concerned with the origin and history of a specific mythical notion than he is with the growth of a specific textual unit. Nonetheless, four basic aspects of his investigative method have special relevance also for traditio-historical research:

(1) *Gunkel deduces the foreign origin of elements on the basis of the Old Testament text itself.* The following is the picture he gives of his collaboration with the Assyriologist Heinrich Zimmern: "the theologian [*scil.*: Gunkel] recognized, starting from inner-theological observations, the foreign character of a substance and for more general reasons postulated a Babylonian origin for it. He attempted to reconstruct its original form and then presented the results to the Assyriologist for confirmation."[11] Two such inner-theological factors are: the appearance of תהום (Gen 1:2) without the article; the significance given "water" (as the enemy of the creator) in this account in contrast to Gen 2—suggesting an origin in a different climatic area than Palestine, e.g., in Mesopotamia.[12] His conclusion that the Gen 1 tradition was originally foreign to Israel is thus based on internal evidence. What importance does this finding have for the traditio-historical method? Gunkel's thesis is that

---

11. *Schöpfung und Chaos*, vii–viii.
12. Ibid., 6–16.

our criteria for determining whether an Old Testament text is or contains a tradition are to be found in the present form of the text itself: "certain features, which once had good meaning in the earlier context, are transmitted in a new association to which they have in the meantime lost connection. Such old features—fragments of an earlier whole, without connection in the present account and hardly understandable in the intellectual situation of the narrator—betray to the researcher the existence of, and individual features of, an earlier form of the present narrative."[13] This thesis may have special significance for the study of religio-historical ideas and motifs, but it indicates no less the methodological point of departure for the tradition historian. Von Rad's work four decades later proceeds from this same awareness.[14]

(2) *If one wants to assert that foreign materials have been borrowed, one must be able to trace this historical path of dependence*. Gunkel is fully aware that the simple existence of analogous myths in two different cultures is no proof of a relationship of dependency or causality, and to avoid the danger of committing the fallacy of *post hoc ergo propter hoc*, he describes specific criteria for determining a genetic tie.[15] Since on these grounds it can be assumed that the myth in Gen 1 stemmed originally from Babylonia, Gunkel must suggest a feasible and probable path connecting them. Literary dependency is unthinkable, so he develops a *traditio-historical* solution: At the level of oral tradition, the original form of the Babylonian Marduk-myth was received by the Hebrews, adapted to Jahweh-worship, developed in numerous poetic renditions (of which Gunkel provides thorough examinations), and finally put into the prose form of Gen 1. Thus Gunkel's *Schöpfung und Chaos* contains virtually the first attempt to reconstruct the history of a developing tradition, and the catalyst for this effort was none other than the search for the religio-historical dimension of Gen 1.

(3) *Gunkel is at least as interested in the post-history of an Old Testament idea or tradition as he is in its prehistory*. This fact is obvious in his analysis of Lev 12, which he concludes to be the final link in the long chain of Israelite and Judaic tradition about the mythological creation. In this way it can be

---

13. Ibid., 6, also 255–56.
14. Cf. below, pp. 78–80.
15. In his review of Max Reischle's *Theologie und Religionsgeschichte* (1904), in *DLZ* 1904, col. 1106: "Now there are cases in which one *must*, on the basis of analogies, conclude dependency—namely when (1) the phenomenon itself is not to be understood as arising out of its own environment, when (2) an especially striking analogy is available, and when (3) a relationship of dependency, as might here be assumed, can be made probable on other grounds." Cf. also *Schöpfung und Chaos*, 282–83; and Klatt, *Hermann Gunkel*, 58–59.

seen that Gunkel's total study of this idea is a paradigmatic "Vorstellungsgeschichte" of the type carried out later by Steck.[16]

(4) *Religio-historically viewed, Israel put its own impress on its appropriated traditions by submitting them, as felt necessary, to a gradual process of demythologization.* We have observed this move in Gunkel's reconstruction of the development of the Marduk-myth into its present form in Gen 1.[17] In essence, such a procedure is the *precursor to the traditio-historical principle of interpretation and actualization*.[18]

D. Commentary on Genesis: Impulses from Gattungsgeschichte

We have just seen how certain principles of Gunkel's religio-historical method led him into the sphere of traditio-historical research. In *Schöpfung und Chaos* his primary interest was directed toward the *traditum*, although certain questions of *traditio* (oral tradition, path of transmission, reinterpretation) also received attention. But with the publication of his commentary on Genesis[19] his point of gravity shifted from Religionsgeschichte to Literaturgeschichte,[20] putting him directly in the middle of traditio-historical considerations. Gunkel's interest in Literaturgeschichte found concrete expression in the historical investigation of the prime Gattung of Genesis: the *saga*. Inasmuch as the saga by definition is "popular tradition"[21] in opposition to strict historical writing, a history of this Gattung has to take into consideration the sociological and religious footing of these popular pieces as well as the vivid development which they most likely experienced in this preliterary period. Although Gunkel's commentary is carried out in the framework of the accepted results of source criticism, his awareness that these documents constitute only the final stage in a long process dates back to his publication of 1895: "the sagas have already had a history in oral tradition before literary fixation; and this prehistory, ultimately of sole importance, is not to be reached through literary criticism."[22] Gunkel devotes prime—although not exclusive—attention to

---

16. Cf. below, pp. 142–46.
17. Cf. also Klatt, *Hermann Gunkel*, 57, 162–64; and B. W. Anderson, *Creation Versus Chaos: The Reinterpretation of Mythical Symbolism in the Bible*, New York 1967, especially 11–42.
18. Cf. above, pp. 5–6.
19. Gunkel, *Genesis übersetzt und erklärt*, HKAT I/1, 1st ed., Göttingen 1901; 3rd revised ed., 1910; 7th ed. (reprint), 1966, from which all page references here are taken.
20. Klatt, *Hermann Gunkel*, 104ff.
21. *Genesis*, VII f. [ET: *The Legends of Genesis*, trans. W. H. Carruth, New York (1909) 1964, 2].
22. *Schöpfung und Chaos*, 143.

the investigation of this prehistory in his commentary. The traditio-historical significance of this work can be seen especially at six points:

(1) *Gunkel's Gattungsgeschichte of the Genesis sagas established the viability of examining the smallest units of the text.* In *Schöpfung und Chaos* he follows a religio-historical *idea* back to its origin, and this is paralleled in his commentary on Genesis by the retracing of a formally defined *unit* of tradition back to its earliest beginnings. Gunkel is intent on uncovering all details of its historical development, which for the sagas of Genesis means determining the probable foreign origin of each and also describing the process of adaptation or "Israelitizing" that it underwent in Palestine. Even legends that originated among the Israelites frequently experienced material changes ("Verschiebungen") as they were transferred from one location to another.[23] Furthermore, the same saga existing simultaneously in different circles would usually develop varying details and elements in each case.[24] A saga could also be reworked due to such external conditions as contact with the cult or changes in Israelite morality and aesthetics. All of these above considerations serve as criteria for dating the elements of the sagas and for determining the content and form which they had at the various stages of their development.

(2) *The determination of the "Sitz im Leben" of the Gattung provides the point of departure for the traditio-historical search for the specific group that developed and transmitted the individual unit.* Gunkel maintains that the sagas were from their very beginnings found only at the popular, oral level; thus they should be understood as the product of the whole circle in which they were developed. His description of the usual "Sitz im Leben" of these legends is well known: "In the leisure of a winter evening the family sits about the hearth; the grown people, but more especially the children, listen intently to the beautiful old stories of the dawn of the world, which they have heard so often yet never tire of hearing repeated."[25] Although Gunkel does not attempt to specify a special "Sitz im Leben" for each individual saga or pericope in his commentary,[26] his effort to understand the living situation or function of the individual unit in its original milieu promotes the investigation of its developmental history and the determination of specific aspects of *traditio*.

---

23. Cf. Gunkel's general discussion of this whole process, *Genesis*, lvi–lvii.

24. Ibid., lxv [ET: 99]: "It is the characteristic of legend as well as of oral tradition that it exists in the form of variants. Each [narrator], however faithful [he or she] may be, and especially every particular group and every new age, tells [the transmitted story] somewhat differently."

25. Ibid., xxxi [ET: 41]. On the basis of this statement, Nielsen (*Oral Tradition*, 11) classifies Gunkel's approach as "antiquated" and "naive."

26. Klatt, *Hermann Gunkel*, 146.

(3) *Gunkel's revolutionary attention to the preliterary stage of oral formation, composition, and transmission stimulated subsequent research into the oral stage of all parts of Old Testament literature.* His later statement with regard especially to narratives seems categorical: "All ancient literature arose originally not in written but in oral form."[27] Unlike Wellhausen and other literary critics who held the oral stage to be too vague and uncertain to be researched, Gunkel sought ways to penetrate this nebulous mass. He thus became the real precursor and initiator of the approach that Scandinavian scholars (Nyberg, Birkeland, Engnell, Nielsen) claimed as their own. Two points, however, are of special interest in this regard: (a) Gunkel has been charged with relegating oral tradition to the preparatory stage prior to the decisive activity that occurred at the written level.[28] This characterization is inaccurate for his work on Genesis but not wholly unfounded for his picture of the prophetic literature. For the Genesis sagas Gunkel maintains that the formation and even frequently the composition into cycles all took place at the oral stage; when J and E received them, they needed to do little more than collect and record them.[29] Thus for Genesis the formation and composition at the oral level were all-important. On the other hand, however, the oral stage that Gunkel attributes to the prophetic literature could seem less significant in comparison. To be sure, Gunkel's clear perception of the prophets as *speakers* was a great advance beyond the literary-critical view of them as writers.[30] But in comparison with the Scandinavians' (Birkeland, Mowinckel, Engnell, Haldar) view of the *oral stage* as the decisive period for formation of the tradition as well as for the composition of the literature (by the disciples), Gunkel conceives of a shorter oral period and of the development of the literature primarily at the written level, beginning with "Flugblätter."[31] (b) The Scandinavians Nyberg and Engnell posit that the act of recording oral traditions marks no great change of an internal nature since the traditions by this point had already achieved a state of virtual fixity.[32] Gunkel, on the other hand, is of another opinion: "the recording of a tradition serves to stabilize it; oral tradition however cannot permanently maintain itself well and is there-

---

27. Gunkel, *SAT* I/1, 6.

28. So Nielsen, *Oral Tradition*, 11–12; cf. also Mowinckel, "Om tilblivelsen av profetbøkene," *NTT* 39 (1938), 318; and A. H. J. Gunneweg, *Mündliche und schriftliche Tradition der vorexilischen Prophetenbücher als Problem der neueren Prophetenforschung*, FRLANT 73, Göttingen 1959, 7–8.

29. Gunkel, *Genesis*, xxx, lxxx.

30. The idea, however, was not original to Gunkel. More than a century earlier Nachtigal posited also a prophetic oral tradition; cf. above, pp. 50–51.

31. Gunkel, *SAT* II/2, xxxviii ff.

32. Cf. below, pp. 178–80, 200–203.

fore not in a position to become the appropriate receptacle of history."[33] This statement betrays a basic skepticism regarding the historical reliability of oral transmission, a skepticism which Nyberg and Engnell do not share. But more than this, Gunkel recognizes that a basic form-critical alteration occurs when the tradition is removed from its living situation and confined to a literary context.[34] This realization anticipates Lord by 50 years.[35]

(4) *Gunkel was among the first to take seriously the concept of oral composition with regard to Old Testament literature.* According to his picture of the oral process, certain sagas, existing originally as individual and independent units but dealing with the same character(s), similar themes, or related historical occurrences, often became gathered into small cycles ("Sagenkränze") still at the oral level. These combinations then continued to be narrated together as a longer story (e.g., the Jacob–Esau–Laban cycle, the stories about Joseph).[36] The important point is that Gunkel holds the traditionists in the early "Sitz im Leben" for being capable of carrying out the artistic work that literary critics had always assumed could only be accomplished at the writer's desk.

(5) *Gunkel's analytical method begins with the literary-critically defined documents and penetrates all the way back to the earliest periods, embracing thereby the total spectrum of historical development.* In effect, this is *tradition criticism* with its effort to determine each developmental stage along the way; but also diachronic overviews, though sometimes quite brief, are included in his commentary.[37] Gunkel has been criticized for absolutizing the archaic stage of the sagas and neglecting the final compositional form.[38] This estimation of his priorities may at first sight seem to be accurate since he is, above all, striving to determine the absolutely original forms.[39] But in truth Gunkel is concerned with tracing the *whole process* of development and does not absolutize the one or the other stage. "He himself carried traditio-historical questioning so far forward that it flows into Redaktionsgeschichte without interruption. By no means does he absolutize this last stage of the tradition; rather, he conceives of it as a member connected organically to the preceding stages of the tradition."[40] Analytically, Gunkel touches every point along

---

33. Gunkel, *SAT* I/1, 14.
34. Cf. the discussion in Güttgemanns, *Offene Fragen*, 157–61.
35. A. B. Lord, *The Singer of Tales*, Cambridge, Mass. 1960, 124ff.
36. Gunkel, *Genesis*, xxxi–xxxiii.
37. Ibid., e.g., 67–77, 116–31, 159–62, 240–42, 395–401.
38. By von Rad, followed then by Kraus, cf. below, pp. 89-91. Somewhat similarly also Mowinckel, *Prophecy and Tradition*, 12–13, who maintains that Gunkel fails "to reach the final synthesis."
39. Cf. Gunkel, *Genesis*, xxxi–xxxii.
40. Klatt, *Hermann Gunkel*, 159; see also the whole section 156–64.

the way—with the exception perhaps of the final Redaktionsgeschichte, for which however he can presuppose the abundant work of his contemporaries. He does not absolutize the "archaic meaning,"[41] for he places supreme importance in the process by which the Israelites adapted the foreign materials to their own religion.[42]

(6) In conclusion, it remains to be pointed out that Gunkel, although he does not conceive of "tradition history" as a separate field with its own methodology (as do von Rad and Noth), nonetheless *uses the terms "Tradition" and "Überlieferungsgeschichte" to refer to precisely the same period as that which we have specified above: the stage of development prior to literary composition*.[43] Gunkel towers as the first researcher to give full consideration to the historical aspects of both *traditio* and *traditum*. His impact on Old Testament research, while direct and immediate in the fields of Religionsgeschichte and Gattungsgeschichte, was delayed in the area of tradition history—until von Rad and Noth succeeded in feeling its effect.

---

41. So von Rad; cf. below, pp. 89–90.

42. Cf. also Klatt, *Hermann Gunkel*, 161–64; and Klatt, "Die 'Eigentümlichkeit' der israelitischen Religion in der Sicht von Hermann Gunkel," *EvT* 28 (1968), 153–60.

43. Cf. above, ch. 2.

7
From Hugo Gressmann to Albrecht Alt: Securing and Extending the Foundation

A. Hugo Gressmann and Tradition Criticism

Inspired by Gunkel's research and influenced by the religio-historical method stemming from A. Eichhorn and others, Hugo Gressmann (1877–1927) applied to diverse parts of the Old Testament[1] the same type of investigation of ancient traditions that Gunkel had executed for Genesis and the Psalms. As we saw to be the case for Gunkel, Gressmann's work in the field of Religionsgeschichte caused him also to realize that the Old Testament has a depth dimension that must not be neglected. He held it to be axiomatic that everything we meet in the biblical literature—whether formulas, ideas, forms, motifs, or the like—has a prehistory, which each researcher is compelled to explore in order to comprehend the final form and meaning of each item.[2] Especially the origin, nature, and history of each of the small tradition units before they were inserted into a literary "source" must receive attention. Also like Gunkel, he did not intend this work to be in opposition to source criticism; on the contrary, only on the firm basis of literary criticism can an inquiry into the preliterary period have any chance of success.[3] But he showed

---

1. Most notable are Gressmann's *Mose und seine Zeit: Ein Kommentar zu den Mose-Sagen*, FRLANT 18, Göttingen 1913; and *Die Anfänge Israels (von 2. Mose bis Richter und Ruth)*, SAT I/2, 2nd ed., Göttingen 1922. Especially his commentary on Joshua in the latter volume (134–64) illustrates well his precise form-critical and traditio-critical approach: by peeling off the strata one by one he reaches far back into the preliterary period and is able to uncover numerous etiological sagas.
2. Gressmann, *Albert Eichhorn*, 35: "There is no substance in the world that has no prehistory, no concept that has no prior point of contact.... And therefore the question must be raised for each substance and each concept: Whence does it come, and what development has it undergone?"
3. Gressmann, *Mose und seine Zeit*, 368.

no doubt that the latter is an area of study that extends beyond the sphere in which literary criticism can operate.[4]

Gressmann's analytical approach can best be called *tradition criticism*. Its nature becomes especially clear in his study of the narratives about Moses,[5] where he strives to uncover all the stages ("Schichten") in the formation of each tradition about Moses, removing each stratum one after another until he finally arrives at the earliest form of the saga. The additions that come at each level are conceived to be variants within the oral tradition. For the historian all of the strata have their own respective worth, although in writing a history of the Mosaic period only the "Ursagen" will be relevant.[6] In contrast to Noth and von Rad but in accord with earlier literary critics like Wellhausen, Gressmann is of the opinion that Numbers–Deuteronomy provides a basically reliable outline of historical occurrences, and he regards Moses as Israel's authoritative leader throughout all the stages in this linear sequence of events. Only with the full initiation of traditio-historical work does one realize that even this picture of history could be a result of the interpretative process in the Israelite cult.[7] Also in contrast to von Rad after him, Gressmann refuses to carry out the traditio-*historical* step—diachronically arranging his critical results into a relative chronology in order to demonstrate how the "Endstadium" was reached. He makes his method particularly vivid by comparing it with an excavation: just like the archaeologist, the tradition critic is interested in uncovering historical facts about each period, and after this reductive approach the critic should not be expected to put the section back together again.[8] This explicit claim for pri-

---

4. Gressmann, "Die Aufgaben der alttestamentlichen Forschung," *ZAW* 42 (1924) 2-8; also "Ursprung und Entwicklung der Joseph-Sage," *EYXAPIΣTHPION: Festschrift Hermann Gunkel*, I, FRLANT 36, Göttingen 1923, 2, where he notes that, after dividing the Joseph saga into the two sources J and E, there still remain "unevennesses, fissures, and breaks in the presentation which source criticism cannot explain away because they reside in the material itself anterior to the sources and thus lead us into the prehistory of the oral tradition. Therefore, *Stoffkritik* must ally itself, as a supplement, to *source criticism*." By "Stoff" Gressmann is presumably thinking of traditions defined more according to their contents than their form. We have pointed out above (pp. 11–12) that a history of "Stoff" in the sense of unstructured raw materials cannot be written. — Gressmann's position regarding "Stoffgeschichte" and source criticism is shared by J. Begrich; cf. the latter's important study, "Die Paradieserzählung: Eine literargeschichtliche Studie" (1932), *Gesammelte Studien zum Alten Testament*, ed. W. Zimmerli, Munich 1964, 11–38.

5. For a concise description of Gressmann's analysis, cf. R. Smend, *Das Mosebild von Heinrich Ewald bis Martin Noth*, BGBE 3, Tübingen 1959, 16–19.

6. Gressmann, *Mose und seine Zeit*, 367.

7. Cf. below, ch. 8; also von Rad, *Theologie* I, 17–19 (ET: I, 3–5).

8. Note Gressmann's own words (*Mose und seine Zeit*, 22–23): "Indeed, it is occasionally demanded that one should not only remove the strata but must also return them to their

orities would seem to make von Rad's (and Kraus') basic criticism of Gunkel[9] considerably more appropriate for Gressmann's work; *his purposeful drive for the earliest stage of the sagas and thus for their "archaic meaning" (von Rad's term) outdoes by far any such inclination in Gunkel's commentary on Genesis.*

What did Gressmann picture to be the crucial tasks facing the Old Testament critic of his time? In a perceptive article precisely to this point,[10] he gives a predominant position to the further solving of problems connected with the ancient traditions of Israel. He makes it clear that less, not more, literary-critical studies are needed, for they cannot be expected to bring any new information of significance. Of primary concern must be the expanding of our knowledge at the point of the historical development of the ancient religions, cultures, and literature.[11] In particular, Gunkel's call for a Literaturgeschichte and Gattungsgeschichte must receive prime attention through further development and application, and the role and character of oral tradition must be more explicitly defined. And especially, according to Gressmann, the actual origins and history of the traditional materials themselves need to be researched more thoroughly. The prophetic literature is in most need of investigations of this type.[12] Gressmann's challenges to biblical scholarship found eager crusaders in the next generation of researchers, both in Germany and (especially for the prophetic literature) in Scandinavia.

B. Early Understandings of Oral Tradition

The idea of "oral tradition" in Old Testament research is so closely associated with Scandinavian scholars that one tends to overlook the fact that the

---

place, or without the image: one should not consider the source writings solely in isolation but should also assess the present context in which they have been transmitted to us. This must in principle be rejected because it requires the impossible. This can be clarified with the help of the ... image of an excavation. One digs up a mound of ruins in order to allow the ruins to speak and to determine their history. For this purpose one removes stratum after stratum, for only the precise knowledge of the individual strata and of their chronological sequence has scientific significance. When the archaeologist has fulfilled this task, has drawn conclusions, and has painstakingly brought all individual finds into order, then the work is definitely completed. However, the above demand suggests that the archaeologist put the dig back together again, in fact that the reconstructed ruins be evaluated and the jumble meaningfully described! Research has nothing to do with such a task."

9. Cf. above, p. 65; and below, pp. 89–91.
10. *ZAW* 42 (1924), 1–33.
11. Ibid., 2–8. Similar positions with respect to literary criticism and the pressing problems of Old Testament scholarship are taken by W. Staerk, "Zur alttestamentlichen Literarkritik: Grundsätzliches und Methodisches," *ZAW* 42 (1924), 34–74; and I. Hylander, "Den gammaltestamentliga litterärkritikens kris," *SEÅ* 2 (1937), 16–64.
12. Gressmann, *ZAW* 42 (1924), 25ff.

groundwork for this subject was already laid prior to the publications of Nyberg, Mowinckel, Birkeland, and Engnell. In the above sections we have seen that scholars for centuries have conceived of an oral tradition for Genesis, i.e. for the period prior to Moses. Their doctrine of divine inspiration and their interest in securing the *pura doctrina* caused them, however, to qualify this postulated oral tradition in one of two ways: either the traditions were assumed to have been passed down through the faithful testimony of the patriarchs (so Calvin, Chemnitz, Pascal, Bossuet), or the oral tradition was regarded as basically unreliable and therefore was replaced by a series of documents (so Astruc, Ilgen). We have also seen that Nachtigal was the first to consider an oral transmission of post-Mosaic historical materials and of prophetical sayings. The literary critics of the nineteenth century reckoned with a mass of oral and written sources for all the historical books of the Old Testament, but the majority of their critical attention was paid to the authors and redactors who received these traditional materials and created their documents on the basis of them. It was tacitly assumed that the period of oral tradition was too vague and uncertain to merit serious study. Gunkel was apparently the first to emphasize the need and feasibility of researching this oral stage. The state of the discussion from Gunkel onwards to the year 1940 should be sketched at this point—not only to improve our understanding of the background for von Rad's and Noth's traditio-historical studies, but also to impress upon ourselves the fact that Nyberg's thesis of 1934 did not introduce the problem but rather appeared late in the course of an already established discussion.

(1) In accord with the general reaction against the literary-critical preoccupation with the compositional and redactional stages, numerous scholars stressed *the important role played by oral means in the formative and early transmittal stages.*[13] Even for those whose dogmatic doctrine of inspired Scripture caused them to make certain qualifications about oral tradition, it still was a factor with which they reckoned because of the many indications of its existence.[14]

---

13. In addition to Gunkel and Gressmann, cf. also, e.g., C. F. Kent, *Narratives of the Beginnings of Hebrew History*, New York 1904, especially 3–20; A. Jirku, *Die älteste Geschichte Israels im Rahmen lehrhafter Darstellungen*, Leipzig 1917; A. Lods, "Le rôle de la tradition orale dans la formation des récite de l'Ancien Testament," *RHR* 88 (1923), 51–64; S. Gandz, "Oral Tradition in the Bible," *Jewish Studies in Memory of George A. Kohut*, New York 1935, 248–69; Gandz, "The Dawn of Literature: Prolegomena to a History of Unwritten Literature," *Osiris* 7 (1939), 261–522 (the section on Hebrew literature appeared in 1930); J. Hempel, "The Forms of Oral Tradition," *Record and Revelation*, ed. H. W. Robinson, Oxford 1938, 28–44; and W. F. Albright, *From the Stone Age to Christianity*, (1st ed. 1940) 2nd ed., Garden City, N.Y. 1957, 64–76.

14. After an analysis of twenty-eight such Old Testament passages that indicate oral transmission, W. H. Gispen (*Mondelinge Overlevering in het Oude Testament*, Meppel 1932)

(2) It was recognized that oral tradition served *religious, practical, recreational, explanatory purposes* in Israel, and that it therefore must be taken into account for historical, lyrical, legal, and prophetic texts alike.[15]

(3) Scholars became aware of the value of oral traditions as *sources of historical, ethnological, and cultic information.*[16]

(4) It became clear that for much of the literature the oral stage was the *creative stage* and that traditions could also be united into *cycles or small compositions* still at the oral level. These materials tended to be committed to writing near the end of an era for purposes of preserving them for later generations.[17]

(5) The point was made that the question of the *literacy* of the Hebrews has little direct bearing on the issue of oral tradition. The Israelites, just like the Greeks and Arabs, could have developed an oral literature before recording it in writing.[18]

(6) Considerable intensive work on the *oral traditions of other peoples* was being carried out in other literary sciences. Especially studies of folklore and epic techniques fostered the analysis of early Israelite materials.[19]

(7) The question of the *faithfulness and reliability* of oral transmission was answered in various ways. Most recognized that the recipients of traditions

---

draws the following conclusion (181): "The value of oral tradition as a factor in the formation of Scripture is modest. Measured against a purely Scriptural standard, the result [of the examination] is sober. This, however, is not to say that the value [of oral tradition] was modest. It is just that it is impossible for us to prove anything further.... Also here [at the points where oral tradition occurred] the powerful influence of sin was present, but the writers of the Bible were guided by the Holy Spirit so that they would not receive any falsehood whatsoever from the oral tradition."

15. Gunkel, Kent, Jirku, Gandz, Hempel.

16. Gunkel, Kent, Jirku, Gandz.

17. Gunkel, Kent, Jirku, Albright.

18. A. A. Bevan, "Historical Methods in the Old Testament," *Essays on Some Biblical Questions of the Day*, ed. H. B. Swete, London 1909, 5–6.

19. From the large bibliography of studies in this direction, reference can be made to especially the following: M. Jousse, *Études de psychologie linguistique: Le style oral rythmique et mnémotechnique chez les Verbo-moteurs*, Paris 1925 (an unusual book, consisting almost entirely of excerpts from other books dealing with matters of oral tradition, including Israelite—all these quotations organized under specific rubrics); H. M. and N. K. Chadwick, *The Growth of Literature*, Vols. 1–3, Cambridge 1932, 1936, 1940, "Early Hebrew Literature" in vol. 2, 629–777; A. Olrik, "Episke love i folkedigtningen," *DS* 1908, 69–89 (GT: "Epische Gesetze der Volksdichtung," *ZAL* 51 [1909], 1–12; ET: "Epic Laws of Folk Narrative," *The Study of Folklore*, ed. Alan Dundes [Englewood Cliffs: Prentice-Hall, 1965] 129–41); M. Moe, "Episke Grundlove," *Edda* 2 (1914), 1–16, 233–49, and *Edda* 4 (1915), 85–126; Gandz, "The Dawn of Literature"; and the voluminous studies of folklore by James Frazer.

generally had a "great reverence for the past,"[20] even though the personal interests of a given tradent could also be expected to filter into the work. Furthermore, the reliability of transmission will vary according to the type of material in question (e.g., greater for ritual texts than for legends).[21] On the whole the opinion was that oral transmission *can* be considered quite reliable but that as a rule one must put more faith in written than in oral means.[22] For a tradition to remain constant and stable at the oral level, certain transmittal aids were usually necessary—mnemonic devices, poetic structure, institutions, written documents for support and control.[23]

(8) Lods made some concrete suggestions concerning *the process to be followed in studying the history of a tradition at its oral stage*. Text criticism and literary criticism are necessary preliminary steps in the analysis. Like Gunkel, he was quite optimistic about the possibility of retracing the history of an oral tradition, in many cases at least.[24]

(9) Lods also referred to those of his day who virtually rejected the methods and results of one type of criticism (e.g., literary criticism, comparative religions, study of the oral traditions) in favor of another, and he rebuked them for this approach since scholarship is too poorly informed on the history of Israel to be able to afford the luxury of such favoritism.[25]

(10) The general state of the discussion by 1934, the year of Nyberg's publication, was thus that *oral tradition must indeed be taken into quite serious consideration in Old Testament research*. However, it was held that the sources transmitted down from early Israelite history were not solely in oral but also partly in written form. It was in this context that Nyberg presented his categorical thesis: "Transmission in the Orient is seldom purely written; it is predominantly *oral*.... The written Old Testament is a creation of the Jewish community after the exile; what preceded it was surely only in smaller part fixed in writing."[26] In part 2 we will devote more attention to the impact of this idea on Old Testament studies.

---

20. So Lods, *RHR* 88 (1923), 62; also Hempel, in *Record and Revelation*, 50ff.

21. Hempel, in *Record and Revelation*, 31.

22. Ibid., 31; E. C. Richardson, "Oral Tradition, Libraries and the Hexateuch," *PTR* 3 (1905), 196–99.

23. W. F. Albright, *The Archaeology of Palestine and the Bible*, 2nd ed., New York 1933, 144ff.; Albright, "The Israelite Conquest of Canaan in the Light of Archaeology," *BASOR* 74 (1939), 13; Gispen, *Mondelinge Overlevering*, 180.

24. Lods, *RHR* 88 (1923), 56ff.

25. Ibid., 55. As we shall see below in part 2, a criticism much similar to this was lodged against the Uppsala Circle two and three decades later.

26. Cited below, pp. 178–79. For the significance of this thesis in the research, cf. part 2, passim.

C. Albrecht Alt's Fundamental Contributions

With Albrecht Alt (1883-1956) we approach the blossoming of "tradition history" into a field of study in its own right, one with its own scope, tasks, method—and an ever-growing bibliography. Alt's contributions to this research were made in two chief ways, one indirect and the other direct. In the first place, he devoted a great deal of his energies to the task of *reinforcing and improving the historical foundations upon which Old Testament studies are built*. This he accomplished through his intimate knowledge of the Near East and his interminable efforts to assess the historical significance of the archaeological finds and the inscriptions discovered there. This work did not deal directly with traditio-historical research but proved to have significant implications for the studies that were to follow, especially in helping to pass judgment on the historical worth of some of the traditions preserved in the Old Testament. Of greatest importance are perhaps his studies of the topography of the land, the territorial boundaries of the tribes, and the history of the settlement of the land of Palestine.[27] His conclusion about the nature of the settlement of the land became the ruling hypothesis: The half-nomadic tribes from the wilderness and the steppes, in search of grazing land for their herds, gradually entered the arable land of Palestine and with time became settled there; this generally peaceful immigration was followed later by some sporadic skirmishes with neighboring tribes already ensconced there.[28] Also important is his description of the formation of the national state of Israel, its beginnings under Saul but its real unification under David, the catalyst for this being the threat from the Philistines.[29] Together with Noth's epoch-making work on the premonarchical amphictyony,[30] Alt's investigations helped provide a framework in which the early historical periods and the Old Testament traditions dealing with them could be understood.

Also to be mentioned is Alt's form-critical examination of Israelite legal materials. His presupposition: "The making of law is basically not a literary

---

27. Cf. especially his articles: "Das System der Stammesgrenzen im Buche Josua" (1927), reprinted in *Kleine Schriften zur Geschichte des Volkes Israel* (= *Kl. Schr.*), vol. I, Munich 1953, 193–202; "Die Landnahme der Israeliten in Palästina" (1925), *Kl. Schr.* I, 89–125; and "Erwägungen über die Landnahme der Israeliten in Palästina" (1939), *Kl. Schr.* I, 126–75. Translations of several of these and other articles mentioned in this discussion can be found in: *Essays on Old Testament History and Religion*, trans. H.A. Wilson, Oxford 1966.

28. We will see below that Noth's historical reconstruction of this period is based primarily on Alt's thesis. Cf. also the critical responses in ch. 10.

29. "Die Staatenbildung der Israeliten in Palästina" (1930), *Kl. Schr.* II, Munich 1953, 1–65.

30. Noth, *Das System der zwölf Stämme Israels*, BWANT IV/1, Stuttgart 1930.

process at all, but part of the life of a community."[31] On this footing he made his well-known distinction between casuistic law and apodictic law, the former specifying both crime and punishment ("If…, then…") and having a profane "Sitz im Leben" among the people, and the latter having an absolute and unconditional form ("You shall not…") and its "Sitz im Leben" in the cult.[32] Alt's clear concept of the vital basis of Israelite law among the people has provided the point of departure for subsequent investigations into the origin and history of specific legal materials and groupings.

But Alt also made *direct contributions* to traditio-historical research during its inaugural period. Especially two of his studies were executed in such a perceptive manner that they became determinative for the work of von Rad, Noth, and others. The essay "Der Gott der Väter"[33] has in fact been acclaimed as a "superb example of traditio-historical research."[34] Concentrating on Israel's prehistory and on the stages leading up to the establishment of the Jahweh-worship in Palestine, Alt finds in the traditions a concrete basis for drawing historical conclusions about this perplexing period: "the Israelite tradition in fact contains a distinctive religious element of which the peculiar characteristics have not yet been recognized and which, if I judge aright, goes back to the original religious forms used by the individual tribes and groups. This is the tradition of the God of Abraham, and Fear of Isaac, and the Mighty One of Jacob, or in short, of the God of the Fathers."[35] This cult of the "Vätergötter" is a religio-historical type found elsewhere in the ancient Near East. Alt thus understands these three patriarchs as recipients of revelation and as founders of independent cults in the period prior to the settlement of Palestine. The "Sitz im Leben" of the ancestral legends is not so much the campfire (so Gunkel) as the worship of the ancestral gods. With the passage of time these three (or more) divinities became fused together ("verschmolzen") into the figure of the historical God of Israel,[36] and in the same manner the traditions were also joined. The strength of Alt's exposition is his demonstration of the possibility of *using the traditio-historical method to extract early historical information from the traditions* and to assess these materials

---

31. Alt, "Die Ursprünge des israelitischen Rechts" (1934), *Kl. Schr.* I, 284 [ET: 86].

32. Gerstenberger's basic criticism of Alt's understanding of apodictic law is described below, p. 269.

33. From the year 1929; *Kl. Schr.* I, 1–78.

34. W. Zimmerli, "Die historisch-kritische Bibelwissenschaft und die Verkündigungsaufgabe der Kirche," *EvT* 23 (1963), 25; cf. also H. Weidmann, *Die Patriarchen und ihre Religion im Licht der Forschung seit Julius Wellhausen*, FRLANT 94, Göttingen 1968, 172.

35. *Kl. Schr.* I, 9 [ET: 10].

36. *Kl. Schr.* I, 30. Traces of the early distinctions among these divinities can still be seen in some of the pentateuchal traditions, e.g., in Gen 31:42a, 53a.

for their historical worth. In this connection he also makes it clear that Wellhausen's basic skepticism about the historical value of the Genesis legends is unjustified, just as is also an unquestioning acceptance of the entirety of the proclamations as credible.

A second noteworthy study is his article "Josua,"[37] dealing with especially the section Josh 1–11. Building on Gressmann's brief commentary of this book,[38] Alt emphasizes that one principle of criticism is unavoidable: "we must eliminate everything that has been inserted by secondary revision into the originally otherwise constituted materials of the narratives."[39] This secondary material has, of course, value itself for reconstructing the historical situation of the time when it was introduced into the tradition, but it must be separated from the primary elements if we are to determine the *original* or earliest historical background of the tradition. Here Alt is quite in accord with the traditio-critical position of Gressmann.[40] Thus after this necessary removal, the primary material of the book of Joshua is seen to be a Benjaminite saga-complex dealing with events of that tribe in the time of the settlement of the land; and Joshua himself is a secondary element, who as a hero of the Ephraimites is "appropriated" as the general, all-Israel leader when the traditions are retold again and again in later times, especially at the cultic center of Gilgal. Also like Gressmann, Alt stresses the importance of the etiological factor in the shaping of the traditions and the manner in which these legends remained anchored ("Ortsgebundenheit") to their "Haftpunkt."[41] This work on the book of Joshua by Alt and Gressmann reached its culmination in the thorough commentary produced shortly thereafter by Noth.[42]

What then are Alt's general contributions to traditio-historical research? There are several: (1) He emphasized the importance of the cult in the process of tradition growth and composition (e.g., for the ancestral legends). (2) He discovered that not only individual traditions and complexes but even a picture of history (e.g., of the ancestral period) could be developed in the tradition process. (3) He maintained that a central character (e.g., Joshua) in a tradition complex could actually be a secondarily added composition device.[43] (4) He emphasized the importance of the etiological factor and of "Ortsgebundenheit" in tradition development. (5) He demonstrated that otherwise

---

37. From the year 1936; *Kl. Schr.* I, 176–92.
38. Cf. above, p. 67 n. 1.
39. *Kl. Schr.* I, 179.
40. Cf. above, pp. 68–69.
41. *Kl. Schr.* I, 182–84.
42. Noth, *Das Buch Josua*, HAT I,7, Tübingen 1938, 2nd ed. 1953.
43. One is reminded of Noth's later thesis about Moses; cf. below, pp. 116–17.

inaccessible historical information (e.g., of the ancestral period) can often be recovered through traditio-historical means. In these and other ways, Alt made a lasting impression on the research of the Old Testament. His influence was felt above all by the two scholars who gave traditio-historical work its identity—von Rad and particularly Alt's best-known student, Noth.

8
GERHARD VON RAD AND MARTIN NOTH: THE FATHERS OF TRADITIO-HISTORICAL RESEARCH

A. GERHARD VON RAD

There are good reasons for regarding the 1930s as the beginning of a new era in Old Testament research, for it was then that Gerhard von Rad and Martin Noth began to publish studies that opened the flood-gate for a massive inquiry into the history of the traditions and transmission of not only the historical books but of all other parts of the Old Testament as well. Both von Rad and Noth were of course dependent upon the research that preceded them (especially that of Gunkel, Gressmann, Alt, and Mowinckel), but their uniqueness was their ability for perspicacious analysis of the materials, as well as an originality of thought and method which allowed them to go beyond the previous trends in Old Testament work and to become occupied in depth with problems that few prior to them had even recognized as existing. Von Rad himself expressed in the opening statements of his 1938 monograph the boredom with the old trends that drove him into this new field: "No one will ever be able to say that in our time there has been any crisis in the theological study of the Hexateuch. On the contrary, it might be held that we have reached a position of stalemate which many view with considerable anxiety. What is to be done about it?"[1]

---

1. *Das formgeschichtliche Problem des Hexateuch*, BWANT, IV/26, Stuttgart 1938 = von Rad, *Gesammelte Studien zum Alten Testament*, TB 8, 3rd ed., Munich 1956, 9 [ET: *The Problem of the Hexateuch and Other Essays*, trans. E. W. Trueman Dicken, Edinburgh and London 1966, 1]; cf. also von Rad, "Hexateuch oder Pentateuch?" *VF* 1947/48 (1949/50), 52. (Hereafter the title of this monograph will be abbreviated *FPHex*, and page references will be taken from *Ges. Stud.*) It will become clear below in part 2 that this ennui in Old Testament research was also a factor in the rise of the Scandinavian traditio-historical work, although certainly more important for the Scandinavians was a distinct distaste for and even rejection of the "classical" literary-critical research of the Old Testament.

1. The Form-Critical Problem of the Hexateuch

a. Point of Departure

What von Rad (1901–1971) did was to start with the most ancient confessional beliefs found in the Old Testament and, using these as the key, to try to explain the compositional form of the Hexateuch *as a whole* in light of its feasible course of development stretching from the originally separate traditions on to their final form in the present context. Von Rad's primary concern was to analyze the formal principles of the total hexateuchal composition, but in the process of this investigation he also gained insights into the literary, oral, and theological prehistory of its component parts. The role of the *cult* is accorded central significance for this history of the traditions.

A lengthy quotation from von Rad's introductory remarks would allow us to understand better his point of departure:

> Let us run over rapidly in quite general terms the contents of the Hexateuch:[2] God, who created the world, called the first ancestors of Israel and promised them the land of Canaan. Having grown in numbers in Egypt, the people of Israel were led into freedom by Moses, amidst miraculous demonstrations of God's power and favour, and after prolonged wanderings in the desert were granted the promised land.
>
> Now these statements, which summarize the contents of the Hexateuch, are understood in the source documents to be essentially statements of belief.... That which is recounted, from the creation of the world and the call of Abraham to the completion of the conquest under Joshua, is purely and simply a "history of redemption." We might equally well call it a *creed*, a summary of the principal facts of God's redemptive activity.
>
> Let us now consider this creed from the point of view of its outward form. It is a truly immense compilation, an arrangement of the most diverse kinds of material which are all brought into relation with one comparatively simple basic idea. At once we see that we have here the end-term of a process [*Endstadium*], something both final and conclusive. The intricate elaboration of the one basic idea into this tremendous edifice is no first essay, nor is it something which has grown of its own accord to the proportions of classical maturity. Rather, as we have said, it is something pressed to the ultimate limits of what is possible and of what is readable. It must certainly have passed through earlier stages of development.

---

2. Von Rad's use of the term "Hexateuch" is indeed intentional since he posits that the conquest tradition with its conclusion in the book of Joshua is the compositional foundation for the whole of Genesis–Joshua. It constitutes therefore a cardinal difference between him and Noth, who maintains that the conquest tradition is not a part of the final Pentateuch. Cf. below, pp. 111, 120–21; and von Rad, *VF* 1947/48 (1949/50), 52–56.

In other words, the Hexateuch itself may, and indeed must, be understood as representative of a type of literature of which we may expect to be able to recognize the early stages, the circumstances of composition, and the subsequent development until it reached the greatly extended form in which it now lies before us.³

Four points thus become obvious regarding von Rad's approach to the problem.⁴ (1) There exist in the Old Testament certain creeds or "faith-statements" which outline the various "heilsgeschichtliche" events through which God chose Israel and led the people to the promised land. (2) These credenda of Israel served as the prime organizing principle for all of the variegated materials and traditions that went into the building of the Hexateuch. (3) The Hexateuch as a *whole* must be form-critically investigated (in the same way as Gunkel examined its parts) and the "Sitz im Leben" of its earliest beginnings, which are still recognizable in the creedal statements, determined. And finally, (4) in order to gain a better understanding of the Hexateuch as the final stage in a long process, it is necessary to examine carefully the earlier periods when the traditions were living, growing, and being collected; especially the key role of the Jahwist in this process must be properly considered. In von Rad's words: "Many ages, many men, many traditions, and many theologians have contributed to this stupendous work. The Hexateuch will be rightly understood, therefore, not by those who read it superficially, but only by those who study it with a knowledge of its profundities, recognizing that its pages speak of the revelations and religious experiences of many different periods. None of the stages in the age-long development of this work has been wholly superseded; something has been preserved of each phase, and its influence has persisted right down to the final form of the Hexateuch."⁵ This summary statement *affirms the very importance, feasibility, and validity of the traditio-historical task.*

First a further word about von Rad's point of departure: the so-called "kleines geschichtliches Credo," which can be found in three places in the Hexateuch and which von Rad assumes to have played so important a role in the early Israelite cult and consequently also in the formation of the Hexateuch.⁶ According to him, Deut 26:5b-9 contains the credo in probably its oldest form—as a prayer used by the cult to confess the people's common faith in the God who had chosen their fathers, who later liberated them from their

---

3. *FPHex, Ges. Stud.*, 10–11 [ET: 2].
4. Cf. also Kraus, *Geschichte*, 445.
5. *FPHex, Ges. Stud.*, 85 [ET: 77–78], italics omitted.
6. Cf. however J. Barr, *Old and New in Interpretation*, London 1966, 74.

severe bondage in Egypt, and who then led them to the promised land. This credo is clearly much older than its literary context and must have attained through its repeated cultic use a canonical form which the Deuteronomist simply records here.[7] Deuteronomy 6:20–24 is of the same Gattung, with the credo appearing this time as a parenesis. It occurs also in Josh 24:2b–13 in a form dealing with the same chief events, although here with considerably more details. These three texts, especially when one considers the context into which they are put, thus show that the recapitulation of Israel's Heilsgeschichte did not occur in Israel as simply a casual reminiscing, but rather as *a serious recitation of events that had vital significance for the members of the cult.* The three creedal statements followed the same schema but were free enough to add different details as might be desired for the various cultic celebrations. One can also note, asserts von Rad, the striking similarity between the credo and the whole Hexateuch in outline form: "Basically there is one uniform, very simple train of thought, and Joshua xxiv.2–13 may be described as already a Hexateuch in miniature."[8]

---

7. A quite different picture of Deut 26:5–10 is offered persuasively by L. Rost, *Das kleine Credo und andere Studien zum Alten Testament*, Heidelberg 1965, 11–25; cf. also G. Fohrer, ZAW 73 (1961), 16. Rost differentiates between the old "Darbringungsformel" in Deut 26:5aα,10 and the "deuteronomisches Credo" in 26:6–9. He disagrees with von Rad that this credo is so very old and that it exists in the present context "nur in deuteronomischer Übermalung" (so von Rad, FPHex, Ges. Stud., 13, 11); Rost argues instead that it is the creation of an individual author in the Josianic period and in this form of a recapitulation was then inserted into the "Darbringungsformel." This totally different view of the origin and importance of this creedal statement causes us to ask: To what extent is a revision necessary of von Rad's form-critical and traditio-historical theses which are founded on these creedal statements, and indeed primarily on this credo in Deut 26? Can his whole structure and view of the Hexateuch be retained in the same form when its foundation is shown to be faulty or at least suspect? One can of course answer (as does W. Zimmerli, "Alttestamentliche Traditionsgeschichte und Theologie," *Probleme biblischer Theologie*, ed. H. W. Wolff, Munich 1971, 632) that the importance of confessional statements in the life of ancient Israel and in the formation of the Hexateuch is not shaken by the probability that the creed in Deut 26 is of a much later date. (Cf. also von Rad's concise response to Rost, in ATD 2, 9th ed., Göttingen 1972, 3.) However, it should at least be clear that in light of Rost's thesis it is necessary now to reappraise the conclusions that von Rad and others have drawn on the basis of their interpretation of Deut 26. Another significant, perceptive critique of von Rad is offered by W. Richter, "Beobachtungen zur theologischen Systembildung in der alttestamentlichen Literatur anhand des 'kleinen geschichtlichen Credo,'" *Wahrheit und Verkündigung: Festschrift M. Schmaus*, Munich 1967, vol. 1, 175–212; cf. also Richter, *Exegese als Literaturwissenschaft*, 155.

8. Von Rad, *FPHex, Ges. Stud.*, 16 [ET: 8].

b. The Traditio-Historical Independence of the Sinai Tradition from the Exodus-Conquest Complex

The above-mentioned creedal statements as well as numerous lyrical renditions of them (e.g., 1 Sam 12:8; Pss 78; 105; 135; 136) are consistent in omitting references to the Sinai events;[9] Sinai, in fact, is first included in the Heilsgeschichte in the exilic Ps 106 and Neh 9. What can we learn from this fact? First, by way of orientation: We must not forget that there are *two distinct aspects to the relationship between exodus/conquest and Sinai.*[10] On the one hand, the *historical* question: How are the Sinai events to be explained with respect to the events of the exodus/conquest? When did this "Digression" or "Abstecher zum Sinai"[11] occur, and who participated in it? On the other hand, the *traditio-historical* and even *theological* question: Regardless of this historical explanation, are we to suppose that the traditions about these events were unified almost since their beginnings? If however there were two separate tradition complexes with a longer existence independent of each other, how then did they become joined together? What changes or developments in the religious belief of the Israelites were necessary before these two tradition complexes, each with its important theological proclamation, could be brought together? It is this latter group of questions to which von Rad devotes his full attention here.

From the omission of Sinai in the credenda, von Rad draws an all-important conclusion: There existed in ancient Israel two complexes of traditions that were originally distinct and independent from each other—the one complex dealing with the events of the exodus from Egypt and the conquest of the promised land[12] and the other complex dealing with all that happened

---

9. Whereas von Rad finds traditio-historical importance in this absence of the Sinai motifs in the creedal statements, Rost (*Credo*, 19) offers a simpler explanation: the credo in Deut 26:6–9 "could not include mention of the covenant-making at Sinai for the very reason that it would have disrupted the distinct line going from the single, nearly defeated Aramean to the great, mighty and populous people, the oppression in Egypt, the exodus and the entrance into the Promised Land."

10. Cf. also von Rad, *VF* 1953/55 (1956), 131–32; A. S. van der Woude, *Uittocht en Sinai*, Nijkerk 1960, 10–11; and Zimmerli, in: *Probleme biblischer Theologie*, 633–34.

11. Wellhausen, *Prolegomena zur Geschichte Israels*, 6th ed., Berlin/Leipzig 1927, 341–42. As von Rad (*Ges. Stud.*, 20–21) notes, Wellhausen noticed this historical unevenness because of the mention of Massah and Meribah already in Exod 17, before the Sinai event is related in Exod 19ff.

12. Von Rad (*FPHex*, *Ges. Stud.*, 48ff., 60) differentiates indeed between the exodus tradition and the conquest tradition, but their traditio-historical separation and independence from each other are more emphatically stressed by Noth; cf. below, p. 114.

at Sinai (the giving of the law and the covenant).[13] The two complexes have entirely different histories, are concerned with dissimilar matters, and are rooted in separate cultic celebrations. The distinctions between the two complexes can be concisely described in the following manner: "the tradition of the Sinai festival celebrates God's coming to his people, whereas the settlement tradition commemorates his guidance and redemptive activity. The Sinai tradition contains a direct and personal revelation of God, and presents the demands of Yahweh's righteous purpose. The tradition of the settlement takes an accepted historical instance of God's saving purpose and validates it as an article of faith."[14] Or even more pointedly: "The exodus tradition bears witness to the redemptive purpose of God revealed to Israel in its travels from Egypt to Canaan; it is a 'redemptive history'. The Sinai tradition testifies to the divine justice, revealed to the nation and made binding upon it: it is apodeictic law."[15]

On the one hand, the Sinai tradition (its main pericope in Exod 19–24) has as its center the narrative of the theophany and the covenant. This narrative existed at first as a separate, closed tradition; and there eventually accumulated around it a number of different, smaller, originally separate traditions, many of which were etiologies for various cultic elements (e.g., those in Exod 33 regarding tent, name, and face). The tradition was closely connected to the cult[16] and was specifically celebrated by the Jahweh-amphictyony in the covenant-renewal ceremony which was held in Shechem (Deut 27; Josh 24) every seventh year at the Feast of Booths (Deut 31:10–11).[17] On the other hand and completely independent in transmission from the Sinai tradition, the complex of the traditions concerning the exodus[18] and the conquest of the promised land is considerably older than the Sinai tradition and centers in the oldest form of the Israelite credo, that found in Deut 26:5b–9. This credo and the rest of the tradition complex which in time gathered

---

13. Both John Bright (*Early Israel in Recent History Writing*, SBT 19, London 1956, 105) and van der Woude (*Uittocht en Sinai*, 8) point out that von Rad is basically relying on an *argumentum e silentio* here.

14. Von Rad, *FPHex, Ges. Stud.*, 48–49 [ET: 41].

15. Ibid., 26 [ET: 18–19].

16. This conclusion, von Rad reminds us, was reached by Mowinckel in his book, *Le décalogue* (Paris 1927), 129, although Mowinckel suggested that the ceremony took place in the temple at Jerusalem (119–20).

17. Von Rad, *FPHex, Ges. Stud.*, 41–48.

18. This original independence of the Sinai tradition from the exodus tradition is challenged by van der Woude, *Uittocht en Sinai*; W. Beyerlin, *Herkunft und Geschichte der ältesten Sinaitraditionen*, Tübingen 1961. Cf. also J. M. Schmidt, "Erwägungen zum Verhältnis von Auszugs- und Sinaitradition," *ZAW* 82 (1970), 1–31.

around it had a legitimizing function for the Israelites, and it was celebrated at the yearly Feast of Weeks (Num 28:26; Deut 26:2) in the cultic center at Gilgal (the "End- und Zielpunkt" of the tradition complex) where, according to the old tradition, Joshua had divided the land among the tribes.[19] *This immediate connection with the cult is of central importance for the history not only of these two complexes in their entirety but also of their constituent parts.*

c. *The Fusion of the Tradition Complexes by the Jahwist*

On the basis of his form-critical view of the whole Hexateuch, von Rad is thus able to gain important insights about the traditio-historical independence of the Sinai tradition from the exodus–conquest traditions. What then is he able to conclude about the process in which the Hexateuch came to be? Von Rad maintains that the Hexateuch did *not* develop through a long process in which old traditions, through the work of many generations, became gradually heaped like sediment upon some firm basis, viz. the credo; for if this were the case, we should then be able to observe a stratification or stacking of traditions, the younger upon the older. "On the contrary, what we see is a large quantity of detached materials which have been fused into a single whole according to the pattern of one ancient tradition. The various materials all lie as it were in the same stratum. One plan alone governs the whole, and a gigantic structure such as this, the whole conforming to one single plan, does not grow up naturally of its own accord."[20] We will see below that several Scandinavian scholars (e.g., Engnell) are of the opinion that the Israelites were capable of joining traditions and then even larger tradition complexes at the oral level, so that there gradually developed an extensive "oral literature" which was then later recorded in writing. Does von Rad's position, as seen clearly in the passage just quoted, indicate a skepticism with regard to the Israelites' capabilities in oral composition? Does he at this point simply yield to the classical literary-critical solution of authors and documents? The answer to both of these questions is negative. For one thing, von Rad concludes from his examination of the hexateuchal materials that, *whereas this gradual growth is obvious within many of the tradition complexes themselves, the process of crystallization is not to be found in the larger hexateuchal structure as a whole.* And second, for von Rad it is simply most conceivable that an individual—*the Jahwist*[21]—took the initiative to join all of the traditional

---

19. von Rad, FPHex, Ges. Stud., 48–55.
20. Ibid., 59 [ET: 52].
21. That this is not the only possibility is shown by, e.g., Kraus ("Gilgal: Ein Beitrag zur Kultusgeschichte Israels," *VT* 1, 1951, 188ff.), who argues that the Sinai tradition did not become

materials into a fluent, linear whole according to a specific plan—the heilsgeschichtliche events. In other words, the crucial point is that the positioning of traditions beside each other and often the intertwining of them with each other constitute for the Hexateuch a process that could not have occurred by "accident" but *only by design*. We will have occasion below to show that Noth departs from von Rad's position at this point, maintaining (like the Scandinavians) that far more development occurred gradually at the oral stage.

With his discussion of the activity of the Jahwist, von Rad's study becomes concerned with the problems of *"Literaturwerdung"*—the process in which the old, often disparate traditions became collected into a (written) literature.[22] Von Rad indeed makes use of the categories of the Documentary Hypothesis, but it is not to be mistaken that he follows Gunkel in opting for the view of the Jahwist as "Sammler und Gestalter" rather than as "Schriftsteller" (Wellhausen's opinion).[23] At the Jahwist's disposal was an indeterminable mass of individual traditions; there were also many cases in which traditions had already become gradually grouped around some theme or event, with the resulting complex then transmitted further as a closed unit and received as such by the Jahwist (e.g., the exodus traditions in Exod 1–14[24] or the Balaam narrative in Num 22–24). However, according to von Rad the Jahwist was not a neutral collector and editor of these traditions and complexes, for he carried a distinct theology into his work and did not hesitate to change or edit traditional material in order to make it more acceptable to his own religious views.

---

joined with the exodus tradition at the initiative of some individual but that it happened when the central cult of the amphictyony was shifted from Shechem to Gilgal and the two traditions were thus brought in contact.

22. Von Rad, *FPHex, Ges. Stud.*, 55ff. Two things need to be clarified at this point: (a) Von Rad here conceives of literature as a written phenomenon. However, it has often been recognized (Engnell, Gandz, Chadwick, Jousse, Lord, et al.) that oral traditions in a fairly advanced stage of compositional development qualify also as "literature"; cf. especially S. Gandz, "The Dawn of Literature: Prolegomena to a History of Unwritten Literature," *Osiris* 7 (1939), 261–522. (b) Our definition of "tradition history" (cf. above, ch. 2) excludes the stage of composition by an independent individual (like von Rad's Jahwist), but von Rad's exposition nonetheless requires attention here, not only because this stage is usually regarded as part of tradition history (cf. above, chs. 2 and 3), but also because von Rad provides insights into the precompositional period as well.

23. Cf. ibid., 58ff.; and Gunkel, *Genesis*, §5. Von Rad attributes a greater theological persuasion to the Jahwist than Gunkel is inclined to do, and he could therefore probably not agree fully with Gunkel's statement (*Genesis*, lxxxv) that "these compilers [*scil.*, J and E] are not masters but servants of their materials."

24. Von Rad, *FPHex, Ges. Stud.*, 59–60. Note Johannes Pedersen's important study of this tradition complex: "Passahfest und Passahlegende," *ZAW* 52 (1934), 161–75; see also below, p. 206.

"The Yahwist gathered up the materials which were becoming detached from the cultus, and compacted them firmly together within a literary framework."[25] This is important for two reasons: (1) it indicates the time and the occasion for the Jahwist's composition: the traditions were being separated from their original cultic spheres; and (2) the removal of the traditions from the cult and the insertion of them in the Jahwist's theological structure mark such a significant change that it can be identified as *the theological problem of the Jahwist*.[26]

According to von Rad, the Jahwist was committed to the scheme of the tradition complex of the exodus and the conquest, and therefore to the credo on which this complex centered. His theological orientation was not arbitrarily chosen; his concepts represent "an extremely ancient traditional deposit, and there was no alternative to using them."[27] Note von Rad's estimation of the Jahwist's commitment to the conquest tradition as the basis for his composition: "the Yahwist's outline plan, the framework of which supports the whole of his work, is the Settlement tradition.[28] If he also incorporated in his plan a very great number of detached traditions of the most diverse origin and of many different kinds, he has nevertheless avoided giving even to the most important among them a place comparable or superior to that occupied by the Settlement tradition. They do not stand here as elements which exist in their own right, but are wholly subordinated to the Settlement tradition in an ancillary capacity."[29] *This conquest tradition was thus the point of orientation for the editorial activity of the Jahwist*.[30] Here we see a further significant traditio-historical consequence that von Rad draws from the postulated central importance of the credenda in Israel.

Von Rad specifies three radical innovations for which the Jahwist was responsible:[31] (1) The Jahwist was the one who inserted the *Sinai tradition*

---

25. Von Rad, *FPHex, Ges. Stud.*, 57 [ET: 50].
26. Ibid., 75-81.
27. Ibid., 58 [ET: 51].
28. Von Rad's reference to the "Landnahmetradition" is not of requisite clarity. He apparently does not intend to emphasize the *process* of the conquest, i.e. the numerous battles as described in Joshua and Judges; rather, he surely has in mind the *fact* that the Israelites finally gained the land, which they identified theologically as "inheritance" and "gift" from Jahweh. The details of this process are then of secondary importance.
29. Von Rad, *FPHex, Ges. Stud.*, 58 [ET: 51].
30. H. W. Wolff ("Das Kerygma des Jahwisten," *EvT* 24, 1964, 73-98) is of another opinion. He agrees that the theology of the Jahwist is the central compositional principle (of the Tetrateuch), but he maintains that the Jahwistic kerygma is not to be found so much in the promise/fulfillment motif implicit in the conquest tradition (so von Rad) but rather in the proclamations of the ancestral traditions regarding the *blessing* of "all the families of the earth" (Gen 12:3) through Israel.
31. Von Rad, *FPHex, Ges. Stud.*, 60-75.

into this scheme; it was not done before him and was not even accepted on the popular level until exilic times. (2) The *patriarchal traditions*, however, have a much older, even organic connection to the conquest tradition, as many of the creedal statements themselves show (e.g., Deut 26 and 1 Sam 12:8). Using the ancient concepts of "the God of the fathers"[32] and the "promised land,"[33] the Jahwist organized and bound these legendary materials to his total scheme, though the impulse to do so was not his own (as with the Sinai complex) but was traditional. That is to say, the element of the "promised land" was already present in the pre-Jahwistic ancestral traditions, but the Jahwist made it clear that this promise of land was really fulfilled in Joshua's time, not simply with Abraham's migration to Palestine. The Jahwist's contribution thus came in making these ancestral traditions subservient to the conquest tradition.[34] (3) The legends dealing with *primitive history* (Gen 2–11), however, were probably less popular than the ancestral and Mosaic traditions and even circulated in different cultural and religious circles than these.[35] Therefore, the Jahwist was responsible, much more than was the case with the other two tradition complexes, for organizing these legends of the "Urgeschichte" and for placing them as an introduction to the whole of the Hexateuch. His purpose for doing so was to give thereby "the etiology of all Israelite etiologies"—the reason for the sin and decay of the world and God's ultimate purpose in bridging the gap between God and humanity. Genesis 12:1–3 is a free creation of the Jahwist— not an older tradition—to serve as an ad hoc transition between the primitive traditions and the ancestral complex.[36]

These are some of the main ideas in von Rad's pioneering study, *Das formgeschichtliche Problem des Hexateuch*, which since its publication in 1938 has been determinative and influential in Old Testament form-critical, traditio-

---

32. Von Rad (ibid., 65ff.) refers often to the contributions of Alt at this point.

33. This element probably belongs to one of the oldest traditions; cf. also von Rad's article, "Verheissenes Land und Jahwes Land im Hexateuch," *ZDPV* 66 (1943), 191–204 (= *Ges. Stud.*, 87–100). A different picture is offered by W. M. Clark, *The Origin and Development of the Land Promise Theme in the Old Testament*, Diss. Yale 1964. Clark suggests that the Land Promise theme is originally a part of the Land Gift tradition, not of the ancestral traditions. The original recipients were thus not the patriarchs; it was the Jahwist who projected the concept of the Land Promise into the ancestral period. Regarding the origin of the form of the Land Promise, Clark supposes that it derives from the form of the war oracle, the content of which is a promise of victory over a geographical area.

34. Von Rad, *FPHex, Ges. Stud.*, 67–70.

35. Pss 135 and 136 belong to a much later tine.

36. The academic discussion of each of these three points since von Rad's publication is too complex and extensive to be reviewed here. Reference may be made, however, to one article on the final statement: O. H. Steck, "Genesis 12,1–3 und die Urgeschichte des Jahwisten," *Probleme biblischer Theologie*, ed. H. W. Wolff, Munich 1971, 525–54.

historical, compositional, and theological research. Because this study marks virtually a turning-point in Old Testament work and because it is so basic to von Rad's later traditio-historical investigations, we have felt it necessary to treat it here in detail, withholding our critique until later when we can see the effect of this study on von Rad's exegetical and theological method. *Von Rad's primary contribution is in directing attention to the living process that brought individual, independent traditions together to form the Hexateuch as we know it.* Prior to von Rad, Gunkel penetrated back to the earliest, often pre-Israelite forms of the separate traditions: sagas, myths, folk-tales. This research was reinforced by the tradition criticism executed by Gressmann and others. But Gunkel was less concerned with drawing a detailed picture of how all these disparate materials became joined together, especially how the Pentateuch on the whole could have developed. Here lies the innovation found in von Rad's study. He accepts, to be sure, Gunkel's work and results; but for him the crucial question is how the Hexateuch came to be, how the "Endstadium" was reached. With respect to their basic research *tendencies*, Gunkel's work is characterized by the effort to reach back into the past; von Rad's work, however, by the attempt to describe the forward movement of the traditions, i.e. the way in which the traditions developed and were drawn together into larger compositions. Whereas Gunkel is interested in the "Sitz im Leben" of the primitive traditions, von Rad is driven by the desire to discover the "Sitz im Leben" of the creedal statements and thus of the Hexateuch as a whole. Both scholars are concerned with roughly the same tradition period, although their emphases are different. Von Rad's study is not solely a compositional analysis of the Jahwistic stage, for he is very much interested in the process that led up to the Jahwist. To reconstruct this process (with the aid of his credenda-thesis) von Rad takes into direct consideration traditio-historical as well as theological problems. His traditio-historical method is consistent, although not well defined or considered in its details and consequences; and he pays attention to both *traditio* and *traditum*.

2. Commentary on Genesis

We have examined the traditio-historical method and the theological orientation with which von Rad approaches the "form-critical problem of the Hexateuch." His attention to the kerygma on the one hand and to the developmental history of the traditions on the other becomes the foundation for his later studies of the Old Testament.[37] It would therefore be instructive for

---

37. This supreme importance of the 1938-publication on the rest of his work can indeed be maintained despite von Rad's rather obscure reference to this monograph as having been

us to see the consequences which von Rad's program has had, and to do this we will look briefly at his commentary on Genesis and his *Theologie des Alten Testaments*. It need hardly be said that both of these works are of such great importance as to deserve an exhaustive review, but in keeping with the intention of our history of research we will have to be extremely selective here and hope only to make lucid the character, strengths, weaknesses, and consequences of von Rad's traditio-historical investigative method.

In his commentary on Genesis[38] von Rad aims to establish, apply, and demonstrate the general ideas that he outlines in his 1938 publication, especially the theses regarding the significance of confessional statements in Israel, the important traditio-historical role of the Jahwist, and the composition of the Hexateuch (the relevant key-words here: "Ausbau der Väterüberlieferung" and "Vorbau der Urgeschichte"). Avoiding the details of his analysis and exegesis, we restrict ourselves here to the following considerations.

a. Comparison with Gunkel's Commentary on Genesis

In what respect does von Rad intend his commentary to be an improvement on previous commentaries of Genesis, especially that of Gunkel? For one thing, von Rad recognizes and acknowledges that which "is to the undying credit of H. Gunkel"—the isolation and analysis of the original narrative units in Genesis.[39] However, according to von Rad it is necessary to carry the examination one step further: "that we should turn once again to exegesis of the texts in their present form, that is, that we should take up the question of the meaning that was gradually attached to them, not least through their incorporation into a great narrative complex with its specific themes."[40] This "meaning" is implicit in the Israelite credenda, and the decisive historical factor is the activity of the Jahwist and Elohist. We have reviewed above von Rad's arguments on behalf of both points in his 1938-monograph. We might schematically describe the situation in the following manner: Gunkel's commentary on Genesis was written in an age in which most attention was paid to

---

"written much too hastily" (in H. W. Wolff, "Gespräch mit Gerhard von Rad," *Probleme biblischer Theologie*, Munich 1971, 654).

38. *Das erste Buch Mose: Genesis, übersetzt und erklärt*, ATD 2-4, 1st ed., Göttingen 1949ff., 5th ed. 1958, 9th ed. 1972. The author wishes to express his gratitude to the Vandenhoeck & Ruprecht Verlag, Göttingen, for making the proofs of this revised ninth edition available so that it could be considered here. All quotations are taken from the revised English edition except where otherwise noted: *Genesis: A Commentary*, rev. ed., trans. John H. Marks, Philadelphia 1972.

39. Von Rad, *Genesis*, 5th ed. 1958, 22; 9th ed. 1972, 16 [ET: rev. ed., 31].

40. Ibid., 9th ed. 1972, 24–25 (not in earlier editions), also 5 [ET: rev. ed., 42].

the documents J, E, and P; he therefore opted to concentrate on the preliterary stage—the individual, independent narrative sagas.⁴¹ Von Rad, on the other hand, faces a situation in which this archaic, original stage is emphasized, and he consequently finds it requisite to call attention to the later compositional stages. He can accept most of the work that Gunkel carried out, but von Rad maintains that what is of primary importance now is to *gain a correct interpretation of the process leading up to the "Endstadium"*—the meaning that the traditions came to have at the hands of J, E, and P. His treatment of these sources is, however, not to be identified with that of the earlier literary critics; for von Rad does not regard, e.g., the Jahwist as the author and free creator of his materials (so Wellhausen) but rather as the one who receives and collects the transmitted traditions and remolds them according to his pronounced theological convictions.⁴² Furthermore, von Rad seeks in his commentary to illuminate the whole process of "Literaturwerdung," the period during which the disparate traditions became joined into a body of literature.

b. Hermeneutical Priority of the Jahwist's Composition

Von Rad's critical objective, however, is somewhat problematic from the traditio-historical point of view. The question can be phrased so: Should a commentary select one phase or stage in the traditio-historical development of the text and then in effect absolutize this stage at the expense of the other phases, or should not the interpreter be interested in the whole developmental process as the background to the present text? Von Rad has pointed out that a profound weakness in Gunkel's Genesis commentary consists "in reaching back to the archaic primitive forms of the given tradition and in

---

41. We have noted above, pp. 65–66, that Gunkel does *not* neglect the later, literary stages but in fact subordinates his saga-analyses to the meaning of the traditions in their present form. Confusion arises because *Gunkel's analysis proceeds backwards in time*, from the latest to the earliest stages, thereby giving the impression that he extols the earliest form and meaning.

42. Note that von Rad seems to be thinking of the Jahwist and the Elohist as individuals rather than as "Erzählerschulen" (so Gunkel, *Genesis*, lxxxv). It is obviously a moot point, but one can indeed be skeptical that a single *individual* in Israel would have dared or even been able to alter the traditional materials so radically as von Rad postulates. Von Rad's concession (*FPHex, Ges. Stud.*, 61) that some of the Jahwist's changes did not become widely accepted for several centuries (on what does von Rad base this supposition?) implies this very revolutionary character. But would it not be more conceivable that a group of "Jahwists," a "school" of persons with strong theological convictions, carried out these changes in the traditions and that they as a group, perhaps at some cultic center, were able to work more effectively for the acceptance of their composition than a sole individual would have succeeded in doing?

virtually absolutizing this oldest meaning of it."[43] *But is not von Rad also guilty of a similar "absolutizing"—of the Jahwistic compositional stage?* He is entirely correct in asserting that an interpretation of the texts of Genesis must take into consideration the many levels of meaning of a particular pericope or tradition[44]—its original (in Genesis: often pre-Israelite) meaning, its early Israelite, its amphictyonic, its Jahwistic, its Elohistic, its Priestly, its meaning at the hand of the final redactor, and even its Christian reception—to the extent, of course that all of these levels of meaning are recoverable. He is also right in pointing out that the exegesis of Genesis must go beyond Gunkel's discoveries of the primitive meanings, just as one must also regard as insufficient Procksch's separate interpretations of the three sources J, E, and P at the exclusion of any possible interplay or mutual reference of the one source to the other.[45] In other words, the exegete needs to draw a larger picture than that of just one stage.

But the fact is that von Rad in his exegesis devotes proportionally too much attention to the Jahwist. To be sure, his reasons for doing so are derived from hermeneutical considerations and theological convictions. But *traditio-historically* seen, von Rad is as guilty as he finds Gunkel in arbitrarily investing too much critical importance in one of the several developmental stages. Throughout von Rad's analyses one sees again and again the typical approach: often a short introduction to the pericope in question, the interpretation section by section, concluded frequently by a "Nachwort" in which von Rad simply refers to the meaning or etiological character of the original saga and then tries to show how its Jahwistic or later meaning differs from this possible original sense and function. This effort to take the original meaning and purpose of the saga into consideration fails for its brevity—which is probably as much due to the limits of this popular commentary as it is to von Rad's hermeneutical orientation.

A commentary, of course, is faced with special difficulties in that it must be driven by an exegetical, hermeneutical principle that can give it unity. Von Rad solves the problem by concentrating on the meaning that the traditions assumed in the compositional form and context given them by the Jahwist, Elohist, and Priestly writers; and this choice is surely advantageous because it provides the interpreter with a point of departure both temporally (from

---

43. Von Rad, "Das hermeneutische Problem im Buche Genesis," *VF* 1942/46 (1946/47), 44; cf. also Kraus, *EvT* 16 (1956), 381–83; and Kraus, *Geschichte*, 447, 351. We have seen above, p. 65, that Klatt persuasively challenges this interpretation of Gunkel's intent.

44. Gunkel (*Genesis*, xxxi–xxxii) agrees also with this principle.

45. Von Rad, *Genesis*, 9th ed. 1972, 23ff.; *VF* 1942/46 (1946/47), 49–50.

the ninth to the fifth centuries B.C.E.) and structurally limited.⁴⁶ But this is not the only possible starting-point, and even von Rad questions whether the preacher and the teacher will want to tie themselves to this hermeneutical principle.⁴⁷ A traditio-historical and redaction-critical examination of Genesis yields an exceedingly complex picture of the development of these traditions; this much must be remembered when one is reading Gunkel's commentary on the one hand or von Rad's on the other. *The way in which each tends to identify one stage as his analytical goal does not do full justice to the total traditio-historical complexity and depth of the Genesis traditions.*

c. Tradition History in the Service of Old Testament Theology

Von Rad's reason for making J, E, and P the object of his exegesis has more of a theological than a traditio-historical basis. Indeed the Jahwist played an important traditio-historical role not only as a compiler and editor but especially because he effected "a complete abrogation of its [*scil.*: the old material's] ancient immanental meaning and a new illumination of all parts of the narrated material."⁴⁸ Driven by his strong theological convictions, the Jahwist took the sagas and cultic traditions which had already become separated from their cultic sphere and had in part been going through a period of "Spiritualisierung" or "Vergeistlichung,"⁴⁹ and he completed this tendency to subsume these traditions under the conception of the heilsgeschichtliche credo.⁵⁰ The traditio-historical importance of the Jahwist is thus of a *theological* nature;⁵¹ it is this aspect that lies at the base of most of the Jahwistic alterations in *traditum* and composition,⁵² and it is this aspect that von Rad esteems so highly. In his exegesis of each pericope von Rad strives to establish whether and how the Jahwist effected a shift in its theological meaning. We argued above that it is traditio-historically arbitrary for von Rad to pay so great attention to the Jahwist, and now we can see clearly why he chooses to do so: because of

---

46. Von Rad, *Genesis*, 9th ed. 1972, 23; cf. also 5th ed. 1958, 31; and *VF* 1942/46 (1946/47), 49.
47. Von Rad, *Genesis*, 5th ed. 1958, 31; *VF* 1942/46 (1946/47), 49.
48. Von Rad, *Genesis*. 5th ed. 1958, 27; 9th ed. 1972, 20 [ET: rev. ed., 36].
49. Ibid., 5th ed. 1958, 10ff.; 9th ed. 1972, 3ff.
50. Ibid.
51. This fundamental relationship between theology and tradition history can be seen especially clearly and pointedly in von Rad's *Theologie des Alten Testaments*; cf. below, pp. 97–98.
52. This consideration is a central problem to which also Zimmerli (*Probleme biblischer Theologie*, ed. H. W. Wolff, 646) draws attention: the need to explain "how the one name of Jahweh, the God of Israel, could have been proclaimed over the diverse elements of tradition." Cf. also Barr, *Old and New in Interpretation*, 89.

the theological message and conviction of the Jahwist, that which is in von Rad's view of the greatest kerygmatic and confessional importance. *Von Rad is inclined to use traditio-historical research for his theological purposes*, a tendency that reaches its culmination in his *Theologie des Alten Testaments*. We will see later that *this juxtaposition of theology and tradition history constitutes a significant difference between von Rad and Martin Noth*.

d. Assessment of Israel's Sagas

Drawing on the results of the traditio-historical and form-critical research of Genesis, von Rad points out that there are two main tasks that the interpreter of these texts has to fulfill: (1) to come to terms with the phenomenon of "saga" (its meaning, function, form, limitations) and for each tradition to try to determine whether or not an independent, isolated saga with its own original prehistory lies behind the present text; and (2) to interpret the text in its present form—as a descendent of the original saga and as a member now of a larger context.[53] We have seen above how von Rad approaches the second task primarily in terms of the Jahwistic composition, and we have also asserted that in his exegesis of Genesis von Rad—in contrast to Gunkel—ascribes only a secondary hermeneutical importance to the saga and its level of meaning, and thus on the whole does not adequately fulfill the first task that he sets for himself. What, then, is von Rad's precise understanding of "saga," and how does he evaluate its traditio-historical significance?

Like Gunkel, von Rad maintains that our book of Genesis arose from numerous, originally separate sagas of different types and origins—cult etiologies, ethnological etiologies, narratives of anecdotal, poetical character. According to him there are two aspects of the saga—the historical aspect and the theological (or confessional) aspect—both of which are important for the exegete as well as the tradition historian. The question of the "historicity" of the sagas becomes complicated because they deal with past history but cannot be classified as historical records or sources in the modern sense. Instead they are the means chosen by a people to describe, remember, and actualize its past: "In its sagas a people is concerned with itself and the realities in which it finds itself. It is, however, a view and interpretation not only of that which once was but of a past event that is secretly present and decisive for the present."[54] This is the essence of "saga"—and its function in the life of

---

53. Von Rad, *Genesis*, 5th ed. 1958, 22, 137–38; 9th ed. 1972, 16, 125–26.

54. Ibid., 5th ed. 1958, 24; 9th ed. 1972, 17 [ET: rev. ed., 33]. The first of these two statements corresponds completely to Gunkel's view of sagas (*Genesis*, vii ff.); the second observation, however, is original to von Rad.

the people. Von Rad supposes that at its very beginning a saga usually had "a 'historical' fact as its actual crystallizing point,"[55] but after this beginning the historical experiences of the community throughout the centuries became the predominant, formative factor in the life and development of each saga. This development of the tradition, we may note, is what Martin Buber calls "a continuous process of crystallisation."[56]

While Buber's understanding of saga and its relation to history is virtually identical with that of von Rad, a comparison of their estimations of the task confronting the researcher elucidates the weakness that we have identified above in von Rad's commentary. Buber asserts that scholars must take a *reductive approach* to literature that arose from original sagas: they "must attempt to penetrate to that original nucleus of saga which was almost contemporary with the initial event" and "must remove layer after layer from the images as set before [them], in order to arrive at the earliest of all."[57] This task is not to be understood in the positivistic sense of determining the *bruta facta* of history, but rather is to be carried out in order to recover the experiences of the people, the "saga-creating ardour" which left its traces in the sagas.[58] Von Rad concurs with Buber's view of saga and history, but his Genesis commentary does not fulfill the traditio-critical task that Buber describes. By virtually leaving to Gunkel the traditio-critical analysis of the sagas and by concentrating on the later, compositional stage of the Genesis-traditions, *von Rad's commentary gives the distinct impression that the saga form of the material is of secondary importance, not only exegetically but also traditio-historically.*

The theological or confessional aspect of Israelite sagas is especially crucial for von Rad. He emphasizes that these sagas, in contrast to the sagas of many other peoples, were not formed for the purpose of portraying idealized, exemplary hero-figures. Rather, in ancient Israel the primary force in the formation of sagas was the *faith* of the people, resulting in a developmental, reformative process which can roughly be summarized: "The later the version of a saga, the more theologically reflective and less naive it is."[59] Von Rad asserts that the ancestral traditions in their present form deal more with God

---

55. Ibid., 5th ed. 1958, 25; 9th ed. 1972, 18 [ET: rev. ed., 34]; cf. also *TLZ* 88 (1963), col. 411–12.

56. Buber, *Moses*, Zürich 1948, 18ff. (= *Werke* II, Munich 1964, 18ff.) [ET: *Moses*, Oxford and London 1946, 15ff.]. Cf. also Kraus, "Gespräch mit Martin Buber," *EvT* 12 (1952/53), 64ff.; and Kraus, *Geschichte*, 448–49.

57. Buber, *Moses*, 19 (= *Werke* II, 19) [ET: 15–16].

58. This same aim is also emphasized by Gunkel, *Genesis*, lxviii.

59. Von Rad, *Genesis*, 9th ed. 1972, 20; 5th ed. 1958, 27 [ET: rev. ed., 36]. One can justly protest von Rad's use of the term "naive" here, a conception similar to Engnell's view of Wellhausen's religious evolutionism; cf. below, p. 203–5.

than with humans and that the individuals involved are not presented for their own sakes but rather only as objects of divine intentions and actions.⁶⁰ Von Rad is admittedly speaking of the final form that the sagas achieved in the book of Genesis; he only hints—inadequately—that the earlier history of the sagas is more complex.⁶¹ But his emphasis is fully in accord with his overall purpose: *to capture the kerygmatic essence or thrust of the sagas, i.e. of the Genesis traditions in their Jahwistic and final forms*. In his own words: "whoever thinks of sagas as a mixture of history and freely roving, popular fantasy will scarcely find a way from there to these materials which will venture to reflect perpetually newer pictures of God's saving ways."⁶² For von Rad it appears to be only of minor, historical background importance that, for example, the tradition in Gen 18 may have been originally intended to legitimate the cultic center at Mamre, or that the cultic saga in Gen 22 was at the outset meant to explain the release from the necessity to sacrifice children, or that the story in Gen 28 arose in order to describe the origin of the northern sanctuary at Bethel, or that the ethnological saga of Gen 16 was originally designed to answer the question about the origin and nature of the Ishmaelites. Especially surprising is von Rad's virtual disregard of the traditio-historical depth of the flood-story, an aspect which cannot be unimportant for the exegesis of Gen 6ff. In each of these few examples, von Rad indeed mentions the traditio-historical background, but his unequivocally primary concern is for the determination of the kerygmatic impact of the final (or Jahwistic) form of each tradition. In a word: *von Rad uses traditio-historical research in order to arrive at that which for him is theologically important*. This approach, with its roots in his monograph from 1938, is especially obvious throughout his Genesis commentary and reaches its zenith in his *magnum opus*, to which we should now direct our attention.

3. Theology of the Old Testament

We have seen above that von Rad's traditio-historical research is based on the conviction that Israel's faith was the determinative factor in the shaping

---

60. Von Rad, *Genesis*, 9th ed. 1972, 20–21; 5th ed. 1958, 26. Cf. also Buber, *Moses*, 21–22 (= *Werke* II, 20–21).

61. How much more complex and variegated—also theologically—this history is can be seen in Gunkel, *Genesis*, §4, lvi–lxxx. On Noth's opinion, cf. below, pp. 115–16.

62. Von Rad, *Genesis*, 5th ed. 1958, 27 [ET: 1st ed., 36]; cf. also 9th ed. 1972, 21 [ET: rev. ed., 37]. Von Rad could probably subscribe to Buber's idea of a "continuous process of crystallisation" only for the earlier stages of the sagas; the main compositional stage, on the other hand, was carried out by an individual compiler/editor, the Jahwist; *Genesis*, 5th ed. 1958, 137; 9th ed. 1972, 125; cf. also above, p. 83.

of the traditions. For the Hexateuch this faith was incorporated in specific credenda, which in turn provided the compositional framework when the traditions became gathered into a written literature. The essential role of the Jahwist in this process (for the Hexateuch) is emphasized by von Rad. We have also seen that his monograph from the year 1938 (*Das formgeschichtliche Problem des Hexateuch*) is perhaps his most important work because it lays the programmatic foundation for these theses and for his form-critical and traditio-historical research method. His commentary on Genesis explicates and illustrates these ideas more closely on the basis of specific texts. But it is also essential to see von Rad's *Theologie des Alten Testaments*[63] in the same light, for here he executes a consistent continuation of these theses and an extended application of his traditio-historical method on the theological proclamations of the entire Old Testament. For this reason we need now to look somewhat more closely at von Rad's use of the history of tradition in his *Theologie*. This analysis will then provide us with the opportunity to deal with a few specific problems associated with von Rad's understanding of history and Heilsgeschichte.

a. The Subject Matter: Israel's Testimonies to Jahweh's Involvement in History

First a word about the subject matter of his theological investigations, for we can discern already at this point how von Rad builds on the theses from his 1938-monograph. We read: "The subject-matter which concerns the theologian is, of course, not the spiritual and religious worlds of Israel and the conditions of her soul in general, nor is it her world of faith, all of which can only be reconstructed by means of conclusions drawn from the documents: instead, it is *simply Israel's own explicit assertions about Jahweh*. The theologian must above all deal directly with the evidence, that is, with what Israel herself testified concerning Jahweh, and there is no doubt that in many cases he must go back to school again and learn to interrogate each document much more closely than has been done hitherto, as to its specific kerygmatic intention."[64] From this statement it is clear that von Rad is not interested in

---

63. *Band I: Die Theologie der geschichtlichen Überlieferungen Israels*, 5th ed., Munich 1966 (1st ed. 1957); and *Band II: Die Theologie der prophetischen Überlieferungen Israels*, 5th ed., Munich 1968 (1st ed. 1960). Page references in parentheses are from the English translations: *Old Testament Theology, Volume I: The Theology of Israel's Historical Traditions*, New York and Edinburgh 1962; *Volume II: The Theology of Israel's Prophetic Traditions*, New York and Edinburgh 1965; both volumes are translated by D. M. G. Stalker.

64. Von Rad, *Theologie* I, 117–18 (ET: I, 105–6), emphasis added.

writing a history of the Israelite religion,[65] nor a history of Israelite piety.[66] He similarly avoids structuring his *Theologie* thematically according to general concepts, such as is done by Walther Eichrodt, Theodorus Vriezen, Ludwig Köhler, and Edmond Jacob.[67] Von Rad finds it most appropriate to write a theology of the Old Testament that concentrates on the "world made up of testimonies," in which Israel offers a picture not of its faith but of its history with Jahweh.[68] The testimonies and confessions of Israel are thus his subject matter, and in examining the texts he always intends to look for the *"specific kerygmatic intention"* of the traditions.

b. Theological Reception of the Traditio-Historical and Form-Critical Methods

The *conditio sine qua non* for properly understanding the nature of von Rad's *Theologie* is the *recognition of its form-critical and traditio-historical presuppositions and foundations*. What we find in his work is a theological reception of the form-critical and traditio-historical method that von Rad inherited from Gunkel and in turn refined into his own investigative program. As we have seen above, the chosen goal of his *Theologie* is to examine Israel's testimonies to its history with Jahweh, a project that in effect can only be carried out by traditio-historically probing the depths of the various Old Testament kerygmatic proclamations. Von Rad's refusal to structure his *Theologie* around the usual theological concepts leaves him free to investigate the theology of Israel's historical traditions and the theology of Israel's prophetic traditions, as the subtitles of the two volumes indicate. In the process, he is first dependent upon the previously reached results of form-critical and traditio-historical research and is then interested in furthering this research and drawing the theological consequences from the results.

His approach can be seen throughout all sections of his *Theologie*. His use of form-critical categories and results—the determination of all types of cultic texts, rituals, liturgies, sacral legal forms, forms of prophetic speech, and above all old confessional formulas—constitutes the basis of his analysis

---

65. Cf. von Rad, "Offene Fragen im Umkreis einer Theologie des Alten Testaments," *TLZ* 88 (1963), cols. 401ff.; also *Theologie* II, 391 (ET: II, 368); and Hans Conzelmann's response, "Fragen an Gerhard von Rad," *EvT* 24 (1964), 115 n. 8.

66. Cf. however Hesse's opinion, "Kerygma oder geschichtliche Wirklichkeit?" *ZTK* 57 (1960), 17–20.

67. Cf. von Rad, *Theologie* II, 6–7, and I, 124–25 (ET: II, vi–vii, and I, 111–12).

68. Ibid., I, 124 (ET: I, 111). On this decisive *novum* of von Rad's *Theologie* in comparison with the "theologies" produced by others, cf. Chr. Barth, "Grundprobleme einer Theologie des Alten Testaments," *EvT* 23 (1963), 342–72; also the discussion by G. E. Wright, *The Old Testament and Theology*, New York 1969, 50–69.

of Old Testament texts. But his *Theologie* takes its primary point of departure from the research into the history of Old Testament tradition. Here it has been shown that, for example, in the three large historical works—the Hexateuch, the Deuteronomistic History, and the Chronicler's History—the diverse forms of the presentation of the history of Jahweh with Israel must be understood from the dynamic perspective of Israel's interest in grappling with its history and with Jahweh's involvement with his chosen people. This insight reveals the two crystallization points or axes of the historical traditions: (1) The confession that Israel has become Jahweh's chosen people and has received the promised land constitutes the compositional foundation for the Hexateuch, the traditions spanning the time from Abraham to Joshua; and (2) the belief in David's election and the establishment of his throne form the driving force behind the Deuteronomistic and the Chronicler's historical works.[69] These interpretations of the divine acts, these two complexes centering in the covenant at Sinai and the Davidic covenant, in turn form the basis for the rest of the Old Testament traditions: Israel's collective and individual response to Jahweh's involvement,[70] and the prophetic proclamations of Israel's doom and new creation.[71]

Here we can observe the overriding concept with which von Rad wishes to comprehend the entirety of the Old Testament: Israel's repeated efforts to understand Jahweh's contact with her. As *a traditio-historical ascertainment with theological import*, it becomes the guiding principle in von Rad's approach to the individual parts of the Old Testament. The basic relevance of tradition history for a theology of the Old Testament can be summarized in one assertion made by von Rad: "In general, even the simplest fusion of two originally independent units of tradition was in itself already a process of theological interpretation. And, in the course of time, what masses of tradition were welded together to form these blocks!"[72] In other words, traditio-historical analysis serves to uncover the data that the theologian has

---

69. Cf. e.g., von Rad, *Theologie* I, 200ff., 318ff., 366 (ET: I, 187ff., 306ff., 355). The important traditio-historical relationship between these two, originally separate streams of tradition—that of the exodus-Sinai traditions and that of the Davidic-Jerusalemic traditions—was first emphasized by L. Rost, "Sinaibund und Davidsbund," *TLZ* 72 (1947), cols. 129–134. cf. also E. Rohland, *Die Bedeutung der Erwählungstraditionen Israels für die Eschatologie der alttestamentlichen Propheten*, Diss.-Heidelberg 1956; and Zimmerli, in: *Probleme biblischer Theologie*, ed. H. W. Wolff, 634–37.

70. Under this rubric and in these terms von Rad understands and presents the theology implicit in the poetic, psalmic, and wisdom literature of the Old Testament; cf. *Theologie* I, 366ff. (ET: I, 355ff.); and *Weisheit in Israel*, Neukirchen-Vluyn 1970.

71. Von Rad, *Theologie* I, 142; II, 13ff. (ET: I, 128; II, 3ff.).

72. Ibid., I, 19 (ET: I, 5).

to evaluate and consider in the attempt to understand Israel's testimonies to Jahweh. The presupposition is that the traditions were impregnated with impressionable theological meaning. Von Rad's prime contribution consists in his recognizing that the characteristic phenomenon of the Israelite tradition process is *the constant striving to actualize and to come to terms with the traditions of old* and that this in itself results in theological innovations. Therefore the subject matter of von Rad's *Theologie* is at the same time that which must be researched through traditio-historical means: "those ever new attempts to make the divine acts of salvation relevant for every new age and day—this ever new reaching-out to and avowal of God's acts which in the end made the old credal statements grow into such enormous masses of traditions."[73]

However, it has been quite correctly noted[74] that von Rad neglects to clarify systematically the decisive methodological problems concerning the theological evaluation of the *traditio* and the *traditum*. That he operates from the firm conviction that the Old Testament is the "Endstadium" of a long, gradual development can hardly be overlooked. At all points he emphasizes and treats seriously the complex preliterary, semiliterary, and literary stages of development. The intricacies of this growth process of the Old Testament are given their due in his analyses of the accumulation and agglomeration of traditions ("Traditionsballung") around, e.g., the exodus and Sinai events, the Davidic covenant, and the prophetic words.[75] *The horizon, importance, and possibilities of traditio-historical research are clearly widened by employing its results and discoveries for the determination of the theology of the Old Testament.* There are, however, a few problems touching on von Rad's use of tradition history, which we will want to examine more closely.

c. *Tradition and History*

At the risk of oversimplifying a very complex problem, we should say a few words about the relationship between tradition and history,[76] for von Rad's

---

73. Ibid., I, 8 (ET: I, vi).
74. Kraus, *Die Biblische Theologie*, Neukirchen-Vluyn 1970, 357–58.
75. Note, e.g., how his analysis of the Davidic traditions begins by locating the oldest elements and then proceeds backwards and forwards according to the process of the growth of the tradition; von Rad, *Theologie* I, 320 (ET: I, 308). Also his view of the "Traditionsbildung" of the prophetic literature (II, 47–57; ET: II, 39–49) is strikingly similar to the Scandinavian conception of the same; cf. below, pp. 183–85, 194–95.
76. That we are limited here to only a few brief remarks should be obvious in light of the complexity of the problem and the large bibliography already available on this subject. For a good discussion of certain aspects of this problem, cf. G. Wallis, *Geschichte und Überlieferung*, Stuttgart 1968, especially 122–26 for a concise sketch of the debate.

treatment of this problem has had far-reaching influence, notably on the so-called "Pannenberg Circle" with its historical-theological program of "revelation as history."[77]

Von Rad's concept of history in his *Theologie* takes its point of departure in the distinction between the Greek and the Hebrew conceptions of history: "From first to last Israel manifestly takes as her starting-point the absolute priority in theology of event over *logos*. The total difference between this way of thinking and the 'Greek urge towards a universal understanding of the world' is obvious.... Hebrew thinking is thinking in historical traditions; that is, its main concern is with the proper combination of traditions and their theological interpretation, and in the process historical grouping always takes precedence over intellectual and theological grouping."[78] Von Rad's point is two-fold: Israel, in contrast to the Greek and also to the other Eastern conceptions of history, regarded its past as a series of actual events rather than

---

77. Cf. especially the collection of articles edited by W. Pannenberg, *Offenbarung als Geschichte*, KD Beiheft 1, Göttingen 1961, 3rd ed. 1965. Cf. also Pannenberg, "Heilsgeschehen und Geschichte" *KD* 5 (1959), 218-37 and 259-88; Pannenberg, "Kerygma und Geschichte," *Studien zur Theologie der alttestamentlichen Überlieferungen*, ed. R. Rendtorff and K. Koch, Neukirchen 1961, 129-40; R. Rendtorff, "Geschichte und Überlieferung," ibid., 81-94; and Rendtorff, "Hermeneutik des Alten Testaments als Frage nach der Geschichte," *ZTK* 57 (1960), 27-40. A critical response to these and other similar publications can be seen in: F. Mildenberger, *Gottes Tat im Wort*, Gütersloh 1964. —The problems of *revelation and history* and of *revelation and tradition* are of central concern. Both are implicit in von Rad's ideas about "history and tradition." Basic dogmatic considerations can be found in G. Gloege, *Offenbarung und Überlieferung*, TF 6, Hamburg 1954. Barr's incisive discussion of the concepts of history and revelation (*Old and New in Interpretation*, 65-102) must also not be overlooked. He argues that revelation models, including a Christocentric doctrine of revelation, are unsatisfactory for treating the Old Testament and its relation to the New Testament. He opts instead to affirm the antinomies inherent in "history" (ibid., 68). According to him, if we operate with a variable concept of history (ibid., 101-2), we can do more justice to the multiplex, cumulative nature of tradition. Wright (*The Old Testament and Theology*, 46-50) offers a rather bland response to Barr's position. Wright's critique (ibid., 50-69) of von Rad's understanding of theology is more perceptive.

78. Von Rad, *Theologie* I, 129 (ET: I, 116). On this relationship between word and deed and on its connection with von Rad's understanding of revelation, cf. M. Honecker, "Zum Verständnis der Geschichte in Gerhard von Rads Theologie des Alten Testaments," *EvT* 23 (1963), 152ff.; and Kraus, *Die Biblische Theologie*, 135-36. As is well known, fundamental criticism of this usual distinction between Hebrew and Greek thinking has been made by Barr, *Old and New in Interpretation*, 34-63; and especially in his *The Semantics of Biblical Language*, London 1961. Barr has done historical science a real service at this and other points, and it is high time that other scholars (e.g., Wright, *The Old Testament and Theology*, 45) cease dismissing his arguments with the trite and irrelevant criticism that Barr makes only a destructive protest and offers no constructive solution.

as a philosophically or mythologically contrived background.[79] However, this concept of a "linear historical span" is something that Israel gained only during a long process of interpreting the events through tradition formation, fusion, and arrangement.[80]

Therefore, according to von Rad, we are confronted in the Old Testament (especially in the Hexateuch) with *not history but tradition*, i.e., *the Israelite picture of history:* "What we see here is not what we are accustomed to understand as history: the idea of history which Israel worked out was constructed exclusively on the basis of a sequence of acts which God laid down for her salvation."[81] We have seen previously that von Rad maintains that this picture of history became expressed in the creedal statements[82] and also in the various collections of traditions and that it therefore should function as the basic hermeneutical principle in the interpretation of the Old Testament. But there is a further important consequence of this: viz., that *a sharp discrepancy between this Israelite picture of history and the historical-critical reconstruction of the actual happenings* thereby comes to light.[83] Von Rad emphasizes pointedly this discrepancy and its effect on the drawing up of a theology of the historical traditions: "Both at this point and in the sequel, we are of course thinking, when we speak of divine acts in history, of those which the faith of Israel regarded as such—that is, the call of the forefathers, the deliverance from Egypt, the bestowal of the land of Canaan, etc.—and not of the results of modern critical historical scholarship, to which Israel's faith was unrelated."[84] Von Rad holds this difference between the historical reality and the keryg-

---

79. Cf. however the important arguments against this commonly accepted distinction between Israelite historiography and that of the ancient Near East: H. Gese, "Geschichtliches Denken im Alten Orient und im Alten Testament," *ZTK* 55 (1958), 127–45; and Barr, *Old and New in Interpretation*, 71–72.

80. Von Rad, *Theologie* II, 114ff. (ET: II, 105ff.).

81. Ibid., II, 116 (ET: II, 106); cf. also von Rad, *VF* 1953/55 (1956), 131–32; and Rendtorff, "Geschichte und Überlieferung," 81ff. This absolute dependence of Israel's view of history on her concept of God is also emphasized by Pannenberg, *KD* 5 (1959), 220 (= *Probleme alttestamentlicher Hermeneutik*, ed. C. Westermann, 298): "The presuppositions of historical consciousness in Israel lie in her idea of God." Cf. also Barr, *Old and New in Interpretation*, 89.

82. Von Rad, *Theologie* I, 118 (ET: I, 106): "in principle Israel's faith is grounded in a theology of history."

83. Soggin ("Geschichte, Historie und Heilsgeschichte im Alten Testament," *TLZ* 89, 1964, cols. 730ff.) reminds us, though, that there is not sufficient agreement among scholars as to allow us to speak of *the* scientific view of Israelite history, Cf. also W. Herberg, "Five Meanings of the Word 'Historical,'" *The Christian Scholar* 47 (1964), 327–30.

84. Von Rad, *Theologie* I, 118–19 (ET: I, 106).

matic interpretation to be a serious problem,[85] but he allows each its rightful existence and does not try methodologically to overcome the inherent discrepancies between them.[86] A theology of the Old Testament has to do with Israel's kerygmatic picture of her past, and it is the traditio-historical method that helps us to reconstruct the development of this picture.

Von Rad's position with regard to this relationship "history—tradition" (or "history—kerygma") has produced a lively discussion on at least two different points: There are those of his students and followers who have tried in their theology of history to overcome the above-mentioned discrepancy by means of expanding the historical-critical method so that it may be able to verify or at least deal with God's revelation in history.[87] A second consequence of von Rad's presentation has been a critical reaction to his distinction between the historical course of events and the kerygmatic picture of this history in the traditions. Hesse especially accuses von Rad at this point of engaging in "double-tracking" ("Zweigleisigkeit")—on the one hand the history of Israel consigned to the investigative sphere of profane historians, and on the other hand the Israelite kerygmatic presentations prescribed as the sole concern of the theologians.[88] Hesse maintains that the *real course* of Israel's history, in and through which God worked, is more important than Israel's conception of the same; therefore a separation of the historical picture from the kerygmatic picture is untenable.[89] This objection seems to be

---

85. Unfortunately, however, von Rad fails to treat in depth the many crucial consequences and implications of this problem. The extensive debate precipitated by von Rad's distinction is a good indication of the complexity and importance of these issues.

86. Von Rad, *Theologie* I, 119-20 (ET: I, 107-8): "Historical investigation searches for a critically assured minimum—the kerygmatic picture tends towards a theological maximum." "It would be stupid to dispute the right of the one or the other to exist. It would be superfluous to emphasize that each is the product of very different intellectual activities." Cf. also von Rad, *TLZ* 88 (1963), cols. 408-416 (ET in *Theology* II, 417-29).

87. This is advanced by, e.g., Pannenberg, *KD* 5 (1959), 259ff.; and Rendtorff, "Geschichte und Überlieferung," 94. For a critique of this approach, cf. Honecker, *EvT* 23 (1963), 163-66; and Barr, *Old and New in Interpretation*, 68ff. Careful analyses of this historical-theological viewpoint are made especially by H.-G. Geyer, "Geschichte als theologisches Problem," *EvT* 22 (1962), 92-104; and L. Steiger, "Offenbarungsgeschichte und theologische Vernunft: Zur Theologie W. Pannenbergs," *ZTK* 59 (1962), 88-113.

88. F. Hesse, "Die Erforschung der Geschichte Israels als theologische Aufgabe," *KD* 4 (1958), 5ff.

89. Ibid., 13; Hesse, "Kerygma oder geschichtliche Wirklichkeit?" *ZTK* (1960), 24-26; cf. also Honecker, *EvT* 23 (1963), 158-60. Essentially the same points are made also by J. Hempel, "Alttestamentliche Theologie in protestantischer Sicht heute," *BO* 15 (1958), 212ff.; V. Maag, "Historische oder ausserhistorische Begründung alttestamentlicher Theologie," *SThU* 29 (1959), 6-18; W. Eichrodt, *Theologie des Alten Testaments*, Teile II und III, 4th ed., Stuttgart/Göttingen 1961, vii ff.; W. Zimmerli, *VT* 13 (1963), 102-5; Chr. Barth, *EvT* 23 (1963), 360, 367ff.; and

understandable: The acts of salvation occurred within the historical sphere, and these acts themselves must be more important than the people's testimonies to them since these confessions in the final analysis reveal more about the people themselves than about God. But von Rad's response is appropriate: It is virtually impossible to extricate the *bruta facta* from the interpretations of them, and in the end contemporary historical science has no possibility of saying anything about the relation of God to history: "Even the best confirmed event of 'real history' remains silent with respect to divine control of history; its relevance for faith can in no way be verified."[90] Furthermore, "it must be emphasized that Israel, with her assertions, comes out of a depth of historical experience that is inaccessible to the historical-critical method of observation."[91] *History and tradition are not contrary subjects; they are related not antithetically but supplementarily.*[92] If God is revealed in history,[93] it is the *tradition*, or the kerygma, that witnesses to this revelation and that therefore is also the proper subject matter for a theology of the Old Testament.[94]

d. Tradition History and Heilsgeschichte

Kraus has raised an important question with respect to von Rad's investigative method and theological program as seen in his *Theologie*: "How do Überlieferungsgeschichte and Heilsgeschichte relate to each other? Is the Heilsgeschichte de facto—Überlieferungsgeschichte?"[95] The problem is complex—but crucial for our understanding of von Rad's use of the traditio-historical perspective. To answer Kraus's question, we must approach the Old

---

somewhat similarly also F. Baumgärtel, "Gerhard von Rad's 'Theologie des Alten Testaments,'" *TLZ* 86 (1961), cols. 804ff., 897ff. On the proximity of Hesse's position to that of Rendtorff and Pannenberg, cf. Honecker, *EvT* 23 (1963), 159–60; and Wallis, *Geschichte und Überlieferung*, 125–26. Hesse subsequently clarified and modified his position in the debate: "Bewährt sich eine 'Theologie der Heilstatsachen' am Alten Testament? Zum Verhältnis von Faktum und Deutung," *ZAW* 81 (1969), 1–18.

90. Von Rad, *Theologie* II (1st ed. 1960), 9 (not in ET). Cf. also von Rad, "Antwort auf Conzelmanns Fragen," *EvT* 24 (1964), 392–93. Also Mildenberger, *Gottes Tat im Wort*, 17ff.; and B. S. Childs, *Memory and Tradition in Israel*, SBT 37, London 1962, 81–89.

91. Von Rad, *Theologie* I, 120 (not in ET).

92. Ibid., II (1st ed. 1960), 9, 11; also I (5th ed. 1966), 11–12 (not in ET). This is a point made also by Wallis, *Geschichte und Überlieferung*, 127–28; and somewhat similarly by J. A. Soggin, "Alttestamentliche Glaubenszeugnisse und geschichtliche Wirklichkeit," *TZ* 17 (1961), col. 397. Note also Rendtorff's reminder ("Geschichte und Überlieferung," 83ff.) that the tradition itself is also a component part of history.

93. von Rad, *Theologie* II (4th ed. 1965), 359 (ET: II, 338).

94. Ibid., II (1st ed. 1960), 9–10 (not in ET).

95. Kraus, *Die Biblische Theologie*, 138, also 356–57; and Kraus, *Geschichte*, 509.

Testament historical traditions separately from the prophetic traditions, for von Rad's treatment of the former varies significantly from that of the latter.[96]

With respect to the *historical traditions*, von Rad[97] distinguishes between two heilsgeschichtliche periods: (1) that of the "kanonische Heilsgeschichte"—the period from the patriarchs to the conquest of the land (the creation and the Sinai revelation were added later to this), as summarized in the early creedal statements; and (2) that of the "zweite Gottesgeschichte"—the period from the settlement of the land to the exile (including thus the establishment of the Davidic dynasty), as recounted by the Deuteronomist and the Chronicler.[98] For both of these periods a distinct "attitude of mind"[99] was in play, whereby the events of the past were contemplated and interpreted and formed into a linear course of history (for the Hexateuch) or a picture of God's continued activity despite Israel's failures (for the Dtr and Chr)—these events thus being incorporated into a Heilsgeschichte. For von Rad these were *processes of human awareness and interpretation* of divine activity—processes that can be analyzed traditio-historically and that are not identical with the heilsgeschichtliche events themselves.

However, for the *prophetic period* the situation is different, and at this point our answer to the question of whether or not von Rad confuses tradition history with Heilsgeschichte will have to be affirmative. More than most other scholars, von Rad has emphasized the dependence of the prophets on the traditions of the past.[100] But just as decisive for him is the fact that the prophets' message centers in the dissolution of the old and the introduction

---

96. Kraus (*Die Biblische Theologie*, 356ff.) has also called attention to this distinction.

97. The section that is especially revealing is in his *Theologie* I, 135-42 (ET: I, 121-28).

98. In response to von Rad's opinion that David's anointment was not added to the "proper, canonical" Heilsgeschichte, Barr (*Old and New in Interpretation*, 68) suggests that this is actually a definitional and not a real problem. — On the whole, Barr emphasizes that which is often implicit in von Rad's exposition: "There is no 'history' of the acts of God alone, but a history in which the tradition grows and suffers change, in which the tradition itself is affected by the impact of events; and these events may be in some cases acts of God, in others not" (ibid., 19). Barr thus opts for the history of tradition rather than for some concept of Heilsgeschichte. He argues further (ibid., 15ff.) that "the acts of God in history" cannot be made to function as the center of tradition—neither descriptively nor historically. He maintains it would be more appropriate to speak instead of various *situations* that initiate, alter, or affect traditions—e.g., situations of God's word or action, social situations, situations of crisis, cultic situations, and the like (ibid., 26-27).

99. Von Rad, *Theologie* II, 118 (ET: II, 108).

100. Note, e.g., von Rad's characterization of the eighth-century prophets: "indeed, their whole preaching might almost be described as a unique dialogue with the tradition by means of which the latter was made to speak to their own day" (II, 187; ET: II, 177). On this, cf. also the studies of Wolff, "Hoseas geistige Heimat" (1956), *Ges. Stud.*, 232-50; and *Amos' geistige*

of the new age; this is especially noticeable in the preaching of Jeremiah, Ezekiel, Zechariah, and Deutero-Isaiah.[101] They regarded the past as being valid primarily for purposes of comparison—e.g., that Jahweh, analogous to his earlier acts of salvation, would accomplish yet more wondrous marvels for his people. This prophetic method of treating the past according to the needs of the present and the future can best be described as a "charismatic-eclectic process."[102] And this situation has an important theological consequence: "this conviction of [the prophets], that what has existed till now is broken off, places them basically outside the saving history as it had been understood up to then by Israel."[103] The point is that the prophets, by the very act of charismatically preaching judgment or salvation, were the means Jahweh was using to launch a new heilsgeschichtliche period. The message of the prophets was a constituent part of this Heilsgeschichte. That this message itself developed in complexity and diversity according to the actual situations of the day implies the historical basis which it had. The traditions went through stages of expansion, reinterpretation, and reflection—be it on the part of the prophet or the prophet's disciples. The historical development of the *traditum* and the transmittal process itself (charismatic-eclectic) constitute the "Überlieferungsgeschichte" and are the legitimate objects of traditio-historical analysis. The weakness of von Rad's presentation, however, is a methodological and definitional one, viz. that *he in effect equates this history of the prophetic traditions with the Heilsgeschichte, rather than to retain the concept of "history of tradi-*

Heimat, WMANT 18, Neukirchen-Vluyn 1964; also W. Brueggemann, *Tradition for Crisis: A Study in Hosea*, Richmond 1969.

101. Von Rad, *Theologie* I, 142 (ET: I, 128), regarding the preaching of the prophets: "However overpoweringly diverse it may be, it nevertheless has its starting-point in the conviction that Israel's previous history with Jahweh has come to an end, and that he will start something new with her. The prophets seek to convince their contemporaries that for them the hitherto existing saving ordinances have lost their worth, and that, if Israel is to be saved, she must move in faith into a new saving activity of Jahweh, one which is only to come in the future."

102. Ibid., II, 345 (ET: II, 324–25). Note, however, Zimmerli's objection at this point (*VT* 13, 1963, 110–11) to the effect that von Rad, by emphasizing this charismatic new interpretation by the prophets, does not come to terms with the prophets' own proclamations (e.g., Micah 6:8) that they stand under the authority of the old covenant and are not attempting to supersede it with something new. — Yet another position considerably more critical of von Rad's view is that of Fohrer and Vollmer, who emphasize the distinction between tradition and interpretation and argue that the immediate Word of Jahweh is of the greatest importance for the prophets, the tradition having little more than homiletical value. Cf. Fohrer, "Tradition und Interpretation im Alten Testament," *ZAW* 73 (1961), 1–30; J. Vollmer, *Geschichtliche Rückblicke und Motive in der Prophetie des Amos, Hosea und Jesaja*, BZAW 119, Berlin 1971; also M.-L. Henry, *Prophet und Tradition*, BZAW 116, Berlin 1969.

103. Von Rad, *Theologie* I, 142 (ET: I, 128).

tion" in its historical-critical sense—as he does for the historical traditions of the Old Testament.

e. A Traditio-Historical Relationship between Old Testament and New Testament?

The confusion just mentioned—which is not simply a terminological one—becomes especially clear when we regard von Rad's presentation of the relationship between Old Testament and New Testament. We have seen above how von Rad's traditio-historical method concentrates on the *forward* movement of the traditions from their beginnings on to their "Endstadium." This focusing on the evolving traditions seems to be at the base of his then asking whether the Old Testament leads to the New Testament. He postulates: "The Old Testament can only be read as a book of ever increasing anticipation."[104] What is true for the Old Testament is applicable for the New Testament as well: "The history of Jahwism is thus characterized by repeated breaks. God appoints new institutions and fresh starts which inaugurate new eras of tradition."[105] This principle includes thus the prophets' "charismatic-eclectic" reception of the traditions, just as it does also the "early Church's reinterpretation of Old Testament material to make the latter apply to itself"—both procedures being indeed traditionally legitimate and well founded.[106] Indeed this process constitutes the essence of Israelite *traditio*—the desire to actualize for each new epoch the traditions of old concerning the liberating and guiding acts of God.[107]

What, then, is the problem here? We can see the difficulty most clearly at that point at which von Rad explicitly identifies the connection as a *traditio-historical relationship* between the Old Testament and New Testament.[108]

---

104. Ibid., II, 339 (ET: II, 319). On this subject, cf. also Conzelmann, *EvT* 24 (1964), 117ff.
105. Von Rad, *Theologie* II, 340 (ET: II, 319).
106. Ibid., II, 409 (ET: II, 384). The keyword for this charismatic new interpretation by the New Testament of the Old Testament is, according to von Rad, "typology" or "structural analogy"; cf. II, 349ff., 387ff. (ET: II, 328ff., 363ff.). Cf. K. Schwarzwäller, "Das Verhältnis Altes Testament–Neues Testament im Lichte der gegenwärtigen Bestimmungen," *EvT* 29 (1969), 281–307, especially 289ff.; however, also see the basic, critical discussion by Barr, *Old and New in Interpretation*, 103–48.
107. Cf. above, pp. 5–6.
108. Note his own words (*Theologie* II, 341–42; ET: II, 321–22; emphasis added): "Because of the confusion of views on the relationship of the Old Testament to the New and the way in which theological definitions of this contradict one another, it may be worth while to anticipate and say that in the chapters which follow [*scil.*: on the relationship of the Old Testament to the New Testament] we are in fact going to discuss the question from one point of view only, the one which we have already taken as our guide in expounding the traditions within the Old Testament itself, that of the *traditio-historical*. Everything that follows is really intended simply

According to him, the Old Testament implies and leads to the New Testament, and the New Testament makes use of the traditional freedom to interpret the old traditions for its own age. The traditions thus continue to have a history stretching on to the New Testament, especially in consideration of the motifs "promise—fulfillment."[109] Von Rad is thus impressed by two factors: (1) the dynamic *traditio* principle in New Testament times is the same as that in the Old Testament period, namely, charismatic, interpretative reactualization; and (2) the contents of the New Testament and the Old Testament are related inasmuch as the New Testament is seen as the fulfillment of the Old Testament expectations and promises.

However, we must challenge von Rad's description of this as a traditio-historical connection. Von Rad's method of analyzing the growth of the Old Testament from the earliest beginnings on to the "Endstadium" is by all

---

to *carry this familiar procedure a stage further* by trying to understand that the way in which the Old Testament is absorbed in the New is the logical end of a process initiated by the Old Testament itself, and that its 'laws' are to some extent repeated in this final reinterpretation.... The method will be an attempt to show one characteristic way in which the Old Testament leads forward to the New." Cf. also II, 7 (ET: II, viii); also Mildenberger, *Gottes Tat im Wort*, 69ff.; and Pannenberg, "Historieteologi og overleveringshistorie," *NTT* 66 (1965), 137–51, especially 147ff.

109. Essentially this same position has been advocated by H. Gese, "Erwägungen zur Einheit der biblischen Theologie," *ZTK* (1970), 417-36. Note Gese's thesis (ibid., 420): "the Old Testament arises by means of the New Testament; the New Testament constitutes the end of a tradition process that is essentially a unity, a continuum." This radical assertion, accompanied by Gese's (ibid., 424ff.) understanding of "theology as formation of tradition," constitutes the logical conclusion of von Rad's position. Perhaps its corrective is to be found in von Rad's premise itself: In his preface to the *Theologie* (II, 7; ET: II, viii) he asserts that the Old Testament must not be viewed *genetically*, as a closed entity with beginnings, high-points, and conclusions. But is not this precisely what Gese (and von Rad) does with the entire Christian Bible? Drawing the lines between Old Testament and New Testament on the basis of some tradition principle cannot be done consistently and legitimately without also considering the Judaic, the Qumran, the later Christian, and perhaps even the Arabic reception and new interpretation of the Old Testament. In fact if this mode of transmission is the primary criterion, should not *any case* of "aktualisierende Neuinterpretation" of the Old Testament throughout history be included? That von Rad and Gese avoid this—especially for the Judaic transmission—should itself indicate that this problem of the relationship between the Old Testament and New Testament does not in strict, critical terms constitute a traditio-historical connection but something else, viz. a *historical, theological, and confessional relationship*. — For further discussions and key contributions to the problem "promise—fulfillment" (or "prophecy—fulfillment"), cf. F. Baumgärtel, *Verheißung: Zur Frage des evangelischen Verständnisses des Alten Testaments*, Gütersloh 1952; the articles by especially Bultmann, Zimmerli, and Westermann in: *Probleme alttestamentlicher Hermeneutik*, ed. C. Westermann, TB 11, 3rd ed. Munich 1960; also S. Mowinckel, "Kan forholdet mellem Det Gamle og Det Nye Testamente uttrykkes som profeti og oppfyllelse?" *NTT* 62 (1961), 223–37; and the criticisms by Barr, *Old and New in Interpretation*, 122ff.

means methodologically correct; indeed this clear understanding of the progressive growth of the traditions up to their fixation is one of von Rad's prime contributions. But *this traditio-historical method cannot be used to explain the essential relationship between the Old Testament and the New Testament*. Within the Old Testament itself (similarly within the New Testament itself) this growth process reached an end in the various tradition complexes, books, and larger works; and in virtually this form they were eventually canonized. What happened after the final form was reached can only be understood as "Nachinterpretation," "Nachgeschichte," or "Auslegungsgeschichte," that is, as a history of the later interpretation and transmission of the texts in question.[110] This distinction corresponds to Barr's delineation between "tradition before scripture" and "tradition after scripture"; the Judaic and the Christian use of Old Testament scripture belongs, of course, to the latter category.[111] By the time of Christ, Old Testament tradition had already been finalized and fixed as scripture for some time (except for late glosses). The "aktualisierende Neuinterpretation" of the Old Testament by the Christian church therefore cannot be understood as a further transmittal stage in the *formative* history of Old Testament tradition. Von Rad is not arguing this, but it seems that *he overestimates the theological implications of the* traditio,[112] which results in the confusion indicated. The "aktualisierende Neuinterpretation" by the church is a formal aspect of transmission with its historical antecedents in ancient

---

110. Cf. above, pp. 15-16. One could perhaps distinguish between two types of "Nachgeschichte" according to the effect on the transmitted traditions: (1) Old Testament traditions, already virtually fixed in literary form, were exposed to later, usually minor additions, glosses, and textual alterations at the hands of subsequent interpreters and transmitters; cf. e.g., H. W. Hertzberg, "Die Nachgeschichte alttestamentlicher Texte innerhalb des Alten Testaments," BZAW 66 (1936), 110-21 (= Hertzberg, *Beiträge zur Traditionsgeschichte und Theologie des Alten Testaments*, Göttingen 1962, 69-80); also M. Sæbø, *Sacharja 9-14*, BWANT 34, Neukirchen 1969, 101. (2) Old Testament texts, both before and after their final canonization, were continuously interpreted and translated by various interest groups or individuals without any internal effect on the contents or texts of the Hebrew Old Testament itself; cf., e.g., on this type of "Nachgeschichte" of Ezekiel: W. Zimmerli, *Ezechiel*, BKAT 13, Neukirchen-Vluyn 1969, 115*-19*. The New Testament reception and reinterpretation of Old Testament texts belong, of course, to this second category, that of "Auslegungsgeschichte"; there is no evidence of Christians' having brought about any internal changes in the Old Testament. It might be added that this second type of "Nachgeschichte" corresponds essentially to what Gadamer terms "Wirkungsgeschichte"; cf. H.-G. Gadamer, *Wahrheit und Methode*, Tübingen 1960, 284-90.

111. Barr, *Old and New in Interpretation*, 27-29, 162-164. Cf. also P. Grelot, "Tradition as Source and Environment of Scripture," *The Dynamism of Biblical Tradition*, Concilium, vol. 20, New York 1967, 7-28. It can be doubted that the dynamics of tradition in both stages are essentially identical, as Barr (29) asserts and as von Rad also would support. The very fact that a *scripture* was present required all other interpretation to be of an *exegetical* nature.

112. Cf. also Kraus, *Die Biblische Theologie*, 357-58.

Israel; the decisively different situation is that for the early Christians the Old Testament had attained the clear status of scripture, ἡ γραφή. With regard to von Rad's second aspect (internal connection of the type "prophecy—fulfillment"), it is *a theological and confessional statement* for the first Christians—as also for us—to describe the relationship between the Old Testament and the New Testament as one of promise and fulfillment. The New Testament use of the Old Testament—just like the use that Judaism made of the Old Testament—is a chapter of its own and is not traditio-historically connected with the Old Testament, except in the rather specialized sense of "Nachgeschichte." *The Old Testament cannot be traditio-historically projected into the future, into the New Testament. The concept "tradition history" must retain at all points the meaning that von Rad and Noth give it for the historical books of the Old Testament—the process of growth and fusion of tradition units, to be investigated by means of the historical-critical method.*

f. The Importance of von Rad's Use of Tradition History

This concludes our extensive description of von Rad's traditio-historical research. We have followed the path beginning with his initial theses in *Das formgeschichtliche Problem des Hexateuch* (1938) and ending with his use of this method in his *Theologie des Alten Testaments*. Certain topics of importance (e.g., the composition of the Hexateuch, tradition and history, tradition history and Heilsgeschichte) have required more detailed treatment, and on occasion we have pointed out specific weaknesses and inconsistencies in his work. But the latter do not detract from *von Rad's central role in defining and demonstrating the traditio-historical task.*

One item remains: to underline the importance of von Rad's revolutionary use of tradition history in drawing up a theology of the Old Testament. Throughout his *Theologie* he is driven by the desire to let the Old Testament speak for itself and to resist the imposing of ideas and concepts on the Old Testament. Advocating "the great closeness of exegesis and 'introduction' on the one hand and the theology of the Old Testament on the other,"[113] he is especially concerned to bring the abundant literary-critical, form-critical, and traditio-historical results to bear in his theological presentations. We have already made clear how von Rad fashions his theology around the traditio-historical structure of the Old Testament, hoping in this way to achieve the best picture of Israel's growing awareness of the Heilsgeschichte. In other words, von Rad does not take the final form of the Old Testament text as his

---

113. Von Rad, *Theologie* II, 8 (ET: II, vii); cf. also II (1st ed. 1960), 11; and I, 7 (ET: I, v). Interestingly enough, the "history of Israel" is not mentioned here in von Rad's statement.

point of departure. Rather, he treats the material according to the heilsgeschichtliche schema which Israel itself developed. The traditio-historical research results that he presupposes and adopts as the foundation for his *Theologie* thus have to carry the entire weight of his theological structure. The legitimacy,[114] success, and effectiveness[115] of this theological method are indeed open for debate. But for our purposes here we must not lose sight of the decisive, all-important *novum* of von Rad's *Theologie—the elevating of the traditio-historical method to virtually the most important aspect of the "Einleitungswissenschaft" and the establishing of the theological usefulness of this traditio-historical research.*

B. Martin Noth

The traditio-historical work on the Old Testament carried out by von Rad has an equally important counterpart in the publications of Martin Noth (1902–1968). These two scholars, working separately, have succeeded in doing the pioneering work that now in effect serves as the foundation and skeleton of the continued traditio-historical investigation of the Old Testament. And yet we would be mistaken in supposing that von Rad's and Noth's respective methods are nearly identical with each other. The quite diverging pictures of the history of, e.g., pentateuchal traditions are testimonies to varying emphases, viewpoints, and methods. We need now to look more closely at three important traditio-historical studies of Noth, after which we can attempt to compare and contrast the approaches of the two "fathers" of modern traditio-historical research.

1. History of the Pentateuchal Traditions

Departing from the chronological order, we will examine first Noth's *Überlieferungsgeschichte des Pentateuch*,[116] for in this way we will be able to continue

---

114. Note, e.g., Maag's (*SThU* 29, 1959, 11) harsh reference to von Rad's theological method as "the tendentious misuse of [form-critical] results in the context of drawing theological conclusions."

115. Especially noteworthy are the criticisms and the alternative offered by Kraus, *Die Biblische Theologie*, 363ff.; and also those by Barr, *Old and New in Interpretation*, especially 101-2, 149ff.

116. Stuttgart 1948, 3rd ed. 1966; hereafter abbreviated as *ÜPent*. — Another presentation of Noth's approach in *ÜPent* has just appeared: B. W. Anderson, "Martin Noth's Traditio-Historical Approach in the Context of Twentieth-Century Biblical Research," introduction to: Martin Noth, *A History of Pentateuchal Traditions*, translated by B. W. Anderson, Englewood Cliffs, N.J., 1972, xiii–xxxii. Anderson's article provides a good, basic introductory picture of Noth's

the discussion of the Pentateuch/Hexateuch to which we devoted so much attention in the above section on von Rad. It will also have the more important advantage of enabling us to understand more clearly the method employed by Noth in his *Überlieferungsgeschichtliche Studien*.[117]

From the outset one must not overlook the fact that to a certain extent Noth intended his two studies, *ÜSt* and *ÜPent*, to be a response to von Rad's *Das formgeschichtliche Problem des Hexateuch* (1938). Such an observation, however, does not mean that he was interested in refuting von Rad's theses altogether; rather, his primary goal was one of supplementation and expansion: to show that the pre-Jahwistic stage of tradition growth is also an important object of traditio-historical analysis and to demonstrate that the differentiation and critical analysis of tradition is a prerequisite for the synthetic work of the type carried out by von Rad. That some very different results—not least in the question "Pentateuch or Hexateuch?" and in their views of precompositional tradition growth—proceed from the investigations of the two scholars is due only in part to the basic difference between their critical approaches.

a. Task and Point of Departure

At the very beginning of *ÜPent*, Noth sets forth with clarity and precision a *definition of the scope and task of traditio-historical work*:

> The growth and formation of the large body of traditions now found in the extensive and complicated literary structure of the Pentateuch was a long process, nourished by many roots and influenced by manifold interests and tendencies. In the course of this development, traditions which doubtless were circulated and transmitted orally at first were probably written down in time, for reasons that are no longer known to us and to an extent that can no longer be determined with certainty. In any event, later on they were brought together in large literary works and these in turn, through the purely literary labors of the so-called redactors, were finally compiled into the large corpus of the transmitted Pentateuch. It is the task of a "history of Pentateuchal traditions" to investigate this whole process from beginning to end.[118]

---

impact on pentateuchal research. A certain amount of duplication with Anderson's article is unavoidable here.

117. Subtitle: *Die sammelnden und bearbeitenden Geschichtswerke im Alten Testament*, Halle 1943 (SGK, Geisteswiss. Klasse 18, 1943). Page references here are taken from the 3rd ed. (Tübingen 1967), and the book will hereafter be referred to as *ÜSt*.

118. *ÜPent*, 1 [ET: 1].

Noth was virtually the first to present such a precise definition of "Überlieferungsgeschichte," and it is indeed noteworthy that he conceives of it as *the total process stretching from the very beginnings of individual tradition formation all the way to the final redactional stage.*[119] However, since the literary stage of pentateuchal growth has received considerable attention and study previously, Noth decides in *ÜPent* to concentrate primarily on the preliterary history of the traditions. This stage, admittedly, has been investigated also by such scholars as Gunkel and Gressmann, but their analytical goal was primarily to uncover the early history and development of the *individual* materials (e.g., legends and sagas). Thereby numerous important questions are left unanswered, especially regarding the origin, the original significance, and the later changes of not only the "Sagenstoffe" but of the "Sagengestalten" as well. Moreover, the problem of the relation of these numerous "Gestalten" to the individual "Stoffe" must be probed, especially in order to determine whether this relation in each case is primary or secondary.[120]

For Noth, however, the chief task consists of the following: "to ascertain the *basic themes* from which the totality of the transmitted Pentateuch[121] developed, to uncover their roots, to investigate how they were replenished with individual materials, to pursue their connections with each other, and to assess their significance. Thus the task is to understand, in a manner that is historically responsible and proper, the essential content and important concerns of the Pentateuch—which, from its manifold beginnings, variously rooted in cultic situations, to the final stages in the process of its emergence, claims recognition as a great document of faith."[122] From this statement it is obvious that Noth, like von Rad, regards the Pentateuch as an "Endstadium" (or perhaps more precisely: as a composite of "Endstadien"). However, the decisive difference is that instead of operating with von Rad's "credenda" Noth focuses his discussion on more or less neutral Pentateuch *themes*, the pivotal centers of the *traditum*. To be sure, Noth accepts in theory the basic principle guiding von Rad: that "certain statements of faith, grounded in the cult and formulated in a confessional manner, constituted the roots from which

---

119. That we now prefer to restrict this scope of tradition history is described above, pp. 21–22.

120. *ÜPent*, 2–4.

121. Noth uses the word "Pentateuch" to refer to the materials preserved in the books Genesis–Numbers and portions of Deut 31–34. The rest of Deuteronomy, as well as Joshua, belongs to the Deuteronomistic History, which is a closed work independent of the Pentateuch. Cf. *ÜPent* 5–6. This conception of the Pentateuch marks a cardinal deviation from von Rad's view of the Hexateuch.

122. *ÜPent*, 3–4 [ET: 3].

in time, like a mighty tree, the Pentateuch grew."[123] But having agreed to this principle, Noth proceeds, with very little further reference to the credos, to analyze the complex developmental history of each of the themes. Throughout all of this, the remark made in his "Vorwort" must not be forgotten: Noth is interested primarily in raising questions and in presenting possibilities, even when these suggested answers are obviously hypothetical.[124]

Noth takes his point of departure in the accepted, assured results of literary criticism, which we hardly need to review here. Indeed his precise literary analysis of J, E, and P in the Pentateuch betrays his debt to Wellhausen, a position distinguishing Noth from the starting-point of several members of the "Uppsala Circle," especially Engnell. However, for Noth this literary-critical analysis provides him with only a provisional footing for his further analyses, for he indicates that the peculiar problems of the Pentateuch cannot be solved with a purely literary approach. *The formative period of the pentateuchal traditions was the preliterary stage.* Thus even in the area of source criticism Noth makes a contribution of his own[125] which has significance for the study of traditions and which becomes the basis for his further investigations. According to him, J and E have so much in common with each other regarding their contents and construction that they could not have been formulated completely independently from one another. Rejecting the possibility that either one had immediate access to the other, Noth suggests that both J and E had a common *Grundlage* (G) out of which they created their works.[126] Noth does not arrive at G through direct literary-critical means but through a traditio-critical comparison of J and E. G—whether in written or oral form is uncertain—consisted of the elements of the tradition on which J and E agreed, although a detailed reconstruction of G is not possible for us because of the fragmentary condition of E. However, it can be seen that all of the five major themes (which will be discussed below) were already present in G and were therefore older than both J and E. This conclusion goes beyond that of von Rad, who held that the Jahwist was responsible for the "Ausbau der Vätertradition," the "Einbau der Sinaitradition," and the "Vorbau der Urgeschichte."[127] Noth maintains that not only did the individual traditions predate J (and E), but that the "Ausbau" and the "Einbau" were also present

---

123. Ibid., 48 [ET: 46].
124. Ibid., v, also 4.
125. The idea, however, was not entirely original to Noth. A somewhat similar hypothesis regarding a common basis (U = Urüberlieferung, Ursage) for J and E had already been proposed by, e.g., O. Procksch, *Die Genesis übersetzt und erklärt*, KAT 1, Leipzig 1913, 281ff.
126. *ÜPent*, 40–44.
127. Cf. above, pp. 85–86.

in G and thus a part of the transmitted body of connected traditions used by J and E.[128] In this manner a further step is made in the history of tradition in that these postulated *thematic relationships* are to be dated in the period of the judges—the product of the amphictyony, not of the authors of J, E, or P.

b. Isolating the Five Pentateuchal Themes and the Additional Elements of Tradition

Admitting that most of the tradition materials were fundamentally of local, tribal origin, Noth points out that in their present form the pentateuchal traditions have a thorough-going "all-Israelite significance."[129] He concludes, therefore, that the Pentateuch did not arise simply as a conglomeration of individual narratives, but rather that this "all-Israel" scheme became, at a relatively early point, a part of the tradition itself, with the result that the individual materials, in spite of whatever origin they had had, were already so oriented by the time they constituted G. "The origin of the individual materials thus does not belong so much to the history of the Pentateuchal tradition as to its prehistory, at least in many instances. And ... the origin of the Pentateuchal tradition presupposes the existence of the historical phenomenon 'Israel.'"[130] On the basis of this historical presupposition Noth proposes the time of the emergence of the twelve-clan league,[131] after the settlement in Palestine, as the *terminus a quo* for the productive stage of the pentateuchal traditions, whether in oral or written form. The *terminus ad quem* of this process is set at the rise of the monarchy, by which time the tradition with all of its themes was largely fixed.[132]

How then does Noth conceive of the formation of the Pentateuch in this period? Specifically, in what respects does his reconstruction of the history of the tradition vary from von Rad's picture? One primary difference is to be

---

128. Noth (*ÜPent*, 43) agrees with von Rad that the "Vorbau der Urgeschichte" was the work of the Jahwist.

129. *ÜPent*, 45–46 [ET: 42]. This "Gesamtisrael" factor is not to be confused with Gunkel's concept of the "Israelitisierung" of foreign materials; cf. above, pp. 60–62, 65–66.

130. Ibid., 46 [ET: 43].

131. Noth's theses about the amphictyony, as seen in his pioneering work, *Das System der zwölf Stämme Israels*, BWANT IV, 1, Stuttgart 1930, constitute the presuppositions for his placing the production of the pentateuchal traditions in this period. We will have more to say about this amphictyony-thesis below in our discussion of Noth's *Geschichte Israels*. At this point it must suffice to emphasize that this monograph from 1930 provides the foundation for his work in *ÜPent* and *ÜSt*.

132. *ÜPent*, 46ff. Von Rad concurs in this time setting for the productive stage of the pentateuchal traditions; cf. his *Theologie* I, 83 (ET: I, 70).

seen in Noth's idea of "themes." In contrast to von Rad who identified two main tradition complexes, the exodus–conquest tradition and the Sinai tradition (the former of these two being the primary and predominant one), Noth specifies *five major themes* that, listed in the order of their traditio-historical priority, were *already present in G*:[133] Guidance out of Egypt ("Herausführung aus Ägypten"), Guidance into the Arable Land of Palestine ("Hineinführung in das palästinische Kulturland"), Promise to the Patriarchs ("Verheissung an die Erzväter"), Guidance in the Wilderness ("Führung in der Wüste"), and Revelation at Sinai ("Offenbarung am Sinai"). Each of these themes, according to Noth, has an essential core of traditions[134] and has its own history of development, separate and distinct from each of the other themes.[135] An actual historical experience or awareness on the part of some proto-Israelite tribe or group apparently precipitated each theme,[136] although later fusion with other themes was carried out by the amphictyonic community. Thus for the theme "Guidance into the Arable Land of Palestine," for example, Noth points out that it was originally separate from the theme "Guidance out of Egypt"[137] and that, since there was no concerted conquest of Palestine by all the tribes together but rather a gradual, generally peaceful immigration by the various groups, the core of this theme is the traditions of the central-Palestinian tribes, the so-called Rachel-tribes (Benjamin, Manasseh, and Ephraim).[138] Eventually this line of tradition became "Israelitized" and adopted by the other tribes as their own, as well as connected with the traditions concerning the escape of some unidentifiable group from Egypt.[139] In similar manner

---

133. *ÜPent*, 48–67.

134. Ibid., 67.

135. Von Rad admits that the literary findings support Noth's assumption about the independence of the individual themes, but he is nonetheless skeptical about the basic, internal disconnection between the themes: "these single themes themselves always presuppose an idea of the whole. Guidance in the wilderness cannot be thought of apart from the deliverance from Egypt and vice versa. Again, the promise to the patriarchs, after it passed over from the cultic communities of the people belonging to Abraham and Jacob to Israel, was immediately referred to the deliverance from Egypt, etc." (*Theologie* I, 136 n. 21; ET: I, 122 n. 21). How these connections are to be explained if not as a product of the amphictyonic community is, however, not indicated.

136. *ÜPent*, 276. F. M. Cross's criticisms ("The Divine Warrior in Israel's Early Cult," *Biblical Motifs: Origins and Transformations*, ed. A. Altmann, Cambridge 1966, 16–17) are thus fundamentally unfounded. Noth does not deny "actual historical memory"; what he repudiates is that the events at the base of the traditions could have happened to *all* of Israel. Cf. the discussion below, pp. 159–60.

137. We have seen above (pp. 81–83) that von Rad also maintains that the traditions centering on these two events were originally separate.

138. *ÜPent*, 54–58.

139. Ibid., 53.

Noth traces the tradition history of each theme back to its original elements, which he tries to describe in its earliest form as well as in the form in which it is preserved in our present Pentateuch, following its course of transmission and identifying its transmitters and the geographical location ("Haftpunkt") where it was primarily handed down.

Going beyond these five themes, Noth seeks to identify and analyze *the numerous, diverse individual traditions and tradition complexes which fill out and enrich the thematic framework.* Anderson has done us the service of isolating six "guidelines" that Noth appears to follow in separating earlier from later traditions. Noth uses these criteria only as indications which, if they are to aid us in clarifying origins and development of traditions, should at best mutually reinforce one another and be conceivable in the context of tribal life. These *guidelines* are as follows:[140] (1) Earliest traditions are formulated in small units and in concise style in contrast to later material, which tends to appear in large units composed in discursive style. (2) Earliest traditions are attached to places (e.g., Shechem, Bethel) and frequently end with an etiology of the place name. (3) Earliest traditions are usually "cultic" or "theophanic" in character. (4) Earliest traditions tend to be anonymous and to deal with typical figures, while later traditions are more specific and individualized. (5) Earliest traditions usually lie in the background and stand out awkwardly in the received pentateuchal narrative. (6) The cases of bracketing together ("Verklammerungen") of discrete units of tradition are secondary.

Among these early, independent traditions that Noth (following Gunkel) finds, there are many that picture a wide range of human relations, emotions, evils—in short, narratives that deal with specific persons, places or events and that thereby attempt to demonstrate the exemplary good and the evil with its consequent reward or punishment.[141] In their very nature they are "matters of universal human experience or interest and therefore they pervade the narrative material of all peoples."[142] These traditions thus include such as the Egyptian plague stories, conquest episodes, traditions concerning Isaac and Abraham, the murmurings of the people in the wilderness,[143] the covenant

---

140. Cf. Anderson, "Martin Noth's Traditio-Historical Approach," xxiii ff., where more details and examples of each are provided. Somewhat related lists of epic "laws" and indications of oral traditions have been drawn up by, e.g., Olrik and Moe.

141. *ÜPent*, 68.

142. Ibid. [ET: 64]. Von Rad (above, pp. 93–94) is of the opinion that the ancestral sagas— at least in their later form—deal more with God than with humans and that in this regard they are distinctly different from the legendary material of other peoples.

143. Cf. G. W. Coats, *Rebellion in the Wilderness: The Murmuring Motif in the Wilderness Traditions of the Old Testament*, Nashville 1968.

and apostasy at Sinai, the Balaam pericope, and more.[144] For each of these complexes Noth attempts to determine its original elements, its "Haftpunkt," and its transmitters. He goes yet further and analyzes the tradition history of certain key pentateuchal figures, such as Lot, Leah and Rachel, Moses, Aaron, and Joshua. Thus, by way of example, for the figure of Moses[145] the only reliable early elements are the tradition of his grave[146] and the references to his marriage to a foreigner.[147] Moses probably did not belong originally to any of the major themes;[148] but because his grave lay in the traditional path of the "Israelites" on their way into Palestine,[149] he was worked into the theme "Guidance into Palestine" by later narrators, and hence into the other themes.[150]

c. The Merging of the Themes and the Individual Traditions

Most of the traditio-historical processes described by Noth to this point proceeded at the oral level, but with the discussion of how the traditional materials became intricately merged and fused with each other we approach the stage of the oldest literary fixations in the history of the tradition, when it

---

144. Noth deals with these and the other supplementary traditions in *ÜPent*, 70–160. It might be mentioned here that von Rad, *VF* 1947/48 (1949/50), 176–77, suggests that Noth underestimates the significance and stability of a number of these traditions, especially in their early connections with the various themes. Von Rad is thinking here primarily of traditions about certain individuals, such as Jacob and Moses.

145. *ÜPent*, 172–91.

146. This is "the most original element of the Mosaic tradition still preserved.... And in other cases too, a grave tradition usually gives the most reliable indication of the original provenance of a particular figure of tradition" (*ÜPent*, 186 [ET: 169–70]). Cf., however, S. Schwertner, "Erwägungen zu Moses Tod und Grab in Dtn 34,5.6," *ZAW* 84 (1972), 25–46.

147. *ÜPent*, 184–85.

148. *ÜPent*, 191 [ET: 174]: "Moses clearly does not belong to the main substance of one of the Pentateuchal themes but only to the narrative elaboration." Noth has two main reasons for coming to this conclusion: (a) the fact that there is little reference to Moses and no substantial weight placed on his importance in the rest of the Old Testament (*ÜPent*, 172–73); and (b) the analysis of the original contents of each theme, showing that Moses is not an indispensable part of any one of them (e.g., *ÜPent*, 184).

149. *ÜPent*, 190.

150. It can hardly be surprising that Noth's radical view of Moses, which he derives on the basis of traditio-critical criteria, has set loose a long series of publications grappling with the problem. For a discussion of the issues and a bibliography of the literature since Noth, cf. H. Schmid, *Mose: Überlieferung und Geschichte*, BZAW 110, Berlin 1968; also S. Herrmann, "Mose," *EvT* 28 (1968), 310–28; and Anderson, "Martin Noth's Traditio-Historical Approach," xxviii ff. As early as 1953, Zimmerli located a weakness in Noth's method: "Is he not operating with a too coarsely meshed net through which valuable particles can escape?" (Zimmerli, *GGA* 207, 1953, 9).

is no longer easy to determine whether any given process represents primarily oral or literary work.[151] Noth hypothesizes that the theme of the "Promise to the Patriarchs," especially self-contained and isolated from the other themes by virtue of its contents, first underwent an assimilation of the three originally independent ancestral traditions (those concerning Abraham, Isaac, and Jacob).[152] The theme was then connected to the other themes by means of the traditions about Joseph,[153] a complex that arose to show how the ancestors got to Egypt whence they later needed to escape. The fusion of the other four themes with each other, according to Noth,[154] was a more gradual process of one theme "growing into" another. The theme "Guidance out of Egypt," as the "Urbekenntnis Israels," was the "Keimzelle" or "Kristallisationskern" of the entire pentateuchal narrative.[155] The figure of Moses became the primary connecting device, and certain stories about him (e.g., his birth, his flight to the Midianites) arose to make this connection smoother. The theme "Guidance in the Wilderness" became fused with "Revelation at Sinai" primarily because the "mountain of God" (Exod 18), which was a part of the former tradition complex, at some later date became identified with the mountain of Sinai.[156] Furthermore, the connecting of the themes with each other and with individual traditions was often done by means of genealogies[157] and itineraries.[158]

---

151. *ÜPent*, 216.

152. *ÜPent*, 216–18. For an earlier study of the Jacob tradition, cf. H. Eising, *Formgeschichtliche Untersuchung zur Jakobserzählung der Genesis*, Emsdetten 1940, especially 428–48. Varying from Noth's, another reconstruction of the history of the ancestral traditions is made by A. Jepsen, "Zur Überlieferungsgeschichte der Vätergestalten," in *Alt-Festschrift*, WZ Leipzig 3, Gesellschafts- und sprachwiss. Reihe (1953/54), 139–55. H. Weidmann provides a useful summary of the (German) research since Alt; *Die Patriarchen und ihre Religion im Licht der Forschung seit Julius Wellhausen*, FRLANT 94, Göttingen 1968, 126ff.

153. *ÜPent*, 226 [ET: 208]: "This Joseph story, a masterpiece of narrative art, is traditio-historically a latecomer in the sphere of the Pentateuchal narrative. Its function as a connecting piece between the themes 'promise to the patriarchs' and 'guidance out of Egypt' makes this probable at the outset."

154. *ÜPent*, 219ff. Von Rad, VF 1947/48 (1949150), 177, accuses Noth of too formal a picture of this "Zusammenwachsen" of the themes and the traditions; cf. however Kraus, *EvT* 16 (1956), 384ff.

155. *ÜPent*, 52, 54, 222–23. One is reminded here of Klostermann's principle of crystallization; cf. above, pp. 55–56.

156. *ÜPent*, 222–23. Cf. also H. Seebass, *Mose und Aaron, Sinai und Gottesberg*, Bonn 1962; and V. Fritz, *Israel in der Wüste: Traditionsgeschichtliche Untersuchung der Wüstenüberlieferungen des Jahwisten*, Marburg 1970.

157. *ÜPent*, 232–37.

158. By "itineraries" Noth means that, as the narrative followed the movement of the people from one place to another, traditions that were anchored ("ortsgebunden") to some location along the way were often "picked up." Cf. *ÜPent*, 237–46.

Throughout Noth's overall picture of the joining of the various pentateuchal traditions, another pronounced difference between him and von Rad becomes obvious. We have seen above[159] that von Rad maintains that the Hexateuch did not develop through a long process in which the various traditions gradually grew together, but that the Hexateuch is instead the result of an intentional, careful effort (by the Jahwist) to bring all the various tradition complexes together and to melt them into a linear whole according to a specific plan or schema. In contrast to this picture, however, Noth pleads for a *gradual process of "Zusammenwachsen" and "Ineinanderwachsen"* of the individual traditions and themes alike; this process was already well advanced by the time of G, in which all five themes were already present and connected with each other. Furthermore, the Jahwist is to be regarded only as one among many individuals active in this process and is therefore not the prime innovator of all the changes that von Rad assigns to him[160]—except for the placing of the "Urgeschichte" at the beginning, which Noth (like von Rad) attributes to the Jahwist.[161] It was the *amphictyonic community, not the Jahwist,* that was responsible for most of the process in which themes and individual traditions were merged into a kerygmatic whole. This is an important, new traditio-historical insight introduced and emphasized by Noth. *Thus the difference with regard to the* traditum *as we have seen above* (von Rad: theologically oriented tradition complexes formed according to the credenda; Noth: more or less "neutral," traditio-critically isolated themes) *is here accompanied by a distinct divergence in their views of the* traditio.

Tracing the history of the traditions must not, in Noth's eyes, stop short of the point at which the written documents of J, E, and P are composed and finally drawn together into our present Pentateuch. For this stage marks the transition of the pentateuchal narratives from the sphere of the cultic formation of the major themes and the popular development of these themes, to the sphere of the theological reflection and contemplation on the transmitted narratives.[162] Of significance for "Überlieferungsgeschichte" is the attempt to determine "in what way and with what purpose the literary versions reworked and shaped the received narrative material."[163] Generally speaking, the forming of the tradition was primarily carried out in the earlier period of transmission (mainly oral), and literary fixation brought changes

---

159. Cf. above, pp. 83–87.
160. *ÜPent*, 43–44.
161. Ibid., 256.
162. Ibid., 247. Noth thus recognizes the importance of the transitional stage from oral to written literature.
163. Ibid., 250 [ET: 231].

largely in the areas of word usage and style, while the substance and disposition of the narratives underwent little alteration.[164] The writers of each of the sources were guided by a distinguishable plan and theology which influenced their reworking of the traditions coming down to them, which resulted at some points in a new development or idea (e.g., J's setting the primeval-history traditions as the background to the ancestral traditions and formulating Gen 12:1–3 to serve as the transition to the next heilsgeschichtliche event).[165] The process of the fusion of the three sources (Noth's formula: J, enriched and expanded by the elements of E, was worked into the literary framework of P) is of less importance for the history of tradition because it represents a purely literary task in which very little new was introduced.[166] Therein, in fact, lies its main significance: that the editors of the final product felt so bound by the traditions of the past that they refrained from making substantial alterations or additions.

But this description of Noth's *Überlieferungsgeschichte des Pentateuch* has gone into sufficient detail for now. We will have occasion later to refer to the consequences that Noth draws from it for his *Geschichte Israels*. In what we have said above, it should have become clear that *the novum in Noth's work is the consistent combining of traditio-historical with thorough-going traditio-critical analysis*.[167] To be sure, the traditio-critical or traditio-analytical method was employed previously by Gressmann and Hylander, but Noth is careful to subsume it under the diachronic concept of tradition history. He thus relentlessly differentiates primary from secondary materials, seeking to arrive at the original state of isolated, disparate traditions so that he can then be able to retrace step-by-step the process of the fusion of traditions with each other and of themes with each other, arriving thus at the present state of the Pentateuch. Noth's goal is therefore to draw a complete picture of the way in which the Pentateuch could have developed. The hypothetical nature of this reconstruction is unavoidable; that parts of it are hardly conceivable can indeed be regretted. It nonetheless remains that *this book by Noth is one of the most important, seminal studies of the Pentateuch in modern times*. That it is also among the most hotly contested of Noth's works is perhaps to be expected. At any rate, further traditio-historical research into the pentateuchal traditions

---

164. Ibid., 251. We will see below that most Scandinavian scholars, notably Engnell, subscribe to an almost identical thesis.

165. *ÜPent*, 256–57. Noth describes the theology of each of the editors and the role it played in the reworking of the traditions in each case; cf. *ÜPent*, 255–67.

166. Ibid., 268; also *ÜSt*, 206ff.

167. Cf. also Kraus, *EvT* 16 (1956), 383–86; and Kraus, *Geschichte*, 451.

cannot refrain from taking Noth's theses into serious consideration; they must be refuted if they are not to be used as the foundation for subsequent work.

2. Traditio-Historical Study of the Deuteronomist's and of the Chronicler's Compositions

The great importance that we have attributed to Noth's study of the Pentateuch is applicable in full measure as well to his earlier book, *Überlieferungsgeschichtliche Studien: Die sammelnden und bearbeitenden Geschichtswerke im Alten Testament* (1943, 3rd ed. 1967 = *ÜSt*). Indeed it is due primarily to this epoch-making study that the Deuteronomistic History and the work of the Deuteronomistic redactors occupied a central place in the interests of many Old Testament scholars for several decades following its publication. In *ÜSt* Noth presents a different picture of the historical books than that which was postulated by earlier and contemporary literary critics.[168] He proposes to define and characterize two distinct historical works: the Deuteronomistic History (= Dtr)—Deuteronomy, Deuteronomy, Judges, Samuel, and Kings; and the Chronicler's History (= Chr)—Chronicles, Ezra, Nehemiah. These histories are to be set off sharply from the Pentateuch, not only because of their different literary origins and natures but also because of their diverging intentions: for the Pentateuch, to present the bases for faith and life; for Dtr and Chr, to portray from a specific theological point of view the history of the events leading to the exile.[169] We need to look briefly now at Noth's theses, giving special regard to what he has to say about the tradition history of both Dtr and Chr.

a. The Deuteronomistic History

The common literary-critical picture prior to Noth was that the documentary sources (J, E, P) of the Tetrateuch continue on through Deuteronomy and Joshua, and according to some scholars even on to Judges, Samuel, and Kings. Von Rad, working from form-critical and traditio-historical premises, supposes the Hexateuch (Genesis–Joshua) to be a continuous literary unit. Noth's thesis, however, is that the conquest tradition was indeed the implicit end of the pentateuchal themes and was thus also included in JE. Nonetheless, it was omitted by the final redactor of the Pentateuch because it was not

---

168. For orientation in the relationship of Noth's work to that of especially Wellhausen, Caspari, Gressmann, Hölscher, and Jepsen, cf. Kraus, *Geschichte*, 455–60. Not all concur with Noth; cf., e.g., Fohrer, *Einleitung*, 212.

169. *ÜSt*, 1–3.

a component of P, the literary framework used by the redactor for the Pentateuch.[170] Therefore, according to Noth, the conquest tradition must belong to another historical opus. Since there is no sign of Deuteronomistic redaction in the Pentateuch[171] and because Josh 1 seems to presuppose Deut 34 and 31:1–13 with its mention of "this law" (= Deuteronomy),[172] this new literary history must begin with Deut 1 and is thus totally independent from the books Genesis–Numbers.[173] The section Deut 1–3(4), a speech recalling the wilderness wanderings, should be seen as the introduction to the whole of Dtr, not simply to the Deuteronomic law collection.[174] Thus only by excluding the previous results of literary criticism is Noth able to set up his own conception of Dtr, which in turn marks *a key shift in our understanding of the books of Deuteronomy and Joshua.*[175]

What is to be said about the tradition history of Dtr? Inasmuch as Dtr (and Chr as well) consists of historical traditions collected in a quite different way than we have seen to be the case for the Pentateuch, the traditio-historical approach will have to be quite different for Dtr and Chr than for the pentateuchal traditions. Let us start with an important citation from Noth:

> Dtr was not a mere "redactor" but the author[176] of a work of history which collected the traditional, extremely diverse materials from the past and arranged

---

170. Noth, *ÜSt*, 211: "The old sources terminated indeed with the theme of the conquest, but in the process of working them into the framework of the P-narrative the *Pentateuch* arose with the total exclusion of the theme of the conquest of the West Jordanian land. The conquest narrative in the book of Joshua constitutes however part of the work of Dtr, which originated quite independently of the Pentateuch." Engnell (*GT*-I, 209ff.) draws yet a further consequence—that the Tetrateuch was *from the outset* a fully independent, intact collection of traditions. For a summary of the debate, cf. A. S. Kapelrud, "Pentateuch-problemer," *NTT* 56 (1955), 185–201.

171. *ÜSt*, 13. Of another opinion is W. Fuss, *Die deuteronomistische Pentateuchredaktion in Exodus 3–17*, BZAW 126, Berlin 1972.

172. *ÜSt*, 13–14.

173. *ÜSt*, 211 (in italics): "There never existed a 'Hexateuch' in the usual sense of a literary entity which at some point comprised the transmitted books Gen.–Josh. essentially in their present form." For a critique of Noth's view, cf. von Rad, "Hexateuch oder Pentateuch?" *VF* 1947/48 (1949/50), 52–56; and S. Mowinckel, *Tetrateuch—Pentateuch—Hexateuch: Die Berichte über die Landnahme in den drei altisraelitischen Geschichtswerken*, BZAW 90, Berlin 1964.

174. *ÜSt*, 14–15.

175. Noth's basic theses still prevail in the intense debate and research today. For a brief overview of some issues and literature, cf. P. Diepold, *Israels Land*, BWANT 95, Stuttgart 1972, 22–27.

176. Noth conceives of the Deuteronomist as a single individual. Others (e.g., Engnell and Carlson, cf. below, pp. 250–51) prefer to speak of "Deuteronomists" or a "Deuteronomistic school" (Carlson: "D-group").

them according to a carefully developed plan. In doing this, usually Dtr simply followed the wording of the sources that were available in literary form to him, merely joining the individual pieces by means of a connective text. In places, however, he evidently engaged in a systematic selection of the materials he received.[177]

On the basis of this statement, we can detect the four primary traditio-historical concerns: (1) the question of the author; (2) the author's sources (which, of course, must be literary-critically isolated in the text); (3) the composition of the various sections of the Deuteronomistic History; and (4) its theological and historical character and bearing to the past. One can, however, understandably question whether all of this belongs more properly under the concept of "Redaktionsgeschichte" instead of "Überlieferungsgeschichte." Noth would reply in the negative: Not only does his definition and scope of "Überlieferungsgeschichte" embrace the redactional stage,[178] but the prime consideration is that we are dealing here not with an editor but with an author. In other words, it is *a formative stage carried out at the literary level*, building on and adding to already given written sources.[179] Therefore, according to Noth, this phase is also a real part of the history of the traditions. The existence and activity of any later editor[180] would then fall within the sphere of redaction criticism.

What sources did the Deuteronomist, who composed Dtr about the middle of the sixth century B.C.E., have available, and how were they used to achieve the Deuteronomistic purposes? Noth postulates the existence of the following sources (excluding shorter lists and minor sources) for the respective sections of Dtr: for Deuteronomy—the Deuteronomic law and diverse sources on the wilderness wanderings and Moses' death;[181] for Josh

---

177. *ÜSt*, 11 (in italics), also 89; and *ÜPent*, 2.
178. Cf. above, pp. 110–11.
179. Carlson, advocating basically the same point, nonetheless identifies this phase as "redactional history"; cf. *David, the Chosen King*, Stockholm 1964, 22. According to our definition above (ch. 2), this stage is to be understood as "compositional history" and is thus not a part of "tradition history."
180. *ÜSt*, 6. For other efforts to identify the presence of a later editor of Dtr, cf. R. Smend, "Das Gesetz und die Völker: Ein Beitrag zur deuteronomistischen Redaktionsgeschichte," *Probleme biblischer Theologie*, ed. Wolff, 494–509; W. Dietrich, *Prophetie und Geschichte: Eine redaktionsgeschichtliche Untersuchung zum deuteronomistischen Geschichtswerk*, FRLANT 108, Göttingen 1972; also Diepold, *Israels Land*, 24, 204–9.
181. Cf. also von Rad, *Deuteronomium-Studien*, FRLANT 58, 2nd ed., Göttingen 1948; E. W. Nicholson, *Deuteronomy and Tradition*, Philadelphia 1967, 18ff.; and R. P. Merendino, *Das deuteronomische Gesetz: Eine literarkritische, gattungs- und überlieferungsgeschichtliche Untersuchung zu Dt 12–26*, BBB 31, Bonn 1969. For a detailed examination of the pre-Deuteronomistic

1–12 and 23—an intact, literary narrative of the conquest tradition; for Josh 13–22—a description of property distribution among the twelve tribes;[182] for the period of the judges—a series of loosely connected narratives about various tribal heroes and their victorious deeds, and also a list of "minor" judges complete with brief biographical information; for Samuel–1 Kgs 2—a comprehensive complex of traditions about Saul and David, an early fusion of the Saul traditions, the history of David's rise to power, the succession narrative, and miscellaneous elements; for 1 Kgs 3–11—a "book of the acts of Solomon" together with other disparate traditions; for the rest of Kings—the frequently mentioned "book of the chronicles of the kings of Judah/Israel" (apparently unofficial reworkings of official annals).[183] It should be obvious enough that at each of these points Noth is presupposing and building on previous research.[184] For each textual segment, Noth offers a detailed picture of the sources, of the extent to which the Deuteronomist accepted or departed from them, and of the Deuteronomist's own additions and alterations.[185] But in all of his discussion, one aspect is enigmatic from a traditio-historical point of view: Why does Noth restrict his attention to the Dtr and its author? He specifies and describes the sources that the Deuteronomist used, but *he does*

---

redaction of Deuteronomy, cf. G. Seitz, *Redaktionsgeschichtliche Studien zum Deuteronomium*, BWANT, V/13, Stuttgart 1971.

182. This section, Josh 13–22, was apparently added by a later redactor, according to Noth, *ÜSt*, 45–46. Cf. however S. Mowinckel (*Zur Frage nach dokumentarischen Quellen in Josua 13–19*, ANVAO, II. Hist.-Filos. Kl., No. 1, Oslo 1946) who, opposing an alleged "purely literary-critical dictatorship in our academic field" (35), postulates that Josh 13–19 is the product of a *postexilic author drawing on orally transmitted information* about tribal land allotment. For a critique of Mowinckel's hypotheses, cf. Noth, "Überlieferungsgeschichtliches zur zweiten Hälfte des Josuabuches," Festschrift Nötscher, BBB 1, Bonn 1950, 157ff. A completely different solution is offered by Y. Kaufmann, *The Biblical Account of the Conquest of Palestine*, translated by M. Dagut, Jerusalem 1953.

183. Essentially confirming Noth's work, another attempt to explain the history of Kings on the basis of a "synchronistische Chronik" as the source and with three later editorial phases (a priestly, a *nebi*-istic, and a levitical) is made by A. Jepsen, *Die Quellen des Königbuches*, Halle 1953.

184. By way of example, for Joshua he could draw on not only his own commentary (*Das Buch Josua*, HAT 7, Tübingen 1938, 2nd ed. 1953), but also the studies by Gressmann (*SAT* I/2), Alt ("Josua," 1936 = *Kl.Schr.* I, 176–92), and K. Möhlenbrink ("Die Landnahmesagen des Buches Josua," ZAW 56, 1938, 238–68).

185. Cf. especially *ÜSt*, 27–87. Noth (*ÜSt*, 18–27) also calls attention to the importance that the chronological system (480 years from exodus to Solomon's building the temple) had for the Deuteronomist; cf. also W. Richter, *Die Bearbeitungen des "Retterbuches" in der deuteronomischen Epoche*, BBB 21, Bonn 1964, 132ff.; and G. Sauer, "Die chronologischen Angaben in den Büchern Deut. bis 2. Kön.," TZ 24 (1968), 1–14.

not attempt here to uncover the prehistory of these sources.[186] For example, for the post-Solomonic monarchy the Deuteronomist drew on unofficial "Tagebücher," and Noth concentrates on this Deuteronomistic compositional stage and refuses to try to trace these "Tagebücher" back to the official annals.[187] One would expect that attempting to reconstruct the origin and history of these sources also belongs to the traditio-historical task. The composition of the final opus is only one of many stages to be examined, as Noth himself emphasizes in his definition of "Überlieferungsgeschichte."[188]

Noth concludes that, on the whole, the Deuteronomist had a positive attitude and respect for the traditions that came down to him, often even when they did not conform to his own beliefs (e.g., to his negative view of the cult).[189] His treatment of the traditions consisted of collecting them, in some cases selecting certain traditions in favor of others, joining them together and making transitional adjustments when necessary, at times making unintentional or intentional alterations and additions, and at all important points inserting retrospective and forecasting speeches in the mouths of the leaders.[190] The motive of the Deuteronomist and the purpose of Dtr are summed up by Noth as follows: "We are surely confronted here with an individual's work done on his own initiative. The historical catastrophes which he experienced have stirred him to ask about the meaning of these events, and drawing on the available traditions about the history of his people he sought to provide an answer to this question in a comprehensive, continuous historical presentation."[191] The task, under the rubric of "Überlieferungsgeschichte," which Noth here sets for himself is thus to analyze this compositional stage—the Deuteronomist himself and his reworking of the materials.

b. The Chronicler's History

The second half of Noth's *ÜSt* is devoted to the other Old Testament historical compilation, the Chronicler's History (= Chr). As Noth points out, the literary

---

186. A similar situation can be seen in the work of Carlson; cf. below, pp. 245–48, 252–53. Cf. also Kraus, *Geschichte*, 458.
187. *ÜSt*, 73.
188. Cf. above, pp. 110–11.
189. *ÜSt*, 95, 103–4. Cf. also Engnell's distinction, below, p. 207. —It could be revealing to see a precise comparison of Noth's Deuteronomist with von Rad's Jahwist in terms of their compositional techniques, reception of tradition, and theology.
190. *ÜSt*, 96–100, 5.
191. Ibid., 110. A somewhat different identification of the Deuteronomistic kerygma as "return to the God of the Heilsgeschichte" is made by H. W. Wolff, "Das Kerygma des deuteronomistischen Geschichtswerks" (1961), *Ges. Stud.*, 171–86.

unity of Chr, which is composed of 1 and 2 Chronicles, Ezra, and Nehemiah, is well established and does not need additional argumentation, as was necessary for the question of the extent of Dtr.[192] But before he can turn to traditio-historical questions, he addresses himself to two literary-critical tasks: (1) the determination of the original extent of Chr by means of excising all later additions (especially lists, e.g., portions of 1 Chr 2–9; also chs. 12; 15:4–10, 16–24; 23–27; Ezra 10:18, 20–44; Neh 7:6–72; 11:3–36; 12:1–26);[193] and (2) the identification of the sources available to the Chronicler. Regarding the latter, Noth mentions the following: for the genealogies in 1 Chr 1–9—the Pentateuch; for the history of the Judaic kings in 1 Chr 10–2 Chr 36—the books of Samuel and Kings, also miscellaneous notices about military fortresses and battles;[194] for Ezra and Neh 8–10—no continuous source (thus no "Esradenkschrift"); and for the rest of Nehemiah—the memoirs of Nehemiah.[195]

Just as he did for Dtr, Noth's *traditio-historical analysis of Chr concentrates primarily on the Chronicler's reworking of the sources and on the historical and theological character of the composition.*[196] The Chronicler should also be seen as a single author, dated by Noth in the period of 300–200 B.C.E.[197] While the Chronicler also had a basically positive attitude toward his sources, frequently to the extent of copying them verbatim, he felt more freedom than did the Deuteronomist in trying to create a living, vivid, idealized picture of this period in Israel's history, and the result was that nearly half of the material can be seen to be his own innovations and additions.[198] Noth disputes the usual view that the Chronicler's main interest was to vindicate the levitical claims to certain important cultic functions in the temple. Rather, the primary motive of the Chronicler was to legitimize the Davidic monarchy and especially the Jerusalem temple as the authentic center for worshiping Jahweh.[199]

We can thus see that Noth's traditio-historical analysis in *ÜSt* is different from that in *ÜPent*. For the latter, he is interested in uncovering the pre-

---

192. *ÜSt*, 110.
193. Ibid., 111–31.
194. Noth (*ÜSt*, 133ff.) does not accept as reliable most of the references that the Chronicler makes to other sources.
195. For more details on all of these sources, cf. *ÜSt*, 131–50. Other important studies of Ezra and Nehemiah include S. Mowinckel, *Studien zu dem Buche Ezra-Nehemia* I–III, SNVAO, N.S. II. Hist.-Phil. Klasse, No. 3, 5, 7, Oslo 1964–65; and U. Kellermann, *Nehemia: Quellen, Überlieferung und Geschichte*, BZAW 102, Berlin 1967.
196. It is interesting to note that contemporary research has given far less attention to Noth's work on Chr than to his pioneering study of Dtr.
197. *ÜSt*, 111, 150–55.
198. Ibid., 156–57, 166–71.
199. Ibid., 173ff.

history of the traditions, in their disparity and in their thematic relationships. For *ÜSt*, however, he concentrates on the one phase of composition at the hand of an author. Does the difference stem only from the varying materials being studied? To be sure, the two literary bodies are entirely distinct from each other, and the pictures of the complete development of each would be divergent at most points. Not least the fact that the Pentateuch springs from primarily oral, disparate traditions whereas Dtr and Chr go back to mainly written sources would account for the basic difference. But there is a parallel: The Pentateuch, Dtr, and Chr all have compositional stages as well as prehistories to these compositions. If Noth can penetrate behind the Jahwist and even G, what stops him then from attempting analytically to get past the Deuteronomist and the Chronicler? The question here is one of drawing the whole developmental picture or only a part of it. The compositional phase which Noth studies in *ÜSt* falls indeed within his defined span of the history of tradition stretching from the earliest beginnings on down to the last redaction. Nonetheless, one cannot help but be disappointed that Noth does not utilize his analytical skills in trying to discover more about the pre-Deuteronomistic and pre-Chronicler periods of development, *offering thus a total picture in ÜSt* just as he does so superbly in *ÜPent*. He does not shy away from hypothesizing and conjecturing in *ÜPent*, and there is no reason why he should then in *ÜSt—especially if insights might be gained that could improve yet further our understanding of the final form of Dtr and Chr.*

3. History of Israel

We have above characterized von Rad's research tendency as a wedding of the traditio-historical method with an overriding theological interest and orientation, and it may not be unfair to continue this schematism here by asserting that *Noth's traditio-historical work seems to be penultimate to his drive to describe the history of Israel.*[200] One must by no means neglect the decisive influence that Gunkel, Gressmann, and Wellhausen and especially his mentors Kittel and Alt had on Noth's historical, investigative approach.[201] And yet for all of this influence and inheritance, there is something definitely new in

---

200. W. Zimmerli ("In Memoriam Martin Noth," *VT* 18, 1968, 409–13) quite accurately pictures Noth's earlier research as being the preparation and foundation for his *Geschichte Israels*; cf. also *GGA* 207 (1953), 1–13.

201. For a comparison of Noth's with Wellhausen's history, cf. Smend, "Nachruf auf Martin Noth," in: M. Noth, *Ges. Stud.* II, TB 39, Munich 1969, 160ff. Cf. also Anderson, "Martin Noth's Traditio-Historical Approach," xviii–xxiii.

GERHARD VON RAD AND MARTIN NOTH

Noth's *Geschichte Israels*.[202] We will see that this innovation results primarily from his consistently drawing the historical consequences of his traditio-historical conclusions. The originality of Noth's history lies in his treatment of *Israel's premonarchical beginnings*, and we will therefore restrict ourselves here to this section.

The usual way to approach the history of ancient Israel is to begin with the antecedents to Israel's life in Palestine, i.e. to describe the ancient Near Eastern world, the pre-Israelite Palestine, the ancestors (their religion and their migrations), the sojourn in and exodus from Egypt, the trek to and settlement of Palestine—at all of these points drawing heavily on information gained from archaeological finds.[203] Noth's *Geschichte Israels*, however, does not follow this pattern. His history starts with the period of the twelve-tribe confederacy established on Canaanite soil and continues on to the final Jewish revolt against the Romans in 135 C.E. The period prior to 1200 B.C.E. he treats, except for some miscellaneous political and cultural remarks,[204] under the rubric of "the Traditions of the Sacral Confederation of the Twelve Tribes."

What are his reasons for this radical demarcation of the history of Israel? Three considerations seem to be especially decisive for Noth:[205] (1) From all that we can determine, Israel began its collective existence only at that point at which the tribes were settled in Palestine and had launched a confederate system. Prior to this period, the various events attributed to "Israel" in the pentateuchal traditions —ancestral migrations, slavery in Egypt, exodus, wilderness wanderings, the peaceful and militaristic immigrations into Palestine—were all actions involving only specific, separate tribes or groups. We therefore have no historical justification for attributing these happenings to Israel as a whole, and the events themselves do not belong to a history of "Israel" in its proper, precise sense.[206] Noth's consideration in this case is thus *historical*, based on the thesis of the Israelite amphictyony, as developed in

---

202. Göttingen, (1st ed. 1950) 2nd ed. 1954. ET: *The History of Israel*, trans. S. Godman, London 1958.

203. To a greater or lesser degree, this is the approach taken by almost all of the historians of Israel, e.g., Wellhausen, Kittel, Sellin, Jirku, Olmstead, Lods, Oesterley and Robinson, Kaufmann, Albright, Ricciotti, Gordon, Orlinsky, Bright, Neher, Mowinckel, Metzger.

204. Noth offers a more extensive survey of ancient Near Eastern history in *Die Welt des Alten Testaments: Einführung in die Grenzgebiete der alttestamentlichen Wissenschaft*, 4th ed., Berlin 1962.

205. Critical responses to Noth's assessment of the historical situation are discussed below, ch. 10. At this point we refer solely to J. Bright, *Early Israel in Recent History Writing*, SBT 19, London 1956, especially 111ff.

206. Cf. Noth, *Geschichte Israels*, 11ff.; and *ÜPent*, 272ff.

his *Das System der zwölf Stämme Israels* (1930).²⁰⁷ (2) Complementing this historical aspect of "Gesamtisrael," there is a specific consequence that Noth draws from his traditio-historical study of the Pentateuch and expresses explicitly already in the epilogue to his *ÜPent*: "It is no longer possible for us to ascertain any *connections* between these initial stages. For we possess only information about a number of particulars which demonstrably have been brought into connection with each other secondarily in the history of the traditions. Therefore, we cannot include the content of the Pentateuchal narrative in the actual 'history of Israel' but can only speak about particular matters coming out of a prehistory of the Israelite tribes."²⁰⁸ *Noth thus takes his history of the pentateuchal traditions seriously*. It has not shown a linear, connected, commonly shared course of history, and therefore it cannot be included as such in a prehistory of Israel. From these traditions we can gain only disconnected, isolated bits of historical information. The prehistory of the tribes and the colonization of Palestine were considerably more complicated than the Israelites implied in their traditions.²⁰⁹ Noth's historical conception is thus in this case conditioned decidedly by his traditio-historical method. (3) Under what aspect should one then treat the pentateuchal traditions? Noth asserts: "They can only be understood historically as the traditions of the tribes united in Palestine concerning the crucial foundations of their faith. As such they were of fundamental importance."²¹⁰ Thus only as a product of the tribal confederacy do these traditions find their place in the historical course of events. Such an assessment does not, however, exclude our examining these traditions for evidence of pre-Israelite happenings.

Noth thus begins his history of Israel with a reconstruction of the origins of Israel in the land of Palestine. After a description of the geographical distribution of the tribes in the land,²¹¹ he gives a composite picture of the process

---

207. The critical responses to his amphictyony thesis, which Noth derives through tradition analysis as well as by analogy with ancient Greece, must indeed be taken into consideration, for they necessitate a careful reappraisal of Noth's historical starting point and its consequences. Cf. on the one hand such modifications to Noth's thesis as urged by R. Smend, *Jahwekrieg und Stämmebund: Erwägungen zur ältesten Geschichte Israels*, FRLANT 84, 2nd ed., Göttingen 1966; but then also the stronger critiques of H. M. Orlinsky, "The Tribal System of Israel and Related Groups in the Period of the Judges," *OrAnt* 1 (1962), 11–20; and G. Fohrer, "Altes Testament—'Amphiktyonie' und 'Bund'?" *TLZ* 91 (1966), cols. 801–816, 893–904. For a sober assessment of the debate: Smend, "Zur Frage der altisraelitischen Amphiktyonie," *EvT* 31 (1971), 623–30.

208. *ÜPent*, 278 [ET: 258].

209. Noth, *Geschichte Israels*, 70; cf. also von Rad, *VF* 1953/55 (1956), 131–32.

210. Noth, *Geschichte Israels*, 106 [ET: 111].

211. Ibid., 54–67. Noth draws here on the results of the many previous studies which he and Alt have done in this area.

in which the tribes settled in the land—for the most part peacefully and primarily in places unoccupied at that time by other peoples.[212] He describes the way in which the various settled tribes, already gathered into smaller groupings (e.g., the six "Leah-tribes"), became allied into an amphictyony.[213] The sacral character of this confederacy is seen best in its institutions: the central sanctuary, the divine law, the office of "judge," and the holy war.[214] He makes it clear that this sacral confederacy, which continued to exist until the destruction of the Jerusalem temple in 587 B.C.E., has a key importance in the cultic life and in the transmission of traditions.[215] For this whole presentation, Noth draws heavily, indeed primarily, on the internal evidence of the Old Testament, evaluated according to traditio-historical criteria.[216]

In his *ÜPent*, Noth makes an important, although perhaps obvious statement: "The history of the Pentateuchal tradition is itself a part of the history of Israel."[217] Under this aspect Noth takes up the discussion of the traditions circulating among the confederate tribes of Israel. The three important themes are the release from Egypt, the ancestors, and the covenant at Sinai. Noth is *more interested in what these traditions can tell us about the settled tribes than what they indicate of Israel's prehistory*. The historical insight gained from this tradition history has already been emphasized in Noth's *ÜPent*: The traditions—transmitted, fused, and arranged as they are—reveal to us the details of Israel's faith and identify the historical happenings that Israel regarded as

---

212. Noth, *Geschichte Israels*, 67–82. For a good survey of Noth's and Alt's view of the occupation of the land, especially in comparison with the picture offered by the "Albright School," cf. M. Weippert, *Die Landnahme der israelitischen Stämme in der neueren wissenschaftlichen Diskussion*, FRLANT 92, Göttingen 1967.

213. Noth, *Geschichte Israels*, 83–94.

214. Ibid., 94–104.

215. Cf. also Noth, "Die Gesetze im Pentateuch: Ihre Voraussetzungen und ihr Sinn" (1940), *Ges. Stud.*, 3rd ed. 1966, 81ff.

216. According to Anderson ("Martin Noth's Traditio-Historical Approach," xviii–xxiii), Noth follows Wellhausen and not Gunkel in trying to understand the Old Testament from within.

217. *ÜPent*, 272 [ET: 252]. This assertion, it should be noted, is applicable not only for the Pentateuch but for all history of tradition as well. Cf. also Rendtorff, "Geschichte und Überlieferung," 83; on the other hand, however, Herrmann, "Mose," *EvT* 28 (1968), 321: "This however is an unclear statement. The concept of history becomes clouded. For traditions alone do not make history, but are dependent on history. There is no self-manifestation of traditions, no spontaneous introduction of traditions into the lap of the amphictyony. Events accompanying the process and pursuing their specific goal must be fundamental. The history of tradition cannot be detached from history." On Herrmann's critique of von Rad and Noth, cf. below, pp. 155–57.

the sources for this faith.[218] Noth attempts also to align these divinely influenced events into the historical sphere, although he admits pointedly that we are dealing in this case with a realm which escapes historical evaluation.[219] Throughout, Noth's central concern is to isolate and describe Israel's individuality, that which makes its history different and distinctive from the history of any other people.[220]

We have thus been able to see how Noth approaches Israel's beginnings and whence he derives his information for this period.[221] For him traditio-historical examinations must first be carried out separately from historical investigations, and only when specific conclusions have been reached can the two investigative fields be brought together. His understanding of the proper sequence of the analytical steps explains why he concludes *ÜPent* with a section on the historical consequences of his traditio-historical results. These historical implications become, in turn, the subject matter of his *Geschichte Israels*. His drive to examine the Old Testament sources traditio-historically and then to assess and appropriate these results for his history can be seen throughout the book, not only in these sections on Israel's beginnings. Noth executes this procedure consistently and relentlessly, even when the consequence is that he deprives us of any confidence in the Old Testament historical accounts and sequences.[222] *For him the task is to trace the history of Israel—a task which usually entails incorporating the history of tradition but, on some occasions, necessitates relying solely upon it.*

C. Summary

Before proceeding further, let us summarize briefly the discussion up to this point. We have seen above that, while the Old Testament was being studied critically in other respects after the Reformation, it took several centuries for a real awareness of the problems of *traditio* and *traditum* to develop. Beginning with Richard Simon in 1678, several Old Testament scholars seem to have suspected that the various parts of the Old Testament could be the final result of a long process of growth. But this conception of the complex prehistory and a method for systematically and purposively examining it were

---

218. Noth, *Geschichte Israels*, 106.
219. Ibid., 9–11, 106.
220. Cf. also Anderson, "Martin Noth's Traditio-Historical Approach," xx ff.
221. A lively debate has followed in the wake of Noth's work. We will be presenting some of the main arguments of Albright, Bright, Herrmann, and others in our critique below (ch. 10).
222. Cf. also Anderson, "Martin Noth's Traditio-Historical Approach," xxviii ff.; Wallis, *Geschichte und Überlieferung*, 118ff.; and von Rad, *VF* 1947/48 (1949/50), 176–77.

not developed until the twentieth century. Under the influence of the religio-historical drive to investigate origins and partly as an aversion to the literary-critical concentration on documents and authors, Gunkel sought to follow the course of form-critically isolated individual units back to their earliest beginnings. This work was supplemented on the one hand by Gressmann's traditio-critical analysis and on the other hand by Klostermann's characterization of the gradual agglomeration of traditional materials as a process of crystallization. Influences at the points of cult and tradition came also from Scandinavia, especially from Mowinckel and Pedersen. The three scholars—Gunkel, Klostermann, and Gressmann—can be regarded as the immediate "forefathers" of the type of traditio-historical research gaining ground in Germany. Its actual "fathers" are von Rad and Noth. Their work inaugurated a new period of increased activity in Old Testament critical research, for they rendered the invaluable service of once and for all establishing the facticity and the importance of the long prehistory of Old Testament texts and then of demonstrating ways in which this growth process can be researched and reconstructed. Their theses and methods have been determinative and even paradigmatic for the studies that have come in their wake. Their work constitutes the *point de départ* for subsequent tradition historians, the given which one must refute if one does not choose to build upon it. Due to this central importance of von Rad and Noth, it would be helpful for us here to draw *schematic lines of comparison* between them in order to illuminate the prime points of methodological and substantive similarity and divergence.

(1) We have seen that von Rad combines his traditio-historical work with an overriding interest in Old Testament theology, whereas Noth seems to subsume his investigations under the general goal of drawing up a history of Israel. To state it differently: *von Rad is interested in putting the history of tradition at the service of theology; Noth, at the service of history.* To be sure, these two orientations or interests are not exclusive of each other, nor does either von Rad or Noth by any means disregard the other sphere of concerns.[223] It is primarily a matter of emphasis—the main arena in which one tries to draw consequences and seeks to apply the results.

(2) As has become clear especially in their studies of the Pentateuch/Hexateuch, von Rad and Noth employ different methods of investigation, which can in part be explained by the historical phase of the traditions that they are seeking to clarify. Von Rad concentrates primarily on the process of "Literaturwerdung," thereby having to presuppose the critical analysis of

---

223. Von Rad (*VF* 1953/55, 1956, 133–34), in fact, points out that the Old Testament theologian and the historian of Israel both have to deal with the same subject matter: Israel's witness to its history with God. The sphere of profane history extends, though, obviously beyond this.

the traditions as carried out by Gunkel, Gressmann, and others. Beginning with a form-critical assessment of the Hexateuch as a whole (result: credenda provided the conceptual framework), he seeks to explain the process in which the original, disparate traditions became joined together into complexes and finally into their present context. He generally finds cult and individual theologians (especially the Jahwist) to have been the responsible agents in this long process. Noth, on the other hand, begins with a precise traditio-critical analysis of the preliterary stage, following the traditions back into Israel's earliest period in search of fundamental, embracing elements and finding them in the five pentateuchal themes, which he assumes to have served as the skeleton for the whole structure. He then proceeds to show how all the various traditions agglomerated around these themes and how the themes became connected with each other. Noth's traditio-*critical* method, in contrast to Gressmann's, is thus kept decidedly subservient to a traditio-*historical* concept.[224] In their studies of the Pentateuch, *Noth thus diverges from von Rad's approach by proceeding analytically from the final state back into the earliest stages and returning again to the final product, whereas von Rad concentrates on the synthesizing forward movement from early stages to the "Endstadium."* Both presuppose the accepted results of literary criticism.

(3) There is a distinct difference between their understandings of the *traditum*. Von Rad regards *the ancient confessional statements, the credenda*, as the roots of the Hexateuch, as the formative and organizing factors for the whole structure. Noth agrees with the importance of these credenda, but he prefers nonetheless to identify *more or less neutral themes* as the kernels of the contents. Von Rad has criticized Noth of formalism in his conception of tradition,[225] but this is an unfair estimation of Noth's view. Kraus[226] comes closer by asserting that Noth's differentiated, historical exposition disregards the "intentional continuity" of the traditions, the driving and uniting force which von Rad finds in the credenda. This aspect, to be sure, receives only occasional attention in Noth's work,[227] but for us the main question is how far back in history this continuity really could have reached. Von Rad presents a picture of a constant stream of tradition ending in our Hexateuch; he does not

---

224. Cf. also Kraus, *EvT* 16 (1956), 383ff.

225. Von Rad, *VF* 1947/48 (1949/50), 177; similarly Kraus, "Der gegenwärtige Stand der Forschung am Alten Testament," *Die Freiheit des Evangeliums und die Ordnung der Gesellschaft*, BEvT 15, Munich 1952, 111. Kraus also appeals here for a critical clarification of the concept of "Überlieferungsgeschichte."

226. *EvT* 16 (1956), 383ff.

227. Schmidt, *EvT* 30 (1970), 176, attributes this weakness of Noth (his "neglect of the concrete content or of the intentional element of the traditions") to his understanding of "actualization" ("Vergegenwärtigung").

specify when these credenda and the theological impulse on the whole began to play so significant a role in ancient Israel, but one gets the impression that they were present from early beginnings.[228] Noth's view, however, seems to be more plausible, for according to him this confessional aspect was a later historical development, a phenomenon of the amphictyony. It was preceded by the stage of separate, scattered traditions and growing tradition complexes— in which a pervasive continuity could hardly be expected and for which the question of whether sacral or profane can only be answered in each individual case. For Noth, the continuity that existed rested in the themes—actual centers of tradition and not just formalistically contrived devices. Noth's view of the *traditum* thus varies from von Rad's but is by no means less probable or weaker simply due to a de-emphasis of the confessional or sacral element as postulated by von Rad.

(4) A final difference between the two scholars can be seen in their evaluation of the *traditio*. We have already noted[229] that von Rad conceives of the "Literaturwerdung" as *an intentional, careful process (primarily conducted by the Jahwist)* in which the various tradition complexes were organized and fused together according to a specific linear schema. However, what von Rad refuses to accept as an "accidental" process of growth Noth pictures as *a long, gradual course of agglomeration and "Ineinanderwachsen,"* the main features of which were already reached in the pre-Jahwistic G (thus earlier than von Rad is willing to postulate). Even the prime agents in this process are specified differently: for von Rad—the cult and then especially the Jahwist; for Noth—the amphictyonic community (primarily through its cult).

These differences of interests, methodology, and conceptions of *traditum* and *traditio* are striking, but there are many points of similarity and commonality between von Rad and Noth. Their awareness of the sharp discrepancy between the actual course of history and the Israelite conception of it is one such shared position. The central importance of the cult throughout the life of Israel is another. Furthermore, they both maintain that the prime *traditio* principle in Israel consists of interpretation and actualization. And basic to all of their traditio-historical work—not just that on the Pentateuch/Hexateuch—is the realization that the depths and the long prehistory of the Old Testament must be investigated if we hope to gain a better understanding of the present form of the text. Both are aware that the results of their analyses have wide-reaching consequences for the areas of, e.g., history and theology. For this reason their traditio-historical studies—for all of their differences—

---

228. Cf., e.g., von Rad, *Theologie* I, 136 (ET: I, 122).
229. Cf. above, pp. 83–86, 116–19.

should best be seen as *complementary* to each other. Von Rad himself implies as much in his assertion[230] that his *Das formgeschichtliche Problem des Hexateuch* must now be read in conjunction with Noth's *Überlieferungsgeschichte des Pentateuch*.

---

230. Von Rad, *Ges. Stud.*, 3rd ed. 1965, 7.

9
Subsequent Examples of Traditio-Historical Studies

Our history of the rise of the traditio-historical research of the Old Testament has devoted special attention to the contributions of the two scholars who have given this approach its main identity, von Rad and Noth. To be sure, the discussion has been pursued further by other scholars, and the parallel Scandinavian debate, reviewed below in part 2, has also played a key part. As a result of the lively interest in this area since von Rad's and Noth's ground-breaking works, there seems to be no end to the bibliography on the subject now. While we have paid special attention above to the tradition history of the historical literature, other studies have sought to apply the method to the prophetic, lyrical, and sapiential texts of the Old Testament as well. Not least of all, attempts to establish the history of biblical notions, motifs, and themes and to trace the course of specific tradition streams have continued to appear. The goal has been to gain a better understanding of the larger historical contexts of the texts, to draw literarily separate pericopes into connection with each other, and to explain substantive tensions in light of the postulated lines of continuity.

Such is the complex state of traditio-historical research today. Among the diverse studies that have appeared, there are those that are carefully and perceptively executed—but also many others that are imprecise in method and unrestrained in conjecturing. Reviewing all of them here is neither possible nor necessary. Instead we will now examine three exemplary traditio-historical investigations of varied subject matter. Our purpose in each case is to determine the way in which the method is understood and applied and to demonstrate that important results can be attained when the analysis is carefully conducted.

A. Hartmut Gese on Ezekiel 40–48

Our first example comes from the Old Testament prophetic literature. Gese's dissertation on Ezek 40–48 provides us with an exemplary investigation of an intricate tradition complex.[1] We are presented in these chapters with a conglomeration of various materials organized according to a strict structural plan—a visionary guidance through and description of the future temple (chs. 40–42), a catalogue of the ordinances of this temple (chs. 43–46), and a picture of the land surrounding the temple (chs. 47–48). The whole appears in Ezekiel as a "Verfassungsentwurf," a program for future reconstruction of Israel. As indicated in Gese's title and emphasized in his introduction,[2] the task which he sets for himself is above all a traditio-historical one: to analyze the developmental and the compositional processes which lie behind our present text. The fragmentation, unevenness, and conflicts between various sections cannot be explained through a text-critical attempt to regain the original text;[3] and these problems can find only a partial solution by means of a literary-critical search for the sources of Ezek 40–48. The predominant question, according to Gese, is of a traditio-historical nature: "to what extent within such a source precisely this material, rather than something else, is presented in such a sequence and in such a structure."[4] Gese is thus in his study concentrating on the preliterary stage of the text, extending also to the redactional period when the disparate sections were formed into "literature." For him a history of the traditions includes *the determination of the earliest materials, the illumination of how the individual elements became joined with each other insofar as these connections were not original, the uncovering of any tradition strata and their component parts, and the identification of agents and historical factors determinative in the growth of the tradition*. His conception of the traditio-historical method is essentially the same as Noth's: traditio-critical analysis, aided by the other critical tools, first approaches the material reductively before the attempt is made to reconstruct the growth process of the traditions on to the final redactional stage.

Gese's exact analyses are guided throughout by this clarity of purpose and method, and this brings dividends in the traditio-historical conclusions which he is able to draw. His first step is to remove the firm compositional

---

1. H. Gese, *Der Verfassungsentwurf des Ezechiel (Kap. 40–48) traditionsgeschichtlich untersucht*, BHT 25, Tübingen 1957.
2. Ibid., 1ff.
3. Parts of the text of Ezek 40–48 are recognized as among the more poorly preserved of the Old Testament. Gese admits (ibid., 3–5) that the text-critical attempt to reconstruct the original Hebrew text through consideration of all known Hebrew and versional variants is a prerequisite for a traditio-historical analysis of the type executed in his study. However, he generally refrains from presenting all the results of his own text-critical work; exceptions are at those points where text-critical insights have direct relevance for the tradition history itself. More details on Ezek 40–41, though, are given in an appendix, ibid., 129–84.
4. Ibid., p.2.

schema of the visionary guidance through the future temple and land. With this done, the text breaks into many individual, often fragmentary elements.⁵ He employs primarily literary-critical and form-critical criteria here: unevenness, internal conflicts, introductory formulas, and so forth. Certain groupings according to content and form become obvious; especially Ezek 40–42, the description of the temple, must be held strictly separate from Ezek 43–48. Gese's analytical procedure is to start with an extensive examination of each individual section in the six text groupings. This analysis of each pericope is carried out as far as possible without having to refer to other adjacent texts. Only after all individual elements in a specific grouping have been examined can certain preliminary traditio-historical consequences be drawn for the whole complex in question. And when he has completed this for all of the groupings, he then attempts to sketch the tradition history of the entire Ezek 40–48. Gese's analytical method is thus to investigate first all of the smallest, isolated parts and then, on the basis of these results and the preliminary conclusions about the intermediate groupings, to draw everything together into a total picture.

What specific traditio-historical results does Gese derive from his analyses? First of all, *Ezek 40–42* originated independently of and prior to Ezek 43–48, as can be seen in the introductions to each section as well as in the later additions to chapters 43–48. The earliest portion of chapters 40–42 is the original account of the vision in 40:1–37, 47–49; 41:1–4. This account stems probably from Ezekiel himself or from the exilic circles during or immediately after his time. It offers a plan of the temple that takes virtually no historical architectural data into consideration, and therefore it was supplemented by successively later additions in order to correct it according to the actual historical building of the Second Temple.⁶ The sections 41:5–15a and 41:15b–26 came first, perhaps both from the same author but originally not in the form of a vision. These were followed later by 42:1–14 and 42:15–20, which also were made to conform to the visionary account. Yet later additions can be seen in 40:38–43, 44–46a, and 46b.

The tradition history of *Ezek 43–48* is more complicated—although also more evident.⁷ Gese identifies three separate tradition strata: (1) The oldest (exilic or late exilic) is the נשיא-stratum: 44:1–3; 45:21–25; 46:1–10, 12. It is characterized by the designations עם הארץ for the people and נשיא for their

---

5. Ibid., 6–8.
6. Ibid., 108. Zimmerli (*Ezechiel* II, *BK* 13/2, Neukirchen 1969, 1249) regards this as rather improbable because the plan in Ezek 40ff. does not correspond enough to the actual details of the Zerubbabel-temple.
7. Cf. Gese, *Verfassungsentwurf*, 109ff.

representative, who has important cultic prerogatives. The contents of this stratum center in sacrificial ordinances and cultic regulations for the congregation and the נשיא. (2) Somewhat younger are the plans for the allotment of the land, the original plan being preserved in 48:1–29. This is related in content to the נשיא-stratum and in fact can be seen as an expansion and supplementation of this first stratum. Whereas the allotment plan in chapter 48 is not aware of the third stratum, the later rendition of the land allotment in 45:1–8a presupposes 44:6ff., the center of the (3) Zadokite-stratum. This stratum—primarily 44:6–16 plus the additions 44:17ff. and 45:13–15—was in no way related to the נשיא-stratum, and the contrasts between the two were never fully smoothed out. The main characteristic is the limitation of the priestly rights to the Zadokites and the degradation of the other priests (Levites) to virtual temple assistants. Regarding the date of the Zadokite-stratum, he sets as the *terminus ante quem* the governorship of Zerubbabel, thus perhaps during the time of Shesh-bazzar. Having specified the three main strata of chapters 43–48, Gese then attempts to explain how all of the parts could have been welded together into the present composition.[8] The tradition in 43:1–11 is constitutive for this composition, and the prime redactional device employed for connecting the materials is the visionary guidance. Gese concludes—like Noth—by asking what *historical consequences* can be drawn from his history of the tradition.[9] Of primary importance here are the office of the נשיא and that of the high priest. Gese assumes that the נשיא in the earliest stratum was a historical figure, a Davidide—perhaps Ostanes, as mentioned in the Elephantine texts. Sheshbazzar and Zerubbabel were the last Davidides with the dignity of a נשיא as well as of a פחה, and after them the office of high priest began steadily to overshadow the office of נשיא. The absence of any mention of the high priest in the Zadokite stratum explains Gese's date for this stratum. Regarding the relationship of Ezek 44:6ff. to the P regulations in Num 18, Gese postulates that some early formulations about two classes of priests began at some point to develop in two different directions and thus produced the varying accounts present in these two texts.

In conclusion we can emphasize that Gese's study evinces a clear, refined concept of tradition history. His analyses tend not to stray from traditio-historical matters, although he does tend to neglect various aspects of *traditio*. We have pointed out a few similarities between his work and that of Noth, especially in its traditio-critical procedure and in the desire to draw historical consequences from his analytical results. Gese's analyses and conclusions have

---

8. Ibid., 114–15. Zimmerli's reconstruction (*Ezechiel* II, 1240ff.) corresponds with Gese's at almost all points.

9. Gese, *Verfassungsentwurf*, 116ff.

met with generally favorable reception, as is evident especially in Zimmerli's thorough, traditio-historically and form-critically oriented commentary of Ezek 40–48.

B. Wolfgang Richter on Judges 3–9

Our second example of contemporary traditio-historical studies deals with a segment from the historical traditions, Judg 3–9.[10] Richter carries out a particularly calculated, sophisticated analysis of these chapters. It is difficult to place his understanding of tradition history and his analytical method in either Noth's or von Rad's direction; he tends to be independent and eclectic in these respects, leaning though perhaps more toward Noth's method. He does not offer a precise, prefatory picture of his conceptions and purposes, but it becomes clear in his study that *he understands tradition history as the stratification of the whole developmental process—whether oral or written—from the earliest beginnings on down to the final gloss*,[11] and in this he concurs with Noth. Richter does not suppose that every Old Testament text is or contains a tradition. The purpose of tradition *criticism* is to establish on the basis of specific criteria whether the text in question contains pregiven elements or traditions. On the basis of these results, the tradition *history* then presents a relative chronology of the various stages, describing the mutual influences among the traditions, the participation of transmitters and the effect of any institutions behind them, and the spiritual and intellectual background of the traditions.[12] Two points are especially noteworthy: Basic to Richter's study is the conviction that *tradition history is possible only through a methodologically consistent analysis of the text*; "Textgebundenheit" is thus a prerequisite for gaining a history of the tradition, that is, for uncovering the prehistory of a specific text and its smaller units.[13] Second, Richter tends to give analytical priority to the formal aspects of tradition, taking the contents into consideration only after the premolded elements and units have been literary-critically

---

10. W. Richter, *Traditionsgeschichtliche Untersuchungen zum Richterbuch*, BBB 18, (1st ed. 1963) 2nd ed., Bonn 1966. Richter's method and intentions are stated more clearly in his methodological program, *Exegese als Literaturwissenschaft*, Göttingen 1971, to which we have made frequent reference in the course of our history of the research.

11. Cf. also Richter, *Exegese als Literaturwissenschaft*, 152–53 n. 4, where he indicates that he now prefers to separate tradition from redaction. His former idea that "tradition history" embraces the whole process is, however, very common, as we have seen above, p. 18 n. 8.

12. Richter, *Exegese als Literaturwissenschaft*, 153ff., especially 164–65.

13. Cf. also ibid., 158; and Richter, *Die sogenannten vorprophetischen Berufungsberichte*, FRLANT 101, Göttingen 1970, 11–12. This corresponds also to Sæbø's position; cf. below, pp. 276–77.

and Gattung-critically determined.[14] Also the question of historicity is of secondary importance to the effort to determine the origin and evolution of the traditions down to their final form in the present text.

Richter's traditio-historical conception and method are obvious in the analytical procedure followed in his study of Judg 3–9. Omitting from discussion the later Deuteronomic and Deuteronomistic redactions,[15] he examines successively the four tradition complexes of the text: Ehud (Judg 3), Deborah-Barak (Judg 4–5), Gideon-Jerubbaal (Judg 6–8), and Abimelech (Judg 9). Each of these complexes is analyzed according to Richter's principle of making a clear delineation between the methodological steps: First a literary criticism on the basis of the standard criteria; secondly a Gattung criticism, including a form analysis followed then by a determination of Gattung and Sitz im Leben. When these steps have been carried out for each of the smallest units and elements, tradition criticism sets in to establish whether the identified Gattungen, formulas, and premolded schemas are indicative of previous traditions. Here in this reductive process he tries to locate signs of tension between traditional elements, any alterations which may have occurred in the course of time, and also the transmitters responsible for each stage. Finally, at the conclusion of his discussion of each of the four tradition complexes, these findings are gathered together and assessed in a concise, chronological sketch of the successive traditio-historical strata from the earliest beginnings on to the final form. These are essentially summaries of the results[16] and appear in each case under the rubric "Traditionsgeschichte" or "Überlieferungsgeschichte."

Richter's refined analytical methods, especially his Gattung criticism, enable him to reach results previously unimagined. On the whole his literary criticism leads him to dispute the two-document hypothesis for Judg 3–9, and in its place he sets a composite picture of *smaller units, tradition strata, a series of schemata and formulas, and an early composition produced by some author*. His tradition history of the Abimelech complex in Judg 9 can serve as a good illustration. Richter uncovers two independent traditions in the chapter: an "Erzählungskranz" in 9:26–40, 46–54 and a fable in 9:9–15. The former contains yet older, premonarchical "Schlachtberichte"; especially 9:26–38 is

---

14. Cf. also *Exegese als Literaturwissenschaft*, 156–57 Barth and Steck (*Exegese des Alten Testaments*, 96) criticize Richter's overemphasis on the linguistic, structural indices at the cost of material, substantial factors.

15. Richter, *Richterbuch*, xiii–xiv. These are treated in his separate study, *Die Bearbeitungen des "Retterbuches" in der deuteronomischen Epoche*, BBB 21, Bonn 1964.

16. Cf. Richter, *Richterbuch*, e.g., 316: "The summary of the results reached in the analysis of each chapter constitutes also its tradition history."

conspicuous as a fragmentarily retained unit depicting with fascination the greatness of Abimelech. These narrative units were collected most likely in the Davidic-Solomonic era, whereas the fable originated later, perhaps in the northern kingdom shortly after the political division. The next stage was that of an author who received the narrative complex and the fable and reworked them into a connected whole with the help of freely composed additions (viz., 9:1–7, 16a, 19b–21, 23–24, 41–45, 56–57). The final stage was a redactional attempt to "Israelitize" the author's work by means of inserting 9:16b–19a, 22, 55. Richter's tradition history here thus offers a simple, plausible explanation of how this chapter came to be. Internal tensions are explained on the basis of the author that joined the older traditions with his own additions in order to make a fluent composition; the two-document hypothesis finds no footing in this chapter and can therefore be rejected.

Reference should be made to one more important result gained in Richter's study. His detailed analyses allow him to reconstruct a *pre-Deuteronomistic literary composition*, which he calls a "Retterbuch" and restricts to Judg 3–9.[17] This was the product of the single author mentioned above, who took the diverse traditional stories, reworked them as he felt necessary, and added numerous sections in order to achieve a literary whole.[18] In composing this work, he employed a geographical framework and, for Judg 6–9, a chronological succession. He was driven especially by the desire to show the ideal nature of the old institutions, primarily that of the chosen deliverer in Jahweh's wars; indirectly he was therefore also attacking the monarchy. In one respect he is more similar to the Deuteronomist than to the Jahwist or Elohist: The accomplishment of his purposes is more important to him than is faithfulness to the traditions. Richter contrasts this with the usual historiography: The type of literature found here in the "Retterbuch" "does not look to the past for its own sake—but to the past in order to address the present on that basis, indeed in order to derive from it criteria and standards for the present."[19] Richter gives good reasons for locating the author in the northern kingdom, probably in the proximity of prophetic circles; the work was quite certainly composed in the second half of the ninth century B.C.E. but prior to the death of Jehu.

In summary: A noteworthy feature of Richter's analyses can be seen in his care to define and limit strictly the method and scope of each of his investiga-

---

17. Ibid., 319–43.
18. We referred to this stage in our review of Richter's tradition history of Judg 9. The sections that Richter attributes to this author are: Judg 3:13, 27–29; 4:4a, 6–9,11, 17b; 6:2b–5, 11b–17, 25–27a, 31bβ, 32, 33–34; 7:1, 9–11a, 22, 23–24, 25–8:3, 4, 10–13, 22–23, 29, 31; 9:1–7, 16a, 19b–21, 23–24, 41–45, 56–57.
19. Richter, *Richterbuch*, 341, also 329.

tive steps. This enables him to keep clear control of his results and to assess them properly. Methodologically, however, he takes perhaps too little consideration of the contents in the earlier stages of his work, concentrating instead on linguistic and form-critical criteria; but on the other hand there is also much to be said for this effort to neutralize all "Denkschemata"—conscious as well as unconscious presuppositions.[20]

The entirety of his analysis aims at drawing up the tradition history of the individual complexes and the whole of Judg 3–9. The stratified pictures of the tradition history which he presents at the conclusion to each complex may sometimes seem incredible for their simplicity, but a careful reading of his foregoing analyses tends to persuade one of their correctness. It can indeed be doubted that we can attain such clear, probable results for most other parts of the Old Testament; but on the other hand the attempt is too seldom made to carry out as complete, calculated, and purposeful an analysis as we find here in Richter's study.

C. Odil Hannes Steck's History of a Notion

Having looked at two contemporary traditio-historical studies, one of prophetic and one of historical literature, we turn now to a third exemplary analysis of a quite different type of subject matter. Odil Hannes Steck (1935–2001) produced in 1967 an exhaustive study of *the notion of the violent fate of the prophets*.[21] Since this notion or conception is obviously not to be equated with a specific, limited text, what is meant by "tradition history" in this connection? We have seen above[22] that Steck proposes to distinguish sharply between "Überlieferungsgeschichte" and "Traditionsgeschichte." The former corresponds more or less to our definition of tradition history and is illustrated by the two studies of Gese and Richter which we have just discussed. According to Steck, "Überlieferungsgeschichte" is the examination

---

20. Richter, *Exegese als Literaturwissenschaft*, 10–17, 28, 174ff.

21. His Heidelberg dissertation: *Israel und das gewaltsame Geschick der Propheten: Untersuchungen zur Überlieferung des deuteronomistischen Geschichtsbildes im Alten Testament, Spätjudentum und Urchristentum*, WMANT 23, Neukirchen-Vluyn 1967. Like Richter, Steck has also produced a methodological manual: Barth/Steck, *Exegese des Alten Testaments. Leitfaden der Methodik*, 2nd ed., Neukirchen-Vluyn 1971. This latter book, to which we referred above in our introduction (chs. 1–2), clarifies Steck's method while also bringing some minor alterations in the methodology and terminology seen in his publication of 1967.

22. Above, pp. 18–19, 23. This distinction is not as clear in Steck's dissertation as in his *Exegese des Alten Testaments*, xi, 3–5, 37ff., 70ff.

of the (primarily oral) prehistory of a *specific text*[23] and comprises two steps: the *analytical* (= traditio-critical) recovery of the preliterary stages of a text all the way back to its earliest form; and the *synthetic* reconstruction of the forward-moving process of the tradition until its first literary fixation, taking into consideration historical influences, the transmitters, and the governing message or intent of the tradition. "Traditionsgeschichte," on the other hand, is the investigation of *individual conceptions or notions* ("Vorstellungen")[24] as well as *tradition streams* ("theologische Strömungen").[25] These indeed find their concrete expression in specific texts, but they thrive actually in certain tradition centers that exist prior to, current with, and posterior to the origin and formation of any individual text in which the given notion may appear. Such a conception or such a tradition stream must be examined to determine its nature, origin, development, transmittal path and location, modifications, and transmitters. *For each of the texts in which the notion appears, this background information can illuminate the specific message in terms of the traditional use.* Pioneers of this type of research were A. Eichhorn and Gunkel[26] for the connection between Israelite and extra-Israelite traditions and Gunkel, Bousset, and Dibelius for the thematic bonds between Old Testament, late Judaic, and early Christian proclamations. This sense of "Traditionsgeschichte," also to be termed "Vorstellungsgeschichte," characterizes Steck's thoroughgoing analysis of the concept of the violent fate of the prophets. It remains only to be noted that Steck uses the term "tradition" to include the aspects of both *traditio* and *traditum*,[27] and each aspect receives its due in his history of the notion in question.

Steck's analytical procedure is oriented toward the task he sets for himself: "to investigate the rise, transmission, and use of the general notion of the violent fate of the prophets as it continued on into primitive and early Christianity."[28] His study presupposes the text criticism, literary criticism,

---

23. Steck's limitation of "Überlieferungsgeschichte" to the oral sphere alone is advocated in his *Exegese des Alten Testaments*. It differs from his (also Richter's) previous view of its embracing as well the literary stage that continues on to the finalization of the text in its present form; cf. Steck, *Überlieferung und Zeitgeschichte in den Elia-Erzählungen*, WMANT 26, Neukirchen-Vluyn 1968, 6 n. 3.

24. Cf. above, pp. 13–14. Steck emphasizes (*Elia-Erzählungen*, 103 n. 3) that these "Vorstellungen" are not to be confused with abstract ideas or isolated motifs.

25. Cf. above, pp. 14–15; also Steck, "Das Problem theologischer Strömungen in nachexilischer Zeit," *EvT* 28 (1968), 445–58.

26. Cf. above, pp. 61–62.

27. *Israel und das gewaltsame Geschick*, 18. However, in his *Exegese des Alten Testaments*, 70–71, Steck chooses to limit "Traditionsgeschichte" to the *traditum*.

28. *Israel und das gewaltsame Geschick*, 18.

form criticism, and redaction criticism of the relevant texts; the results of these analyses are at all points made to serve his investigation of the continuity and modifications of this specific conception throughout its history. After a preliminary examination of difficult references to the violent fate of the prophets in the Synoptic Gospels, the *first main step* is to describe and analyze this notion in its earliest Old Testament form. The defining characteristics of any "Vorstellung" are at this point checked: "fixed linguistic field, characteristic formulatory structure, specific notional contour and ... typical line of assertion (logic of material)."[29] Furthermore he attempts to determine the traditio-historical background of the notion, which he finds to be the tradition of the Deuteronomistic prophetic proclamations. Steck's *second main step* is then to examine the "Gestalt" of this notion many centuries later—in the Josephic, rabbinic, and early Christian literature—for the purpose of seeing whether the notion here of the violent fate of the prophets can be brought into relationship with the established original "Gestalt" of such proclamations. Of decisive importance is a convergence in the "formulatory structure" and "linguistic field." Having determined such a convergence and thus a traditio-historical connection between the Old Testament statements and these later occurrences of the notion (whereby this connection is not due to the immediate literary influence of the Old Testament proclamations), Steck can then in his *third step* turn to an exhaustive analysis of this notion in the interim period, i.e. in late Judaism. For him it is especially important to trace the history of the notion not only as such but especially as a phenomenon anchored in Israelite-Judaic history, in other words, to deal with the Judaic interest in the notion, with its "Sitz im Leben," and with its transmitters. After completing this history the only *remaining task* is to explain and illuminate the reception of the tradition by Hellenistic and Palestinian primitive Christianity. With these steps accomplished, the total history of this specific notion has been traced from its beginnings to the early Christian period.

What are the results of Steck's traditio-historical analyses? It must suffice here to give only a sketch of his history of the tradition and to avoid the details and reasons which he offers at every point. The historically inaccurate statement that Israel's prophets as a whole experienced a violent fate and even death at the hands of their people is to be found not only in early Christianity but in fact also in the Old Testament and Palestinian Judaism, as well as in primitive Christian, rabbinic, and Koranic tradition. This notion is not characterized by a biographical interest in the prophets but rather by a theo-

---

29. Barth/Steck, *Exegese des Alten Testaments*, 74. Cf. also *Israel und das gewaltsame Geschick*, 19, 61ff.

logical persuasion of Israel as the responsible agent of this act. The earliest extant occurrence of this proclamation is in Neh 9:26, part of a penitentiary prayer. This text indicates that the notion of the violent fate of the prophets is actually *an aspect of a larger conceptual whole—the Deuteronomistic picture of history*. To be more precise, the notion of the prophets' fate is a component of a two-part proclamation about the prophets: about their continuous work in preexilic Israel and about the repeated rejection of the prophets by the people of God. This proclamation is one element of the Deuteronomistic picture of history, in which the events of 722 and 587 B.C.E. are interpreted as judgments of God. *The idea of the people's violent treatment of the prophets was thus formed in order to express the people's continuous, fateful resistance to God's will*. Steck is able to describe for this notion a specific "linguistic field" which remains surprisingly constant for centuries thereafter. The notion of the fate of the prophets was not passed on primarily as a literary but as a living tradition, especially during late Judaism. To identify the transmitters and the religious anchorage of this notion, we must see it as one of several components of the Deuteronomistic picture of history. The traditio-historical roots of this latter complex are to be found in the Levitical-prophetic movement of the northern kingdom, and the Levites continued to be the transmitters of the tradition until Seleucid times. The Hasidim then took it over, followed by a Palestinian eschatologically oriented "Umkehrbewegung" in the late Judaism of the first centuries B.C.E. and C.E. From this sphere it was picked up by early Christianity and by the rabbinic tradition. The "Sitz im Leben" of the tradition of this "Geschichtsbild" is to be found in Israel's penitence for its sins offered at various ceremonies and secondly in the preaching of conversion and in the teaching of the law. Only in this total context can the notion of the violent fate of the prophets be understood, not least for the late Judaic and early Christian periods. The notion was used to accentuate Israel's continuous resistance to the law and to God's message through the prophets. Whether Jesus himself employed the concept is uncertain, but it is likely that the Jewish Christians in Palestine were not only familiar with it but also used it in reference to Jesus' violent death. For the Hellenistic Christians, whose missionary efforts the Jews sought to thwart, it was an indication of the permanent stubbornness of the Jews and thus also a reason for the rejection of Israel as God's elected people. After Matt. this notion of the violent fate of the prophets became essentially a motif to be used, isolated from its earlier context, primarily as a parenetic and polemical topos.

Steck's study of this tradition thus succeeds in tracing the complete history from earliest stages on to early Christian use. It is particularly noteworthy how he is able to follow it in its historical, theological, and intellectual contexts. Constancy and modifications of the tradition throughout its history receive special attention. Steck's investigation is one of very few such exhaustive treatments of the history of a specific notion. Its importance rests in the illumination of theological and historical bonds between Israel and later periods, especially Judaism and early Christianity. As such, the extent to which the New Testament sayings stand in direct line with Old Testament proclamations becomes clarified. *Steck has established the feasibility and importance of conducting such a "Traditionsgeschichte," which in turn underscores the need for additional work of this type.*

10
Critical Reaction to Traditio-Historical Research

The insights gained from the above history of research and from our methodological discussion indicate *a plurality of ways in which the traditio-historical method is understood and applied.* There is no basic agreement about its scope: whether the entire history of a given literary piece, or only its predocumentary period, or exclusively its oral stage, or also the history of elements of content (notions, motifs, streams) as well. There is also little unanimity as to whether the traditio-historical method embraces all the other exegetical methods or is only one in a series of several investigative steps. Furthermore, there exists a remarkable variety of ways in which Old Testament scholars attempt to uncover the developmental history of texts—as can be seen especially in the divergent results reached. In comparison with the literary-critical, form-critical, and text-critical methods, the traditio-historical approach lags far behind in terms of refined and generally accepted techniques and criteria. At many points it may even seem that the guiding principle is solely an intuitive conjecturing. With the efforts to define the method by above all Koch, Barth/Steck, and Richter, a certain clarity has been gained, and it can be hoped that further methodological advances are imminent. Only then will tradition historians be able to approach their subject with the confidence of attaining plausible, helpful information about the prehistory of the texts. And when supplemented with the insights gained in the other methodological steps, tradition history will in turn contribute considerably to the overall goals of interpreting the texts and understanding the times that produced them.

Traditio-historical research, in all its pluralism, has not proceeded undisturbed by critical opposition. On the contrary, the type of investigations initiated and carried out especially by German researchers has been exposed to sharp criticisms not only from their own compatriots but, above all, from Anglo-American and Scandinavian scholars. Differentiation at this point is necessary, for many biblical critics (e.g., in North America) have responded positively to the German work and have been strongly influenced by the methods practiced and the results attained so far. But loud protests against these methods and results have been raised, notably by Herrmann, Wright, Bright, Albright, and Engnell. These basic criticisms—we are thus disregarding the disputes over the innumerable individual points—deserve serious consideration here, for *they have at times drawn attention to definite weaknesses and have instigated precise responses, clarifications, and modifications* on the part of the main exponents of the traditio-historical approach. Characteristically, the debate has concentrated more on the Pentateuch than the prophetic traditions and more on Noth than von Rad. This critique can be systematized under the following points.

A. The Dependency of Traditio-Historical Analysis on Other Investigative Procedures

1. The Issue of External Evidence

One criticism that has gained a considerable hearing is raised by the "Albright School," especially W. F. Albright, G. E. Wright, and J. Bright,[1] and directed primarily against Noth's treatment of the ancestral, conquest, and other pentateuchal traditions. In essence, Noth is accused of having carried out an *internal analysis* of these traditions without due consideration of the *external evidence* supplied by years of archaeological and linguistic work on the premonarchic era. This criticism seems on the surface to be of a methodological nature, but closer attention reveals that it is actually conditioned by the fact that the consequences that Noth draws from his traditio-historical analysis diverge sharply from the view that Albright and others consider substantiated by archaeology. At any rate, if we are to do justice to this criticism, we must differentiate between different levels of it. By way of example, on the one hand we find blanket statements about "Noth's complete refusal to make use of archaeological data"[2] and about his "negativistic" and "nihilistic" attitude

---

1. Cf. especially: W. F. Albright, "The Israelite Conquest of Canaan in the Light of Archaeology," *BASOR* 74 (1939), 11–23; Albright, *From the Stone Age to Christianity*, Garden City 1957; J. Bright, *Early Israel in Recent History Writing: A Study in Method*, SBT 19, London 1956; G. E. Wright, "Archaeology and Old Testament Studies," *JBL* 77 (1958), 39–51; and D. N. Freedman, "The Interpretation of Scripture III: On Method in Biblical Studies: The Old Testament," *Int* 17 (1963), 308–18.

2. Wright, *JBL* 77 (1958), 48.

with regard to such data.³ Noth's caustic reaction to these unjust generalizations can be understood.⁴

However, a more pertinent aspect is treated by Bright—the questions of "proof" and "balance of probability."⁵ Bright concedes that archaeology is unable to supply evidence to prove the truth of any single item in the entire hexateuchal tradition. Instead of waiting for irrefragable proof as Noth seems to do, Bright maintains that it is necessary for the historian to weigh the related or divergent indices (from the traditions, culture, geography, inscriptions, history of the Hebrew language) in order to determine the *balance of probability*. An internal analysis of the biblical sources on the basis of criteria of form and Gattung is by itself too narrow and insecure a foundation for Noth, Alt, and others to draw the far-reaching historical consequences which we have seen above, particularly with relation to the ancestors and the conquest of the land. External evidence, Bright declares, is available and must be considered before prematurely drawing conclusions.⁶

Now it is true that Noth's analysis of Genesis–Joshua is primarily internal in character, that his aim is to probe the traditions which constitute the primary source of information about the premonarchic period.⁷ The main point of controversy, however, is *the value of archaeological data* and the extent to which these can contribute to our attempts to reconstruct the history of this period. That Noth had a thorough knowledge of the land of Israel and of the various archaeological finds prior to the writing of his *ÜSt* and *ÜPent* is not to be contested.⁸ However, he was *not convinced that the results of archaeology required a different picture of Israel's early history* than that which can be gained from a literary and traditio-historical examination of the Old Testament textual heritage remaining from those times. Such was Noth's opinion at

---

3. E.g., Albright, *BASOR* 74 (1939), 12; and Bright, *Early Israel*, 31.
4. Noth, "Der Beitrag der Archäologie zur Geschichte Israels," VTSup 7 (1960), 263 n. 1, 272 n. 2.
5. Bright, *Early Israel*, 87–89.
6. This position of Bright, Albright, and others is well summarized and treated by M. Weippert, *Die Landnahme der israelitischen Stämme in der neueren wissenschaftlichen Diskussion: Ein kritischer Bericht*, FRLANT 92, Göttingen 1967, especially 51–59, 123ff.
7. This is pointed out also by B. W. Anderson, "Martin Noth's Traditio-Historical Approach," xxii–xxiii.
8. This is recognized also by Albright, *BASOR* 74 (1939), 12; and Bright, *Early Israel*, 31. According to personal information obtained from Prof. Rudolf Smend, Jr., Noth made three trips to Palestine before 1933, first in 1925 with Alt, each time remaining there several months. Moreover, he read continuously and eagerly the various archaeological reports, so his knowledge of archaeological data ranked perhaps second only to Alt's among German scholars. This familiarity with the land and with archaeology is especially evident in Noth's commentary on Joshua (HAT 1938).

the outset of the debate[9] as well as two decades later[10] in response to Wright and Bright. In Noth's own words, "what is scientifically at stake is not whether we use 'external evidence' but whether we have 'external evidence.'"[11] When considered closely, archaeological data may be of little or no help in dating, describing, and classifying the ancestors historically. With regard to the conquest, archaeological evidence also fails to support the biblical account; if anything, these nonuniform finds seem to confirm the complicated picture that traditio-historical analysis draws of the gradual settlement and federation of the tribes.[12] Simply because of the inability of archaeology to produce an incontestable total picture of a historical process and because of the possibility of divergent interpretations of the scattered data, Noth maintains that a literary and traditio-historical analysis, enhanced and supplemented by archaeological insights, is essential.[13]

What important residue remains from this debate on the usefulness of external evidence? The danger of polarization, nurtured by polemicism, has been close at hand since the outset of this controversy.[14] However, if the prime question is whether or not "external evidence" should be employed, then there does not appear to be much difference among the scholars in question, for each one of them advocates the need to use all means and methods

---

9. Noth, "Grundsätzliches zur geschichtlichen Deutung archäologischer Befunde auf dem Boden Palästinas," *PJ* 34 (1938), 7–22.

10. Noth, VTSup 7 (1960), 262–82; Noth, "As One Historian to Another," *Int* 15 (1961), 63ff.; and Noth, "Hat die Bibel doch recht?," *Festschrift für Günther Dehn*, ed. W. Schneemelcher, Neukirchen Kreis Moers 1957, 7–22.

11. Noth, VTSup 7 (1960), 271 n. 1.

12. Ibid., 265–78; also above, pp. 73, 127–30.

13. Noth, VTSup 7 (1960), 278: "Since the results of archaeology are dealing at any given time with individual historical incidents which have left behind visible tracks, it is requisite to determine with great precision what a tradition, to which reference may be made, really asserts and can assert and what it does not assert and cannot assert. Traditio-historical research in the area of the Old Testament is indeed also involved in the archaeological enterprise of unlocking the ancient Orient to us today. It is constantly nourished by the increasing insight into the diversity and reality of ancient Oriental life, as it has been demonstrated so graphically by the discovery of archaeological fragments that go beyond the merely literary remains."

14. The immaterial, inaccurate, but frequent accusations of "nihilism" and "negativism," as expressed often by Albright, Wright, and Bright, deserve the sound refutation that Noth gave them (VTSup 7, 1960, 263, n. 1.). However, Noth has also been guilty of repaying in like coinage, e.g., his accusation that Bright's motto is "External evidence at any price" (Noth, *Int* 15, 1961, 64). Noth's suspicion that many American scholars often use archaeological data for apologetic purposes is perhaps not wholly unfounded; cf. also M. Smith, "The Present State of Old Testament Studies," *JBL* 88 (1969), 30ff.

available for investigating past history.[15] It also seems advisable to conduct the methodological steps one after another, and perhaps even respectively by different scholars.[16] The issue is therefore not one of correlation of the content of a tradition with archaeological and linguistic evidence, but rather of criticism—in the sense of *careful differentiation between all data available, "internal" and "external," and a relentless examination of each individual item before conclusions are drawn*.[17] And for the benefit of research, the present state of the discussion in the numerous areas is in need of an objective, assiduous appraisal. Weippert has attempted it for the debate on the conquest of Palestine;[18] a similar effort to evaluate the past work and ideas regarding the patriarchal age, especially in consideration of the internal and external data, would now be helpful.[19] Weippert's conclusion regarding the conquest[20] may well prove even more applicable to the ancestral period: *the literary, formal, and traditio-historical criticism of the Old Testament accounts is indispensable because it provides us with the greatest connected insights into some of the historical and traditional processes in question.*

2. Traditio-Historical Criteria and the Question of Historicity

The above argument about the need for external evidence to supplement internal analyses implies the incapability of traditio-historical work alone to

---

15. Cf., e.g., Noth, VTSup (1960), 262–63; Wright, *JBL* 77 (1958), 51; Bright, *Early Israel*, 123; Anderson, "Martin Noth's Traditio-Historical Approach," xxx.

16. Cf. also Smith, *JBL* 88 (1969), 34.

17. Noth, VTSup 7 (1960), 262, 272.

18. Weippert, *Landnahme*, 1967.

19. Weidmann's useful survey of the ancestral studies since Wellhausen generally disregards this side of the question, dismissing it in fact categorically: "'Extrabiblical finds,' which could help us out of our deficient knowledge about Israel's beginnings, are not in our possession" (*Patriarchen*, 173). This general statement hardly does justice to the considerable efforts of some to find extrabiblical evidence for this period. Weidmann, however, is optimistic about the possibilities of traditio-historical research in this area: "The consistently applied traditio-historical method is indeed the only method that enables us to derive historical information from the ancient Israelite traditions. But it always involves a calculation of probability with several unknowns that must be considered at the same time. Consequently, the 'results' reached with the traditio-historical method can, as a rule, only be hypotheses with greater or lesser probability" (ibid.). [Note: Coincidentally, at roughly the same time as the present study was written, i.e., in the early 1970s, two other investigations were in process that specifically addressed issues regarding the ancestral period and traditions: Thomas L. Thompson, *The Historicity of the Patriarchal Narratives: The Quest for the Historical Abraham*, BZAW 133 (Berlin: de Gruyter, 1974); and John Van Seters, *Abraham in History and Tradition* (New Haven: Yale University Press, 1975).]

20. Weippert, *Landnahme*, 132.

provide us with a fairly conclusive, reliable reconstruction of historical happenings. This fundamental accusation has been raised especially by Albright, Bright, and Herrmann. The latter challenges generally the legitimacy of allowing traditio-historical analysis to pass judgment on historical events, especially when the history of the tradition becomes in effect substituted for history proper.[21] Going into specifics, Albright attacks Alt's and Noth's use of form-critical and traditio-historical criteria, Albright's point being that "the ultimate historicity of a given datum is never conclusively established or disproved by the literary framework in which it is imbedded."[22] It does not do, he continues, to suspect automatically the historical accuracy of any tradition with an etiological element (e.g., in Josh 2ff.), for such etiological explanations could just as conceivably have originated as a mnemonic and didactic aid for a genuine historical tradition already in existence.[23] Also the matter of "Ortsgebundenheit" is inconclusive since traditions connected with places are often known to "wander."[24] Bright[25] has continued the attack on these criteria, calling into question the validity and accuracy of histories of tradition which are founded primarily on these analytical principles. Wright[26] is also critical of efforts to align the contents of a tradition too closely with its form. He maintains that the classification of the form does not by itself cast doubts on the historicity of the contents; external checkpoints are necessary for settling the issue of historical background and origin.

Noth, in his subsequent response to Albright's, Bright's, and Wright's criticisms at these points,[27] takes a noticeably more careful position with regard to etiologies. He admits the basic relationship of etiological narratives to history and maintains that it is the task of the historian and critic to attempt to decide, on the basis of literary and other factors, whether this relationship is

---

21. Herrmann, "Mose," *EvT* 28 (1968), 302–3, 324–25.
22. Albright, *BASOR* 74 (1939), 12.
23. Ibid., 13: "It is, therefore, *a priori* impossible to say whether a given 'aetiological' statement is based on authentic tradition or is the result of a combination *ad hoc*. Only when there is definite external evidence can we be sure of our ground."
24. Ibid., 14ff., with examples.
25. *Early Israel*, 91ff.
26. *JBL* 77 (1958), 50–51.
27. Noth, VTSup 7 (1960), 278–82. Mowinckel, in an excursus on this debate over etiologies (*Tetrateuch—Pentateuch—Hexateuch*, BZAW 90, Berlin 1964, 78–86), aligns himself unequivocally with the position of Noth and Alt (as well as Gunkel and Gressmann) against Albright. Referring to an ancient mode of thinking which he terms "etiological thinking," Mowinckel warns especially against postulating the historical accuracy of the nuclei of etiologies (as Albright does)—and more than this, against assuming an intimate relationship between history and etiology on the whole.

original or not. Weippert[28] is of roughly the same opinion, though he treats the arguments of Albright and Bright too lightly. For us it is necessary to recognize that *this question about how a given etiology may be related to history cannot be answered singularly for all cases, and furthermore that this etiological element must not be overrated as a traditio-critical criterion for distinguishing between earlier and later traditions.*[29] This much needs to be conceded to Albright and Bright. The discussion has been complicated also by a difference of opinion regarding the marks of an etiological story. Notably Childs[30] has demonstrated persuasively that the formula "until this day," which Alt and Noth regard as a clear indication of the etiological form, appears in the Old Testament for the most as a later redactional commentary on existing traditions. The study by Burke Long[31] of certain "etiological motifs" has helped to clarify formal problems. But the course of the discussion leads one to conclude that the critic will need to be careful and circumspect in appealing to etiological elements for drawing traditio-historical conclusions. The matter of etiology and "Ortsgebundenheit" constitutes, though, only one of several traditio-historical criteria, and it need hardly be said that the various criteria and indications of earlier or later stages in the traditions should at best mutually reinforce or complement one another.[32]

But with these qualifications about the limitations of traditio-historical criteria, the matter of historicity is not settled. A further consideration of importance is that *we must avoid misusing traditio-historical as well as "external" criteria in the drive to establish the historicity of reported events.* Two prevalent tactics thus need to be abandoned: (a) the effort to show that the *"essential truth"* of narratives (e.g., of ancestral legends) can be "confirmed" by external (especially archaeological) evidence;[33] and (b) the conservative tendency to use tradition history for the purpose of *early dating* of contents

---

28. *Landnahme*, 134–39.

29. Cf. also Richter, *Exegese als Literaturwissenschaft*, 155–56, and the literature mentioned there; also F. Golka, "Zur Erforschung der Ätiologien im Alten Testament," *VT* 20 (1970), 90–98.

30. B. S. Childs, "A Study of the Formula 'Until this Day,'" *JBL* 82 (1963), 279–92. Note also Smend's important thesis about "the role of etiology as a main motif for Israel's historical thinking in all its stages"; Smend, *Elemente alttestamentlichen Geschichtsdenkens*, ThSt 95, Zurich 1968, quotation from 18.

31. B. O. Long, *The Problem of Etiological Narrative in the Old Testament*, BZAW 108, Berlin 1968. Especially significant in this regard is Westermann's discussion in his "Arten der Erzählung in der Genesis," *Forschung am Alten Testament*, TB 24, Munich 1964, 39–47.

32. This has already been emphasized above, p. 115, with regard to Noth's analytical procedure in *ÜPent*.

33. Cf. M. Smith, *JBL* 88 (1969), 28–32.

and for seeking to establish a centuries-long continuity of thought and belief in successive, connected tradition circles.[34] Both of these tactics can often be seen in the debate we have reviewed, and neither side seems to have been aware of these basic faults. Childs, though, in a perceptive monograph on memory and tradition,[35] addresses himself directly to this misuse of the idea of historicity. He criticizes especially Albright's position at two points: His prime interest in *bruta facta* minimizes the centrality of the interpretation of the events and thus distorts the essence of history; and secondly, Israel's redemptive history cannot be reduced to a series of scientifically verifiable, historical data to which religious interpretations have been added. "The point at issue is whether historical research has as its function to illumine the *interpreted* event, or to attempt to play the so-called 'objective' event against its interpretation."[36] This is essentially the issue between von Rad and Hesse.[37] The conclusion should be obvious: *It is wisest to avoid making "historicity" the central concern in our analyses, for this is inevitably done at the expense of Israel's interpretation of the "original" event. And it is this interpretational process that is the proper subject matter of traditio-historical research.*

B. The Question of Traditio-Historical Overkill

One criticism heard and read quite frequently is that the enthusiasm of discovery has too often caused tradition historians to lose sight of the boundaries of their methods and to draw conclusions that are artificial, subjective, and unconvincing.[38] This accusation, often made quite generally and vaguely, is implied in the characterization of traditio-historical research as "nihilistic."[39] Such a nonspecific, diffuse criticism about excessiveness contributes little to the discussion since it only attacks the general nature and results of the research without dealing with concrete problems of methodology. However, two specific aspects of this criticism deserve closer attention.

1. Overextension of the Method

The essence of the first is that the traditio-historical task and method are in themselves legitimate and necessary but that certain tradition historians over-

---

34. Ibid., 28–29; von Rad, *VF* 1947/48 (1949/50), 175; Smend, *VF* 1960/62 (1963/65), 36.
35. Childs, *Memory and Tradition in Israel*, SBT 37, London 1962.
36. Ibid., 86.
37. Cf. above, pp. 101–2.
38. This criticism is first found in Albright, *BASOR* 74 (1939), 12; cf. also, Wright, *JBL* 77 (1958), 47–51.
39. Cf. above, pp. 148–49; and in response, Noth, VTSup 7 (1960), 263.

estimate this method and fail to see that it is inherently limited in being able to uncover fully reliable historical data. Like the previously discussed criticisms, this is usually directed *in concreto* against Noth, though also against von Rad. Thus Bright asserts: "though Noth's work is a masterpiece of logical erudition and contains much of lasting value, one feels that it exceeds the objective data and presses form-critical methods beyond their rightful limits.... It raises the question if, just as literary criticism reached limits of nicety beyond which it could not go without subjectivism, similar limits do not impose themselves an the tracing of the history of tradition in its predocumentary form."[40] This analogy with past literary-critical excesses in finding sources is meant as an ominous warning.

The point is made with particular force in Herrmann's provocative appraisal of traditio-historical research in general and of Noth's treatment of Moses in particular.[41] He also does not challenge the legitimacy of this research per se but rather the tendency to overestimate its possibilities.[42] According to him, this takes its most dangerous form in a "granting of autonomy to tradition history." Thus the traditio-historical method develops an inner logic which allows hypotheses to be confirmed and used as self-evident stepping-stones for making further conjectures, which assume the garb of "conclusions"; an example is the heuristic function of Noth's isolation of the five pentateuchal themes—actually a working-hypothesis and nothing more.[43] When tradition history makes itself autonomous like this, it loses contact with the relations of history itself and tends even to substitute its own historical outline for history proper.[44] In Herrmann's own words: "It is inevitable that these logically consistent text analyses were and are unable finally to advance historical scholarship. Rather, in their emphasis on form-critical kerygmatic structures they went almost to the extreme of a philosophy of history, with an independent theologoumenon developed out of the relation between tradition and history."[45] Herrmann suggests a way out of this *circulus vitiosus*: The tradition historian should assume the basic reliability of the

---

40. Bright, "Modern Study of Old Testament Literature," in *The Bible and the Ancient Near East* (W. F. Albright Festschrift), ed. G. E. Wright, 25; cf. also Bright, *Early Israel*, 80–83.

41. Herrmann, "Mose," *EvT* 28 (1968), 301–28.

42. Cf. ibid., especially 302ff. and 320–28, where more details are provided for the arguments presented here in condensed form.

43. Wright, *JBL* 77 (1958), 51, touched on this criticism earlier: "To use such liturgical separation of themes as proof of the historical separation of the traditions goes far beyond the evidence which the method of research used permits."

44. This same point is made also by Anderson, "Martin Noth's Traditio-Historical Approach," xxviii.

45. Herrmann, *EvT* 28 (1968), 323.

essential historical outline offered in, for example, the Pentateuch. His task is then to determine "that and to what extent, starting from the fundamentals of the tradition, there occurred in the course of time a considerable reflecting on details, with these then being incorporated in the Pentateuch."[46] In this way traditio-historical work can avoid becoming a subjective enterprise of hypothesizing at will; it can be held in limits because it begins with a serious consideration of the probability that the historical sequence reported in the traditions really is accurate.

It should at once be obvious that Herrmann raises issues and problems here that are of crucial importance. He addresses himself to the fundament of previous tradition criticism and challenges the very validity and effectiveness of the direction of work taken by especially Noth, one of the founders and chief representatives of traditio-historical research. Herrmann's alternative is a viable option which can hardly be easily dismissed; indeed it may in some ways even be preferable to Noth's. Three points, however, need to be made by way of qualification: (a) Herrmann is surely correct in accusing Noth of a certain arbitrariness in deciding what is "primary" and what is "secondary." But he goes too far in doubting whether such a distinction can or even need be made.[47] In effect Herrmann's position corresponds to Birkeland's and Engnell's reluctance to stratify the prophetic traditions, their reason being that the materials passed through the "Schmelzofen der Gemeinschaft."[48] Be this true for the prophetic traditions, it seems nonetheless certain that Israel's historical traditions, affected as they were by cultic, political, and social factors, experienced a pattern of successive growth which can be detected. It is fully legitimate and necessary for the critical historian to develop means for distinguishing between these earlier and later elements. And this implies *the need to examine the sources for their reliability and credibility*—a task to which Herrmann attributes only secondary importance[49] and yet which is a mandatory, indispensable aspect of all history writing—especially when, as in the case of the Old Testament, the sources are the consequence of repeated reinterpretations by a people concerned religiously and existentially with its past. (b) In his polemics against Noth, Herrmann is guilty of distinguishing too radically between history and tradition history. He portrays it at times even as an oppositional relationship with which one must reckon in a methodological program.[50] *This putative con-*

---

46. Ibid., 327–28. Cf. also Kraus, *Geschichte*, 491–93.
47. Herrmann, *EvT* 28 (1968), 324ff.
48. Cf. below, p. 184.
49. Herrmann, *EvT* 28 (1968), 323.
50. Cf. ibid., e.g., 327: "... the tradition preserves its credibility also in those places where supposedly traditio-historical grounds contest historical truth."

trariness, however, gives a contorted picture of a delicate balance between the two entities.[51] Traditio-historical investigation serves in its critical analyses the interests of historical science. "The historical reality was only a *singular entity*; it is our task to research it with all means available to us."[52] The legitimate and plausible insights and conclusions of tradition history must be incorporated in—not played off against—the total historical reconstruction of the period in question. (c) Herrmann objects to a premature drawing of conclusions, i.e. before all methodological steps have been carried out and all factors considered.[53] Here Herrmann touches again on a central point but gives a somewhat misleading picture of it. To be sure, a specific method should not be overtaxed, made to carry the whole weight in the total effort of history writing. But on the other hand, *it is incumbent upon the researcher to make concrete decisions on the basis of the data examined at each of the methodological steps along the way*.[54] From these decisions consequences will be drawn for use and testing in subsequent investigative stages. This tactic taken by Noth and others is thus fully legitimate, though Herrmann is also correct in emphasizing that provisional results must not be overrated until all the evidence has been duly weighed.

2. IMPLAUSIBILITY OF THE RESULTS

This accusation that the traditio-historical method has been overestimated has a corollary: the complaint that the results of the analysis are extreme, radical, and incredible. The essence of this reproach is that *the results themselves refute the method and the criteria*. Thus Bright poses the question which he then answers in the negative: "even if this method be used with caution, is it in any event possible on the basis of present knowledge to write a 'History of Tradition' on the scale, and with the exactitude, that Noth attempts?"[55] It is very doubtful, so the argument goes, whether we can attain to such details and to such precise stratifications of the traditions as are presented in many traditio-historical studies, such as Noth's *ÜPent* or even Sæbø's work on Deu-

---

51. Cf. above, p. 102.
52. Noth, VTSup 7 (1960), 263–64.
53. Herrmann, *EvT* 28 (1968), 302–3: "In full appreciation of scholarly premises, however, the question might be raised whether at any point along the path of the research method it is not possible to reach conclusions that are indeed compelling based on the logical consistency of an applied method but that are in conflict with other factors of both literary and historical potency and that thus become false conclusions when the method is ranked higher than the small circle of what is really probable and persuasive."
54. Cf. also Richter, *Exegese als Literaturwissenschaft*, 38–39.
55. Bright, *Early Israel*, 104, in italics.

tero-Zechariah.[56] Even if such conclusions seem to follow logically from the critical analyses, it is better to exhibit a basic carefulness, wariness, and reticence than to engage in excessive hypothesizing.

Like most of the other criticisms discussed above there is indeed something important and truthful in this. Tradition historians will have to concede this much and so avoid the tendency to provide every question with an answer. To be sure, Noth himself gave precedence to the questions over the answers, and he recognized the basic hypothetical nature of his analytical results;[57] yet one receives the impression from the details of his studies (especially in *ÜPent*) that he seemed to forget this in his eagerness to construct his system. But a complete, detailed history of tradition is in most every case not possible at the present state of the research—if ever. Furthermore, the frequent tendency to postulate all types of traditio-historical connections, tradition streams, and theological orientations must be done with more restraint in the future. *The term "traditio-historical" must not be used to glorify guesses.*

But there is another side to the matter of historical plausibility. Noth's treatment of Moses' place in the pentateuchal tradition has become the example *par excellence* of excessive, implausible, "nihilistic" traditio-historical conclusions. However, precisely at this point Noth did not feel that he was being radical—but *careful*.[58] He sought only to attain solid ground and reliable reference points, and he felt that these could be found solely in the traditions about Moses' foreign marriage and his grave.[59] He was of the opinion that *this tactic of gaining the certain minimum is far preferable to assuming too much*.[60] This principle is also a rule of thumb that must not be sacrificed to the subjective criterion of plausibility. Yet having gained this critical minimum, any edifice constructed on this basis—whether with traditio-historical means (like Noth's) or through historical assumptions and archaeological support (like Bright's)—will be exposed to scrutiny by others. Whether either structure is found to be acceptable or objectionable—in a word: plausible—is usually a question of one's own presuppositions and starting points.

---

56. Cf. below, pp. 276–86.
57. Cf. Noth, *ÜPent*, v, 4; also Smend, "Nachruf auf Martin Noth," in Noth's *Ges. Stud.* II, 165.
58. So according to personal information from Prof. Rudolf Smend, Jr.
59. Cf. above, p. 116.
60. Noth (*Int* 15, 1961, 63) accuses Bright, for example, of stretching the evidence too far in his attempt to date the patriarchs.

C. The Need for a Basic Trust in the Traditional Outline of History

We have mentioned often above that the "Albright School," followed also by Herrmann, attributes a basic historical skepticism to Noth, von Rad, and their followers. This skepticism consists supposedly of the basic "assumption that the biblical pattern is automatically wrong and that the first principle of operation is to discard it for something else."[61] The alternative approach to this "negative" treatment of the biblical sources takes its starting point in *the willingness to grant the basic authenticity of the texts (and traditions) until historical and archaeological study shows them to be suspect*. We have already described above Herrmann's suggestion somewhat similar to this. According to this "respectful approach" (not in a theological or reverential sense, but rather in a scholarly sense), the biblical scholar can safely trust the traditional outline of history because of a premonarchic phenomenon described variously as an "actual historical memory,"[62] a "genuine historical recollection,"[63] or an "Urerinnerung."[64] Only in this way can we find an adequate explanation for the origin of Israel and its faith—a noticeable weakness in Noth's reconstruction.[65] As Cross explains it, "the thrust of historical events, recognized as crucial and ultimately meaningful, alone had the power to displace the mythic pattern.... While it is true, obviously, that all elements of later twelve-tribe Israel did not engage in these epic events, but came to share them as historical memories through the 'actualizing' of them in the covenantal cultus, it also must be insisted that the pattern—Exodus from Egypt, Covenant at Sinai, Conquest of Canaan—is prior, cultically and historically, to the several elements in the pattern or Gestalt."[66] The task for the tradition historian would thus be "to begin with the biblical pattern, not uncritically but not unsympa-

---

61. Freedman, *Int* 17 (1963), 313. This characterization and also the accusation of skepticism, nihilism, and negativism are misleading and unjust. Noth and his followers do not approach the sources with an automatic, basic skepticism or doubt. Rather, they are concerned with suspending judgment until the investigation has been completed, *refusing to presuppose precisely that which has to be proved*. This approach may in its end effect appear to be skeptical, but it should be clear that an objective weighing of the possibilities is the only legitimate method viable for the historian. This is especially applicable for the Old (and New) Testament, which is not history writing in the scientific sense but rather the product of a community with vested (religious and national) interests in its past.

62. F. M. Cross, Jr., "The Divine Warrior in Israel's Early Cult," *Biblical Motifs: Origins and Transformations*, ed. A. Altmann, Cambridge, Mass., 1966, 16.

63. Bright, *Early Israel*, 122.

64. Herrmann, *EvT* 28 (1968), 326.

65. So Bright, *Early Israel*, 84.

66. Cross, "The Divine Warrior," 16–17.

thetically, either."⁶⁷ Without immediately suggesting another hypothesis he must test the biblical picture of the historical process and then correct, adapt, and if necessary discard any parts of it, as the total evidence dictates. In addition to this the tradition historian will want to examine the traces of Israel's reflecting on these "fundamentals of the tradition."⁶⁸

We are faced here, of course, with two fundamentally different approaches to the sources, and it is certainly unwise to try to force a compromise between them. In view of the fact that the debate between the two positions has often enough brought agreement or at least correction and modification at one point or the other, we are probably best advised—in the interests of on-going scholarship—to recognize these basic differences and to encourage the further effort to attain advancement on individual matters by means of stimulation, critique, and combination.⁶⁹ With time it may become obvious which basic position seems the most justified and which set of hypotheses answers the most questions and explains the phenomena the most adequately. But this much should be certain: *The traditio-historical approach in itself necessitates neither the one nor the other position.* It is for each individual tradition historian to decide for himself whether the given historical framework can be accepted (so Herrmann, Cross, Bright, *et al.*) or whether the evidence makes it more probable that even the Israelite picture of history is a product of the long process of tradition growth and interpretation (so Noth, von Rad).

D. The Necessity of Avoiding Modern Cultural Presuppositions

A final basic, general criticism of especially German traditio-historical research has cone from the ranks of Scandinavian scholars; since we will have occasion in the following sections to treat this in more detail, it can suffice to refer to it very briefly here. Especially Pedersen and Engnell, but others as well, have accused German scholars of approaching Old Testament texts and traditions with a Western cultural point of view. The result is then an underestimation of the important role of oral means in Israel during the formation and transmission of historical, legendary, and prophetic traditions. Although Gunkel and his successors recognized this phenomenon of oral tradition, they could not free themselves from an anachronistic "bookish view" of the ancient Near East. Thus—so Pedersen and Engnell argued—these scholars did not abandon the strong literary-critical approach of Wellhausen but chose

---

67. Freedman, *Int* 17 (1963), 315.
68. Herrmann, *EvT* 28 (1968), 328–29.
69. Cf. also Noth, VTSup 7 (1960), 263; and Rast, *Tradition History and the Old Testament*, 31–32.

instead to try to incorporate literary criticism into their traditio-historical analyses—a combination which is doomed to failure and frustration. The alternative is for the tradition historian to break radically with the literary-critical method and to adopt an analytic as well as synthetic method which aims at viewing the Old Testament as a product of its Near Eastern environment, yet with its own distinctiveness, and which assesses properly the range and reliability of oral tradition and its effect on the ultimate text of the Old Testament.[70]

It will become clear below that this criticism is part of a general attempt among certain Scandinavian scholars to replace the German critical approach with one of their own making. Quite obviously this position in its earlier, often extreme and even absolutistic form is not defensible, but we must not overlook the fact that these views have been submitted to considerable modification and even rejection among the Scandinavians themselves. For example, literary criticism is no longer identified with excessive source criticism but is now accepted as a legitimate means for determining the unity or the composite character of a given text. On the whole, the Scandinavians' insistence on the importance of oral tradition and their reminder that biblical scholars and historians must avoid approaching the Old Testament with set "anachronistic" convictions constitute important contributions to the discussion and have generally had a positive effect on non-Scandinavian traditio-historical work.

E. Summary

By way of conclusion we can observe that there has been no general rejection of the traditio-historical method per se. The common opinion is that scholarship should avail itself of these devised techniques for probing the prehistory of the Old Testament texts and that this research can bring worthwhile dividends for exegesis, historiography, and theology. The criticisms that have been expressed are directed primarily at the subjectivity and the presuppositions of individual tradition historians, and this more for the work on the historical literature than for the studies of the prophetic and other traditions. The efforts to correct, modify, and supplement the established analytical procedures have promoted methodological clarity—despite the frequently polemical, at times even hostile manner in which the complaints have been registered. It is not to be denied that traditio-historical research has opened new horizons and that biblical studies have benefited from the improvements and refinements

---

70. Cf., e.g., I. Engnell, "Methodological Aspects of Old Testament Study," VTSup 7 (1960), 21ff.

urged on the practitioners of this method. But the unfortunate fact remains that this field (unlike literary criticism and even form criticism) lacks distinct, commonly accepted criteria and analytical procedures. This absence is perhaps inevitable since traditio-historical research deals with a sphere in which essentially only hypotheses and conjectures can thrive. The failure to reach unanimity at most points of method, to say nothing of the investigative results, is therefore hardly surprising.

PART 2

THE SCANDINAVIAN DEBATE ON TRADITIO-HISTORICAL PROBLEMS

Preliminary Remarks

A noteworthy phenomenon of Old Testament research during the twentieth century is the important role that Scandinavian scholars played and the directions their studies have taken. Such is the case above all in the area of traditio-historical work, for a substantial number of these researchers have repeatedly addressed themselves to its problems and have sought to apply its method to the literature of the Old Testament. The result has been the development of an approach which at many points is different from that which characterizes especially German research. It must not be supposed, however, that there has been total or even general agreement among all of the Scandinavians involved in these studies—no more than could be said for their colleagues in other lands. Thus several of the researchers have at times defended a rather distinctive "hard line" (e.g., Nyberg, Engnell, Kapelrud, Nielsen, Carlson), others have taken up a position quite critical to this (Widengren, Bentzen), and yet others have opted for a place somewhere in the middle where they could choose what they felt to be best in Scandinavian, Continental, and Anglo-American camps (Mowinckel, Ringgren). It must also be noted that over time there has definitely been less of a tendency among Scandinavian scholars to see themselves in a position opposed to that held commonly by non-Scandinavian tradition historians. Indeed there are now several publications (e.g., Sæbø's) which one could just as well suppose to have been produced by, for example, a German scholar.

For our purposes there is validity in isolating and reviewing separately the traditio-historical work carried out by the Scandinavians. One often finds a tendency among many researchers elsewhere to consider Scandinavian Old Testament studies as a homogeneous lot, to be quick to attack this work or simply to disregard it *en bloc*, and even to categorize it as "extreme" and thus to dismiss it uncritically. A careful look at the history of Scandinavian research reveals how unjust such treatments really are. Not only have substantial contributions come from Northern Europe, but it can also be shown that the picture of these scholars as members of a uniform, monolithic school is in fact a caricature.

However, we must not obscure the fact that much of this research varies decidedly—admittedly more in its earlier than in its later stages—from that reviewed above in part 1. To be more specific, this difference is seen most clearly in the *presuppositions* and the *methodology* of the Scandinavian tradition historians. Whereas the question of methodology will crop up frequently in the following history of the research, it would be advisable for us here to attempt to get a clear picture of the points of departure and the recurring themes which characterize to a greater or lesser degree the work of these Old Testament scholars—and which in many cases even appear to be unassailable presuppositions basic to their research. The following are generally seen to be *the primary characteristics* (in each case the originator and/or main proponent[s] are identified): (1) the necessity, established by Pedersen, to regard and research *the cultural history of Israel for its own sake*—indeed in light of its environment, and yet removed from the nonrealistic conceptions traditionally invested in it by the Christian church; for traditio-historical research the consequence of this is that the traditions must be seen against the backdrop of their actual historical milieu; (2) the stress on *the psychological characteristics* and the mental history of the Israelite people (this factor also due especially to the contributions of Pedersen), e.g., the question of the role of ecstasy among the prophets (Mowinckel); (3) an emphasis on the central, positive influence of *the cult as creative drama and the important role of both king and prophet* in the cultic activities (Grønbech, Mowinckel, and the "Myth and Ritual School"); the cult can thus be seen as the Sitz im Leben for the development and transmission of many traditions; (4) the religio-historical idea of *divine or sacral kingship* (Mowinckel, Engnell) and the substitution of the *"high-god" theory* for the usual evolutionistic interpretation of the history of religion (Söderblom, Engnell); these ideas provide the sources for the content and character of numerous traditions and motifs; (5) a high regard for *the reliability of tradition*[1] (Pedersen, Nyberg); (6) the stressing of *oral transmission* as the predominant means used in the formation and preservation of the majority of Old Testament traditions (Nyberg, Engnell, though with roots reaching back to Gunkel, Mowinckel, and others); (7) an *"antievolutionism"* in religio-historical, ideological, and traditionary questions, combined with a denunciation of any examination of Old Testament traditions which amounts to an *interpretatio europeica moderna* (Pedersen, Engnell); and (8) an *abandonment of minute literary criticism* (Pedersen). Especially the last four of these characteristics have become central elements of much of the

---

1. For Nyberg, Engnell, and others a corollary of this principle is the strong preference of the Masoretic text over the LXX and other versions.

Scandinavian traditio-historical research, as will become clear in the survey that follows.

Although many of the important articles and books written by the Scandinavian researchers have appeared in the English, German, or French languages, a sizable number of definitely significant publications have never been translated out of the original Norwegian, Swedish, or Danish. Consequently this literature has remained inaccessible—except on a second-hand basis[2]—to the vast majority of Old Testament scholars. The purpose of the following survey is to present as comprehensively as possible *the major developmental lines of the Scandinavian research into the history of Israelite tradition*, quoting liberally (usually in translation) from literature not available to most non-Scandinavians and yet trying to avoid duplication of the relevant materials reviewed elsewhere. Our aim here therefore varies somewhat from that of part 1, in which we sought to sketch the rise of the consciousness of traditio-historical problems and the development of a method to deal with them. In the section below we are more interested in describing the course of a debate which has focused on a few specific points. This debate is best reviewed chronologically rather than thematically, for it is necessary to show that significant development has occurred at many points, positions were altered or modified with time, and more extreme ideas were eventually abandoned. All of this will be depicted in the following, and the work of certain scholars (especially Mowinckel, Nyberg, Engnell, Widengren, Carlson, Nielsen, Sæbø) will be given greater attention in order to illustrate high points in the course of the research. We hope also to demonstrate that the Scandinavians have made some of their greatest traditio-historical contributions in the area of the prophetic literature. A systematic critique of general problems (especially concerning oral tradition and the importance of religio-historical questions) follows in chapter 15.

One must at all costs avoid isolating Scandinavian work from non-Scandinavian research, and vice versa. The debate pictured in the following must be seen as running parallel to the work described above in chapters 7–10. The influence of especially Gunkel, von Rad, Noth, and British scholars has been significant. Just as we have referred often above to discussions below, so also must cross-referencing continue in the following sections so that this connection remains evident.

---

2. Several, usually brief reviews of portions of the Scandinavian research have provided help in this regard; cf. the literature listed below, ch. 15.

11
The Beginnings

A. Sigmund Mowinckel's Early Work on Prophetic Tradition

The earliest Scandinavian contributions to traditio-historical research came from the Norwegian scholar Sigmund Mowinckel (1884–1965), probably the best known of all Scandinavian Old Testament specialists. Mowinckel has not infrequently been criticized by certain of his colleagues in the North (especially Engnell[1]) for operating with a basically literary-critical orientation. Whether or not this criticism is justified or even important, it must nonetheless be acknowledged that Mowinckel anticipated by several years numerous tenets to which his later critics were to subscribe so enthusiastically—or which they at least had to take into serious consideration in their attempts to answer traditio-historical questions. For example, already in 1916 Mowinckel recognized that the prophetic words and traditions were originally collected and transmitted at the oral stage before having been committed to writing in a later period.[2] Also of prime importance are Mowinckel's contributions

---

1. Cf. below, p. 218.
2. *Statholderen Nehemia: Studier til den jödiske menighets historie og litteratur*; Kristiania (= Oslo) 1916, 116–17. We have seen above (pp. 49–51 and 64–65) that Nachtigal and Gunkel preceded Mowinckel in this. Apart from his emphasis on the primacy of the oral transmission of prophetic literature, Mowinckel deals here with no other aspects of *traditio* nor with the tracing of the development of the traditions themselves. His words are nonetheless worth noting, for they anticipated Nyberg's thesis by almost twenty years: "Here it is of greatest importance to note that the prophetic books are not written by the prophet in question himself. They therefore have nothing whatsoever to do with autobiography or memoirs or pages from a diary. The prophets did not write; they talked. Their words were of the moment, born of a sudden, rushing, ecstatic or enthusiastic condition—not composed by means of pen and ink. Oral improvisation is the essence of prophecy.... If the prophets wrote at all, it was the short, mysterious oracle, written down on a tablet as proof that a future event was correctly predicted; such an inscription consisted of one or two words (Isa. 8:1f.; 30:7f.). The prophetic books in their present form are compilations according to an oral tradition, just as the Gospels are. The various, individual, for the most very short oracles have first circulated in oral tradition for a long time and then gradu-

regarding the centrality of the cult in the worship of ancient Israel and the existence of cultic prophets among whom psalms and prophetic sayings came to expression.[3] From this point it is a small step to the idea of a circle of prophetic disciples who preserved and transmitted the materials inherited from the master. Moreover, with the emphasis on the centrality of the cult the answer is often provided for the question of where the development and transmission of certain traditions have taken place.

In Mowinckel's later studies his contributions to traditio-historical work became more pronounced as he realized the importance of trying to trace the origin and development of Israel's traditions. In 1926 he published (in Norwegian) a monograph on the disciples of Isaiah.[4] Here Mowinckel is particularly preoccupied with the preexilic prophecy of judgment in its transformation to a nationalistic prophecy of happiness, to deal with which he posits that *Isaiah's ministry created a prophetic community which preserved, interpreted, transmitted, and finally set in writing the message of Isaiah*. This group of disciples was expressly chosen by Isaiah for the purpose of preserving his message,[5] a practice quite common in the East. They also became responsible for the preservation of the proclamations of Amos and Hosea, whose words had at first existed only at the oral level.[6] Also within the circle of these disciples were preserved the major sections of Micah, Zephaniah, Nahum, Habakkuk, the Song of Moses, and some of the Deuteronomic laws.[7] As disciples of Isaiah they learned the prophetic "technique," how to live the life of a mystic, and how

---

ally became recorded and collected and ascribed to the various prophets whose names had held fast in the memory of posterity."

3. Cf. especially Mowinckel, *Psalmenstudien III: Kultprophetie und prophetische Psalmen*, Kristiania 1923. Mowinckel's views regarding these matters are well known; suffice it here to quote a passage from his introduction to *Psalmenstudien* III (3), where his thesis is made clear: "The prophetic form of certain psalms corresponds to a cultic reality. Understanding prophetic words as those which came as God's answer to a petition in a certain cultic situation and which are given by one who is regarded by himself and by his contemporaries as a prophetically gifted, though perhaps also a permanently attached official of the cult, then these prophetic words had a fixed place in the cult, and most if not all prophetic psalms in the Psalter are really cultic psalms and must be understood in this cultic situation."

4. *Jesaja-disiplene: Profetien fra Jesaja til Jeremia*, Oslo 1926. This is a continuation of his earlier study: *Profeten Jesaja*, Oslo 1925. In this latter book he anticipated his work of 1926 at a number of places, e.g., on 19 and 32.

5. Mowinckel speaks of the disciples more as "preservers" than as transmitters of the prophetic tradition (e.g., *Jesaja-disiplene*, 127), but he makes it clear in a later publication (*Prophecy and Tradition*, Oslo 1946, 109 n. 97) that in *Jesaja-disiplene* he understood the process as a transmission and transformation of the traditionary materials.

6. *Jesaja-disiplene*, 128.

7. Ibid., 13, 127, 140.

to perform the bodily and spiritual exercises so that they also could experience ecstatic, visionary revelations.[8] People would come to these disciples and ask for an oracle from Jahweh, and many of the nongenuine proclamations contained in the book of Isaiah originated precisely in this way. The prophecies existed from their beginning as an oral "literature" since there was no need for them to be recorded.[9] It was Isaiah himself, just like Jeremiah, who caused his disciples to commit the prophecies to writing so that they might be preserved for a more receptive and believing audience than existed in his generation. Thus, according to Mowinckel, the idea of recording the prophecies arose when they became something more than proclamations directed to some particular situation, when they were recognized as having significance and relevance for all the people regarding Jahweh's will and plan.[10]

Mowinckel's prime contributions to the beginnings of the Scandinavian debate were thus related to the ideas of *prophetic circles, oral transmission of the prophetic words, and the central role of the cult in Israelite life*. That he was aware of other problems of tradition as well is obvious in the concise "Literaturgeschichte" that he published in 1934.[11] Here he attributes a considerable importance to the traditions, asserting that many of them were borrowed and adapted from the Canaanites and other peoples, that numerous traditions are clearly etiologies, that early traditions existed separately from each other but eventually became gathered into groupings, that the historicity of the various events is hard to prove but at any rate is of minor importance, and that oral transmission is a factor with which one must reckon for the laws, the wisdom literature, and the prophetic materials.[12] These and other ideas were destined to receive prime attention in the Scandinavian research of the following two decades.

B. Johannes Pedersen: Initial Opposition to Literary Criticism

The roots for the antipathy that many of the Scandinavian scholars have showed toward literary criticism go back primarily to the publications of Johannes Pedersen (1883-1977) of Copenhagen.[13] Indeed for his role in this

---

8. Ibid., 10-11.
9. Ibid., 126-27.
10. Ibid., 126-28.
11. *Hvordan Det gamle testament er blitt til (Israelitisk-jödisk litteraturhistorie)*, Oslo 1934, 2nd ed. 1968; translation of title: "How the Old Testament Came into Existence."
12. Cf. *Hvordan Det gamle testament*, especially 10ff. Oral transmission is postulated for the laws on 56, 60; for wisdom literature on 64; and for prophetic materials on 102ff.
13. Pedersen, however, was hardly the only one to raise his voice against the excesses of literary criticism and the Documentary Hypothesis. We have seen above (pp. 58-59 and

regard he has even been called "the 'father' or founder of the Scandinavian branch of the 'traditio-historical school.'"[14] In an article written in 1931,[15] Pedersen indicates that one of the chief reasons for his skepticism toward the literary-critical method is that Wellhausen was clearly influenced by Vatke, who was a strong Hegelian.[16] This rationalism was supposedly combined with evolutionary conceptions, and the result was that Wellhausen's presentation of Israel's history became simplistic and unreal, especially when based on the methods of literary criticism. This argument of "guilt by association" leads Pedersen to conclude that literary criticism can have only limited value in our study of the Old Testament, especially the Pentateuch: "This source-critical method undoubtedly has significance for antiquity when one is interested in determining events and external facts. But it must be greatly restricted when one aims to describe the culture of a people. If we are aware of this, we will also be able to see that a neat division of diverse strata of the pentateuchal sources and their distribution among specific points of time are problematic with respect to history."[17]

What then was Pedersen's alternative to this? According to him, JE, D, and P should be seen as *collections of heterogeneous materials that stem indeed from ancient times but yet were fused together into these collections in later, primarily postexilic epochs*. JE, D, and P therefore do not represent evolutionistic lines of development but rather parallel tendencies which, taken together, provide a picture of the variegated culture of Israel.[18] It thus follows that simply by assigning a date to one of these "sources" nothing is said about the age of the various traditions which it contains; and the reason for this, if we understand ancient Israelite psychology, is quite simple: "All Pentateuchal sources are as well preexilic as postexilic. When we are working with them

---

67–69) that also Gunkel, Gressmann, and Staerk were dissatisfied with the exclusive use of the literary-critical method. Others who influenced the Scandinavians in this regard were: P. Volz and W. Rudolph, *Der Elohist als Erzähler: Ein Irrweg der Pentateuchkritik?*, BZAW 63, Gießen 1933; and U. Cassuto, *La Questione della Genesi*, Florence 1934. Cf. also articles by the Dane Paul V. Rubow, "De tre Fortællere i Pentateuchen," *DTT* 3 (1940), 101–8; and "Kildene til første Mosebog," in his *Reflexioner over dansk og fremmed Litteratur. Nye kritiske Studier*, Copenhagen 1942, 122–65.

14. E. Nielsen, *The Ten Commandments in New Perspective: A Traditio-Historical Approach*, SBT, Second Series 7, London 1968, 3.

15. "Die Auffassung vom Alten Testament," *ZAW* 49 (1931), 161–81; Danish edition in *NTT* 32 (1931), 137–62.

16. Note however Mowinckel's criticism of this, in *Prophecy and Tradition*, Oslo 1946, 111–12 n. 120; and now especially Perlitt, *Vatke und Wellhausen*, BZAW 94, Berlin 1965, 161ff.

17. *ZAW* 49 (1931), 175.

18. Ibid., 178.

and the other sources, there is no other way but that of internal appraisal. In each individual case the character of the substance must be examined, and the background which it presupposes must be inferred. That is precisely the task of the historian."[19] Pedersen, in the drawing up of his monumental account of the mental history of Israel,[20] attempts to operate in this manner and thus to tap the traditional sources preserved in the Old Testament. He places his emphasis on the *character, origin, and relative age of the materials* and thereby minimizes the importance of the recording of the traditions and the collecting of them into a body of literature. Frequent criticisms of literary-critical methods and conclusions are included throughout the book.[21]

Pedersen's main importance in the Scandinavian debate is thus two-fold: negatively, *his skepticism toward the literary-critical approach;* and positively, *his emphasis an the great age of the pentateuchal materials and on the historical importance of their early forms.* His idea of the postexilic composition of the documents functioned as the catalyst for Nyberg's bombastic thesis about the predominance of oral tradition throughout Israel's history. Furthermore, Pedersen's hypothesis that the transmission process in Israel produced a nearly indecipherable mixture of old and new elements was taken over and developed by Engnell.

---

19. Ibid., 179.
20. *Israel, Its Life and Culture*, I–II (Danish: 1st ed. Copenhagen 1920, 2nd ed. 1934; English: London 1926) and III–IV (Danish: 1st ed. Copenhagen 1934, 2nd ed. 1960; English: London 1940).
21. Particular attention is called to the concluding footnote (*Israel* III–IV, 725–27 of the English edition) where Pedersen attempts to give a brief view of his alternative to the usual literary-critical interpretation of the composition of the Old Testament. Cf. also his "Passahfest und Passahlegende," ZAW 52 (1934), 161–75. —Mowinckel, in a review of Pedersen's *Israel* ("Hellighet og guddommelighet i det gamle Israel: Johs. Pedersens Israel III–IV," NTT 38, 1937, 1–72), calls Pedersen to task for his often irresponsible criticism of literary-critical analysis. Devoting a special section (65–72) of his review to this problem, Mowinckel points to several instances where he feels that Pedersen himself has not carried out the necessary analysis of the materials or has not considered carefully enough the literary-critical arguments. Mowinckel, in this perceptive critique, also observes a line of development in Pedersen's own thinking: In the first Danish edition (1920) of *Israel* I–II, as also in the first English edition (1926; e.g., 27ff.), Pedersen shared generally the current critical view of the four pentateuchal sources, tending however to be somewhat hesitant regarding the detailed separation of J from E. It was in his 1931 article (described above) that Pedersen expressed pointedly his opposition to the Documentary Hypothesis and to the usual literary criticism. This position was then developed further in the second Danish edition of I–II (1934; e.g., 20ff.) and in III–IV (Danish, 1934; e.g., 543ff.): The Pentateuch comprises heterogeneous elements stemming from different ages, the final redaction being postexilic; source criticism, however, is methodologically unreliable and its results are unverifiable because of the complex combination of old and new elements in the various traditions.

C. Ivar Hylander and Basic Problems of Method

1. The Traditio-Critical Task

In his dissertation[22] submitted in 1932, Ivar Hylander (1900-1982) carried out an examination of the traditions in 1 Sam 1-15. His methodology was essentially one of motif analysis and tradition *criticism*—quite similar to the approach taken by Gressmann.[23] To be sure, this is precisely how Hylander defines the first stage of traditio-historical research: " 'Traditio-historical' means first of all: do traditio-critical work."[24] In his study of the traditions of Samuel, the ark of the covenant, and Saul, Hylander therefore begins with the attempt to isolate the smallest possible units in which the contents of the traditions existed; and having described the relations of these units to each other, he then shows how they became grouped into layers ("Schichten"), from which the final form of the traditions emerged.[25] It thus seems that Hylander was among the first to become conscious of the two necessary steps of the investigation: first a determined tradition criticism, the results of which should then be gathered into a traditio-historical picture showing how the final product was reached. This is the same method adopted by von Rad and especially Noth in the following decade.

Whereas Hylander emphasizes that he would not be able to operate within the bounds of pure literary criticism, his examination of the materials is at many paints guided strongly by literary-critical methods and principles—a tendency which many of the later Scandinavian scholars sought to abandon. It is to Hylander's credit, however, that *he seeks repeatedly to probe the relation of the traditions to history*:

> The tradition is rooted ... in history and can from the outset be significantly determined also by this source. Considering that tradition is constituted by the mutuality of substance and motifs, it can be disastrous to disregard even just *one* possible influence on it. And at this point it seems to me that the relationship between history and tradition is double in nature. Of course, new motifs bringing new, even foreign materials can be added, but they almost always meet with an old substance that, borne by an old motif, retains constantly formative power.

---

22. *Der literarische Samuel-Saul-Komplex (I. Sam. 1-15) traditionsgeschichtlich untersucht*, Diss. Uppsala, 1932.
23. See above, pp. 67-69.
24. Hylander, *Samuel-Saul-Komplex*, 1.
25. Ibid., e.g., 207ff.

In the formation of tradition, therefore, the relationship between substance and motif is reciprocal.[26]

Thus materials from another age which remain in the traditions have important historical worth for us as well. Moreover, it is the goal of traditio-historical analysis not only to uncover the historical foundation of a tradition but especially to understand and evaluate the different threads of the tradition as reflections of actual history.[27]

2. Literary Criticism and Tradition History

In an important article on what he termed the crisis of Old Testament literary criticism,[28] Hylander clarifies his own position regarding the task of tracing the history of traditions, and also the relationship between literary criticism and traditio-historical research. Hylander points out that his own previous works have often been misunderstood as efforts to regain "pure" primary texts, in other words as if he were executing a type of text criticism. His intention, he counters, has quite simply been "to attempt to show the conditions for the existence of tradition—not only through formalistic-literary criticism but also with the use of motif analysis and traditio-historical methods."[29] He does not evince an antagonism toward Wellhausen nor toward literary criticism as an approach; indeed, he agrees that literary criticism is necessary if we are to gain a correct historical view of the stages and processes of the literary development of the Old Testament.[30] However, the form-historical, motif-analytical, and traditio-historical research which has been carried out since Gunkel has submitted the principles of literary criticism to renewed examination.[31] The situation that developed within Old Testament research, he observes, was one of a polarization of efforts and interests into two general camps: (a) the literary-critical research, concentrating its attention optimistically on the literary form of the traditions, this research being primarily

---

26. Ibid., 3–4. Thus already here with Hylander we find an awareness of the complementary relationship between tradition and history, as stressed by von Rad two decades later; cf. above, pp. 101–2.
27. In this regard cf. also Hylander's "Det profetiska ordet," *SEÅ* 4 (1939), 5–12.
28. Hylander, "Den gammaltestamentliga litterärkritikens kris: Ett bidrag till traditionsproblemet i nyare religionsvetenskaplig forskning," *SEÅ* 2 (1937), 16–64. The article appeared, of course, after the publication of Nyberg's *Studien zum Hoseabuche* (1935), which played an important part in the situation discussed here by Hylander.
29. *SEÅ* 2 (1937), 61 n. 67.
30. Ibid., 19–20.
31. Cf. ibid., 22–37, for a good, brief history of this developing research.

analytical but with an increasing need being felt to answer also questions of synthesis; and on the other hand, (b) a research into the Old Testament materials themselves—their forms and "Sitze im Leben" and with special interest directed toward oral transmission and the development of traditions—a study that involves questions primarily of synthesis but also of analysis. *A crisis has developed from this polarization because of the lack of success in defining the boundaries between the two methods and between their working-hypotheses.* The result of this confusion has been frequent antagonisms and hostilities between the two groups—rather than an effort to work out a division of tasks and thus establish a spirit of co-operation.[32]

How does Hylander seek to resolve this conflict between tradition history and literary criticism? He makes a number of specific comments about the tasks of traditio-historical research,[33] and these amount to *the first attempt to clarify precise problems of method*: (a) The historian must take into account *two tendencies which characterized the transmitters* of Israel's traditions: on the one hand "an effort to keep the tradition unviolated, this effort being both grounded in natural traditionalism as well as strengthened by a religiously motivated respect of reality, and on the other hand a need to form the tradition aesthetically—even in oral tradition—and thereby, again out of the peculiar religious character of the formation of Old Testament tradition, an effort to press into it reality according to a religious scheme."[34] (b) An important task of traditio-historical research is to test the historical claim, i.e. *the historicity*, of the tradition in question.[35] (a) For each type of literary tradition and with respect given to its presuppositions in oral transmission it is necessary to find the best viewpoints and methods; there is *no general rule* which can apply to the study of the organic development of every type of tradition.[36] (d) For a *critical-analytical examination* of the traditions the following methodology should be observed: (α) The point of departure should not be a literary-critically oriented hypothesis, but rather quite simply the larger units of related traditions themselves. (β) The first task is to examine these units of traditions according to character, general ideology, internal connections, and leading viewpoints. In this way a preliminary separation of dissimilar material parts of the tradition

---

32. Ibid., 19, 28–29, 35–37. Hylander points out that, regarding the question of whether the oral or the literary stage of transmission was the formative and predominant one, disputes analogous to those within Old Testament research have arisen also, e.g., in Homeric studies, in the research into Icelandic folklore, and in the studies of Synoptic Gospels.
33. Ibid., 46–50, 63–64.
34. Ibid., 47.
35. Ibid., 48.
36. Ibid.

is achieved. (γ) By means of motif- and "Stoff"-analysis the larger but perhaps secondarily amassed bodies of materials must be broken down into their original component parts—as far as this is possible.[37] (e) These component parts should be classified and described according to their original character (e.g., cultic legend, historical recollection, a general or a localized saga, etc.).[38] (f) The attempt must be made to determine *the causes or occasions through which the elements of the traditions became "fixed"* in the traditio-historical sense; this applies both to the smaller, original components and to the larger narrative collections.[39] (g) The researcher must also seek an answer to the question of whether a *continuing oral tradition* influenced or altered in any way the tradition in question after it became literarily fixed to a certain degree.[40] Hylander affirms that for most of these tasks literary criticism can and should be employed in order to aid in the solution of the problem in each case.[41]

We can thus observe that Hylander was concerned to clarify aspects of the traditio-historical method, especially the relationship of these to literary criticism. In this regard he rejected the idea that the tradition historian has little or no use for the literary-critical analysis of the text. In his measured reliance on this latter method and in his clear conception of the need to stratify the traditions and to try to reach back to the origins of the materials, he defended an approach which was quite different from that adapted by his colleagues, especially Nyberg, Birkeland, and Engnell. We will see that the conflict over the legitimacy of literary criticism in Old Testament studies worsened rather than improved in Scandinavia, despite Hylander's efforts.

D. Henrik Samuel Nyberg: The Thesis of a Predominant Oral Tradition

Most of the Scandinavian scholars date the real beginning of their direction in traditio-historical research with the work published in 1935 by H. S. Nyberg

---

37. Ibid., 48–49.
38. Ibid., 63.
39. Ibid.
40. Ibid., 64.
41. Hylander (ibid., 50–63) illustrates the traditio-historical method with an examination of the tradition of the ark in 1 Sam 4–6. Here he shows that a literary criticism of the text is helpful but by no means adequate by itself to answer the traditio-historical questions. He concludes that the original form of the material in 1 Sam 5–6 is a Danite tradition with three basic motifs: the cultic motif in 5:2,4,5,; the cultic motif in 5:6,7a, etc.; and the cultic motif of the returning of the ark, the primary interest of this being the founding of the cult itself. It was primarily oral tradition which was responsible for the development of this tradition into its final form, the rise of doublets and variants, and the appearance of narrative embellishments; some of this, though, is to be attributed to the literary stage.

(1889–1974), *Studien zum Hoseabuche: Zugleich ein Beitrag zur Klärung des Problems der alttestamentlichen Textkritik*.[42] It is a book of less than one hundred fifty pages, dealing primarily with the textual criticism of Hosea but containing also an introduction in which the question of the origin and transmission of the Old Testament materials, especially of the prophetic books, is briefly discussed. Nyberg's theses are delivered categorically and firmly, and one can only be amazed that they attracted so much attention and thereby precipitated a debate lasting two decades and longer. His followers sought to confirm and apply his ideas; his opponents, to disprove and discredit them. We would do well to appraise these foundational ideas quite carefully at this point.

1. The Nature of Transmission in Israel

In this programmatic statement Nyberg formulates his own propositions as antitheses to the usually accepted literary-critical tenets. He maintains that *the Hebrew text of the Old Testament is dependent on an oral tradition, trustworthy and reliable, which preserved the legend, myth, law, and prophecy in the period prior to the exile*. His basis for this thesis is quite simple: "Transmission in the Orient is seldom purely written; it is predominantly *oral*. Living speech in the Orient played from time immemorial and plays still a greater role than written statements. Almost every recording of a work in writing was preceded in the Orient, up to most recent times, by a longer or shorter oral transmission, and even after this recording oral transmission remains the normal form for continuing and using a work."[43] As support for this broad contention he cites only two facts, the traditional manner in which the Koran is used and the recitation of the Yasna by the Parsi priests. Nyberg speaks in unequivocal terms about the necessity for researchers to realize how important oral tradition has been in the Orient: "whoever does not pay due attention to the ancient, firmly rooted Oriental custom of preferring oral speech to the writ-

---

42. UUÅ 1935:6 (Uppsala). The section of this monograph (5–9) which occupies our attention here was published in almost identical form one year earlier in Nyberg's article, "Das textkritische Problem des Alten Testaments, am Hoseabuche demonstriert," *ZAW* 52 (1934), 241–54 (especially 242–46). For critiques of Nyberg's work, cf. especially J. van der Ploeg, "Le rôle de la tradition orale dans la transmission du texte de l'Ancien Testament," *RB* 54 (1947), 5–41; and Gunneweg, *Tradition*, 51–55.

43. *Studien zum Hoseabuche*, 7. In his book, *Irans forntida religioner* (Stockholm 1937, 9–15; German edition: *Die Religionen des alten Iran*, MVÄG 43, 1938, 8ff.), Nyberg reiterates this principle with regard to the East in general and the Avesta in particular. Cf. also Nyberg, "Die schwedischen Beiträge zur alttestamentlichen Forschung in diesem Jahrhundert," VTSup 22 (1972), 6, 9–10.

ten word blocks his own passage to understanding every Oriental body of literature."⁴⁴

If oral transmission was indeed so predominant in ancient Israel, what then was the role played by writing and written transmission with regard to Old Testament materials? Nyberg's dictum: *"The written Old Testament is a creation of the Jewish community after the Exile; what preceded it was surely only in smaller part fixed in writing."*⁴⁵ There was, of course, writing prior to this time in Palestine, but it was used more for practical than for purely literary purposes (e.g., in contracts, memorials, official listings, letters). Regarding what exists in the Old Testament, however, "the concrete historical traditions, the epic narratives, the cultic legends, undoubtedly also the laws in general must have been transmitted orally. Certainly only with the greatest reserve is one to reckon with writers among the prophets and poets."⁴⁶ The material was preserved and passed on by circles or centers of traditions; and this was accomplished, not by mechanical, passive repetition, but with adaptation and expansion through succeeding generations. Thus what should occupy our attention, Nyberg maintains, is *the organic growth and transformation of living materials*, not corruptions of written texts.⁴⁷ For ancient Near Eastern culture

---

44. *Studien zum Hoseabuche*, 8.

45. Ibid., 8 (emphasis added). In an additional note (128), Nyberg points out that, regarding the purely literary activity in preexilic times, he allows it less "Spielraum" than Eissfeldt does in his *Einleitung in das Alte Testament* (1934). As Nyberg sees the problem, "the present composition of the Old Testament books corresponds entirely to the working of one who is standing in the middle of a stream of living oral tradition and is endeavoring to hold onto the individual features. A literature fixed in writing places constraints on its user in a quite different way; it binds his hands and forces its external form on him." He concedes that certain basic laws must have been fixed in writing very early; but on the whole, oral transmission is primary and predominant: "What is decisive for me is that written products of that older epoch did not lead an independent existence as written literature designed for reading in our sense, but that they served *solely as supports for the oral tradition, which always constituted the primary entity*" (italics added).

46. Nyberg, *Studien zum Hoseabuche*, 8. For earlier ideas about oral tradition in Israel, cf. above, pp. 69-72.

47. The task facing the text critic is thereby also limited: "to recover the oldest written tradition of the Jewish community" (ibid., 9). The text critic is thus bound to the literary product, and it is not for him but for the exegete to decide whether any given material belongs originally to the tradition collection in question. For text-critical work Nyberg maintains that the Masoretic text should be allotted more and the versions less importance than is normally done. Birkeland, who otherwise follows Nyberg quite closely, suggests that this view of the status of the MT and the versions is exaggerated; "Profeten Hoseas forkynnelse," *NTT* 38 (1937), 303ff. Also Begrich argues strongly against Nyberg's text-critical method; "Zur Frage der alttestamentlichen Textkritik," *OLZ* 42 (1939), cols. 473-83. L. G. Rignell, on the other hand, is quite convinced that his study of Zechariah's nocturnal visions confirms Nyberg's thesis about the reliability of

memory was much more reliable as a method of preserving the contents of a tradition ("die primitiven Stoffe"). The important implication of this fact is that Old Testament scholarship ought to reconsider seriously the possibility of getting back to the *ipsissima verba* of, for example, the prophets. We must be content, Nyberg says, with accepting the tradition about what they said.[48] Especially this latter suggestion about the unimportance of recovering the earliest stages of the tradition became later the subject of a heated debate between Mowinckel and Engnell.

2. Tradition History of Numbers 16–17

After the appearance of this brief discussion in *Studien zum Hoseabuche*, there came little from Nyberg's pen either in the way of further elaboration of and support for his theses, or in the way of application of these viewpoints to the text by means of traditio-historical studies. An important exception to the latter is his article on Korah's revolt in Num 16–17, this study being presented as a contribution to the traditio-historical method.[49] Here the opposition to literary criticism is especially apparent. The usual literary-critical view is that, while Num 17 is the work of P, Num 16 is a fusion of two sources—JE's (or only J's) narrative about the revolt of Dathan and Abiram against the political leadership of Moses (vv. 1b, 2a, 12–15, 25–26, 17b–34), and of P's account of the revolt by Korah and the 250 men against Moses and Aaron (this latter narrative is also often seen as having originally had two forms, one older and one younger). A postexilic redactor was responsible for the weaving of these different narratives into one story. For Nyberg, however, this literary-critical analysis is problematical, for he simply finds it difficult to imagine a literary process in which a redactor took excerpts from diverse narratives and worked them into a "mosaic."[50] Rather than presupposing such a process, he chooses to base his study on the *assumption that the development of the tradition occurred at the oral rather than at the written level*. The result is that "the whole question of unevennesses and contradictions in his [*scil.*,

---

the MT; *Die Nachtgesichte des Sacharja: Eine exegetische Studie*, Lund 1950, especially 246–48, 10–14.

48. Nyberg, *Studien zum Hoseabuche*, 9: "Only the tradition of those words is given us, and it is doubtful to the highest degree whether any sources for it other than the oral tradition ever existed. For a long time now research of the Gospels has not been concerned with determining in detail the *ipsissima verba* of Jesus. It is first and foremost occupied with only the tradition of these words. In principle it is no different for Old Testament research."

49. "Ḳoraḥs uppror (Num. 16f.): Ett bidrag till frågan om traditionshistorisk metod," *SEÅ* 12 (1947), 230–52 (also in *SEÅ* 12, 1948, 214–36).

50. *SEÅ* 12 (1947), 244–45.

the 'redactor's'] material comes then into a new light. It is no longer a question of disparate and contradictory written sources, but of diverse streams and complexes of traditions which intersect with each other and of material which he does not bother to develop further.[51] Whether certain parts of the material existed in writing at some early time, whether the whole narrative was immediately recorded or existed first for a shorter or longer time in oral tradition, whether the final written form is a verbatim reproduction of the oral form or rather a free rendition of it—we do not know the answers now to all of these questions, and we probably never will be able to answer them with certainty. What is of primary importance for us is to realize that "the narratives are recorded especially as the writer heard them, and that the narrators themselves did not use written sources but oral traditions";[52] all analyses of the traditions must be founded on these basic facts. In the case of Num 16–17, Nyberg maintains that the narrator was interested in presenting a closed, dramatic course of events; and the existence of repetitions in the story are evidence of the oral, narrative style.[53] The double line in the story is primary, and the tradition as such can rightly be regarded as being very old, probably dating in fact from the time of the amphictyony. The references to the same revolt in Num 26:9–11 and 27:1–3 support this fact, according to Nyberg.[54] His study of this pericope thus illustrates well the importance that the oral-transmission thesis had for the critical work of Nyberg and his followers: It provided them with an alternative to the usual literary-critical solutions.

3. CONTRIBUTIONS TO THE DEBATE

In what ways did Nyberg make an impact on the research of his colleagues? Which of his ideas were taken up and pursued—or challenged and rejected—in the years that followed? The following are the most significant:

(a) Oral transmission was more important than writing in the East.

---

51. Ibid., 246. Cf. however Bentzen, *Introduction to the Old Testament* II, Copenhagen 1958, 26.
52. Nyberg, *SEÅ* 12 (1947), 247.
53. Ibid., 247–48. Here we can see vividly a phenomenon which occurs so frequently when one compares opposing methods of research: A given fact (in this case, the existence of repetitions in the text) is used, seemingly arbitrarily, as "proof" for two contradictory theses—for literary critics repetitions constitute the evidence of two or more written sources which were joined into one, whereas for Nyberg this same fact "proves" that the story was told and developed orally by narrators.
54. Ibid., 248–51.

(b) The proper appreciation of oral tradition is a prerequisite for understanding ancient Near Eastern texts.
(c) Oral transmission in the East is trustworthy and reliable.
(d) In Israel legends, myths, laws, and prophecies were generally preserved orally until the exile.
(e) The tradition "lived" in circles or centers; here it was reinterpreted and transformed in the transmission process.
(f) The written Old Testament is a product of the exilic community.
(g) The biblical scholar should accept the tradition as it is and not try to separate early elements from later ones.
(h) Repetitions and unevenness in the text are more likely due to oral tradition than to literary activity.

E. Harris Birkeland: Establishing the Thesis and Demonstrating Its Consequences

A major weakness in Nyberg's presentation was that it lacked the battery of convincing support and evidence which must accompany the introduction of a new thesis. Moreover, he did not demonstrate how his principles of transmission would alter our understandings of the various Old Testament materials themselves. These two deficiencies became, in part, the tasks to which the Norwegian scholar Harris Birkeland (1904–1961) addressed himself in his book, *Zum hebräischen Traditionswesen: Die Komposition der prophetischen Bücher des Alten Testaments*.[55] Birkeland, a student of Mowinckel as well as Nyberg, took the theses set forth by the latter as his point of departure: "The Semitic-Oriental method of transmission, as also that of certainly any nonmodern people, is decidedly of oral character."[56] Birkeland submitted that this can be substantiated in part by a study of *Islamic traditions*; for the Koran, although supposedly committed to writing even before the death of Muhammad, existed for centuries side by side a complete oral tradition of it. Also for pre-Islamic poetry and for the later *ḥadīth*-collections oral transmission was predominant. The function of a written rendition was to protect the oral from being lost, but the Arabs often tended to prefer the latter, as can be seen by the mistrust which the historian Abu-l-Qāsim ibn ʿAsākir (twelfth century C.E.) showed for the written text: "My friend! Strive zealously to attain (traditions), and receive them from the men themselves, (directly) without mediation. Receive them not from written records, that

---

55. ANVAO, II. Hist.-Filos. Kl., 1938: No. 1, Oslo 1938.
56. Ibid., 6.

they not be smitten by the disease of textual corruption."[57] The written texts, in fact, were not infrequently corrected by that which existed in the oral traditions.[58]

What, however, does this have to do with the Old Testament materials, which arose a millennium and more before the time of the Koran? Birkeland maintains that the Arab mentality and their preference for the spoken word were characteristics common also to the Israelites. Although we cannot exclude the possibility that, e.g., the prophets could have written down some of their prophecies, we must be guided by the principle that oral transmission was by far the primary and predominant means. This dictates then *the methodological sequence which our investigations must follow: first traditio-historical examination and then literary criticism of the text.*[59] For pentateuchal studies, the consequences can be significant: For example, the relationship between J and E might be such that J, as a written source (which itself can be questioned), existed side by side an oral tradition (which we call "E") and was gradually corrected by it, the result being what we refer to as "JE."[60]

Birkeland's study is devoted primarily to the prophetic literature. The Scandinavian work done on this corpus has brought the most significant of their contributions, and Birkeland's monograph secured the foundation (Mowinckel was the precursor) for the particular traditio-historical direction taken by them. How does he view the situation? Birkeland maintains that, for the study of the composition of the prophetic books, the following concepts impose themselves upon us: "*Tradition, complexes, circles instead of: notes, larger literary products, writers at a desk.*"[61] What was preserved of the prophet's own words in each case were essentially only those prophecies which were of interest to the prophet's disciples and which were found to be socially effec-

---

57. Quoted by Birkeland, ibid., 11. Pedersen (*Den arabiske bog*, Copenhagen 1946) concurs basically with Birkeland, whereas Widengren gives a quite different picture of Arabic transmission habits; cf. below, pp. 232–34.

58. Birkeland, *Zum hebräischen Traditionswesen*, 7–13; cf. also his *The Lord Guideth: Studies on Primitive Islam*, SNVAO, II. Hist.-Filos. Kl., 1956:2, Oslo 1956, 6–12 and 133–35.

59. *Zum hebräischen Traditionswesen*, 13–14. The idea of carrying out a traditio-historical examination prior to the literary-critical determination of unevenness in the text may seem quite strange to us today, for we have come to see that literary criticism provides the necessary basis for the other investigative steps; cf. also above, p. 24. Birkeland's conception, however, is due to his associating tradition history with oral tradition, and literary criticism with written sources; if Israelite transmission was *ex hypothesi* preponderantly oral, and our texts are essentially oral tradition frozen in writing, then tradition history should be given methodological priority, according to him.

60. *Zum hebräischen Traditionswesen*, 20. Cf. also Mowinckel, *NTT* 38 (1937), 71.

61. *Zum hebräischen Traditionswesen*, 22 (emphasis original).

tive and relevant; usually only those predictions that were fulfilled continued to be handed down. In other words, as in biology, it was the principle of "the survival of the fittest" that determined what was retained through the various selection processes.[62] Only at the beginning stages were individual prophecies transmitted independently of one another; they soon became grouped into oral tradition complexes of various sizes, connected by means of catchwords, material associations, the need for more abstract proclamations to have the concrete support of some historical account, and so forth. The words of a prophet were propagated primarily by means of the "initially usually small, though gradually increasing circle around the prophet, which grew and continued to function after his death and thus transmitted and remoulded the material throughout generations."[63] *Reinterpretation and gradual composition were thus integral aspects of the oral transmission process.* The control which the circle of disciples had over the tradition was so great that we will never be able with certainty to separate the prophet's own words from that which was added or altered by his followers. However, to the extent that questions about the prophet's *ipsissima verba* can be answered, it is achieved only by following traditio-historical, not literary-critical methods.[64] What we have before us in the prophetic books is a relatively late literary fixation of the oral tradition. Birkeland, concurring here with Nyberg, is very clear and unrelenting at this point:

> Nothing is more erroneous than to speak of literature in connection with prophetic words. For the preserved product has passed through the *smelting-furnace of the community* ('Schmelzofen der Gemeinschaft'). In most cases it will therefore be extremely difficult for us to recover the product of the great geniuses themselves. We see mostly only their effect.... Regarding method, it is highly important that we are clear about this peculiarity of prophetic books and that we do not become victims of false optimism with respect to finding the real words: *We will never be free of the work of the circles.*[65]

Only occasionally are we able to gain impressions of the great personalities who motivated and inspired their successors. We will see below that Engnell extended this idea to its methodological limit, maintaining that we must give up trying to penetrate back to earlier stages of the tradition. Birkeland, having

---

62. Ibid., 15–16. Cf. also below, pp. 225–26.
63. Ibid., 18.
64. Ibid., 22.
65. Ibid., 23–24 (emphasis added). Cf. also Birkeland, "Zur Kompositionsfrage des Buches Jeremia," *MO* 31 (1937), 50–51. This latter article, it may be noted, deals briefly with several traditio-historical problems of the book of Jeremiah.

thus described the principles and methodology which should guide scholars in the study of the prophets, launches into a cursory analysis of the composition of the individual prophetic books, operating from the assumption that most of the difficulties are easily explainable "when one regards oral transmission as carrier of the tradition."[66]

What then are Birkeland's primary contributions with respect to prophetic tradition? Inasmuch as he definitely preferred the traditio-historical method to literary criticism—a position that Engnell carried to its extreme—Birkeland's basic ideas and the methodological consequences which he drew from them are important:

(1) Birkeland described more clearly than Nyberg the process of oral composition, the principles by which the prophet's disciples gathered together the sayings into ever-larger collections.
(2) The disciples, by means of reinterpretation and selection, are responsible for deciding what was retained in the tradition.
(3) This transmission process is conceived of being, not "reliable" or "faithful," but one of reworking and revamping, thus the image of the "Schmelzofen."
(4) The consequence of this is that we have little chance to penetrate back to the earliest stages with any certainty.
(5) To the extent that information about the prophets themselves can be gained, this can be accomplished only through traditio-historical rather than literary-critical means.

F. Johannes Lindblom's Research: Evidence of the Force of These Ideas

The wide range of Old Testament studies carried out by the Swede Johannes Lindblom (1882-1974) has given him the reputation of being a careful and competent researcher.[67] His contributions to the traditio-historical research of the Old Testament are not many, but it is significant to note that he consistently held himself at a distance from the extremism which was developing in this area of studies in Scandinavia and which culminated in the initial position represented by Engnell. He was, however, no "Bahnbrecher" in this work, and his interest in traditio-historical problems was indeed probably aroused due to the ever-increasing activity in the field among other Scandinavian

---

66. *Zum hebräischen Traditionswesen*, 90.
67. Cf. also G.W. Anderson, "Johannes Lindblom's Contribution to Biblical Studies," *ASTI* 6 (1968), 4–19.

researchers; there exists little evidence that he had a sensitivity for these problems earlier in his career.[68] For our purposes here it may be best to review his contributions by examining first his studies of the prophetic literature and secondly his work on the book of Job.

1. THE PROPHETIC LITERATURE

Lindblom's research in the prophetic literature has from the beginning been characterized by an attempt to understand it as "revelation literature," and in order to clarify this interpretation he has usually sought parallels in the revelation literature of the medieval Christian mystics. Already in his first important work on the prophets[69] Lindblom asserts that it is false to see the prophets *simply* as public speakers or preachers or to assume that our present prophetic books contain the remains of these speeches: "The so-called speeches of prophetic literature are in and of themselves not speeches but, psychologically viewed, revelations or auditions which the prophets in an inspired condition received from their God. They become speeches only because they are presented to the public. In the moment when they were delivered to the people they naturally became transformed somewhat."[70] These revelations remain for us to this day only because they were *recorded quite early*, either by the prophet himself or by one of his listeners or followers; the reason for this recording was to gain a wider audience for these prophecies and also to enable later generations, after the predictions had been fulfilled, to see that the prophet had spoken the truth. Lindblom maintains that these recorded prophetic revelations underwent a *long literary history* before reaching their present form. If we are to understand the way in which the numerous smaller pieces developed into the final body of prophetic literature, we need first—operating from the premise that the proper prophetic "Gattung" is the word of revelation—to isolate the individual, separate revelatory units from each other, being care-

---

68. E.g., in a manual written for students, *Gamla testamentets skrifter* (1st ed., Stockholm 1910, 2nd ed. 1921), Lindblom's position varied little from that taken by Gunkel. He shows no antipathy toward literary criticism, and only occasionally does he touch on traditio-historical matters, as in the following general statement (p. 23 of the second edition): "The Books of Moses are the ripened fruit of a long literary process lasting several centuries. Oral and written traditions have gradually been accumulated into ever larger literary units, narrative cycles, collections and books, until they finally assumed the form in which we now recognize them. Many factors in this literary process remain in the dark, but thanks to recent research its principal features are nonetheless clear to us." This statement is then followed by a brief description of the four pentateuchal sources.

69. *Die literarische Gattung der prophetischen Literatur: Eine literargeschichtliche Untersuchung zum Alten Testament*, UUÅ 1924: Teologi, 1, Uppsala 1924.

70. Ibid., 56, 15.

ful to avoid the common error of making these units too small.[71] Lindblom demonstrates his hypothesis and method by analyzing the book of Amos, and in two later monographs he does the same with Hosea[72] and Micah.[73] In the latter of these two works his understanding of the nature of prophetic literature and his methodology are more precisely expressed. Here he admits that not all of the prophetic literature can be regarded as revelation literature.[74] Lindblom thus proposes that there are usually three different possibilities which we have to consider regarding the writing down of prophecies: the given prophetic text is either a recording of a public speech, or a recording of a revelation which later served as a basis for a speech, or a recording of a revelation which was to be distributed in written form as a "Flugblatt."[75]

In these earlier studies on the whole, Lindblom tends to minimize (or simply to disregard) the role of a continuing oral transmission, especially one which played an important part in the formative stage of the tradition. Lindblom's *magnum opus* on the prophets, *Profetismen i Israel*,[76] includes a chapter (590-649) in which the above outlined principles are treated in considerably more detail, though with little substantial change from his earlier theses. It is first in his book, *Prophecy in Ancient Israel*,[77] that Lindblom fully demonstrates his awareness of the living, developmental process of the prophetic traditions.[78] While retaining his original thesis regarding the revelatory character of the prophetic literature, he acknowledges here the importance played by oral transmission and by the transmitters (disciples) and collectors of the traditions after the time of the prophets.[79] He furthermore takes pains frequently to discuss the traditio-historical studies of the prophets carried out by other Scandinavians since his book of 1934, and it may be noted in this regard that he expresses himself amenable to the positions usually held by Birkeland and Mowinckel.[80]

---

71. Ibid., 58-65.
72. *Hosea literarisch untersucht*, AAAbo 1927: Humaniora, V:2, Åbo 1927.
73. *Micha literarisch untersucht*, AAAbo 1929: Humaniora, VI:2, Åbo 1929.
74. Ibid., 7-8.
75. Ibid., 8-9.
76. Stockholm 1934.
77. Oxford 1962. Lindblom accurately emphasizes in the preface that this book is by no means a simple translation of the Swedish publication but is rather a completely new study. Especially the fourth chapter (220-91) is important for us here.
78. For shorter notes touching on traditio-historical problems, cf. "Einige Grundfragen der alttestamentlichen Wissenschaft," *Festschrift für Alfred Bertholet*, Tübingen 1950, 332ff.; and *A Study on the Immanuel Section in Isaiah, Isa. vii,1-ix*, 6, SM, 1957-1958:4, Lund 1958, 5.
79. *Prophecy in Ancient Israel*, 69ff., 159ff., 226ff.
80. Ibid., e.g., 235, 239, 264, 424.

2. Tradition History of the Book of Job

Whereas Lindblom's work on the prophets offers little to traditio-historical research that is striking and original, his studies of the book of Job make substantial contributions to this growing field of research. His *Boken om Job och hans lidande*,[81] which should be ranked among the best introductions to Job up to the time of its publication, deals more in its second edition (1966) than in its first (1940) with traditio-historical problems. These, however, receive his direct attention in two articles, "Joblegenden traditionshistoriskt undersökt"[82] and "La composition du livre de Job."[83] In the former of these articles Lindblom executes an exemplary examination of the Job-legend (i.e., the story of Job according to the prologue and epilogue of the book), and his conclusions are as follows: The kernel of this legend originated in Edom and was later introduced into Israel where it underwent revision and expansion by the Israelite narrators. In addition to inserting the name of Jahweh into the Edomite legend, these narrators added three other elements, each of which occurs in the present prologue but is conspicuously missing in the epilogue: the motif of Satan (added by the Jewish narrators who regarded it as being unthinkable that God could have been immediately responsible for Job's misfortune), the motif of Job's sickness (added in order to heighten Job's misery), and the motif of Job's nagging wife (introduced in order to emphasize Job's steadfastness to his God). Because of the discrepancy between Job 2:13 and 42:7, Lindblom suggests that there originally existed prior to 42:7 a conversation between Job and his friends which would have stirred up God's wrath against the friends but that this conversation was later suppressed and replaced by the present dialogue which suited better the interests of the Israelite narrators.[84] The conclusion of the Job-legend also bears the marks of having gone through a similar development: The original Edomite ending is found in 42:12–15, whereas the conclusion in verses 10–11 is a later, more polished ending composed and introduced here by the Israelite narrators. The final two verses of the chapter are a later redactional ending. Lindblom asserts that *the greater part of this development of the legend took place during the stage of*

---

[81] 1st ed., Lund 1940, 2nd ed. 1966.

[82] *SEÅ* 5 (1940), 29–42. This article is essentially a summary of the second chapter of his book (36–65 of the first edition)—a new formulation of the ideas with special attention to tradition history.

[83] Kungliga humanistiska vetenskapssamfundets i Lund, årsberättelse, 1944–1945, III, Lund 1945.

[84] *SEÅ* 5 (1940), 34–39. Lindblom disagrees with the proposal advanced by F. Buhl ("Zur Vorgeschichte des Buches Hiob," BZAW 41, Festschrift für K. Marti, 1925, 52–61) that a remnant of this missing conversation can be found in 27:5–11.

oral transmission. Only by employing the traditio-historical method are we able to analyze this development and arrive at the conclusions described above.

In "La composition du livre de Job" Lindblom, in addition to reiterating the history of the development of the Job-legend, addresses himself to the problem of the rise of *the dialogue section* of the book of Job. In this case he concludes that it is *the literary product of a Jewish author* who, having omitted the original conversation between Job and his friends, used the Job-legend as a framework for a poetic composition dealing with divine retribution and justice. This dialogue underwent further expansions at the hands of yet later authors who introduced the poem in Job 28, the discourse of Elihu, the poems about Behemoth and Leviathan, and the sections Job 40:6–14 and 42:1–6.[85] Lindblom submits an important principle for traditio-historical research in his answer to the question of whether the author of the poem knew the Job-legend in its oral or in its written form: "This question is unimportant, for a narrative completely fixed in oral tradition is no different, with respect to form, from a written document. The Edomite story has surely been transmitted to the Israelites in an oral form. One cannot respond with certitude to the question whether or not it has been committed to writing since ancient times on Hebrew soil."[86] Lindblom supposes that the author had the legend already in its written form, but he emphasizes that it is neither possible nor important to answer this question with absolute certitude. *The difference between a tradition fixed and firmed in the memory and one committed to writing was certainly negligible*, according to him.

In conclusion we can observe that Lindblom gives us the impression of one whose moderate interests in traditio-historical problems were awakened by others—not of one who was a pioneer or a driving force during the rise of this work in Scandinavia. His early studies of the prophetic literature give little sign of cognizance of the traditio-historical dimension, although he takes these matters into account in his publications after 1950. His attempt to examine traditio-historically the book of Job (in 1940) provides evidence of the impact of Nyberg and Birkeland on Scandinavian work. But Lindblom was aware that there was little essential difference between oral and literary sources, and we will see below[87] that Mowinckel used the same argument against Engnell in pointing out that it is therefore just as legitimate to examine critically the oral sources as it is the written materials.

---

85. "La composition du livre de Job," 35ff., 90ff.
86. Ibid., 34.
87. Cf. below, pp. 209–11.

REDISCOVERING THE TRADITIONS OF ISRAEL

G. Sigmund Mowinckel's Further Studies

It has been demonstrated above[88] that Mowinckel in his studies prior to 1930 was fully aware of four important aspects of tradition: that prophetic sayings were preserved and collected into small compositions still at the oral level, that disciples of the prophets (especially of Isaiah) were responsible for this work and for adding prophecies of their own to the collections, that the prophets themselves often caused the collections to be recorded, and that the cult played a central role in the formation of prophecies, psalms, and other traditions. In the work that was done in the following years by Pedersen, Hylander, Nyberg, and Birkeland, two aspects were especially emphasized: the nature and extent of oral tradition in Israel and the precedence of the traditio-historical method over literary-critical investigations. Both of these matters assumed central positions in the debate during the 1940s, and specific issues were settled so that a more moderate direction could be followed by the Scandinavian scholars beginning in the next decade. Two conflicts, one between Mowinckel and Engnell and the other between Widengren and Engnell, were the most crucial in this regard. Our first task now is to clarify Mowinckel's position on the issues of literary criticism and oral tradition, the latter with respect primarily to the prophetic literature.

1. The Indispensable Work of Literary Criticism

Mowinckel has frequently come under attack by some of the Scandinavian tradition historians (especially by Engnell[89]) for his continued use of literary criticism despite an interest in tradition history. It is true that Mowinckel was not willing to jettison literary-critical research as several of his colleagues seemed eager to do, but at the same time there is no justification for the criticism that he adhered to a strict, unrelenting use of minute literary criticism. In fact, the course he tried to steer was one which kept him from either extreme and enabled him to balance his Old Testament studies with the methods and results of literary-critical, form-critical, and traditio-historical investigations.

In his review of Pedersen's *Israel*,[90] Mowinckel addresses himself to the question of the validity of literary criticism and in so doing renders as well some personal comments about his own research methods and interests. He rebukes those (in this case Pedersen) who suppose that literary critics still operate under the impression that the Old Testament is a literary creation

---

88. Cf. above, pp. 169–71.
89. Cf. below, p. 218.
90. *NTT* 38 (1937), especially 65–72; cf. also above, p. 173 n. 21.

rather than a collection of heterogeneous materials stemming from different ages and places. Mowinckel points out that even Wellhausen was aware of this heterogeneity, and that especially at the present time "we who are adherents to literary criticism know very well that, when it concerns motif criticism and tradition history, a 'mechanical' division between the sentences and the words in the individual narrative or tradition cannot lead to the desired end."[91] However, he continues, *this does not imply that we should refrain from trying to separate older elements from younger, or material of one character from that of another;* precisely these tasks, in fact, are important and necessary. Mowinckel admits that he himself has sometimes been inclined to regard literary-critical work as tedious and boring in comparison with the analysis of motifs and contents but that his research for the commentary on Joshua–Kings (*GTMMM* II)[92] required that he once again take up this literary-critical task, and the result was that he became more than ever convinced of the correctness and importance of the parallel-source hypothesis—not only for the Pentateuch but for the historical books as well. Attempts at explaining away the obvious distinctions between the various sources usually bring only unsatisfactory and inconclusive results.[93] *Literary criticism, Mowinckel concludes, is not carried out at the expense of traditio-historical considerations but incorporates them into its analyses.* Like Hylander, he thus refused to accept an intrinsic conflict between the two methods. He did not make Birkeland's mistake of positing the methodological priority of tradition history just because of the predominance of oral tradition. Rather, it was clear to him that literary criticism, form criticism, and tradition history are three separate investigative steps, each with its proper subject matter. We will see that Engnell was of a quite different opinion in this regard.

2. The Rise of the Prophetic Literature

Because of his familiarity with literary criticism and his acceptance of its reasonable results, Mowinckel was able to produce a number of traditio-historical studies which have become programmatic and determinative for further work done in these areas. Perhaps the most important of these is his Norwegian article of 1942 on the subject of the rise of the prophetic lit-

---

91. Ibid., 69.

92. *Det Gamle Testamente: De tidligere profeter*, translated by S. Michelet and S. Mowinckel, Oslo 1935.

93. Mowinckel (*NTT* 38, 1937, 70) refers, by way of example, to Pedersen's treatment of Num 16–17 (*Israel*, III–IV, 283ff. of the English edition).

erature.⁹⁴ This work is significant not only as a prelude to his *Prophecy and Tradition* (1946), but also as a clear statement of the nature of prophetic transmission and of the critical tasks facing the researcher. His ideas have been foundational for later debate,⁹⁵ and the fact that this article has never been translated and therefore has received so little attention outside Scandinavia makes it advisable to review it at some length at this point.

a. Oral Tradition as the Foundation

Mowinckel takes as his point of departure the premise that the prophets—both the older ones (like Elijah and Elisha) as well as the younger, so-called "literary prophets"—always issued their prophecies first at the oral level and that these prophetic messages were transmitted to later generations principally by oral means, with writing being only a secondary and occasional method of transmission.⁹⁶ Furthermore, an examination of the relatively few times that the prophets make specific reference to their own use of script (e.g., as in Jer 29; 51:59ff.; and even Baruch's scroll, mentioned in Jer 36:1ff.; Isa 8:1ff.; 30:8; Hab 2:2) indicates that writing was used each time only to serve some unusual demand or purpose, or as a support for the oral tradition. Mowinckel's own description of the situation is noteworthy:⁹⁷

> It is the oral tradition and the well-exercised memory, not paper and ink, which were and are the means of preserving and handing down all such products of the mind that in present Europe constitute "literature." To this day virtually all transmission of intellectual things, also of holy texts, regardless of length, occurs principally in the memory and orally; instruction and further transmission take place orally; the texts *shall* be learned and remembered, by continual oral repetition, even if they are in a language which in fact the learned only with great pains can understand. That which is written is only a secondary means of sup-

---

94. "Oppkomsten av profetlitteraturen," *NTT* 43 (1942), 65–111. Essentially the same material is reproduced in briefer form in Mowinckel's introduction to *GTMMM* III, *De senere profeter*, Oslo 1944, 34–37. Cf. also Mowinckel's *Prophecy and Tradition*, Oslo 1946, 77.
95. Cf. e.g., D. Jones, "The Traditio of the Oracles of Isaiah of Jerusalem," *ZAW* 67 (1955), 226–46; and von Rad, *Theologie* II, 47ff. (ET: II, 39ff.).
96. *NTT* 43 (1942), 66–68; cf. also above, pp. 169–71. Mowinckel refers liberally at this point and elsewhere to the contributions made by Nyberg and Birkeland, and it is quite obvious that their theses have influenced him strongly.
97. *NTT* 43 (1942), 80–81. Mowinckel (104) asserts, however, that despite this principle of the predominance of oral tradition there probably are certain sections of our present prophetic literature which existed from the very beginning in written form, i.e. that they were composed as literary prophecy; examples of this might be Ezek 40ff.; Isa 24–27; 34–35; Jer 30–31; 50–51; the apocalypse of Joel.

port for the memory and enjoys only a secondary status in relation to the oral tradition; the oral is the real; the written in case of doubt is corrected and supplemented according to the actual or supposedly better information in the oral tradition (Nyberg).

Given these facts, asks Mowinckel, what was it that caused the prophets' oral proclamations, born of the inspiration of the moment, to be committed to writing at some later date and then even to be collected into a body of prophetic literature? This transition, he asserts, marks a very important shift in the nature and essence of prophecy, as well as of its psychological presuppositions.[98]

b. The Prophetic Word as Authoritative

Mowinckel maintains that, if we are to come to an answer to this question, it is necessary first to recognize the position held by the prophets in Israel, viz. as *spiritual, religious, divinely ordained authorities*. Whereas the legends about Elijah and Elisha contain only incidental prophetic proclamations, beginning with the time of Isaiah and his two immediate predecessors, Amos and Hosea, proclamations were preserved and transmitted in detail and obviously for their own sake, very often without background or biographical information. This was because in certain circles (especially at first among the prophets' own disciples) these prophecies were regarded as *authoritative*: "The words of the prophet were not dead capital; they were *living*; they were again and again reactualized in new, analogous situations by men who showed themselves to be authorized, inspired transmitters and perpetuators of the heritage, with spiritual right to direct the sting of God's word also against the conditions in their own land and their own time."[99] These authoritative prophecies, moreover, became with the passing of time something *traditional*; their original, radical character dwindled as they began to constitute the spiritual and moral tradition of the circle of the faithful.[100] This "circle" was, from the outset, the school of disciples ("the sons of the prophets") which the prophet himself founded for the dual purpose of preserving his message and of training the disciples to be prophets themselves.[101] Isaiah's school of disciples is probably the most important of all such groups, for not only did it preserve the prophecies of Isaiah and other like-minded prophets (such as Amos and Hosea), but

---

98. Ibid., 68–69.
99. Ibid., 83.
100. Ibid., 83–84.
101. Ibid., 81ff. Cf. Isa 8:16. See also the discussion above, pp. 170–71, of Mowinckel's *Jesaja-disiplene*.

some of the disciples became prominent prophets themselves (e.g., Micah, Habakkuk, Nahum, Zephaniah). In this way the master's thoughts and methods gained a much greater sphere of influence.

c. Interpretation and Actualization among the Disciples

It is only to be expected that there occurred within the various circles of disciples a great amount of discussion and speculation about the meanings of the preserved proclamations, and the resulting interpretations were not infrequently introduced into the traditional materials and transmitted further as the words of the master.[102] This represents a very important developmental stage—the transition "from prophecy to theology, from creative inspiration to inspiration-supported learning, from free inspiration to the inspiration of a calling."[103] In addition to this, the disciples left their marks on the materials as they collected, organized, and arranged the prophetic proclamations in the oral tradition, for they were psychologically and sociologically guided by the interests which the materials should serve.[104] However, while this stage of collecting and editing was primarily a process of filling out and building upon the traditions (a process which lasted from the time of the prophets to the canonization of the text, ca. 100 C.E.), this was not carried out arbitrarily, for the disciples and their successors often felt bound by traditional interpretations and by the manner in which the proclamations were transmitted in numerous tradition complexes.[105] An important addition, though, was the scheme which the disciples chose to follow in the arranging of the prophecies, both in the smaller complexes and in the books as a whole—*prophecy of doom followed by prophecy of promise and hope*. This, asserts Mowinckel, marks a change in the prophecy, "a new segment in the course of revelation history,"[106] a work of new creation which caused the whole prophetic tradition to become bearer of the message of revelation—that if doom is pronounced, it is in order that the people might be saved. The double task facing Old Testament scholars in this regard is to determine the original meaning and background of

---

102. *NTT* 43 (1942), 85–86.
103. Ibid., 88.
104. Ibid., 89: "The tradition did not develop out of historical or biographical or literary interests, but out of the practical demands of life, the need to possess as completely and clearly as possible the authoritative word of God, which should show the direction for the life of the people—the congregation—both now and in the future, but with that also the need to actualize the words and make them suitable to the necessities of life that in each age are felt the most."
105. This double nature of the transmittal process—conserving and interpreting—was emphasized previously by Hylander; cf. above, p. 176.
106. *NTT* 43 (1942), 94.

each prophecy (especially the prophecies of doom), and also to examine each in its later context of salvation and promise.[107]

d. Creation of the Written Literature

To the question of why the prophecies were committed to writing, Mowinckel first answers that the oral stage was the formative and transformative stage and that any early writing down of the prophetic proclamations played no decisive role in the transmission.[108] As the art of writing became more and more popular and as professional scribes arose and were attached to the temple, the tendency developed to write down that which existed in oral tradition. Since the prophecies were already arranged orally by the disciples into tradition complexes, the work facing the scribes consisted primarily of *recording and arranging these complexes into order according to certain principles of composition*. An oral tradition however, probably often existed side by side the written one as a correcting agent until the written form was canonized. At some point indeterminable to us (probably when Hebrew became a dead language and therefore difficult to remember, especially for Diaspora Jews), the written form of the tradition became the principal one, and the materials were transmitted further in this form. At any rate, the *terminus ad quem* for written fixation of the prophetic books would be prior to the time of Daniel.[109]

3. SUMMARY

What position then did Mowinckel occupy at this point in the Scandinavian debate? Two specific directions in his research were becoming pronounced: *Methodologically*, he refused to believe that literary criticism and tradition history should be mutually exclusive, and he made it clear that the critical analyses should not just stop with the text but must be carried out also for the traditions at the oral level. In especially this latter point he differed directly with Birkeland and subsequently also Engnell, both of whom discouraged attempts to recover the *ipsissima verba* of the prophets or to identify the later interpretations stemming from the disciples. Thus in his critical method Mowinckel did not conform to the direction that was gaining in popularity

---

107. Ibid., 97. Engnell, in direct opposition to Mowinckel, maintains that this scheme of doom–promise is primary to the prophets themselves and thus part of the inherited goods which the disciples received; cf. below, pp. 213–16, 218.

108. *NTT* 43 (1942), 90. This applies also to the few prophecies which the prophets themselves wrote or ordered written; cf. ibid., 101, 104.

109. Ibid., 100–103.

among his colleagues. However, with regard to the nature and extent of *oral tradition* in the prophetic literature, he was quite in alignment with the theses of Nyberg and Birkeland. To be sure, he had already posited the oral character of prophecy in his writings two decades earlier, but in his 1942 article the considerable detail with which he developed this idea gives clear indication of the influence of Nyberg and Birkeland. Mowinckel even postulated a more extensive oral tradition of the prophetic materials than did Engnell after him, as we will see below. Mowinckel's influence in these areas was considerable, not least on von Rad (*Theologie* II) with respect to the matters of oral composition and the process of interpretation and actualization among the disciples. His methodological position also eventually forced Engnell to certain concessions. These problems will occupy our attention in the following chapter.

At this point it remains to be emphasized that Mowinckel's traditio-historical research was by no means limited to the prophetic literature. We refer elsewhere in the present work to some of his contributions in the areas of the pentateuchal, historical, and psalmic traditions. But for the Scandinavian debate that eventually focused on Engnell, his ideas about both method and the prophetic literature are the most important.

12
Ivan Engnell: The Center of the Debate

We have reached the point where it is necessary to evaluate the work of Ivan Engnell (1906–1964), former professor of Old Testament at Uppsala. Of all his colleagues he is the one most closely identified with the characteristic direction taken by the Scandinavian tradition historians, and he is not infrequently regarded as the head or founder of the "Uppsala School." The majority of Engnell's publications appeared only in Swedish, and his direct influence on non-Scandinavian scholars has therefore been minimal indeed—to say nothing of the fact that he has so often been misunderstood and misrepresented. In addition to making key contributions in the area of the history of religions,[1] Engnell sought to apply thoroughly and consistently to the whole of the Old Testament the thesis of Nyberg (his teacher in Semitics) regarding the predominance of oral tradition in the East. Engnell carried this out chiefly through his "traditio-historical introduction" to the Old Testament[2] and his work as editor and chief contributor to the Swedish Bible Encyclopedia.[3] But his influence was felt equally well as the teacher of a generation of Old Testament scholars in Sweden; through his inspiration and encouragement numerous other traditio-historical tasks in varied sections of the literature were carried out by his students. Yet it should not be supposed that we are faced here with a monolithic "school" with set opinions and unchangeable directions. Not only did all of his students gradually modify their ideas

---

1. Cf. above all his dissertation, *Studies in Divine Kingship in the Ancient Near East*, Uppsala 1943; now in its second edition, Oxford 1967.

2. *Gamla Testamentet: En traditionshistorisk inledning*, I, Stockholm 1945; hereafter referred to as *GT*–I.

3. I. Engnell and A. Fridrichsen, ed., *Svenskt Bibliskt Uppslagsverk*, Gävle, vol. 1 in 1948, vol. 2 in 1952; 2nd edition ed. by I. Engnell, Stockholm, vol. 1 in 1962, vol. 2 in 1963. Thirteen key articles by Engnell from the 2nd ed. of *SBU* have now been published in translation: Engnell, *Critical Essays on the Old Testament*, trans. and ed. by J. T. Willis with the collaboration of H. Ringgren, London 1970; American edition: *A Rigid Scrutiny: Critical Essays on the Old Testament*, Nashville 1969.

and redirect their interests during the following decades, but Engnell himself also found it necessary to alter, expand, and even abandon some of his early ideas as the Scandinavian debate continued.[4] In the following we will want to examine his views under the immediate influence of Nyberg and Birkeland and then to demonstrate the changes that eventually occurred, both of a methodological as well as of a substantive nature.

A. Engnell's Traditio-Historical Introduction to the Old Testament

Only the first part of Engnell's *Gamla Testamentet* has been published. The second volume never appeared, although Engnell stated in the Foreword to GT–I that already at that time (1945) most of the second volume was in proof;[5] frequent references are made to it in the course of his discussions. The first volume, giving as it does a more or less detailed presentation of the viewpoints and opinions to which Engnell and other Scandinavian scholars had come, met with considerable criticism—both among non-Scandinavian researchers as well as from several individuals in Norway, Sweden, and Denmark.[6] Typical is Bentzen's opinion regarding Engnell's strong polemical tendencies and the nature of the book as a whole: The volume, he writes,

> has all its good attributes, but also many questionable aspects. With respect to the history of scholarship, the book—as an introduction for beginners—is not very instructive. It seems that Engnell's joy of discovery often leads him to elevate his new perceptions resplendent against the background of the dark age of his predecessors' ignorance.... Moreover, the book is designated by the author himself as something preliminary. That can be criticized insofar as a work, which is characterized by the author in this manner, should be intended as a textbook for beginners.[7]

---

4. Cf. also J. T. Willis, "I. Engnell's Contributions to Old Testament Scholarship," *TZ* 26 (1970), 385.

5. Professor Helmer Ringgren of Uppsala has kindly made available to the writer the entire proof-sheets for the second volume. Not more than 107 pages in length, it consists solely of a survey of the contents of Genesis through Isa 55, essentially in the form of very brief exegetical and religio-historical notes together with references to relevant literature. Apparently a few copies of these proof-sheets have been in the possession of some of the Swedish scholars, for one occasionally finds direct references to this second volume.

6. See, e.g., the critiques by Mowinckel, Widengren, Bentzen, Noth, Gunneweg, Schrey, and others. Some of these reactions to Engnell's book will be mentioned below.

7. Bentzen, *TRu*, NS 17, 1948/49, 321–22.

This and similar criticisms notwithstanding, it is indeed a curious fact that the book, for all of its importance in the field of Old Testament studies[8]—especially as the prime example of the products of the "Uppsala Circle"—has never been translated from the Swedish into a more widely used academic language. Because it thus has not been directly accessible to the vast majority of Old Testament scholars, we choose to present his views here in some detail. Critical reactions will be saved for later sections, especially in connection with Engnell's debate with Mowinckel and Widengren; our own evaluation is found below in chapter 15. In the following, certain key questions will need to be answered: What does Engnell mean by a "*traditio-historical* introduction" to the Old Testament? To what extent does he adopt and even carry further the theses of his predecessors? At what specific points are similarities and differences to be found with the work of Noth and others? What, in a word, is Engnell's critical method?

1. The Importance Given Tradition History

In a brief opening statement Engnell attempts to set the stage for his book. Old Testament criticism, he points out, has in the past century gone through three main stages: (a) the source- or literary-critical stage, associated especially with the name of Wellhausen and characterized by "logicism and rationalism together with its often naïve historicism, marked by an evolutionistic orientation in the writing of history and the history of religion";[9] (b) the form-literary stage, initiated by Gunkel and strengthened by the comparative-religion method, thus serving as a corrective to the Wellhausenian approach; and finally (c) the traditio-historical stage, which alone is methodologically satisfactory because of its combination of synthesis and analysis and its much more positive approach to the reliability of tradition. This final type, says Engnell, is the method which in this book is guiding him in his attempt to find a new orientation for the problems inherent to Old Testament introductions. The study is carried out, admits Engnell, with reservation about certain fun-

---

8. Note Gunneweg's (*Tradition*, 12) estimation of Engnell's book: "The significance of this work lies less in its clearly working out the 'traditio-historical' theses, for at this point Engnell basically repeats what has been considered the 'traditio-historical viewpoint' since Nyberg. Rather, its significance comes much more from the fact that Engnell is now attempting to develop, starting from this viewpoint, a new basis for introductions. That, however, would be a goal that could hardly be reached in a writing of the modest size of Engnell's *Gamla Testamentet*."

9. *GT*–I, 10.

damentals and details; of most importance for him, however, is the "question of proper directions, not of definitive results."[10]

According to Engnell, "tradition history" is not limited to the oral or precompositional stage of the texts. For him *it embraces all critical questions concerned with the study of the literature*, including problems of the text, literary forms, compositional techniques, mythical and cultic background, the religio-historical dimension, and historical aspects. Inasmuch as the role of oral tradition in Israel was *ex hypothesi* so central, this matter colors all considerations throughout his book. This traditio-historical perspective given the various problems connected with Old Testament introduction needs now to be examined at specific points.

2. Oral Tradition and Its Significance for Text Criticism

Following a brief chapter on the history of the canon, Engnell addresses himself to the problems of the text of the Old Testament. Already at this point does Engnell's dependence on Nyberg and other Scandinavian scholars become evident. Here in a brief discussion of textual criticism Engnell declares that the attempt to get "behind" the Masoretic text and to arrive at "the original text" is little more than "wishful dreaming." The hopelessness of such efforts is due to the primarily oral character of the initial stages of transmission of most of the Old Testament materials; because of this fact, textual errors could just as well be of an auditory as of a purely graphic nature.[11] This primacy of oral transmission is attested as well by comparison with other Eastern literature, so that for the composition of the majority of the Old Testament the case is clear: "What we have before us are living, oral traditions, committed indeed to writing, but firmly formed and fixed already in the oral stage so that even the written form signifies in itself nothing absolutely new and revolutionary."[12] We must reckon with a "living" process of development and modification of the traditions during the period of oral transmission; and the literary fixation of the Old Testament, which occurred in postexilic times, was based on this comprehensive, unbroken tradition. We are therefore compelled to have a *basically positive attitude toward the recorded traditions*—not like the disbelief and suspicion which characterized Wellhausen and his followers. The task of the textual critic is only to attempt to restore as far as possible the written, consonantal text; it is for the exegete—not the textual

---

10. Ibid., 11.
11. Ibid., 28. That it is possible in some cases to distinguish between these has been shown by Ringgren; cf. below, pp. 238–40.
12. *GT-I*, 29.

critic—to try to separate "primary" from "secondary" elements in the traditions,[13] although because of the nature of traditions and transmission this can rarely be done with success.

Engnell's argument here thus has three aspects: (a) *The tradition as we have it in its final form is of most importance.* It is therefore not necessary to try to find the *ipsissima verba* of, e.g., the prophets, to divide between "original" material and "secondary" accretions. (b) This applies also to the text. Our task as text critics is to try to recover *the final form of the text of the Jewish community*, not to attempt to reconstruct an "Urtext." (c) Even if we did want to isolate the original elements in the tradition itself, it would be a *hopeless task* because the traditions have been so reworked and transformed by the transmitters that we can no longer determine what is primary and what is secondary. *We are bound in this regard to accept the traditions which the text records.*[14] Thus we should not say, "So says Isaiah," rather —"According to the tradition, so says Isaiah." In Engnell's opinion, attempts to recover the prophets' *ipsissima verba* are based ultimately on residues of the doctrine of verbal inspiration and thus lack the correct understanding of the character of revelation—whereby a prophetic saying retains its worth whether it is seen as originating from the prophet himself or from one of his disciples.[15] *Tradition is cumulative, and its final form is decisive.* For Engnell, this basic principle of tradition, which at some points has found acceptance among other scholars as well,[16] thus dictates also the text-critical task.

---

13. Ibid., 28, 30. Engnell is following Nyberg and Birkeland at this point; cf. above, pp. 179–80 n. 47. Sæbø is of a different opinion regarding the text-critical goal; cf. below, pp. 277–81.

14. *GT*-I, 28–30. This became a main point of conflict between Engnell and Mowinckel; cf. below, pp. 209–11.

15. *GT*-I, 30. It is interesting to note that Mowinckel (*NTT* 38, 1937, 65, 72) uses basically the same argument but directs it *against* the position which Pedersen represents (and which Engnell shares to a degree). Whereas Engnell accuses the textual critic of often being influenced by the doctrine of verbal inspiration, Mowinckel—defending in part the literary criticism of the Old Testament—argues that Pedersen, in using as sources the prophetic books in their present form with no appreciable omissions, is operating from a conservatism and piety that ironically bring about the reverse effect of Judaizing and thus depreciating (at least from the standpoint of the history of revelation) the prophetic materials. For Mowinckel's direct response to Engnell's criticism here, see *Prophecy and Tradition*, 112 n. 130. Cf. Engnell's clarification in "Profetia och tradition," *SEÅ* 12 (1947), 134 n. 51.

16. For example, both Zimmerli and von Rad agree that it is unacceptable to devaluate the secondary additions to the prophetic words and that the categories "genuine/ nongenuine" have only relative importance; cf. above, p. 10.

3. The Literary Forms

The third chapter of the book deals with literary forms, and there is little to be found here that is substantially new in comparison with Gunkel's and Hylmö's[17] discussions of the same—although Engnell maintains[18] that the difference is his own attempt to *see the forms consistently in light of the cult and from the traditio-historical viewpoint*. What does he mean by this? As he did with regard to the text of the Old Testament, Engnell emphasizes here the problems connected with transmission and with the committing of the traditions to writing. Like Nyberg, Birkeland, and Mowinckel before him, Engnell posits the existence of certain circles and schools that transmitted the traditions by word of mouth for decades and even centuries. Because of this it is wrong for us to think in terms of "redactors" who "with scissors and paste composed a written mosaic using clippings from various written sources."[19] The circles or schools of traditionists varied according to the kind of material that was being preserved: The wisdom literature was transmitted by the scribes and the wise; the psalms by priests and singers at the temple; the collections of laws by other groups of priests; the prophetic literature by schools of the disciples of the prophets; the proverbs by the מֹשְׁלִים (Num 21:27); the lamentations by professional mourners; and the narrative traditions by a type of storyteller similar to the Arabian *rawi*.[20] These circles worked not only with smaller units but also with complexes or integrated collections of traditional materials. The result was the rise of an "oral literature," that is, a diversified body of traditions "prepared already in oral form, fixed in firm complexes."[21] Why then was the need felt to commit these well-developed traditions to writing? The reason for this transition, in Engnell's opinion, is best attributed to a "crisis of credit" ("förtroendekris"), to a certain period of time when faith in the spoken word became weakened.[22] Another factor was possibly that the written word was believed to have some "magical" power. Although this shift

---

17. Gunnar Hylmö, *Gamla Testamentets Litteraturhistoria*, Lund 1938. This book is a good presentation and description of the multitudinous forms in Old Testament literature, examined in a manner similar to the works of Gunkel, Budde, and Hempel. Although Hylmö makes occasional comments regarding oral tradition, the transmitters, etc., there is no systematic, conscious effort to trace the developmental history of the forms and traditions.
18. *GT-I*, 39, n. 1.
19. Ibid., 41.
20. Ibid., 41.
21. Ibid., 40, 42. We have seen above (pp. 70–72) that this idea of an "oral literature" was current prior to Nyberg and Engnell.
22. Gunneweg (*Tradition*, 13) criticizes Engnell for his lack of detail at this point: "It is not so very clear what he means precisely by this—e.g., a weakening of trust in the faithfulness

from oral to written literature occurred at different times—for some materials (e.g., some law-collections, cultic-poetic texts) even quite early—we can with certainty conclude that the majority of our Old Testament was first written down in the exilic and postexilic period.[23] This "conclusion," of course, corresponds entirely with Nyberg's dictum about the Old Testament being a creation of the postexilic Jewish community.

4. Tradition History as an Alternative to Literary Criticism

The fifth and final chapter[24] of *GT–I* is crucial for us: "The Problem of the Pentateuch."[25] It is at this point that Engnell's opposition to literary criticism becomes particularly sharp and relentless, especially in his brief overview of the development of literary criticism as a research method, both in its classical form and in the form it took after the time of Wellhausen.[26] He is especially impatient with much of the Old Testament research done prior to him in the twentieth century, both that which is inclined to atomize the sources (the result being a new fragment hypothesis), as well as that which is guided by form and motif criticism (Gunkel and Gressmann) and tends almost toward a new supplementary hypothesis.

Why is the polemic against Wellhausen so important for Engnell, and how does he counter some of the classical principles of literary-critical research? It is, of course, not unusual for a researcher espousing a new method to criticize previous methods on the grounds of error, inadequacy, or simply boredom; such was the case, we have seen, with Gunkel,[27] von Rad,[28] and Nyberg.[29]

---

of oral tradition or more in a general sense—and how this crisis of credit then affected the means of transmission."

23. *GT–I*, 42–43.

24. The fourth chapter of Engnell's book is a survey of his religio-historical views and does not have much bearing on the traditio-historical research of the Old Testament—except that this discussion is included in a *traditio-historical introduction*. Suffice it to say that Engnell is militantly opposed to the evolutionistic theory of religious development, and in its place he sets the "high-god" theory. Great importance is placed on the role of the cult and kings, especially David. He presupposes the complete fusion of Canaanite religion with Israelite religion, though there was a "Jahwistic reaction" in terms of a demand for exclusive loyalty to the God whom the fathers knew in the wilderness. For a more detailed review of Engnell's ideas here, cf. G. W. Anderson, *HTR* 43 (1950), 249–53; and Anderson, in *OTMS*, 287–89 and 296–97.

25. Engnell thus offers no survey of the prophetic literature in his *GT–I*.

26. *GT–I*, 168–85.

27. Cf. above, pp. 58–59.

28. Cf. above, p. 77.

29. Cf. above, pp. 178–79. Nyberg even employed a thesis/antithesis construction to dramatize his opposition to literary criticism.

But beyond this, Engnell feels that there is significant precedent for rejecting the methods and results of literary criticism, whether in its moderate or extreme form; and he presents a summary of the diverse reasons for which some recent scholars have departed from Wellhausen's methods.[30] Among Scandinavians this opposition has been, as we have seen, primarily due to the new appreciation of the role played by oral transmission (Nyberg) as well as to the new understanding of Hebrew psychology (Pedersen). Engnell's own objections to the usual literary-critical arguments fall into three groups: (a) The existence of doublets or variations in the text is proof of the process of the oral transmission of the materials—not evidence of separate documentary sources. Furthermore, obscurities and seeming contradictions can usually be understood when one becomes familiar with Hebrew logic and psychology.[31] (b) Regarding stylistic differences, the argument appealing to "linguistic constants" (i.e., that there are certain words or idioms which are peculiar to the different sources) is not conclusive because the use of these "constants" is often arbitrary and not by any means restricted to the respective sources. For example, the "documents" are not consistent in using the divine names characteristic to them. This is because "whichever divine name is employed depends on the traditionist's own choice. He alternates more or less consciously between the various names for stylistic or 'theological' reasons—*he* alternates, not the writers of the sources."[32] (c) Concerning "theological constants," such as certain religious, cultic, and moral ideas peculiar to the various sources, Engnell asserts that these differences also are often arbitrary and artificial—"subtle differences which only the predisposed, hyperlogical source-critics can detect."[33] By way of example, if J and E do not make the claim for the centralization of the cult, this cannot be used as a criterion for dating these sources, for it simply means that these traditions arose outside of Jerusalem.[34] On the whole Engnell concedes that some forms of literature (e.g., some laws, genealogies, various listings[35]) were committed to writing early and that literary criticism can be practiced on these materials—although much success should not be expected in terms of separating secondary from primary elements or tracing in detail the history of written documents.[36]

---

30. *GT–I*, 186–90. Engnell points to such scholars as Wiener, Halévy, Jacob, Cassuto, Rupprecht, Green, Dahse, König, Klostermann, Kittel, Yahuda, Pedersen.
31. *GT–I*, 191–94.
32. Ibid., 199.
33. Ibid., 206. Engnell admits (203) that the Deuteronomist does have a distinctive theological emphasis; but this, he maintains, is best explained in traditio-historical terms.
34. Ibid., 203–4. For support, Engnell appeals to Pedersen, *ZAW* 49 (1931), 178.
35. *GT–I*, 104–5.
36. Concerning literary criticism and the Chronicler's work, see below, p. 207.

What then is the essence of Engnell's attack on literary criticism? As we have observed for Birkeland prior to him,[37] Engnell is especially motivated by the thesis of a predominant oral tradition. The vast majority of Old Testament materials were developed and composed at the oral level, and our texts of these are basically traditions frozen in writing. Literary criticism, which presupposes development and redaction at the written level, therefore has no relevance in these cases. Only for the few forms of literature that were recorded early or that were even composed at a desk does literary criticism have any work to do. Furthermore, argues Engnell, all of the usual literary-critical criteria either are arbitrary or artificial in themselves or are just as explainable on the basis of the oral tradition or the Hebrew mentality. Thus only tradition history, which can properly assess the oral period, is valid for these texts. Engnell's position on the absolute priority of tradition history, set down here in *GT–I*, remained constant throughout the rest of his life.

5. Tradition History of the Pentateuch

A brief look at Engnell's positive presentation of the traditio-historical view of the Old Testament is now in order. He provides only a very general overview of the Tetrateuch, Dtr, and Chr.[38] Throughout this part references are made repeatedly to Noth[39] and Pedersen,[40] and Engnell's debt to them (or, as the case may be, his similarities with them) is obvious. Especially his descriptions of Dtr and Chr vary from Noth's[41] only at minor points, so we will restrict ourselves here mainly to Engnell's ideas about the Tetrateuch.

Using the literary-critical designations, Engnell asserts that D is entirely missing in the Tetrateuch and that J, E, and P do not stretch beyond the book of Numbers. He opposes the thesis held by Noth and others that P constituted the literary basis for the collection and that J and E were worked in by redaction.[42] It is "both more natural and simpler," in Engnell's opinion,[43] "to consider that 'P' quite simply is the last transmitter and editor of the 'P-work', or the 'Tetrateuch'.... This 'P' (whether one person or many) is then at

---

37. Cf. above, p. 183 n. 59.
38. *GT–I*, 209–59.
39. *ÜSt*, 1943. Engnell (*GT–I*, 210–11 n. 3) feels it necessary to point out that Noth's book is "a work with which I first became acquainted long after my own position became clear." Although Noth and Engnell have much in common, Noth is nonetheless criticized for having a basically literary-critical orientation.
40. *Israel: Its Life and Culture*, I–II.
41. Cf. above, pp. 120–26.
42. *ÜSt*, 206ff.
43. *GT–I*, 212–13.

the same time responsible for the collections of laws which form the actual material behind 'P' and has also ... put his theological stamp on the work."[44] The Tetrateuch falls into two major divisions—the narrative material and the legal material, each of these having, of course, its own independent origin and tradition history. The *narrative sections* taken together show a fairly distinct line of development stretching from the creation on to Moses' death (the last chapter of Deuteronomy belongs at the end of Numbers), and the traditions (both separately and in complexes) that comprise these sections had for the most a long and intricate period of oral transmission and development that resists definitive and detailed description.[45] Like Noth,[46] Engnell believes that the transmitters generally had a positive, conservative attitude toward the traditions they received, and in particular that the basic structure of J's narrative was undoubtedly normative for P. Within the Tetrateuch the traditions contained in Genesis are in content, character, and origin clearly different from those of the other three books; one can even with right regard the whole of Genesis as an introduction to all that follows.[47] The real center of the Tetrateuch is the tradition complex in Exod 1–15, the cultic "Passover-legend," in Pedersen's terms.[48] This is the core which drew to itself the preceding Genesis narratives and the following Sinai tradition complex.[49] The *legal material* in the Tetrateuch consists essentially of local collections of laws that "grew out of the oracular and judicial function practiced by the priesthood connected to the various holy places, with particular emphasis placed on the priesthood's ideological union with the royal-sacral institution."[50] We can assume that the various laws were committed to writing relatively early but did not achieve their final form until postexilic times; this, however, does not exclude the possibil-

---

44. Engnell (221–25) wants to assign P to an earlier date than Wellhausen did, and in this respect he follows the arguments put forth by J. Kaufmann ("Probleme der israelitisch-jüdischen Religionsgeschichte," *ZAW* 48, 1930, 23–43). Engnell, in opposition to Wellhausen, denies that P is antimonarchical and that the centralization of the cult is presupposed in P. Engnell sees Moses, not Aaron, as "the primal king" and the central figure in P; and he agrees with Kaufmann that P, at close examination, proves to be a "codex for the worship of the Most High, which Judaism could adapt to centralization only artificially and laboriously" (Kaufmann, *ZAW* 48, 1930, 32). See also the article by Kj. Jensen, "Om de mosaiske Lovskrifters Alder," *DTT* 5, 1942, 1–14, where it is suggested that the legal materials of P are older than the Deuteronomistic law.

45. *GT-I*, 213–14.
46. Cf., e.g., *ÜSt*, 207.
47. *GT-I*, 215, 218.
48. Pedersen, "Passahfest und Passahlegende," *ZAW* 52 (1934), 161–75.
49. *GT-I*, 218ff. One is reminded of Klostermann's crystallization hypothesis, according to which the kernel was the Sinaitic law; cf. above, pp. 55–56.
50. *GT-I*, 225.

ity of their continuing existence and transmission at the oral level during this period as well. The Tetrateuch as a whole, with its cultic interest being predominant, went through a long period of growth and expansion—the details of which process are no longer transparent to us—and was brought by P to its ultimate form also in the postexilic times.[51]

The most striking part of Engnell's picture of the Tetrateuch is the way he avoids the literary-critical language of documents and sources. For him JE and P are more like tradition strands than clearly defined documents, and his notion of P as the final transmitter departs clearly from the usual view. He takes pains as well to emphasize the role of oral tradition in this entire process.

By way of concluding this review of Engnell's *GT–I*, we refer to two noteworthy ideas about the Dtr and the Chr. In describing the Deuteronomist's basically positive use of the sources and traditions available to him, Engnell makes an important distinction that Noth does not specify:

> One may be able to say that the 'Deuteronomist's' manner of relating to his material is temperate and strongly positive with respect to the older epochs, but of a more far-reaching and revisional nature the closer he cones to his own time. This may seem to be astonishing at first, but considering the work itself it is natural enough: conservatism when faced by the old traditions, but on the other hand a more personal involvement in the judging of the conditions closer to his own time.[52]

Engnell is of the opinion that this general attitude can explain much of the compositional details in Dtr. And with respect to the Chronicler who had considerably more written sources at his disposal[53] than was the case with P or the Deuteronomist, Engnell, who had generally ruled out literary criticism for the rest of the historical books, feels that it can address itself to the problems inherent here in Chr.[54]

---

51. Ibid., 229–30.
52. Ibid., 240–41 n. 4; also 232.
53. According to Engnell (ibid., 249–53), the sources used by the Chronicler were primarily the Tetrateuch, Dtr, the special sources which he himself refers to, and diverse documents for the composition of Ezra and Nehemiah. Engnell, however, refers (ibid., 249 n. 1) with approval to Kapelrud, *The Question of Authorship in the Ezra-Narrative* (Oslo 1944), where the significance of oral transmission in Chr is emphasized. Noth (*ÜSt*, 131ff.) is criticized for disregarding this role of oral tradition; cf. *GT–I*, 250 n. 1.
54. Engnell however is quite skeptical that literary criticism even here can achieve very much: "Whether these documentary sources can in detail then be isolated and cleared of secondary additions, etc.—concerning that, it seems to me, one can entertain legitimate doubts. The literary critics, in the meantime, retain in this case also their usual optimism, although one

B. Prophecy and Tradition: Mowinckel versus Engnell

Engnell's *GT–I* elicited two major critical responses in Scandinavia—the one regarding method (Mowinckel) and the other concerning the thesis of a predominant oral tradition (Widengren).[55] The controversy between Mowinckel and Engnell was carried out in two publications entitled "Prophecy and Tradition." Mowinckel's study[56] appeared the year after *GT–I* and must in many ways be regarded as being of equal if not greater importance than Engnell's book. The significance of the latter lies in its representation of certain extreme views from the early period of the "Uppsala Circle" and in its attempt to write an Old Testament introduction from a consistently traditio-historical point of view (i.e., as Engnell understood it). The importance of Mowinckel's *Prophecy and Tradition*, however, rests in its reasoned, programmatic statement of the tasks, purpose, and place of traditio-historical research.[57] It was one of the first published responses to Engnell's book, and considering the basic arguments it raises and the weaknesses it indicates in Engnell's methodology and conclusions, it has been normative in the evaluation of Engnell's position. Especially to be noted in this regard are the discussions about the relation of traditio-historical research to literary criticism and about the possibility and desirability of determining the *ipsissima verba* of the prophets.

1. Mowinckel

a. The Need for Both Traditio-Historical and Literary-Critical Research

Mowinckel's monograph is divided into two chapters, the first dealing with the general questions of traditio-historical research and the second attempting to see the prophetic literature in this light. In a thematic sketch of the development of the research,[58] Mowinckel describes several reasons for the rise of traditio-historical criticism, the impulses and insights provided by Gunkel and Gressmann, the realization of the importance of the oral transmission of Old Testament materials, and the relation of traditio-historical

---

might suppose that the very divergent results of their research should agree with each other" (*GT–I*, 249).

55. Widengren's arguments are presented in detail below, pp. 228–37.

56. *Prophecy and Tradition: The Prophetic Books in the Light of the Study of the Growth and History of the Tradition*, ANVAO, II. Hist.-Filos. Kl., 1946, No. 3, Oslo 1946.

57. Geo Widengren (*Literary and Psychological Aspects of the Hebrew Prophets*, UUÅ 1948:10, 8), however, criticizes Mowinckel for his polemical opposition to Engnell and for his being "especially interested in saving literary criticism."

58. Mowinckel, *Prophecy and Tradition*, 5–19.

research to form criticism, religio-historical criticism, and the like. Mowinckel emphasizes that, whereas the schematism of literary criticism has been rejected, among scholars everywhere the traditio-historical method has developed in Old Testament research "without its being felt as a breach in principle with the method of literary criticism in itself."[59] Thus Engnell's proclamation of the "complete bankruptcy of 'literary criticism' and its inadequacy with regard to the material" is unwise methodologically and unsound materially.[60] By stressing the interaction between oral and written transmission of Israel's traditions, Mowinckel asserts that in many cases the methods of literary criticism are, within their limits, justified and necessary.[61] Therefore, we should not be faced with an exclusive set of alternatives—*either* oral or written transmission—*either* traditio-historical research or literary criticism—but with a *both/and*.[62] In his own words, "the method of O.T. research can neither be a purely literary criticism nor an exclusive stressing of the fact of oral tradition; it must be a working together of literary criticism and traditio-historical analysis and research."[63]

b. *The Critical Stratification of the Tradition*

At another critical point of opposition to Engnell's *GT–I*, Mowinckel addresses himself to the question of *the purpose and scope of traditio-historical research*. Engnell, according to Mowinckel, uses the terms "history of tradition" and "consistently traditio-historical method" almost as if they were slogans.[64] In truth, however, Engnell holds that because of the process of oral transmission it is unnecessary and inadvisable in principle to attempt to get behind the tradition in its present form, to try to gain, for example, the *ipsissima verba* of the prophets.[65] From this Mowinckel concludes that Engnell, with his emphasis on *tradition*, has lost contact with the essence of this research—

---

59. Ibid., 16.
60. Ibid., 17ff., 26. Mowinckel's characterization (86–87) of Engnell's opposition to the literary criticism of the Old Testament is interesting: "The constant polemic blows that from certain quarters are aimed at the older school or the one-sided setting of the problem as a pro or contra Wellhausen often have the appearance of a fight against windmills or of cheap rhetorical victories."
61. Ibid., 20ff. Unfortunately, Mowinckel offers no specific examples from the Pentateuch where literary criticism is held to be necessary, for it is here that Engnell is most impatient with literary critics.
62. Ibid., 6–7, 34, 66.
63. Ibid., 34.
64. Ibid., 18, 6, 35.
65. Ibid., 18, 36, 88, 112.

the *history* of the traditions. For Engnell " 'tradition' sometimes appears to be understood as something static rather than as a dynamic process, as a real *history*."[66] In Mowinckel's opinion, however, what is necessary is to attempt to distinguish between the "strata" of the traditions, between the older and the younger parts, the primary and the secondary. It is furthermore "important to grasp the interests and the historical forces that have carried on the tradition, and the influences that have had a formative—and transformative—effect on it during the transmission." Mowinckel states his principle categorically: "A tradition history which does not want to distinguish between 'strata' in the tradition is no tradition history, still less a 'consistently traditio-historical discussion.' "[67] Mowinckel illustrates in the second part of his book the appropriate approach with regard to the prophetic literature: The original, short, thematic, situation-determined sayings of the prophets were preserved by "schools" or "circles" of disciples who with time often transformed, adapted, and arranged the prophecies (sometimes at the oral, sometimes at the written stage[68]) according to the scheme "disaster—salvation." *It is the task of traditio-historical criticism, using all the means at its disposal, to attempt first to isolate the original units and then to trace the entire developmental process*—to the extent possible in each given case.

c. Source Analysis of Oral Tradition

With respect also to the question of oral transmission Mowinckel goes beyond the contributions of Nyberg and Engnell. According to Mowinckel, by replacing the idea of a transmission through written sources with the idea of "a transmission through inculcation and further learning," that is, through oral tradition, nothing essentially is gained in terms of "our knowledge of the real character of the material" nor regarding our gaining "any greater certainty as to the originality or reliability of the tradition. The problem of the value of the material as sources still remains a problem demanding solution."[69] Thus one important part of traditio-historical criticism is to submit the oral tradition itself to a kind of "source analysis."[70] Furthermore, answers must be sought for the question of how the transmitted materials developed, why

---

66. Ibid., 19.
67. Ibid., 86; cf. also 18–19, 30, 36–37, 84ff.
68. O. Eissfeldt, however, criticizes Mowinckel for giving too little significance to the role of the written transmission of prophetic material; cf. Eissfeldt, "Zur Überlieferungsgeschichte der Prophetenbücher des Alten Testaments," *TLZ* 73 (1948), col. 533 (= *Kl. Schr.* Ill, 1966, 59).
69. Mowinckel, *Prophecy and Tradition*, 23.
70. Ibid., 33. Cf. also below, pp. 291–92.

they became gathered into tradition complexes, how they obtained their final form, and what their historical value is.[71] Mowinckel admits that many times the researcher will be frustrated in his attempts to trace the history of all the traditions, but on the whole he is optimistic that this task often can be completed and that many of the above questions can be answered.[72]

d. General Principles of Israelite Tradition

In terms of Mowinckel's emphasis on the importance of the *history* of the tradition and based on past research into both biblical and popular traditions, he submits the following programmatic theses as conditions for traditio-historical studies.[73] (α) For all tradition the original traditionary unit and thus the starting-point for the formation of the tradition is the separate narrative, the separate anecdote, the separate prophetic saying, and so forth. (β) All tradition has been anchored deeply in life; therefore its form, development, and alteration patterns are dependent on the psychological, sociological, and artistic laws connected to its place in life. As a rule, only in its final stage does the tradition become fixed and unchangeable. (γ) The tradition material bears certain formal and factual traces of this complex history of development and enables the researcher, to a certain extent, to analyze and follow the origin, growth, and life of the separate traditions and tradition complexes. This constitutes the work of traditio-historical research. (δ) These general laws of tradition apply as well to Old Testament and Eastern traditions. (ε) One important factor to be considered in this history of a tradition is the role possibly played by the recording of the tradition or by the influence from written sources and from already recorded traditions.

Mowinckel concludes his monograph with an unequivocal stand against Engnell's denunciation of attempts to get behind the traditions as delivered to us and to determine the *ipsissima verba* of the prophets. Mowinckel's message

---

71. Ibid., 30. In an interesting aside on the research done into Norwegian family traditions, Mowinckel states (31) that the conclusion reached in these studies is that, "with regard to the 'that' of the happenings, an oral tradition may preserve the memory for some 300 years, whereas all further particulars, the separate 'how's' and 'why's' and the words spoken, already before that time have become 'tales,' epic fiction; after some 300 years there is no longer any guarantee worth mentioning of the correctness even of the 'that' of the happenings. The Oriental and O.T. oral traditions are dependent upon the same psychological and sociological laws as all other tradition." Mowinckel makes no distinction between religious and profane traditions—a difference which Engnell holds as the decisive factor in the reliability of oral transmission in Israel; cf. below, p. 218 n. 103.

72. Mowinckel, *Prophecy and Tradition*, 35, 88.

73. Ibid., 35–36

here is in many ways typical (except for its romantic character) of the book and deserves to be quoted in its entirety:

> Science submits to no "Verbot" but according to its own inherent nature adopts the same attitude to such orders as our own "illegal" struggle did to the thousands of "Verbote" of the occupants.[74] And in this case there is also no reason why science should respect the prohibitions. "Behind the tradition" there loom, after all, the powerful figures of the prophets, who have created that very tradition, and in a number of cases their 'own words' speak to us so clearly that we cannot take amiss. We are not going to allow anybody to deprive us of the right to attempt to let them speak as clearly as possible. In many cases we have perhaps to give it up; the voice of the prophet sounds there more like a powerful leading melody or as a deep undertone in the chorus of the tradition, or more subdued, flooded by the many-stringed accompaniment of the tradition. However, where there appears to be a possibility to ascertain their own words, get hold of the original sayings, approximately such as they once sounded in the streets and market-places of Jerusalem and by the gates of the temple, there we will try to find them by all the means in our power both those of form history, tradition history and literary criticism.[75]

2. Engnell

Engnell's response to Mowinckel's criticism appeared the following year in a Swedish article in the Lindblom-Festskrift.[76] It focuses ostensibly on the question of the originality of messianic elements among the prophets, but Engnell uses the occasion to present an elaboration, clarification, and defense of his position regarding the tasks and methodology of traditio-historical research. He reiterates here among other things his continued impatience with "schematic" literary criticism and adherence to an anachronistic evolutionistic view of the development of traditionary materials.[77] What, however, are Engnell's specific rejoinders to the key criticisms directed against him by Mowinckel, and what—if any—changes from Engnell's previous positions are thereby expressed? Three areas are important:

---

74. Mowinckel's reference here is to the Norwegian opposition to German occupation in World War II.

75. Ibid., 88.

76. "Profetia och tradition: Några synpunkter på ett gammaltestamentligt centralproblem," *SEÅ* 12 (1947) 110–39; published also in *SEÅ* 12 (1948), 94–123.

77. *SEÅ* 12 (1947), 111ff., 131ff.

a. Limiting the Range of Oral Tradition

Mowinckel criticized Engnell for his "axiom" that almost all of the Old Testament literature was originally transmitted orally.[78] To this charge Engnell replies that this is by no means his opinion and that he expressly stated[79] in *GT*–I that the circumstances varied according to the different parts of the Old Testament. He furthermore regards it as necessary for researchers to do justice to the fact that "the two means of transmission, the oral and the written, go hand in hand and should not be played off against each other as mutually exclusive alternatives."[80] Engnell in fact tries to turn the tables on Mowinckel and criticizes the latter for his own extreme, generalized statement regarding the oral transmission of the prophetic materials.[81]

Engnell introduces a distinction between two different types of prophetic literature: the liturgy-type and the *diwān*-type.[82] In the *liturgy-type* (examples are Joel, Nahum,[83] Habakkuk, and Deutero-Isaiah) the materials are the creations of individual prophetic personalities, were probably recorded in writing from the beginning, and are therefore less the result of an active, formative handling by a circle of disciples—although in some cases they may have been transmitted orally to a certain extent. In contrast to this, the *diwān-type*, of which Amos, Hosea, Jeremiah, and Proto-Isaiah are examples, represents "the collected results of predominantly oral traditions, of prophetic words and traditions about the prophet, handed down and disseminated within a circle of disciples and traditionists who hide themselves behind the authoritative name of the prophetic master."[84] Engnell warns against "playing the circle of traditionists off against the master," for the two "constitute an indissoluble unity."[85] Thus we are not justified, for example, in attributing the doom—restoration scheme or the catch-word principle to the disciples, for the impulse

---

78. Cf. Mowinckel, *Prophecy and Tradition*, 18.
79. *GT*–I, 29, 40ff. Cf. also above, pp. 202–4.
80. *SEÅ* 12 (1947), 127 n. 38. J. van der Ploeg (*RB* 54, 1947, 5ff.) is criticized for his failure at this point.
81. Engnell (*SEÅ* 12, 1947, 127–28) is referring to Mowinckel's statement in "Komposisjonen av Jesajaboken kap. 1–39," *NTT* 44 (1943), 160: "All of the transmitted prophetic books are to be seen, not as 'original works' of the prophet in question, but as collected works based on original oral tradition."
82. Engnell, *SEÅ* 12 (1947), 128–31. The *diwān*-type is described in *GT*–I, 43–44, but no explicit distinction between it and the liturgy-type is given there, as Gunneweg (*Tradition*, 13) erroneously states.
83. For Engnell's disagreement with Haldar concerning Nahum, cf. below, p. 227.
84. *SEÅ* 12 (1947), 129.
85. Ibid., 130.

to organize the prophecies in this way could just as well have come from the prophet himself.

On the whole, Engnell's arguments here represent *a modification of his original position regarding the predominance of oral transmission*, but there still remain questionable and problematic matters with which he does not deal. For one thing, Engnell does not spell out the *criteria* for determining which of the prophecies were originally orally transmitted and which were transmitted by writing. Furthermore, it should be pointed out that Engnell neglected to address himself to one of Mowinckel's most perceptive and telling observations—that simply by asserting that a given tradition was handed down orally instead of by writing, nothing is essentially gained in terms of tracing the traditio-historical development of the material itself (the *traditum*). Moreover, as Mowinckel says, should we perhaps submit the oral tradition itself to a kind of "source analysis"?[86] It would have been beneficial to have received Engnell's replies to these matters.

b. Ipsissima verba *and Tradition*

A second of Mowinckel's criticisms was directed against Engnell's disinterest in trying to determine the *ipsissima verba* of the prophets.[87] In response to this, Engnell asserts that only in certain cases can the genuine words of the prophets be isolated, but he maintains his original position that "to hunt for them is in principle wrong"[88] because the prophet's words and the disciples' additions to and reworkings of them are inextricably enmeshed in one another. However, according to Engnell one of the principles of the traditio-historical method is to *believe a tradition* that clearly claims to be reproducing the master's word in some concrete situation.[89] Here we can see how important the notion of "respect for tradition" is for Engnell.

c. The Analytical Task

One of the most important of Mowinckel's criticisms dealt with Engnell's general understanding of the purpose and methodology of traditio-historical research and its relation to other types of research, in particular to literary criticism.[90] Engnell's answer to Mowinckel's charge appears to be less stringent

---

86. Cf. above, pp. 210–11.
87. Cf. above, pp. 209–12.
88. *SEÅ* 12 (1947), 134.
89. Ibid. Cf. also above, pp. 200–201.
90. Cf. above, pp. 208–10.

and less categorical than was the position he held in *GT–I*. Here in "Profetia och tradition" Engnell lays the foundation for the traditio-historical methodology by stating directly that it implies from its outset an *analysis* of the materials. This analytical examination, however, must begin anew—independent from and unrestricted by authoritative figures and working-principles that happen to be fashionable at the moment. By way of example, a good deal of the detailed work and results of literary criticism can be used to our benefit, but we must not succumb to the tendency of many literary critics to operate with a mechanical, evolutionistic method, the result of this being an *interpretatio europeica moderna*. In a statement obviously parallel to one of Mowinckel's axioms,[91] Engnell affirms that analytical research must proceed with the assistance of all available means—form-literary, stylistic, philological, religio-historical, motif-analytical methods, etc. Three warnings, however, should be heeded: these analytical methods (e.g., form-literary investigation) should not be carried to the extreme of past literary criticism so that one uses them to try to isolate "secondary additions" from the primary materials; the task of analysis must not so occupy one's attention that one overlooks the work of "synthesis"; and one must also learn not to expect detailed and certain results nearly every time.[92] Engnell's declarations here lead him to define what he sees to be the purpose and goal of traditio-historical research: *to provide us with a clearer picture of the distinctive character of Israel and of the Old Testament, seen in its historical context and environment.*[93] This curious specification of the purpose of this method—quite different from Mowinckel's and from our own—is understandable only in light of Engnell's view of tradition history as a comprehensive whole embracing *all* steps in the examination of the Old Testament.

d. General Principles of Tradition History

In addition to giving the above responses to Mowinckel's criticisms, Engnell renders a number of opinions on diverse aspects of tradition history which deserve to be summarized here: (α) It is erroneous in principle to presuppose that the messianic character of many of the prophecies and the tendency to arrange prophetic proclamations according to the principle of doom-salvation originated in the circle of disciples, for both of these elements were in all likelihood present already among the prophets themselves—if not even prior to them—and then became an integral part of the traditional goods inherited

---

91. Cf. above, pp. 209, 212.
92. *SEÅ* 12 (1947), 135–37.
93. Ibid., 138–39.

by the disciples.⁹⁴ (β) The main reason why our prophetic "books" have developed and survived is because they (in contrast to the prophetic traditions of, e.g., Elijah and Elisha) have had the proper "driving motif"—"the Jahwistic tendency, especially in its positive-messianic aspect…, laying claim to authoritative validity."⁹⁵ (γ) When we are faced with a formula, an expression, or a traditionary unit which appears in more than one context (e.g., Amos 1:2 and Joel 3:16; cf. also Jer 25:30), we should refrain from thinking immediately of "borrowings," "citations," or the priority of one to the other. Rather, in most cases we would do best to consider that "the prophets and the circles of pious persons behind them carry and transmit further a living, religious, often cultically rooted tradition and thought-pattern which expresses itself in traditional forms, drawn from a *common fund* of stylistic-formal and terminological material."⁹⁶ Without specifying it, Engnell seems to be referring here to streams of tradition. (δ) It is an anachronism to see the prophets as creative artists in the modern sense, for the prophets stood as links in a long chain of tradition stretching back to the Canaanite cultic prophets, and "artistry" for them therefore meant "the knowledge of the forms given by tradition and the ability to use all of these diverse elements as well as to combine them according to given patterns."⁹⁷ (ε) Engnell asserts that the traditio-historical problems facing us with respect to the prophetic materials and the relationship of the dominating influence of the prophet to the transmittal, formative, and transformative work of the disciples have a striking parallel to the situation facing New Testament researchers of the traditions preserved from Jesus and his disciples. In both cases the master has left his mark not only on many of the proclamations but also on the circle of disciples as a whole.⁹⁸

3. The Result of the Debate

Due to this controversy with Mowinckel, Engnell thus modified his exposition in *GT–I* in two significant ways: (a) With his distinction between the liturgy-type and the *diwān*-type, he limited the extent of oral tradition in the prophetic literature; and (b) without softening his attack on literary criticism he admitted to a task of analysis implicit in traditio-historical work. But there remained a chief methodological difference of opinion between him

---

94. *SEÅ* 12 (1947), 123–24, 126, 130–33. This statement is, in part, directed against Mowinckel's thesis that the doom—salvation scheme is secondary; cf. above, pp. 194–95, 210.
95. *SEÅ* 12 (1947), 127 n. 38; cf. also Engnell's *The Call of Isaiah*, UUÅ 1949:4, 60.
96. *SEÅ* 12 (1947), 122–23.
97. Ibid. 123, 121.
98. Ibid., 134–35.

and Mowinckel: Engnell refused to allow a critical stratification of the tradition into primary and secondary elements. He defended his position with the argument that the process of transmission (like Birkeland's "Schmelzofen") has formed the tradition in such a way that it now resists virtually all differentiation. He thus held fast to his principle that we can only examine the final form of the tradition—a position with which Mowinckel (and most other scholars) disagreed vigorously.

C. Engnell's Subsequent Work

Engnell maintained his stand on the character and importance of traditio-historical research until his death in 1964. Indeed, most of his later pronouncements on the traditio-historical method, the value of literary criticism, and the tradition history of both the Pentateuch and the prophetic literature (which had received much of his attention in his earlier studies) are so repetitious of his previous statements that little would be gained by reviewing them again in this connection. We will restrict ourselves to only a few specific themes.

1. Oral Tradition

As a result of the criticism by Mowinckel, van der Ploeg, Widengren, and others, Engnell became noticeably more cautious in specifying the extent of oral tradition in Israel. Thus with regard to the prophetic literature he could state: "I reckon with, most likely, about half less of orally transmitted material than do Mowinckel, Birkeland, and Nyberg."[99] He does not, however, withdraw his claim that most of the Old Testament traditions were not fixed in writing until exilic or postexilic times.[100] The evidence for this major role of oral tradition is derived not only by analogy from other Near Eastern literature, but most importantly by an internal analysis of the relevant Old Testament literature itself.[101] Engnell rejects the criticism that he, by stressing the stability and reliability of oral tradition, has retreated to a new orthodoxy. He makes it clear that for him oral transmission "by no means implies the

---

99. *The Call of Isaiah*, UUÅ 1949:4, 55 n. 3.
100. Ibid., 56–57.
101. Engnell asserts (ibid., 57–58), however, that the ancient Near Eastern—or even just the Western Semitic—culture was not so uniform and homogeneous that the discovery of early evidences of writing at, e.g., Ras Shamra should lead one to some general conclusion about written transmission in ancient Israel. He argues (admittedly *e silentio*) that it is indeed noteworthy that no early writing has been discovered in Israel analogous to those texts found elsewhere. Cf., however, Widengren, below pp. 231–36.

preservation of the tradition material as an unchangeable and absolute unity, but a living remodelling"[102]—although Israelite oral tradition, because of its anchorage in the life-situation, was generally able to resist changes and corruptions.[103]

2. "Primary" versus "Secondary" Elements

Engnell did not falter in his opinion that one must avoid stratifying the tradition. He reasoned that, since it is false in principle (because of the nature of transmission) for literary critics to attempt to distinguish between "primary" and "secondary" elements in the text, it is also wrong for tradition historians to be interested in doing this with respect to the traditions. Thus Mowinckel, for example, despite his laudable emphasis on oral transmission, is not seen as a true tradition historian because he is interested in searching for the *ipsissima verba* of the prophets and because he holds that messianism and the doom—salvation scheme are secondary features added by the prophets' disciples.[104] Engnell maintains, as we have seen already,[105] that both the messianic impulse and the alternation-pattern are original with the prophets themselves.[106] We can observe, however, that Engnell himself did in fact plunge "valiantly and resolutely into the depth"[107] at two points: to describe the background of religio-historical motifs or orientations[108] and to identify sources of the historical books.[109] But in each case he is concerned with *only the first and then the final stages—not with the stages of development and transformation connecting them.*

---

102. *The Call of Isaiah*, 58.
103. Ibid., 59. Due to this religious rooting of Old Testament traditions Engnell concludes that "every comparison with a profane literature, be it otherwise ever so related, becomes fallacious."
104. Ibid., 21–24. Engnell suggests (21) that Mowinckel's later traditio-historical research appears to be "a mere change of terminology" from his earlier literary criticism, and when Mowinckel is seen by others (e.g., Pfeiffer, *JBL*, 1947, 480–81) as the main exponent of the traditio-historical approach, Engnell responds that "in Sweden, at least, we know better" (24 n. 2).
105. Cf. above, pp. 213–16.
106. *The Call of Isaiah*, 22ff., 60; also Engnell, "The 'Ebed Yahweh Songs and the Suffering Messiah in 'Deutero-Isaiah,'" *BJRL* 31 (1948), 54–55.
107. Ringgren, *TLZ* 91 (1966), col. 646.
108. E.g., the divine-kingship ideology, the originality of messianism, etc.
109. E.g., for the book of Samuel; cf. Willis, *TZ* 26 (1970), 390–91.

3. The Traditio-Historical Method

In a programmatic article in SBU,[110] Engnell describes the traditio-historical method as moving along the following lines: (a) an unbiased analysis of the traditions, the aim of this being to delimit as far as possible the tradition collections, complexes, individual units and also the strata within oral tradition; (b) to this end, the employment of all available means and methods (linguistic, literary-historical, motif-analytical, psychological-sociological, archaeological, cultural-historical, religio-historical, etc.); (c) synthesis, or the interpretation of the smaller units in relation to their contexts; (d) a proper appreciation of the role played by oral tradition, without playing it over against the part taken by written transmission; (e) a general acceptance of the reliability of oral transmission in preserving traditionary materials; and (f) a recognition that the proper starting-point is with the *internal* investigation of the Old Testament, using comparative materials wisely and with restraint. Here it becomes especially clear that for Engnell traditio-historical research is restricted primarily to the study of the *traditio*, the process of transmission; the tracing of the developmental history of the *traditum* itself is for him not so important. His investigations into the traditionary materials are thus limited virtually to compositional analyses of the end products.

4. The Primacy of Traditio-Historical Research

Engnell did not lose his antagonism to literary criticism, to which he occasionally referred as "l'école" or "l'école chirurgicale."[111] Even late in his life he could still maintain resolutely:

> I would like to state then, that the break with the literary-critical method must be radical; no compromise is possible. The old method must be replaced by a new one. And the only possible alternative is, as far as I can see, what is in Scandinavia called the traditio-historical method. Its fundamental principle is a disengagement from the anachronistic bookish mode of view, and a realistic insertion of the O.T. literature in its Near Eastern environment, though ... contemporaneously always with the aim of working out the special Israelite character.[112]

---

110. "Traditionshistorisk metod," *SBU* II, 1st ed. cols. 1429ff. As can be seen, most of these points were presented in earlier publications (and discussed above); the main significance of this article is that they are here formulated into a series of principles. Cf. VTSup 7 (1960), 22–24, for an English translation of portions of this article; also Engnell, *Critical Essays*, 3ff.

111. *The Call of Isaiah*, 5, 24, 56.

112. Engnell, "Methodological Aspects of Old Testament Study," VTSup 7 (1960), 21–22.

Despite this unshakable stand, Engnell is willing to admit that traditio-historical research is still in its infancy and that many of its results are therefore only preliminary. He expresses no doubts, though, that it is the working-hypothesis that "solves most of the problems and leaves the least number of question marks, and at the same time from a general scientific-historical viewpoint appears as the most realistic and therefore the most trustworthy one."[113] Moreover, traditio-historical research remains for him not a single method of subordinate importance, but the larger approach which embraces other methods and means in the carrying out of its tasks.[114]

---

113. Ibid., 28; cf. however Rendtorff, *EvT* 27 (1967), 149.
114. VTSup 7 (1960), 28.

13
The "Uppsala Circle"

The particular direction in traditio-historical research taken by especially Nyberg and Engnell did not remain long their private possession but soon elicited response and reaction within the ranks of Old Testament scholars, both inside and outside Scandinavia. This response has ranged from acceptance to rejection, from basically adopting this position as a starting-point for further research, to virtually refusing to give it any serious consideration at all. In our attempt to evaluate the importance that the work and the theses described in the above sections have had for our understanding of the history of Old Testament traditions, it is perhaps best for us to see first how the discussion has developed at its own home base, in Uppsala, where this research direction first established its own identity. There at the old Swedish university a group was formed of Old Testament scholars and students, and traditio-historical theses and the consequences of these were discussed among the members, as well as researched by them individually. There were certain recurring themes—the role of oral transmission, religio-historical motifs and patterns (especially sacral kingship, the high-god theory, and the role of the cult), the viability of literary criticism—but the discussion gained a breadth and depth during the production of the *Svenskt Bibliskt Uppslagsverk* and also because of individual research projects in process. Engnell emerged as the head of this circle and inspired his students to develop and prove some of the bold theses which he had formulated but not worked out in detail. Indeed one can concur with Bentzen when he expresses his "admiration for the erudition, the freshness of viewpoints, the philological proficiency, the enthusiasm and the energy, with which work is carried out."[1]

It would be inaccurate to suppose that there existed a far-reaching uniformity or invariability among these Uppsala scholars, for differences of opinion even at basic points as well as a gradual shift away from the earlier,

---

1. Bentzen, *TRu*, NS 17 (1948/49), 319.

more extreme and dogmatic positions of Nyberg and Engnell characterize the history of this debate, as will become clearer in our discussions below. Indeed we have already seen how even Engnell himself has, in the course of time, modified and altered his own earlier theses. This lack of homogeneity and uniformity of opinion precipitates a terminological problem for us which must be clarified before we proceed further. Are we justified in speaking of an "Uppsala School," as is generally done? If one understands the term "school" as an integrated group of scholars who share a common method, tend to ask basically similar questions, and retain a certain conformity in the answers to these questions, then our employing this term for the Uppsala scholars is problematic for the following reasons: (1) Especially Widengren, who plays such an important role within this group at the points of religio-historical and motif-historical questions, could hardly be included in this "school" with regard to his position on the oral/written transmission problem. (2) Engnell himself has always insisted that an "Uppsala School" does not exist,[2] although he has on occasion also used the term.[3] (3) The diversity of interests and opinions among the Uppsala scholars militates against the use of a term which effectually implies homogeneity. (4) Furthermore, even the component "Uppsala" in the term "Uppsala School" is hardly appropriate, for there are several non-Swedish scholars (e.g., Kapelrud and Nielsen) who have much in common with the methods and interests found among the "Uppsalenser" and should actually be included in such a group. Also, many of the theses advocated in Uppsala have been supported, developed, and often even initiated by other Scandinavian (and non-Scandinavian) scholars as well. Indeed one is tempted to define the term "school" quite loosely as a "common emphasis, a common approach, and a common *type* of solution"[4] and then to speak of a "Scandinavian School," noting especially the important part played by Mowinckel and Pedersen.[5] However, with respect to traditio-historical research, we choose to use the terms "Scandinavian direction" and "Uppsala *Circle*." The latter phrase might sound strange in the ears of those used to hearing "Uppsala School," but it should become clear below that "Circle" is preferable and historically accurate when understood as a group of scholars who, because of a common location, are continually in discussion with

---

2. Cf. Ringgren's "Foreword" to Engnell's *Critical Essays*, ix; and North's "Appreciation," in Engnell's *Studies in Divine Kingship*, 2nd ed., Oxford 1967, xv.

3. E.g., in his article, "Traditionshistorisk metod," *SBU* II (1st ed. 1952), cols. 1430–31; and in *Israel and the Law* (SymBU, 2nd ed. Lund 1954), 1.

4. Cf. Anderson, *HTR* 43 (1950), 239.

5. This was proposed by Ringgren in his presidential "Address of Welcome" at the VIIth Congress of the International Organization for the Study of the Old Testament, Uppsala 1971.

each other about the applicability of certain specific problems or theses to their diverse interest areas and about the validity of one another's solutions. *The term "Uppsala Circle" thus provides adequate latitude for the commonality, controversy, and development that are obvious in the publications of the Uppsala scholars.* It also justifies our handling Kapelrud and Nielsen under the subsequent category of "Influence of the Uppsala Circle." Furthermore, inasmuch as the phrase "Uppsala School" has been "like a red flag for most traditional exegetes,"[6] our use of the word "Circle" should serve to discourage non-Scandinavian researchers from treating the Uppsala scholars as a band of like-minded extremists who can be dismissed *en bloc*.

The purpose of the following section is to determine *the extent to which this circle of scholars adopted, rejected, modified, developed, or went beyond the theses, presuppositions, and methodological programs introduced by the Scandinavian researchers already reviewed above.* A primary consideration in this connection is the movement away from more or less extreme positions and the attempt to work out a broader, more refined understanding of the traditio-historical task which can integrate in it especially the German research methods (primarily literary criticism) that had been assaulted so categorically by Engnell and others at the beginning. One further remark needs to be made at this point: the Uppsala Circle has been exceedingly active in the areas of comparative religions and the history of motifs. Although the Scandinavian contributions here are of very great importance, the histories of the motifs pose a multiplicity of problems that require separate, extensive handling alone. Consequently, in the discussions below the significance of individual religio-historical themes for Old Testament traditions will have to yield first place to the main questions of *traditio* and *traditum* and to the general understanding of the traditio-historical task.

A. Alfred Haldar: Prophetic Circles And Transmission

One of the first members[7] of the Uppsala Circle to demonstrate through publication the influence of Nyberg's and Engnell's traditio-historical theses

---

6. Ringgren, in Engnell's *Critical Essays*, x.

7. Another is Gunnar Östborn, whose works have less immediate importance for traditio-historical research and will consequently not be reviewed here. His Uppsala dissertation (*Tōrā in the Old Testament: A Semantic Study*, Lund 1945) is reviewed by Engnell in *Israel and the Law*, 1–16. Also noteworthy is Östborn's *Yahweh's Words and Deeds: A Preliminary Study into the Old Testament Presentation of History* (UUÅ 1951:7). Another of his studies, *Cult and Canon: A Study in the Canonization of the Old Testament* (UUÅ 1950:10), has relevance for the question "tradition and canon." —Two others who submitted Old Testament dissertations at Uppsala but who have played no appreciable part in the Uppsala Circle are G. A. Danell, *Studies*

was the Swede Alfred Haldar (1907–1986). In his dissertation[8] he seeks to establish the existence, character, and functions of prophetic and priestly associations or guilds in the ancient Near East, within which the development and transmission of many traditions supposedly occurred. Even before reviewing his study we should observe, though, that Haldar has been brought severely to task—and not least by his own colleagues—for his tendency to obscure the differences between analogous phenomena and for his being too quick to draw conclusions on the basis of a rather superficial parallelization of Old Testament texts with other ancient Near Eastern records.[9] However, it is important for us to look more closely at this work in order to gain a better view of the consequences that the traditio-historical emphases in Uppsala have had.

1. Associations of Cult Prophets

Haldar's thesis is that the Old Testament prophets, including the earlier prophetic figures as well as the later "literary prophets," belonged to cultic, divinatory associations similar to the ones found in other ancient Near Eastern cultures.[10] Operating from the assumption that "Israelite prophecy must ... be regarded as an off-shoot of a cultic phenomenon common to the whole Near East,"[11] he supports his thesis by studying the evidence for cultic associations in ancient Mesopotamia and in the general West-Semitic region, as well as the hints in Arabic literature of similar pre-Islamic priestly associations. Haldar attempts to show that these associations throughout the whole Semitic area were regarded as having been founded by some mythical cultic figure (Moses in Israel) who is depicted as a sacral king, with the present king usually functioning as the leader of his associations.[12] Especially for Sumero-Akkadian and Israelite associations Haldar minimizes the differences between prophet,

---

in the Name of Israel in the Old Testament, Diss. Uppsala 1946 (cf. Engnell's review, *Israel and the Law*, 16–33); and Curt Lindhagen, *The Servant Motif in the Old Testament: A Preliminary Study to the 'Ebed-Yahweh Problem' in Deutero-Isaiah*, Diss. Uppsala 1950.

8. *Associations of Cult Prophets among the Ancient Semites*, Diss. Uppsala 1945.

9. Cf., e.g., Bentzen, *TRu*, NS 17 (1948/49), 324–25; and Eissfeldt's review in *TLZ* 73 (1948), cols. 151–55.

10. This idea that the נביאים are cultic prophets dates, of course, back to Mowinckel (cf. above, pp. 169–71), Pedersen (*Israel: Its Life and Culture*, III–IV, 115ff.), and A.R. Johnson (*The Cultic Prophet in Ancient Israel*, Cardiff 1944); cf. also H.H. Rowley, "Ritual and the Hebrew Prophets," *JSS* 1 (1956), 338–60; J. Lindblom, *Prophecy in Ancient Israel*, Oxford 1967; and G. Quell, "Der Kultprophet," *TLZ* 81 (1956) cols. 401–404.

11. Haldar, *Associations*, 110–11, 91, 74, 134.

12. Ibid., 92, 140–41, 200. Cf. however Eissfeldt, *TLZ* 73 (1948), col. 153.

priest, and seer, preferring rather to see here a *"cumulation of functions"* shared by these leaders in cult, in society (as diviners, judges, and even physicians), and in political and military affairs.[13] Haldar goes yet further than Mowinckel and Johnson and maintains that not only the earlier נביאים were cultic prophets but that also the later "literary prophets," as the successors to these, should similarly be regarded as cultic prophets.[14] Haldar thus chooses to stress the element of "continuity," rejecting thereby the "evolutionary view" that sees a development from the cult prophets to the later "literary prophets."[15]

2. Prophetic Tradition and Transmission

In what ways are these ideas related to the traditio-historical theses that had been gaining acceptance in Uppsala prior to the appearance of Haldar's treatise? What consequences do his views have on our understanding of the rise of the prophetic literature and of the prophetic figures themselves? First, it must be said that Haldar accepts unquestioningly the Nyberg/Birkeland/Mowinckel/Engnell hypothesis that the prophetic literature is the result of a long process of transmission within prophetic circles and that this transmission was for the most part of an oral nature.[16] For Haldar this thesis has the same important consequences that it has for Engnell:[17] if the prophetic books are indeed "the outcome of a long process of tradition preservation in the different prophetic circles"[18] then (a) it is impossible for us to determine which sections of the prophetic books are "authentic" (i.e., which date back the initiator of the tradition),[19] and consequently (b) we are rarely able

---

13. Ibid., p.199: "Applied to oracle giving, this [*scil.*: cumulation of functions'] means that no clear distinction can be made between 'sacerdotal' and 'prophetic' oracles; the Accadian bārû priest can take part in the ecstatic rites and the maḫḫû priest busy himself with divination by the observation of omens, while the West-Semitic kōhēn is an ecstatic too and the nābî' imparted oracles obtained by means of 'technical oracle methods'"; cf. also 124ff., 155, 200–201; and Engnell, *GT*–I, 69–77.

14. Cf. also Gunneweg (*Mündliche und schriftliche Tradition*, 14–15, 94–98, 114ff.), who, while criticizing Haldar for a "Nivellierung" of the distinction between the *nabis* and the literary prophets, nonetheless himself arrives at a modified version of this position.

15. Haldar, *Associations*, 199.

16. Ibid., 122, 156, 158. In an additional note (ibid., 206–7), Haldar gives evidence as well for the fact that oral transmission of texts occurred also in Mesopotamia, although probably not to the extent that this was the case in Palestine.

17. Cf. above, pp. 200–201, 214.

18. Haldar, *Associations*, 122.

19. In another article, "On the Problem of Tradition in Ancient Semitic Religious Literature" (extract from *MO* 34, Lund 1946, 1–17), Haldar makes a similar point with respect to the intertwining of poetic and prose materials in Arabic traditions.

to say anything conclusive about the individual prophetic figures which are behind these traditions. "The customary idea of these figures is of course—at least in part—the result of regarding them as the 'authors' of the 'books' that bear their names."[20] In contrast to this idea, Haldar concurs with Birkeland's conception of the tradition process as a "Schmelzofen": If the formative and transformative handling of traditions within the prophetic associations was truly significant and deep-reaching, then we cannot be sure what stems from one prophet or another in the same circle. However, according to Haldar it is also not of the greatest importance, since the concept of "continuity" suggests an unbroken line from one prophetic generation to the next. Thus we can see here that Haldar assumes the same stance as Engnell and Nyberg regarding the impossibility of reconstructing the historical development of the traditions.

With these consequences of Haldar's theses in mind it may be well for us to look somewhat more closely at his understanding of the *transmission* carried out within these prophetic circles. Haldar suggests that, as members of the associations, the prophets and priests functioned as transmitters of religious as well as of political and historical traditions. According to him, this fact becomes especially clear if we remember that one of the important duties of these individuals was the recital of cultic texts at the big annual festivals.[21] The associations transmitted in addition to cultic texts also prophetic oracles and legal traditions; indeed many of the oracles and laws originated in these circles because of the functions of the priests and prophets.[22] Selection, alteration, and censorship are all seen to be facets of the transmission process, but Haldar goes on to discuss an additional principle which was operative because of the intimate relationship between politics and religion. This is the fact that political predictions were preserved only if they were fulfilled;[23] this principle is especially relevant for large sections of Isaiah, Jeremiah, and so forth.[24] Haldar also shares Engnell's opinion that the scheme of alternating

---

20. Haldar, *Associations*, 122.
21. Ibid., 155ff., 201. Deut 33:9c–10a is seen as evidence of the Levites' part in this process of preservation and transmission; ibid., 100–101, 3–4.
22. Ibid., 155ff.
23. A similar idea was suggested earlier by Birkeland; cf. above, pp. 183–84.
24. Haldar, *Associations*, 159. By way of example, Haldar refers to the conflict between Elijah and his circle on the one hand and the prophets supporting King Ahab on the other (1 Kgs 18ff.). When Ahab was defeated in the battle, Elijah's words became verified and were therefore preserved. However, says Haldar, if Ahab and Jehoshaphat had won the battle and thus Jehu's revolt had failed, then the circle of prophets around Ahab would have been the dominant one, and the tradition which we would now have about this incident would have been developed by Ahab's prophets and would naturally have cast Elijah and his associates in the light of

between prophecies of doom and prophecies of salvation is, as a phenomenon common to the prophetic literature of the whole ancient Near East, of a very early date and thus part of the cultic, traditional materials transmitted down to the Old Testament prophets.[25]

In his work on the book of Nahum[26] Haldar demonstrates the significance which, in his opinion, this idea of cultic associations can have for Old Testament studies. In opposition both to the "traditional view of literary criticism" (that the book is a written creation composed prior to the fall of Nineveh) and also to Humbert's thesis that the book is a prophetic liturgy,[27] Haldar maintains that what we have here is a collection of several political-religious prophecies, originating not with just one person but rather in such a cultic association or circle as is described above, in the years prior to Nineveh's collapse in 612 B.C.E. It is thus evidence of the *political activity* of such associations, as well as of their familiarity with mythico-ritual texts (in Nahum the picture is of a struggle between Jahweh and his foes) and their ability to use these materials in their political propagandizing.[28] The written text of these prophecies was "composed by an unknown member of a cultic association," and the name of the prophet Nahum was ascribed to it at a later date.[29]

To conclude this section we must emphasize two contributions that Haldar made in his work on the prophets. First, he furthered the effort to understand the prophets as members of a traditional line closely associated with the cult, rather than as lonely individuals with a deep-set opposition to the cult. Second, he demonstrated the importance of objectively viewing

---

false prophets, for in such political affairs "it is only to be expected that the tradition should be accommodated to suit the victorious party, the other side being rendered powerless" (ibid., 159).

25. Ibid., 213 (referring to p. 129). Cf. above, pp. 213–16, 218.
26. *Studies in the Book of Nahum*, UUÅ 1946:7.
27. Ibid., 2–5. Cf. P. Humbert, "Le problème du livre de Nahoum," *RHPR* 12 (1932), 1–15.
28. *Studies in the Book of Nahum*, 6, 88, 145, 148ff.
29. Ibid., 148. It is interesting to note that Engnell himself differs sharply with Haldar on this interpretation of the origin of the book of Nahum. In "Profetia och Tradition" (*SEÅ* 12, 1947, 128–29) Engnell states that "one cannot simply postulate that a collective, a circle of traditionists, stands behind it; rather here one must at least examine closer the possibility of individual prophetic figures as originators, as 'writers,' in accordance with what the tradition itself informs us." Contending that Haldar has not offered sufficient evidence for his suggestion that the book of Nahum stems from a cultic circle, Engnell tends to agree with Humbert's view of it as a prophetic liturgy. —Precisely at this point we can see how seemingly arbitrarily Engnell approaches the text. When should the critic accept "what the tradition itself informs us," and when not? What explicitly are Engnell's *criteria* for distinguishing between the liturgy-type and the *dīwān*-type of prophetic literature?

the prophets against the background of the ancient Near East, where phenomena similar to those in Israel can be found. But precisely in both of these points lies also the weakness of Haldar's work, for he obscures the differences between earlier and later prophets in Israel and likewise fails to distinguish adequately between the various prophetic circles in the Semitic culture. He thus *covers over the individuality and particularity of Israelite elements*—precisely contrary to the central task that Engnell sets for tradition historians.[30] Indeed Haldar's postulated prophetic associations become ideal producers and transmitters of traditions, but his easy leap from analogy to dependency in trying to establish his basic thesis regarding the associations has put his exposition in a questionable light and thereby has *minimized his positive contributions to the course of traditio-historical research*. His argument about the "Schmelzofen" effect of the transmission process in prophetic circles and his position concerning the infeasibility of critically stratifying prophetic tradition were both simply taken over from Birkeland and Engnell.

B. Geo Widengren's Refutation of the Thesis of a Predominant Oral Tradition

The reason for our employing the wider term "Uppsala Circle" instead of "Uppsala School" becomes clear when we assess the contributions made to the ongoing discussions by Geo Widengren (1907–1996), the professor of the history of religions in Uppsala. We have seen above that, in addition to philological work, the research activity in Uppsala—especially that of a traditio-historical nature—seems to center on two focal points: (a) the role played by oral transmission in Israel and (b) the religio-historical background and history of the motifs. Whereas Widengren is fully in accord with the other Uppsala scholars at the second point,[31] he differs decidedly from them—especially from Nyberg and Engnell—regarding the first issue. If we were to hold to the term "Uppsala School," then in its strict sense Widengren would not be a member because of his divergent views on this central issue of oral transmission and the consequences which this factor is assumed to have for the history of Old Testament tradition. However, he is very much a member of the "Uppsala Circle" in the sense that from the outset he participated actively in the discussion of these issues, even if his opinions regarding oral transmission resulted practically in an open controversy between him and especially Engnell. Widengren's special field, though, is the history of religion, and

---

30. Cf. above, p. 215.
31. Cf. also Bentzen, *TRu*, NS 17 (1948/49), 320, 322; Anderson, *HTR* 43 (1950), 246–48; and Schrey, *TZ* 7 (1951), 321–24.

with regard to the sacral-kingship ideology and the high-god theory he has been one of the pioneers and chief proponents of the direction taken by the Uppsala scholars.[32] His contributions in this area are of prime importance; indeed he has devoted most of his efforts to these questions. However, for our purposes we will concentrate on his treatment of the question of oral transmission[33] and on his role in the Scandinavian debate on this aspect of *traditio*.

1. THE IMPORTANCE OF WRITING IN THE ANCIENT NEAR EAST

To review briefly the general state of the discussion by 1948, the year of Widengren's publication: The thesis advanced by Nyberg, Birkeland, and Engnell and supported to a greater or lesser extent by Pedersen, Mowinckel, Lindblom, and Haldar is that the primary means of transmission of Old Testament traditions was oral. Further, although situations varied somewhat according to the type of literature under consideration, the usual process was for traditions to originate separately and independently, to be handed down from generation to generation usually among professional or semiprofessional

---

32. For Widengren's work in these areas attention is directed especially to his following publications: *Hochgottglaube im alten Iran*, UUÅ 1938:6; *Psalm 110 och det sakrala kungadömet i Israel*, UUÅ 1941:7,1; "Det sakrala kungadömet bland öst- och västsemiter," *RoB* 2 (1943), 49–75; *Till det sakrala kungadömets historia i Israel*, HS I 3, Stockholm 1947; *The King and the Tree of Life in Ancient Near Eastern Religion*, UUÅ 1951:4; *Religionens värld*, 2nd ed., Stockholm 1953 (German edition: *Religionsphänomenologie*, Berlin 1969); *Sakrales Königtum im Alten Testament und im Judentum*, Stuttgart 1955; and "King and Covenant," *JSS* 2 (1957), 1–32.

33. Widengren's key works in this area are *Literary and Psychological Aspects of the Hebrew Prophets*, UUÅ 1948:10; and "Oral Tradition and Written Literature among the Hebrews in the Light of Arabic Evidence, with Special Regard to Prose Narratives," *AcOr* 23 (1959), 201–62. Another important article is his "Tradition and Literature in Early Judaism and in the Early Church," *Numen* 10 (1963), 42–83, a critique of Birger Gerhardsson's *Memory and Manuscript: Oral Tradition and Written Transmission in Rabbinic Judaism and Early Christianity*, Uppsala 1961. In this article Widengren attempts to show that Gerhardsson has underrated the role of written transmission both in Judaism and in early Christianity. Gerhardsson's study is important regarding oral and written transmission among both the Jews and the Christians in the early centuries C.E., but it should not be read without reference to Widengren's article and especially to the review by M. Smith, "A Comparison of Early Christian and Early Rabbinic Tradition," *JBL* 82 (1963), 169–76. Note also Gerhardsson's response to the latter, *Tradition and Transmission in Early Christianity*, CN 20, Lund and Copenhagen 1964. —At this point we may mention that both Gerhardsson and Harald Riesenfeld have been influenced decidedly by Engnell and consequently attempted to carry over to New Testament literature some of his traditio-historical and religio-historical methods and theses—for Gerhardsson especially the thesis about oral transmission, and for Riesenfeld primarily the work in the history of religious motifs; cf. the latter's dissertation, *Jésus transfiguré*, ASNU 16, Uppsala and Copenhagen 1947 (cf. Noth, *Ges. Stud.*, 198–99, 227ff.).

transmitters (or, for prophetic traditions, among the disciples), to undergo some internal transformation as well as gradual assimilation into tradition complexes still at the oral level, and then finally for this fixed, oral form to be committed to writing, for most of the traditions this recording occurring first in exilic or postexilic times. What, however, is Widengren's alternative solution to this problem of transmission, and what evidence does he offer to support his thesis?

From the outset, Widengren asserts that the role and the trustworthiness of oral transmission among the Israelites have been grossly exaggerated by Engnell and other Scandinavian scholars, and that this has been the case above all with regard to the prophetic literature.[34] According to Widengren, a basic fault committed by these researchers has been *a misinterpretation of the data provided by the other Near Eastern cultures*, for the fact is that among Israel's neighbors the art of writing and the tendency to commit traditions to written form were considerably more widespread than is generally admitted by his Uppsala colleagues. Using the distinction first instituted by Stig Wikander,[35] Widengren maintains that a definite difference can be observed between Indo-European (especially Indian, Iranian, Greek, Latin, Germanic, and Celtic) and Near Eastern (including Egyptian) religions: The former were from the outset characterized by an absence of written religious texts, cult-images, and temples, but having an authoritative priesthood trained in oral transmission; the latter, on the other hand, have since early times generally had temples, idols, and holy writings. Therefore, Widengren points out, simply contending that oral transmission was predominant in Near Eastern cultures and then appealing to Indo-European practices for support for this contention is misleading, unsatisfactory, and inconclusive. One must not be so indiscriminate in searching for analogic evidence in support of his theses.

With this principle we must agree fully, but the problem does not end at this point. In examining Widengren's use of comparative materials, one at times has reason to suspect that he also treats his Semitic evidence too flatly and without differentiation. There is, of course, justification in his claim that, in light of the absence of sufficient evidence in the Old Testament, the researcher is obliged to turn to external (Near Eastern) witnesses in order to be able to gain a better impression of situations in Israel.[36] But in so doing *one must not become insensitive to any essential differences present between cultures*

---

34. Widengren, *Literary and Psychological Aspects*, 93.
35. Wikander's work has not been published, though certain aspects of the Indo-European religion are touched in his article, "Indoeuropeisk religion," *RoB* 20 (1961), 3–13. Cf. also Widengren, *AcOr* 23 (1959), 225–26; and *Religionsphänomenologie*, 569–71.
36. Cf. below, p. 291.

separated by as much time and space as were ancient Mesopotamia and Israel, or Israel and the Islamic countries.[37] Nonetheless, Widengren's close analysis of transmittal means in other Semitic cultures did enable him to sketch a quite different picture of the situation than that offered by Engnell, and this corrective measure in the question of *traditio* is one of Widengren's prime contributions.

2. SUPPORTIVE EVIDENCE

Widengren's thesis is that *one cannot give an unequivocal answer to the question of whether oral means or written means was the primary transmittal method in the ancient Near East*. In his own words, "it is wrong to contrast oral and written tradition too much in an ancient Semitic culture."[38] Wid-

---

37. Widengren's use of external analysis and comparative, analogic materials provided the substance for a sharp difference in principle and method between him and Engnell. In *The Call of Isaiah* (1949, 57–58), in the article "Traditionshistorisk metod" in *SBU* II (1st ed. 1952, cols. 1433–34), and again in his article in VTSup 7 (1960, 24–27), Engnell rebukes Widengren by asserting that, concerning questions of tradition and transmission, "the *internal* investigation of the literature of the O.T. should be the *self-evident starting-point*" (VTSup 7, 1960, 24) and that appeal to comparative materials should be made only with extreme care, taking always into consideration differences of time, place, environment, setting in life, and the Israelite transmittal conservatism. Engnell criticizes especially the appeal to Arabic literature and conditions because of "the deep differences in time and space, from the cultic and religious point of view" (*The Call of Isaiah*, 57). Curiously enough, as Widengren points out (*AcOr* 23, 1959, 226ff., 215), this emphasis on internal analysis and the hesitancy to use analogic materials mark a significant shift in Engnell's method, for in previous works (e.g., *GT-I*, 40) as well as in his agreement with Nyberg and Birkeland he supports his thesis of the predominance of oral transmission by appealing to the general employment of oral means throughout the ancient Near East; and of course such external investigation of other Semitic cultures is the *sine qua non* for his motif-historical or religio-historical work in the Old Testament. But this fact of Engnell's inconsistency here does not by itself refute Engnell's charge against Widengren. As to the legitimacy of using Arabic analogies, Widengren appeals to little more than the fact of similar cultural patterns between Arabs and Israelites, as well as to their common Semitic attitude toward the spoken and the written word; cf. *Literary and Psychological Aspects*, 9–10, 55–57, 65–66, 122; and *AcOr* 23 (1959), 215, 225–29. —One is indeed left with the impression that the issue still remains unsettled regarding the value and legitimacy of appealing to outside sources in order to draw conclusions about conditions in Israel. The days of Pan-Babylonianism are long past, and we have learned that there was both truth and falsity in the theories of the "Babel-Bible" advocates. However, the question about the precise validity of comparative research for Israel and the Old Testament is surely an issue which yet needs to be thoroughly and systematically examined. Until this is done, such references as those made by Widengren and others to putatively parallel circumstances must be regarded as provisionally helpful—but not as conclusive. Cf. also Ahlström, *HTR* 59 (1966), 70–71 n. 7.

38. *Literary and Psychological Aspects*, 56; cf. also 92 and 121–22.

engren provides the evidence for his thesis first from the ancient Near East in general and then from the Arabic lands in particular.

a. Mesopotamia

Archaeology has shown that the alphabet and the inclination to use writing were early developments in Mesopotamia. Although relatively shorter songs and poems of a mythic-epic character were probably circulated and transmitted orally at the beginning, they were very soon recorded in writing; a good example of this is the Gilgamesh Epic.[39] After a tradition was written down, this became the primary means of transmitting it to later generations—even though it still may have been memorized and recited for centuries thereafter.[40] Also the Ugaritic texts are apparently the written form of an oral tradition, recorded as soon as the alphabet with cuneiform characters was developed. Whereas earlier inscriptions and texts have been found in abundance in other parts of the Near East, the importance of the Ras Shamra texts for us is that they "testify to the writing down among the ancient Western Semites of their religious, i.e. chiefly mythic, and ritual texts," accomplished prior to or near the time of the settling of the Israelite tribes in Palestine.[41]

b. Arabic Cultures

The situation in Arabic lands is also an admixture of oral and written means of transmission, with greater reliance apparently invested in the latter.[42] Among

---

39. *AcOr* 23 (1959), 218–21. J. Læssøe ("Literacy and Oral Tradition in Ancient Mesopotamia," *Studia Orientalia Ioanni Pedersen ... dictata*, Hauniae 1953, 205–18) comes to a conclusion similar to Widengren's regarding the basic predominance of written transmission in Mesopotamia. Læssøe also appeals to the Gilgamesh Epic as a good example of how the use of writing made possible the complex combination of diverse sources into one connected epic composition. The great importance which Babylonian and Hittite chroniclers put on written documents is shown also by H. G. Güterbock, "Die historischen Traditionen und ihre literarische Gestaltung bei Babyloniern und Hethitern bis 1200," *ZA* 42 (1934), 1–91; 44 (1938), 45–149.

40. Widengren, *Literary and Psychological Aspects*, 58ff., 90–91. The same thesis was submitted by Gunneweg, *Mündliche und schriftliche Tradition*, 48–50, 77–78, 119–22. Referring to the close relationship between writing and recitation, Widengren (91) quotes the Sumerian proverb: "Writing is the mother of orators, and the father of artisans."

41. *Literary and Psychological Aspects*, 58; cf. also *AcOr* 23 (1959), 222–23. Widengren (*AcOr* 23, 1959, 223–24.) dismisses summarily Engnell's *e silentio* argument about the fact that no analogous written texts have been discovered in Palestine; cf. above, p. 217 n. 101.

42. Cf. also Læssøe, "Literacy and Oral Tradition," 207–8; but then also Ringgren, *ST* 3 (1949), 35–39; and Pedersen, *Den arabiske bog*, København 1946, 5–6, 14–15, 21ff., 31ff.

pre-Islamic Arabs writing was quite well known and used in the towns and to a more limited extent even among bedouins, especially those under the influence of Christianity.[43] The manner of transmission was on the one hand thus dependent on the state of the literary and scribal culture in the different districts, but on the other hand also dependent on the literary form of the material in question. Poetry and wisdom sayings were probably recorded quite early after only a relatively short period of oral transmission,[44] whereas the prose narratives (the *ayyām al-'Arab*) apparently existed at the oral level for about two centuries before being fixed in writing.[45] For the early Islamic era and the preservation of the religious traditions, the evidence indicates again the presence of both oral and written means of transmission rather than the exclusive predominance of the one or the other. The learned historical literature, the *sīrah* and the *ḥadīth*, most likely existed in writing almost from the outset, at least from the first Muslim generation.[46] Concerning the origin of the Koran, Widengren emphasizes that Muhammad was intent on preserving his *sūrahs* by both oral and written means: he dictated them to his secretaries to be written down and also recited them to his believers that they might learn them by heart. Here can be seen clearly the close relationship between the written and the spoken word, for "the holy word is written down not only in order to be preserved, but also in order to be read aloud and recited."[47] Another important fact is that Muhammad himself is responsible for occasional variations of and interpolations in his earlier revelations.[48]

Widengren's studies of the transmission of certain pre-Islamic and Islamic traditions have brought him also to several miscellaneous, general

---

43. *Literary and Psychological Aspects*, 11–20, 29.

44. The ancient poems that were handed down orally by the popular *rāwīs* gradually became more and more corrupted. Consequently many poets in the period just prior to and after the beginning of the Muhammadan era either wrote or caused their poems to be written down. For example, Dū-l-Rummah (a bedouin poet living at the beginning of the eighth century C.E.) advised his listeners to write down his poems, for: "A book does not forget or alter words or phrases which have taken the poet a long time to compose" (quoted by Widengren, *Literary and Psychological Aspects*, 24, cf. also 21–33). Contrast this, though, with the antiscribal statements expressed in a later era, e.g., the passage quoted by Birkeland, above, pp. 182–83. It is obviously possible to find evidence supporting any thesis—even two opposing ones.

45. *Literary and Psychological Aspects*, 33–34 For more details on the oral and written transmission of the *ayyām*-literature, cf. *AcOr* 23 (1959), 232–43. Also J. R. Porter argues that studying this pre-Islamic literature can contribute to our understanding of the Old Testament narrative traditions; "Pre-Islamic Arabic Historical Traditions and the Early Historical Narratives of the Old Testament," *JBL* 87 (1968), 17–26.

46. *Literary and Psychological Aspects*, 35–45.

47. *Religionsphänomenologie*, 567; cf. also *Literary and Psychological Aspects*, 45–47.

48. *Literary and Psychological Aspects*, 48–54.

conclusions which we can simply mention here: "The single tradition is more trustworthy than the context where it is found."⁴⁹ The separate tradition is often preserved verbatim for centuries, this fidelity to tradition being due to written, not to oral, transmission (because of the usual brevity of the oral period).⁵⁰ A relatively young source may in certain cases have preserved an old tradition in better form than an earlier source has succeeded in doing.⁵¹ Traditions possessing a rather complicated plot often develop inaccuracies, confusions, and repetitions when transmitted orally by nonprofessional traditionists.⁵² And these poorly transmitted stories are often "improved" when they are recorded in writing.⁵³

c. The Old Testament

Concerning the Old Testament materials, Widengren draws conclusions similar to those reached above for general ancient Near Eastern and Arabic conditions. When seen alongside the work done by his predecessors and contemporaries, he offers here little evidence and few arguments that are new, except possibly for his comparisons of Israelite with Arabic and Mesopotamian conditions. This fact, however, is precisely what is so striking: how the *same* data can be interpreted in such contrary ways and thus lead to such diverse conclusions. For example, citing the well-known references to writing and written sources in the narrative books (e.g., Judg 8:14; Exod 34:28; 17:14; Num 21:14; 2 Sam 1:18) and in the prophetic literature (e.g., Isa 8:1, 16; 30:8; Jer 36:2, 4, 32; 51:60; Ezek 2:9–10; 43:11; Hab 2:2; Hos 8:12), Widengren does not draw the same conclusion as, for example, Mowinckel, Birkeland, Engnell, and Nielsen—that the very mentioning of something having been written implies that this was a special, unusual situation, that is, the exception rather than the rule. Rather, Widengren maintains that we are provided here with the indications that writing was in fact employed very early and is therefore mentioned occasionally in the traditions; however, we should not suppose that these were the only places where writing occurred from the outset, for its use was relatively commonplace.⁵⁴ In other words, according to Widengren

---

49. *AcOr* 23 (1959), 235.
50. Ibid., 258.
51. Ibid., 253.
52. Ibid., 261–62.
53. Ibid., 262.
54. Widengren, *Literary and Psychological Aspects*, 60ff. Engnell (VTSup 7, 1960, 27) accuses Widengren of confusing "the *ability* of writing, especially its use in what was earlier called 'magical' connexions, with the factual transmission of a 'literature.'" A similar point was made long ago by A. A. Bevan, "Historical Methods in the Old Testament," *Essays on Some*

these passages indicate that *writing was the rule rather than the exception*. Of course oral transmission was also present to some extent, especially for the narrative traditions of the conquest of Palestine[55] and the sagas of creation, the flood, and the patriarchs. These traditions, however, are contrasted with, e.g., the books of Samuel and Kings, which were intentionally designed as historical *oeuvres*, based both on written records (official lists, royal annals) and on oral traditions presumably written down shortly after the events described. The general rule is that "only for such Hebrew literature as reflects the conditions of a nomadic or seminomadic people may we assume a more prolonged oral transmission of historical and poetical traditions and narratives."[56] This is a chief presupposition for Widengren's thesis about transmittal habits in Israel. He agrees that oral traditions were present but maintains that they were recorded as soon as an urban life permitted it. The literary stage is also important because it was usually in this period that the diverse traditions, already in written form, were collected into tradition complexes. One should not conclude from these statements, however, that Widengren adheres to the methods and theses of literary criticism, for he objects strongly to the minutiae of classical literary-critical investigations and even submits that "all the work of literary criticism is to be remade."[57]

Since Widengren associates oral transmission with the nomads and literary transmission with the settled culture—a distinction which in this form is perhaps too general and simplistic—the implication of this viewpoint for the *prophetic literature* is clear, for the prophets operated for the most in an urban civilization where writing was supposedly the natural means of preserving the spoken word.[58] For Isaiah, Jeremiah, and Ezekiel we know that they themselves wrote down or dictated part of their prophecies, and there is no reason to doubt that this was also the case with Amos and Hosea, whose prophecies are

---

Biblical Questions, ed. Swete, London 1909, 6. Widengren (*Literary and Psychological Aspects*, 90–92), on the other hand, maintains that the fact that traditions were memorized or recited does not mean that this was the only or primary manner of transmission. Gunneweg argues similarly; cf. below, pp. 289–90 n. 8.

55. Widengren (*Literary and Psychological Aspects*, 63ff.) compares these with the prose traditions *ayyām al-'Arab*.

56. Ibid., 122, cf. also 62–68. Van der Ploeg (*RB* 54, 1947, 41) also makes this distinction, attributing oral transmission more to the desert or nomadic life and written transmission more to settled peoples. Cf. however Bentzen, below, pp. 256–57.

57. Widengren, *Literary and Psychological Aspects*, 65. Widengren does not spell out what form this restructuring of literary criticism is to take.

58. Ibid., 92–93. Note that Gunneweg asserts that writing was the *authoritative, official* means at the sanctuaries and courts, whereas oral transmission was the *normal* means among the common people; cf. below, pp. 289–90 n. 8.

preserved in a better text than oral transmission probably could have managed.[59] According to Widengren, Jeremiah corresponds well to the Arabian pattern of a prophet dictating the prophecies to a scribe to ensure that they are written down while the prophet is still alive; one difference is that there is no mention in the book of Jeremiah that any of his disciples preserved his words in their memory, whereas this was the case with Muhammad.[60] Widengren also emphasizes the idea of the Heavenly Book, the revealed, written Word which the prophet receives and for which he accordingly attempts to produce an earthly counterpart. This is true not only for Ezekiel and Muhammad but can also be seen to be a common phenomenon in the ancient Near East.[61] A further factor worth considering is that the complicated, often turbulent visions of the prophets (e.g., Ezekiel) most likely had to be recorded in writing very early in order that their pictorial details would not be forgotten.[62] Quite generally stated, Widengren tends to attribute the majority of the material of the prophetic literature to the prophets themselves rather than to their disciples, opposing thus the frequent attempts of literary critics to show that, e.g., prose sermons and messianic prophecies are later additions.[63]

3. Conclusions

To sum up Widengren's opinions about the handing down of Old Testament materials, his point is that we have evidence for the use of written transmission, but little or no proof of a putatively predominant role played by oral

---

59. Widengren, *Literary and Psychological Aspects*, 77–78.
60. Ibid., 71–74, 47–48.
61. Widengren, *Religionsphänomenologie*, 569: "The revealed word is the written word! … The holy word, which is proclaimed by the mediator of revelation, is in heavenly, pre-existent form in a heavenly book. The prophet receives revelations from this heavenly book and strives to create an earthly counterpart to it. This is a phenomenon that we find in Israel as well as in Islam." Cf. also *Literary and Psychological Aspects*, 74–76; Widengren, *The Ascension of the Apostle and the Heavenly Book*, UUÅ 1950:7; as well as Pedersen, *Den arabiske bog*, 10ff.; and Læssøe, "Literacy and Oral Tradition," 208–9. —A related problem is whether a belief in the magical power of the written word may have occasioned early literary fixation of the prophetic messages; cf. Gunneweg, *Mündliche und schriftliche Tradition*, 49, 74–75, with his references to A. Bertholet, *Die Macht der Schrift in Glauben und Aberglauben*, AAB, Phil.hist. Kl. 1948,1, Berlin 1949; also recently M. H. Woudstra, "Prophecy, Magic, and the Written Word," *CTJ* 2 (1967), 53–56.
62. Widengren, *Literary and Psychological Aspects*, 116–21.
63. Ibid., 80–90. Widengren bases his arguments in part on a comparison with Muhammad's development through the stages of poet, teacher, and lawgiver.

transmission.⁶⁴ Criticizing Engnell's hypothesis on the importance of the *traditio oralis*, Widengren asks pointedly: "Where do we find in the O.T. a passage mentioning a circle of traditionists faithfully preserving by means of oral tradition some prose narratives of the character found in the Pentateuch?"⁶⁵ By no means, however, does Widengren deny the existence of associations of prophets and disciples, in which some materials (especially biographical traditions, as was also the case with traditions about Muhammad) may have remained for a time in the memories of the disciples before being written down.⁶⁶ Moreover, it is indeed possible that for a majority of the traditions an oral stage—however short—may have been the foundation of the written accounts. There thus remain two important conclusions on the basis of Widengren's studies: First, we should *avoid contrasting strictly the two means of transmission, oral and literary*; for in all likelihood there existed an interplay, a hand-in-hand relationship, between them.⁶⁷ But secondly, *the tendency in the Near East and thus also in Israel*, as we have seen, *was to commit oral traditions to writing quite early* and in this way to try to preserve them from transformation, corruption, or loss.⁶⁸ With these two theses and the thorough, comparative foundation given them by Widengren, his work has served as a corrective, as a necessary braking device for the excesses accumulating in the scheme championed by Nyberg and Engnell in their earlier writings. That the other members of the Uppsala Circle, including also Engnell, later adopted a more moderate position with regard to the oral-transmission question is perhaps due above all to Widengren's efforts.

---

64. Ibid., 77. In contrast to Nyberg (above, pp. 180–81), Engnell (above, p. 204), and Birkeland (*Zum hebräischen Traditionswesen*, 48), Widengren (80) maintains that the occurrence of doublets does *not* per se prove the presence of oral transmission any more than it indicates the joining of several literary sources, for the doublets could just as well have resulted from the prophet's own repetition of the proclamation, as was the case with Muhammad.

65. Widengren, *AcOr* 23 (1959), 229. Here Widengren is clearly as guilty of arguing *e silentio* as was Engnell at an earlier point (above, p. 232 n. 41).

66. Widengren, *Literary and Psychological Aspects*, 92–93, 115–16, 121.

67. This interplay between oral and written means of transmission is indeed mentioned by Birkeland, Mowinckel, Engnell, and Haldar; cf. Gunneweg, *Mündliche und schriftliche Tradition*, 74–76; and below, p. 293. However, the others in their studies regard the oral transmission of prophetic traditions as having been predominant and decisive, whereas Widengren stresses above all this fact of the interplay.

68. Here Widengren admittedly (*AcOr* 23, 1959, 208–9) has much in common with van der Ploeg, *RB* 54 (1947), 5–41. Widengren's views are also quite similar to Gunneweg's (*Mündliche und schriftliche Tradition*), although it is striking how seldom the latter refers to Widengren's work.

C. Helmer Ringgren

Engnell's successor as professor of Old Testament at the University of Uppsala is Helmer Ringgren. His interests lie above all in the history of Israelite religion, but he has also made important contributions to traditio-historical research at two specific points, viz. the possibility of oral transmission as the cause of variant readings and the methodological relationship between traditio-historical work and other types of Old Testament research.

1. Oral Transmission as Explanation for Certain Variant Readings

In his article "Oral and Written Transmission in the O.T.: Some Observations,"[69] Ringgren begins by summarizing the accepted results of the research: "Two things may be said to remain established: firstly, that oral and written transmission should not be played off against one another: they do not exclude each other but may be regarded as complementary; and secondly, that the question of the mode of transmission of the O.T. texts must be judged from case to case, and that special investigations of each book or each complex of traditions are sorely needed."[70] Ringgren recognizes that one is often forced to argue on the basis of analogy in determining the role of written and oral transmission in the Old Testament,[71] but in this article he turns to what he points out is a little-used method of internal examination—the comparing of the points of variance between two preserved renderings of an Old Testament tradition.[72] The pericopes he chooses are from the Psalms and from the prophetic literature—traditions transmitted and preserved in two different

---

69. *ST* 3 (1949), 34–59.
70. Ibid., 34.
71. As we have seen above (p. 231 n. 37), Engnell, in contrast to Widengren, was unwilling to accept analogic, external evidence in this regard.
72. A similar method, Ringgren observes, has been useful in trying to establish the mode of transmission of Egyptian texts and Arabic poetry; Ringgren includes a number of examples of the latter. For the Egyptian material scholars have compared different copies of the literary text in question, and the variants discovered can be grouped into three categories: (1) those that are solely graphic (e.g., the misinterpretation of signs), showing that the text at this point was copied directly from a written original; (2) those that are apparently due to mistakes of hearing in the course of dictation; and (3) those that must be attributed to slips of memory, occurring either (a) while the teacher dictates from memory what he knows by heart, or (b) while the scribe writes what he knows by heart, or (c) when the pupil writing from dictation forgets the correct wording read by the teacher. Cases (a) and (b) represent a sort of oral transmission. (Cf. Ringgren, *ST* 3, 1949, 34–35.) For the Old Testament we possess almost no divergent texts, and for this reason Ringgren restricts his examination to passages that are recorded twice in the Old Testament.

contexts and usually under the authority of two distinct circles of traditionists.[73] How are we to explain the slight variations between two such texts, and what would most probably have caused these divergences?

Taking as an example Ringgren's examination of *Ps 18 and 2 Sam 22*, we see that he finds four types of variants.[74] (a) Many variants are obviously graphic, arising from mistakes made in the process of copying (e.g., metathesis, visual confusion). (b) There are several variants that consist of only a different vocalization of the same consonants. Ringgren suggests that it is more likely that such different interpretations of the written consonantal text stem from an oral tradition concerning the correct reading of the text, rather than that they result from scribal conjectures. (c) There are also a number of grammatical and stylistic variants which may be the consequence either of intentional revisions of the text or of dialectical differences within the Hebrew language; the latter possibility would then indicate an oral transmission. And finally, (d) there are quite a few variants that apparently are slips of memory occurring during the process of oral transmission; some examples of these are found in (versification here identical in Ps 18 and 2 Sam 22): verses 7 (אשוע—אקרא), 8 (השמים—הרים), 25 (כברי—כבר ידי), 28 (ועינים רמות—ועיניך על רמים), 39, 43a, 48 (ומוריד—וידבר), and 49 (מוציאי—מפלטי). These traces of an oral transmittal stage found here and in the other psalm texts can also be observed in the prophetic traditions preserved twice in the Old Testament.[75] The conclusion drawn by Ringgren is thus that, *although many variant readings are undoubtedly graphic, there is a greater number which must be due to mistakes occurring during an oral transmission of the texts*. However, he cautions, "even if it seems clear that some or many of the texts of the O.T. were transmitted orally for a certain time, we have no evidence that the same holds true for them all"; the evidence must be judged from case to case.[76] Ringgren does not make clear whether he thinks that oral transmission played the predominant role in the formation and handing down of these traditions (so Nyberg and Engnell) or whether written means were employed relatively early (so

---

73. He examines comparatively: Ps 18 and 2 Sam 22; Ps 14 and Ps 53; Ps 40:14–18 and Ps 70; Ps 57, 60 and Ps 108; Ps 105, 96, 106:1, 47 and 1 Chr 16:8–36; Isa 2:2–4 and Mic 4:1–3; Isa 16:6–12 and Jer 48:29–36; Isa 37:22–35 and 2 Kgs 19:21–34; Obad 1:1–6 and Jer 49:14–16, 9–10; Jer 6:12–15 and Jer 8:10–12; Jer 6:22–24, 49:19–21 and Jer 50:41–46; Jer 10:12–16 and Jer 51:15–19. The variants found in the Jerusalem scroll are also discussed at the relevant places.

74. Ringgren, *ST* 3 (1949), 39–45.

75. Ringgren points out that his conclusions concerning the Isaiah texts correspond to the results reached by: M. Burrows, "Variant Readings in the Isaiah Manuscript," *BASOR* 111 (1948), 16–24, and *BASOR* 113 (1949), 24–32; and R. J. Tournay, "Les anciens manuscrits hébreux récemment découverts," *RB* 56 (1949), 231.

76. Ringgren, *ST* 3 (1949), 57–59.

Widengren, van der Ploeg, and Gunneweg). He admits, though, that *it is very difficult to determine when any given text was first committed to writing*. At any rate, it is probable that there existed up to the time of the Masoretes a parallel oral tradition concerning the correct way of reading the consonantal text.[77]

2. The Place of Tradition History in Old Testament Research

It can thus be seen that Ringgren assumes a *mediating position in the Uppsala Circle*, striking a balance as he does between the views forwarded by Engnell on the one side and Widengren on the other. Another welcome aspect of his works is an absence of the polemicizing engaged in so frequently by these latter two men. In addition to Ringgren's contributions regarding the question of variant readings, his treatment of the relationships among the literary-critical, form-critical, and traditio-historical methods of Old Testament research is important.[78] Here he asserts that these three methods should be seen as *complementing* rather than excluding each other, and thus he seeks to avoid the antagonism which Engnell often showed for literary criticism. In Ringgren's own words: "What we need today is a synthesis in which all means and methods can work together to reach the common goal, namely to recover the milieu that produced the texts and the function that they had in this milieu,[79] and thereby to determine their real meaning."[80] He also tends to minimize

---

77. Ibid., 59.

78. Ringgren, "Literarkritik, Formgeschichte, Überlieferungsgeschichte: Erwägungen zur Methodenfrage der alttestamentlichen Exegese," *TLZ* 91 (1966), cols. 641–650; and in a substantially somewhat different form: "Litterärkritik, formhistoria, traditionshistoria—eller vad?," *RoB* 25 (1966), 45–56.

79. This idea of *function* as a replacement for "Sitz im Leben" has been especially well developed by the Finnish scholar Ilmari Soisalon-Soininen in his article, "Begreppet funktion i gammaltestamentlig traditionsforskning," *SEÅ* 33 (1968), 55–67. Suggesting orally (August 1971) that the notion of the function of a tradition is also applicable—but in altered form—to other Old Testament genres (e.g., prophetic traditions), Soisalon-Soininen has demonstrated its usefulness in connection with the Patriarch-traditions (*Aabrahamista Joosefiin*, Helsinki 1965; and "Der Charakter der ältesten alttestamentlichen Erzähltraditionen," *Temenos* 4, 1969, 128–39) and the traditions of Gen 2–11 ("Die Urgeschichte im Geschichtswerk des Jahwisten," *Temenos* 6, 1970, 130–41). On the importance of the notion of "function" in the science of folklore, cf. Alver, "Category and Function," *Fabula* 9 (1967), 63–69; and L. Honko, *Geisterglaube in Ingermanland*, Helsinki 1962, 140ff. On the functional importance of religion in general, cf. H. Ringgren, *Religionens form och funktion*, Lund 1968.

80. *TLZ* 91 (1966), col. 647. A concise example of this type of investigation may be Ringgren's "Är den bibliska skapelseberättelsen en kulttext?," *SEÅ* 13 (1948), 9–21, in which he shows that Gen 1 in its present form is hardly to be regarded as a cultic text of the New Year festival, but is rather a revised and de-mythologized rendition of such an originally used myth. Cf. also *TLZ* 91 (1966), cols. 648–49; Ringgren's article "Skapelse" in *SBU* II; Engnell, "'Knowledge' and

the difference between Scandinavian and German tradition historians, referring especially to Engnell's appeal for a combination of analytic and synthetic methods.[81] On the whole, Ringgren is both optimistic and realistic about the capability of traditio-historical research to discover some of the early stages in the history of Old Testament traditions, especially when this research is combined with motif-historical examinations. In this way questions that are of significance for the historical growth of the traditions but that are beyond the reach of literary criticism and form criticism can often be answered.[82]

D. Gösta W. Ahlström

1. Tradition History of Psalm 89

Attention should also be directed to some of the insights offered by the Uppsala scholar Gösta W. Ahlström (1918–1992), long-time professor at the University of Chicago. His study of Ps 89 casts light not only on the tradition history of this specific psalm, but also on the developmental history of psalms in general.[83] In accordance with the accepted opinion, Ahlström agrees that the "Sitz im Leben" of most psalms is the cult, the center of the religious life of the people.[84] However, precisely because of this locus two problematic factors have distinct bearing on their tradition history. First, because the Israelites took over and gradually "Israelitized" many of the Canaanite cultic centers, we need to be on the guard for Canaanite traditions and rituals which the Israelites retained and incorporated into the psalms.[85] And secondly, due to the exile and the destruction of the temple an "Umkultisierung" in exilic and postexilic times probably disrupted not only the transmission

---

'Life' in the Creation Story," VTSup 3 (1955), 103–19; and F. Hvidberg, "The Canaanite Background of Gen. I–III," *VT* 10 (1960), 285–94.

81. Cf. above, p. 219; *TLZ* 91 (1966), cols. 647–48.

82. *TLZ* 91 (1966), cols. 645, 648ff. In his book, *Israelitische Religion* (Stuttgart 1963), Ringgren makes frequent references to the contributions of traditio-historical research and at many points uses these results in tracing the history of Israelite religion; cf., e.g., 6ff., 15ff., 36ff., 92ff., 229ff.

83. *Psalm 89: Eine Liturgie aus dem Ritual des leidenden Königs*, Lund 1959. On the general history of the psalms, see also S. Holm-Nielsen, "Den gammeltestamentlige salmetradition," *DTT* 18 (1955), 135–48, 193–215; H.-J. Kraus, *Psalmen* I, BK 15, 3rd ed., Neukirchen-Vluyn 1966, lxi–lxiii; and Becker, *Israel deutet seine Psalmen*, especially 10–39.

84. That this cultic interpretation of the psalms has been exaggerated too greatly by several Scandinavian scholars can indeed be maintained; cf., e.g., Kraus, *Psalmen* I, xxxix–xl.

85. Ahlström, *Psalm 89*, 13. Cf. also his monograph, *Aspects of Syncretism in Israelite Religion*, HS V, Lund 1963.

but also the contents of some of the psalms.[86] In light of both of these factors we cannot always be sure whether a psalm in its present form is identical with its preexilic cultic form. Ahlström maintains that *the psalms generally originated and were transmitted among the circles of the priests and singers at the various cultic centers*, and in this he differs slightly from Gunkel, Mowinckel, and Causse, who seem to be thinking more of the lower priesthood of the Jerusalem temple.[87] Ahlström agrees with Nyberg's thesis about the predominance of oral transmission in the ancient Near East, and he thus asserts that the priests and singers must have known by heart the psalms and liturgical materials. These traditions were regarded as holy and of divine origin and were therefore probably recorded quite early; however, this written form did not displace the oral transmission but rather functioned "partly as support for the memory in recitation and partly as teaching material for the priests' pupils in the temple schools."[88]

Concerning *Ps 89* specifically, Ahlström suggests that it *originally belonged to the ceremony of the Canaanite vegetation-god Dwd and was a part of the renewal-of-life ritual of the annual festival*.[89] According to him this hypothesis is supported by the superscript משכיל, which he—like Engnell—maintains to be the name for a psalm used at the annual festival—especially a psalm which deals with the resurrection of the king in the vegetation rites and his renewed ascension to the throne.[90] Due to the Deuteronomistic exclusiveness, the direct references to this original association to the Dwd-cult were gradually eliminated, while its motifs of suffering, death, and resurrection remained.[91] The psalm itself must therefore be regarded as being very old, its

---

86. *Psalm 89*, 11: "Many psalms could be adapted to the partially new conditions in the Second Temple; others, to the synagogal worship. Then when the psalmic material was collected, the tradition was no longer in its original state. That is confirmed, among other places, in the fact that the Masoretes occasionally read something other than what was written or that in certain cases they were even doubtful about the meaning of some words." Cf. also Holm-Nielsen, *DTT* 18 (1955), 214–15.

87. Cf. *Psalm 89*, 14, for literature references. Ahlström, however, does not seem to distinguish adequately here between the origin and the "Sitz im Leben" of the psalms; that the two are not identical has been shown by Kraus, *Psalmen* I, xlviii, lxi–lxiii.

88. *Psalm 89*, 15. Cf. also Engnell, VTSup 7 (1960), 23.

89. *Psalm 89*, 163–73. On Ahlström's concurrence with other Scandinavians regarding the mythic interpretation of Psalm 89, cf. Kraus, *Psalmen* II, 616–18.

90. *Psalm 89*, 21–26, 11; Engnell, *BJRL* 31 (1948), 76–77. Cf. however Kraus, *Psalmen* I, xxii–xxiii, xxix–xxx, and especially xl (in reference to Ahlström's understanding of the superscript משכיל): "It is a very hazardous enterprise to use a dominant cult theory to appropriate the obscure superscriptions of the psalms and to give them questionable translations, all in order to introduce ritual groupings with them."

91. Ahlström, *Psalm 89*, 172–73.

oracle in verses 20ff. apparently always having been used at the enthronement of the king. Consequently Ahlström, in opposition to the usual view, maintains that Ps 89 must be prior to the prophecy of Nathan in 2 Sam 7.[92] The psalm in its present form is a unity,[93] although it does contain older elements which originally could not have belonged to the Jerusalem tradition. Its place of origin is uncertain, but its present form and unity were probably achieved in Jerusalem circles.[94]

2. The "Oral/Written" Debate

Like many of the other Scandinavian scholars, Ahlström has published an article dealing with general matters of traditio-historical research, in his case with the methods or technique of transmission.[95] One principle that he seeks to emphasize is that *the reliability of oral transmission is not a fact that can be generally affirmed, for it is dependent upon the circle of tradents that in each respective case has been active*.[96] His list of the characteristics of an oral-composition technique do not vary much from Nielsen's earlier discussion of same,[97] although Ahlström cautions expressly that these criteria cannot prove with any certitude that a given tradition originated or was transmitted as an oral composition.[98] Ahlström also disagrees with Engnell's thesis that the greater part of the Old Testament literature was first recorded in exilic and postexilic times. In addition to much of the law materials (which Engnell admitted to having been recorded quite early), many of the prophetical utterances and the temple traditions were, according to Ahlström, also written down at an early date, in many cases probably with no prior period of oral transmission.[99] As evidence for the custom of writing down the laws he refers to Hos 8:12, Jer 2:8 (ותפשי התורה, the verb תפש having the meaning "to take, to grasp, to seize something or to handle a concrete thing"), 1 Sam 10:25, and Josh 24:25–26. The law is thus understood as holy script, although it should at the same time always be read, recited, and memorized.[100] Turning to the prophetic literature, Ahlström dismisses the hypothesis that the words of the prophets were circu-

---

92. Ibid., 182–85; cf. also his article, "Der Prophet Nathan und der Tempelbau," *VT* 11 (1961), 113–27 (= in Swedish, *SEÅ* 25, 1960, 5–22).
93. Gunkel is not of this opinion; cf. Ahlström, *Psalm 89*, 9, 12, 184.
94. Ibid., 182ff.
95. "Oral and Written Transmission: Some Considerations," *HTR* 59 (1966), 69–81.
96. Ibid., 69–70.
97. See below, pp. 267–68.
98. *HTR* 59 (1966), 71–72. Cf. also Richter, *Exegese als Literaturwissenschaft*, 159.
99. Ahlström, *HTR* 59 (1966), 72–73.
100. Ibid., 73–75.

lated from the outset in pamphlet form; he assumes, with Widengren, that an oral tradition served as "the foundation of the written accounts."[101] Ahlström suggests that we can presuppose a basically reliable transmission of these prophetical utterances for three reasons.[102] (a) The prophet himself was aware of the importance of his role as "the mouth of the deity," as the messenger of the words of Jahweh. (b) At least some of the prophets had disciples who probably also regarded the prophetical utterances as divine words and who were thus "the natural keepers of the tradition."[103] These disciples also would have been the recipients of the prophets' own interpretations. While admitting that the disciples may often have adapted an oracle to a new situation, Ahlström assumes that "the disciples of a prophet would not have allowed other utterances into the prophetic tradition which were not in accordance with the mind and the intentions of their master."[104] (c) From the case of Jeremiah we learn that the oral transmission, and in his case also the written transmission, was initiated by the prophet master himself, not by his listeners or disciples.[105] While writing was sometimes used from the beginning, it is impossible for us to isolate these passages in the present prophetic books, according to Ahlström.

In all of this it should be clear that Ahlström does not introduce many new, significant arguments or pieces of evidence for the "oral/written" debate, but it is nonetheless important for our purposes to realize that he, like Ringgren, adopts a sober, moderate position with regard to this question. To be sure, *Ahlström holds it to be necessary to take the factor of oral transmission into consideration, but he tones down markedly the importance which was invested in it in the early publications of other Uppsala scholars.* With regard to the larger field of traditio-historical research, Ahlström's primary contribution is certainly his work on the psalms—even though his postulated mythical background for Ps 89 may be problematic in itself.

---

101. Widengren, *Literary and Psychological Aspects*, 88; cf. also *AcOr* 23 (1959), 215; Ahlström *HTR* 59 (1966), 77.

102. *HTR* 59 (1966), 76–81.

103. Ibid., 78. Ahlström does not comment on how the words of the prophets without disciples could have been transmitted and preserved if these words were not, as he maintains, circulated from the outset in pamphlet form.

104. Ibid., 81; cf. also 78.

105. We have seen above (p. 236) that Widengren points out that the Arabian prophet also initiated the written and oral transmission of his words.

E. R. A. Carlson on Second Samuel

It would perhaps be well to conclude this section on the Uppsala Circle with a review of one of its later members,[106] R. A. Carlson (1928–2001), for his work[107]—probably more than that of any of his colleagues—is basically in alignment with the investigative approach and method championed from the beginning by Engnell. Carlson's interest in the "history of tradition" and his special debt to Scandinavian work in this area become clear in his Prolegomena, in which he spells out his methodological orientation. However, in this we must not lose sight of a definite modification and refinement of the traditio-historical method and theses characteristic of the early work of especially Nyberg, Engnell, Kapelrud, and Nielsen.

1. Traditio-Historical Method and Scope

The following aspects of Carlson's methodological considerations are important. (a) Carlson understands the term "history of tradition" in its usual sense: a description of the process of growth of a tradition—"the various phases through which a narrative or a complex of traditions has passed before receiving its final form."[108] Like Mowinckel,[109] he places emphasis decidedly on the second element, "traditio-*historical*," indicating thereby that this type of investigation is "ultimately concerned with following and describing certain aspects of the history of the various types of material in the OT, from formation to final redaction."[110] In this scope of the traditio-historical task

---

106. We are thereby—somewhat arbitrarily—omitting from discussion Magnus Ottosson's dissertation, *Gilead: Tradition and History*, Coniectanea Biblica, Old Testament Series 3, Lund 1969. Ottosson belongs also to the Uppsala Circle and, like Carlson, is considerably influenced by Engnell's traditio-historical method. This is obvious especially in the introductory remarks to his book. With his investigation Ottosson seeks to clarify two points: (a) the history of the area of Gilead and especially its role in the history of Israel, and (b) the ideological justification of the claim Israel lays on the area. For the second of these he analyzes texts (in Genesis, Numbers, the prologue to Deuteronomy, Joshua, and Judges) which underline Israel's right to Gilead. Ottosson points out (11) that his approach to this ideological aspect coincides with the functional concept of tradition as proposed by Soisalon-Soininen; cf. above, p. 240 n. 79.

107. His dissertation: *David, the Chosen King: A Traditio-Historical Approach to the Second Book of Samuel*, Stockholm/Göteborg/Uppsala 1964; also his Swedish resume of the same, in *SEÅ* 31 (1966), 122–32.

108. *David, the Chosen King*, 9.

109. Cf. above, pp. 209–10. Cf. also Rendtorff, *EvT* 27 (1967), 148–49.

110. *David, the Chosen King*, 11. Carlson thus defines the terms "history of tradition" and "history," but he does not offer us a closer explanation of what he means when he speaks of a

Carlson is thus fully in agreement with Noth,[111] although like Engnell he is skeptical about the possibility of stratifying and separating too distinctly the many phases of this growth process. Under these "certain aspects" of the tradition history Carlson understands the *determination of origins, method of transmission, ideological reshaping of elements, and final redaction*. These are only some of the important questions, for the variety of Old Testament tradition types implies also a variety of traditio-historical problems needing to be solved; for this same reason *stereotyped solutions are hardly defensible*.[112] (b) In order to solve such problems traditio-historical research, as an analytical procedure, should avail itself of such criteria as style, formal constructions, ideological tendency, compositional techniques, and so forth. The traditio-historical method thus embraces linguistic, stylistic, form-critical, ideological, and religio-historical analyses.[113] This comprehensive view of traditio-historical work corresponds wholly to what Engnell[114] prior to him and Sæbø[115] subsequent to him advocate.

(c) To aid the discovering of the *history* of tradition through this comprehensive *analysis* of the present state of the tradition, Carlson maintains that it is essential to gain an *external, comparative perspective*, that is, to examine the historical, ancient Near Eastern background of a given tradition in order to gain a better understanding of its ideological, thematic, and formal aspects, as well as the relation of the tradition to that background. Carlson emphasizes the importance of this comparative perspective: "Complete analytical understanding of the literary form, transmission, tendencies and motifs of the OT is in fact impossible without this comparative background, though final judgment must in every case be based on internal analysis."[116] Engnell called for an almost exclusively internal analysis,[117] so it seems in theory that Carlson goes beyond this position in that he recognizes the need for external, comparative work. We will see below, however, that in practice the difference between the two positions is indeed minimal.

"tradition." This failure to fix the precise limits of this term is unfortunately rather typical of traditio-historical researchers.

111. Cf. above, pp. 110–11.
112. Carlson, *David, the Chosen King*, 11.
113. Ibid., 13–14; *SEÅ* 31 (1966), 123–24.
114. Cf. above, pp. 214–15.
115. Cf. below, pp. 276–77.
116. *David, the Chosen King*, 13.
117. Cf. above, pp. 219, 231 n. 37.

(d) Carlson, like Engnell and Nielsen, regards the traditio-historical method as an "analytical alternative" to literary criticism.[118] What he finds objectionable in literary criticism is its general subservience to a particular literary theory of written sources, redactions, and additions.[119] For this reason he maintains that a basic methodological prerequisite should be "to free analytical work from every *a priori* consideration."[120] This, of course, is a very difficult, elusive, if not impossible enterprise, but it has an important implication for Carlson which carries him considerably beyond Nyberg's and Engnell's methodological point of departure. Thus just as it was incorrect for literary critics to assume wide-reaching literary activity at the formative, transmittal, and redactional stages, so also—according to Carlson—must *tradition historians avoid postulating a dominant oral tradition down to the time of the exile*. Carlson does not mince words in appealing to his colleagues to abandon the dogmatic preconceptions which afflicted the work of some of his predecessors: "Nyberg's emphatic thesis on the dominant role of oral transmission in the history of the OT was a necessary reaction against the theories of the literary critics, but cannot in principle serve as a foundation for traditio-historical analysis."[121] The reason for this is that the Old Testament materials are too variegated to be treated according to such a general theory or scheme. The traditio-historical method must, for example, also be applicable to traditions which apparently arose in written form (e.g., the Chronicler's opus); here a "documentary-literary method" should be employed, though still within the framework of traditio-historical research.[122] Regarding the roles of written and oral methods of transmission Carlson opts for the moderate position that was the result of two decades of discussion among Engnell, Widengren, Mowinckel, Ringgren, Nielsen, and others: the two methods, oral and written, must be seen as complementing, not opposing each other. Oral transmission is indeed quite reliable, yet neither oral nor written means

---

118. *David, the Chosen King*, 10; compare the similar position held by Nielsen, below, pp. 265–66. In a conversation with the writer in August 1971, Carlson indicated that this formulation stems from Engnell. Carlson emphasized that, whereas he accepted this while under the influence of Engnell, he has since then come to realize that it is an indefensible exaggeration to regard traditio-historical research as an analytical alternative to literary criticism. Carlson objects to the minute analyses and the "hair-splitting" of earlier literary-critical investigations but holds that more recent literary-critical work is definitely more acceptable and instructive. Cf. also Rendtorff, *EvT* 27 (1967), 139–49.

119. *David, the Chosen King*, 9–11, 16–17.

120. Ibid., 10. Richter concurs; cf. *Exegese als Literaturwissenschaft*, 11–17, 28, 174ff.

121. *David, the Chosen King*, 10; cf. also *SEÅ* 31 (1966), 124.

122. *David, the Chosen King*, 10–11. Carlson is indebted to Engnell for this term; cf. Engnell, "Traditionshistorisk metod," *SBU* II, 1952, col. 1435; 2nd ed., 1963, col. 1260.

inherently offer a guarantee against the occasional rise of considerable variations during the transmittal stage.¹²³

We have thus seen that at several points Carlson's methodological principles mark a decided advancement beyond the positions of Engnell and Nyberg. Does his actual investigative procedure correspond to the method that he spells out in the Prolegomena, the highlights of which we have just described? What are the results and insights he reaches through his traditio-historical analysis of 2 Samuel? As mentioned above in (a), Carlson considers traditio-historical research as dealing with the period extending from the beginnings of the tradition all the way down through the final redactional phase, and in this scope he concurs with Noth. However, the application of his method to the text of 2 Samuel unfortunately continues the parallel, for like Noth Carlson directs almost the entirety of his attention only to redaction and composition. He is thus occupied with the final form of the tradition (the "Endstadium," to use von Rad's term) and *as a rule does not attempt to trace the developmental history of the tradition elements prior to the time of the redactors*¹²⁴—this despite his above-mentioned emphasis on the "certain aspects" of history. Therefore his actual analysis of 2 Samuel is not entirely consistent with the method which he describes. His analytical procedure is, however, quite in accord with Engnell's refusal to go back behind that which the traditionists have delivered to us and to try to stratify historically the tradition.¹²⁵

2. A Pre-Deuteronomic Davidic Epic

An exception to this is seen at the occasional places where Carlson seeks a mythological or comparative-literary background for certain elements or whole traditions. For example, he ascertains close ideological and compositional affinities between the Davidic cycle and the Keret epic from Ugarit.¹²⁶ This can especially be seen in the functional relationship of the Bathsheba episode (2 Sam 10–12) to the following קללה-traditions (2 Sam 13–20), parallel in composition and motifs to the Keret epic.¹²⁷ Carlson concludes from this that this connection between 2 Sam 10–12 and the section 2 Sam 13ff. must have been present already at the pre-Deuteronomic stage, such that the Bathsheba episode served then as a sort of prologue to the rest and thus as "a

---

123. *David, the Chosen King*, 15–19, 49.
124. Cf. also Ringgren, *TLZ* 91 (1966), col. 646.
125. Cf. above, pp. 200–201, 219.
126. Cf. *David, the Chosen King*, e.g., 34, 43.
127. Ibid., 144, 188–93.

turning point in the pre-Deuteronomic Davidic epic, of which the D-group made such good use for their own purposes."[128] With this as an example we can see (a) that Carlson suggests that aspects of our present Davidic traditions go back to legendary traditions from neighboring cultures, and more specifically that "accepted literary patterns have provided a basis for the form given the Davidic story";[129] and (b) that he differentiates between Deuteronomic and pre-Deuteronomic materials, styles, and motifs. Carlson thus *postulates the existence of a Davidic epic*, that is, a complex of traditions about David, which was at the disposal of the Deuteronomists: "The compositional character of 1-2 Sam. ... provides a positive indication that the D-group were able to turn, for their description of the epoch of Saul and David, to a core of material already existing as a whole."[130] This means then that Carlson disagrees with the Rost-Noth-von Rad-Hertzberg thesis that 2 Sam 9-20 + 1 Kgs 1-2 constitute an independent "Thronfolgegeschichte" dating back to an eye-witness account recorded during Solomon's reign.[131] To Carlson, Rost's thesis smacks too much of literary criticism and does not take seriously enough into consideration the cultic, ideological, and traditio-historical aspects of this complex and its stylistic similarities with the rest of the Davidic epic.[132] Carlson finds it more fitting to regard the whole of 1-2 Samuel as a compositional unity already at the pre-Deuteronomic stage—although it is not possible for us to reconstruct this earlier Samuel-Saul-David cycle of tradition.[133]

---

128. Ibid., 189-90.
129. Ibid., 191.
130. Ibid., 43; cf. also 47, 189-90; and *SEÅ* 31 (1966), 128.
131. This is also the position held by R. N. Whybray, *The Succession Narrative: A Study of II Samuel 9-20; I Kings 1 and 2*, SBT, Second Series 9, London 1968.
132. Carlson, *David, the Chosen King*, 42-43, 131-39. —For recent literature on the complex of traditions about David's rise to power, cf. H.-U. Nübel, *Davids Aufstieg in der Frühe israelitischer Geschichtsschreibung*, Diss. Bonn 1959; F. Mildenberger, *Die vordeuteronomistische Saul-Davidüberlieferung*, Diss. Tübingen 1962; A. Weiser, "Die Legitimation des Königs David: Zur Eigenart und Entstehung der sogen. Geschichte von Davids Aufstieg," *VT* 16 (1966), 325-54; R. L. Ward, *The Story of David's Rise: A Traditio-Historical Study of I Samuel xvi - II Samuel v*, Diss. Nashville, Tennessee 1967; and the contributions made by two Danes: H. Gottlieb, "Traditionen om David som hyrde," *DTT* 29 (1966), 11-21 (= "Die Tradition von David als Hirten," *VT* 17, 1967, 190-200); Jakob H. Grønbæk, "David og Goliat: Et bidrag til forståelsen af legenden i 1 Sam. 17 og dennes placering," *DTT* 28 (1965), 65-79; and Grønbæk, *Die Geschichte vom Aufstieg Davids (1. Sam. 15 - 2. Sam. 5): Tradition und Komposition*, ATDan 10, Copenhagen 1971. The latter dissertation is especially noteworthy as a good traditio-historical study of this tradition complex.
133. This idea of a unified Samuel-Saul-David cycle (in contrast to the conception of an independent succession narrative) stems immediately from Carlson's mentor, Ivan Engnell, who—more explicitly than Carlson—contends that this cycle existed in oral form at the disposal

3. COMPOSITIONAL ANALYSIS OF SECOND SAMUEL

Carlson's prime efforts in this book are thus along the lines of a *compositional analysis*,[134] and it would therefore be advisable for us to get a better picture of his conception of the Deuteronomic literary techniques and compositional restructuring of 2 Samuel. By way of orientation it may first be said that he concurs with Noth's and Engnell's conception of the ideological and literary unity of the Deuteronomic history (the "D-work": Deuteronomy–2 Kings).[135] However Carlson opts for the collective, "group" postulate (the "D-group") of Engnell, Hertzberg, Nielsen, and others rather than for the single, individual "Deuteronomist" of Noth.[136] A more significant difference is that, whereas Noth maintains that the Deuteronomist made few other changes in 1 Sam 13–1 Kgs 2 other than to add introductory formulae and "list" material to the sources at his disposal,[137] *Carlson postulates that the D-group was as active in its editing of these traditions as it was in, for example, Judges and 1–2 Kings.* In his own words, the ideological and compositional principles of the Deuteronomic editors "do not merely determine linguistic structure and choice of style, but in fact completely dominate the compositional technique and the arrangement of the material."[138] Nonetheless the D-group was guided by a basic respect for the traditions of the past while at the same time contributing through interpretation, arrangement, addition, deletion, and stylistic alterations at innumerable points.[139] Probably much of this redactional work was carried out in this group at the oral level, for a compositional analysis of the D-work reveals many techniques and patterns ("ring" composition, the

---

of the Deuteronomic circle; cf. "Samuelsböckerna," *SBU* II (1952), cols. 1043–1049; II (2nd ed., 1963), cols. 867–871.

134. Our definition of "tradition history" (cf. above, pp. 21–23) omits indeed the compositional stage, but we are endeavoring throughout this present study to treat instead all that which has been understood as "tradition history" by the various researchers. Therefore consideration and assessment of Carlson's work at this point are essential.

135. Carlson, *David, the Chosen King*, 22–23. Ottosson, *Gilead*, 10ff., also shares Engnell's view of the "D-work" and the "P-work."

136. *David, the Chosen King*, 29–30, 23.

137. Noth, *ÜSt*, 61ff; cf. Carlson, *David, the Chosen King*, 23.

138. Carlson, *SEÅ* 31 (1966), 124; cf. also his article, "Deuteronomisk," *SBU* I (2nd ed., 1962), cols. 413–418. Carlson seems also to assume more editorial activity of the D-group in 2 Samuel than Engnell does. The latter holds moreover that it is hardly possible for us to distinguish the Deuteronomic elements in the sections reworked by the D-group. Cf. Engnell, *SBU* II (1952), cols. 1043–1049.

139. *David, the Chosen King*, 22; cf. Noth, *ÜSt*, 95ff. In light of the far-reaching redactional activity which Carlson assigns to the D-group, one is indeed inclined to ask what this "respect for tradition" *concretely and specifically means.*

principle of association, sevenfold and threefold patterns, etc.) typical of oral transmission.[140]

The D-group was basically antiroyalistic, but its supreme characteristic was its belief that Israel's misfortunes are ultimately grounded in her faithlessness to Jahweh. To indicate this central principle Carlson uses the two words ברכה and קללה—"blessing" when Israel follows Jahweh and "curse" when the people turn away from him. This Deuteronomic theme, according to Carlson, is distinctly expressed in the Davidic traditions of 2 Samuel—although Carlson does not make it clear whether this thematic contrast was present and distinct already in the pre-Deuteronomic Davidic epic, or whether it was entirely a Deuteronomic novelty. At any rate, as editors the D-group used some of the Davidic traditions positively, as in the section 2 Sam 2–7, with its integrating factor abbreviated in Carlson's rubric "David under the Blessing (ברכה)." Carlson suggests that this unit fills a Messianic function for the D-group, whose hopes for the future caused them to transcend their antiroyalism and admit, even in exilic times, that "you may indeed set as king over you him whom Jahweh your God will choose" (Deut 17:15).[141] The second section treated by Carlson is 2 Sam 9–24, its central motif being "David under the Curse (קללה)."[142] Here the D-group makes graphic the pattern of cause and effect, which is dependent on faithfulness/faithlessness to Jahweh. The section is anti-Davidic, although the figure of David is used for a specific didactic, hortative purpose: "the D-group has made use of an ideal figure, who ranks high both in the tradition and in the popular consciousness, to give an authoritative demonstration of their faith in a future made possible by turning again to Yahweh and by devotion to him."[143]

The redactional activity of the D-group in 2 Sam 10–24 can be seen at many points, according to Carlson. The material in 2 Sam 21–24 has been moved from its original location before chapter 9; the traditions of Nathan (ch. 12) and Gad (ch. 24) have been reworked; Ps 18 has been inserted in chapter 22; and numerous alterations reflecting exilic conditions have occurred. Furthermore, the D-group gave this section a clear compositional structure that can be seen through the literary techniques employed. Thus the Bathsheba episode is made to introduce two seven-year קללה-periods of retribution for David's sin: 2 Sam 13–14 and 15–21:14. Each of the sections, chapters 10–12, 13–14, and 15–20, is introduced by the copula ויהי אחרי כן. This redactional

---

140. *David, the Chosen King*, 36. Thus against the view of many, Carlson suggests that "the redactional history was a process of oral character," not necessarily of written; cf. ibid., 18.
141. Ibid., 30–32, 41ff., 263ff.
142. Ibid., 131ff.
143. Ibid., 26.

addition, however, does not justify drawing any traditio-historical conclusions about these three sections being originally separate and independent, for the D-group introduced this device only to "mark the boundaries of three integral sections in an original compositional whole."[144] In addition, Carlson suggests that Chap. 10–20 constitute a שכב-composition, connected associatively by the D-group to correspond to the laws in Deut 22:13ff. Thus 2 Sam 10–12 reflects Deut 22:22; 2 Sam 13–14 is to be compared with Deut 22:28–29; and 2 Sam 15–20 corresponds to Deut 23:1.[145] The section 2 Sam 21–24, located here and edited by the D-group in a manner similar to the compositional editing of Deut 32–33, supports the קללה-motifs of 2 Sam 10–21.[146] The final result is thus the total Deuteronomic picture of David's kingship as a thematic paradigm of the exilic situation.

4. Evaluation of His Traditio-Historical Analysis

Carlson's investigation stimulates us to some reflections of a very basic nature. His penetrating, shrewd analysis of 2 Samuel enables him at many points to separate Deuteronomic additions and changes from the pre-Deuteronomic form of the tradition. Whether his redactional results are correct or not is of course a debatable issue for each of the individual points; indeed it is not even conclusively established whether the D-group was at all—or at least to this extent—active in 2 Samuel. Be this as it may, a more basic, methodological problem commands our attention at this point: the remarkable fact that Carlson does not take the next logical step after his Redaktionsgeschichte—to attempt to describe, as far as possible, the form, extent, function, and structure of these traditions in the state in which the D-group received them, and then on the basis of a traditio-historical examination to try to catch sight of the developmental stages in the prehistory of the same.[147] *Why is it necessary to stop at the Deuteronomic redaction without tracing the history of the tradition back beyond this point* (except simply to mention mythological or literary parallels, as with the Keret epic)? This question applies to Carlson's *David, the Chosen King* as well as to Noth's *Überlieferungsgeschichtliche Studien*, although for each of them the pre-Deuteronomic prehistory would be different since Noth assumes written sources[148] whereas Carlson is apparently thinking more

---

144. Ibid., 42.
145. Ibid., 163–93.
146. Ibid., 194ff.
147. Such a picture is sketched roughly by, e.g., Kaiser, *Einleitung in das Alte Testament*, Gütersloh 1969, 129–30.
148. "Tagebücher" based on official annals; cf. *ÜSt*, 72–73.

in terms of a body of orally formed and transmitted source materials.[149] One would, in fact, be more inclined to assume that a traditio-historical investigation of the early traditions would be more important in Carlson's case since he postulates the existence of a *Davidic epic* which was at the disposal of the Deuteronomists. Such an epic would seem to presuppose a period of growth and development—precisely the proper object of a full traditio-historical analysis. Carlson succeeds in distinguishing Deuteronomic from pre-Deuteronomic materials; what restricts him from then attempting to put these pieces together in order to gain a better picture of this pre-Deuteronomic Davidic epic? His reply: "The task of reconstructing a pre-Deuteronomic cycle of tradition in 1–2 Samuel is so complicated as to be impossible."[150] The reason for this is that the oral techniques, at both the formative and redactional stages, have so obscured the development that it is no longer transparent what occurred at the earlier stages. In other words, Carlson seems to concur with Engnell's thesis of the infeasibility of stratifying the development of the tradition or of seeing through the fog created by oral transmission. But inasmuch as this traditio-historical research is concerned with the tradition from its earliest stages down to its last redaction,[151] *one must not from the outset decline to attempt to investigate the prehistory.* Carlson's interests lie with the redactional stage;[152] his compositional, literary-analytical, ideological investigations of 2 Samuel are indeed perceptive, compelling, and noteworthy—although they fulfill only part of the total traditio-historical task.

---

149. Perhaps a good indication of Carlson's preoccupation with the redactional phase is simply this fact that it is so difficult for the reader to determine exactly what Carlson esteems to be the transmittal nature and extent of the pre-Deuteronomic form of 2 Samuel.

150. Carlson, *David, the Chosen King*, 43; cf. also Noth, *ÜSt*, 73.

151. As we have seen above (pp. 245–46), this is the definition accepted by both Noth and Carlson.

152. This interest in literary techniques and composition is obvious also in his articles, "Élie à l'Horeb," *VT* 19 (1969), 416–39; and "Élisée—le successeur d'Élie," *VT* 20 (1970), 385–405.

14
THE INFLUENCE OF AND RESPONSE TO THE UPPSALA CIRCLE

The Old Testament research directions taken by the Uppsala Circle and the theses propounded by its members have been met variously by Old Testament scholars in other countries. It may be characterized roughly as a somewhat more positive reception in, for example, England than in Germany. However, of special interest is the reaction that the ideas emitting from Uppsala have elicited from their closest neighbors. Whereas the Old Testament scholars in the other Swedish theological department at Lund have shown more interest in philological investigations than in traditio-historical matters, their colleagues in Norway and Denmark have had a research tradition closer to that of Uppsala, as can be seen from the influence that, for example, Mowinckel, Pedersen, and Birkeland have had on the Uppsala Circle. In the following we will therefore turn our attention to four researchers—Bentzen, Nielsen, Kapelrud, and Sæbø—whose works bear the marks of contact with Uppsala. We will see that two of them (Nielsen and Kapelrud) have been influenced more strongly than the other two by the ideas and methods which we have reviewed in the above sections. Our primary interest, however, is not simply to survey historically the effect of an idea, but rather to attempt to *show how the strong points of the traditio-historical research carried out since 1935 in Uppsala have been filtered out from its more problematic aspects and how these positive points have improved or supplemented the methods and ideas current elsewhere.*

A. AAGE BENTZEN

The Dane Aage Bentzen (1894–1953) has earned a reputation of an astute, thorough Old Testament scholar, especially on the basis of his magnum opus, *Introduction to the Old Testament* (two volumes).[1] A Scandinavian who has

---

1. Copenhagen, 1st ed. 1948, 2nd ed. 1952. First Danish edition: *Indledning til det Gamle Testamente*, Copenhagen 1941. References here are made to the second English edition.

had a great deal of contact with German and English scholarship as well, he has rendered the invaluable service of making accessible to the non-Scandinavian world much of the work and ideas that have gained a hearing among his Old Testament compatriots in the North.[2] Because of his effort to keep a foot in each of the two camps, however, it was probably inevitable that he could not please all parties, especially with respect to the controversial ideas championed by certain members of the Uppsala Circle. Thus, for example, regarding questions of the sacral-kingship ideology and the important role of cultic-mythic patterns, Bentzen's basic acceptance—though made with some distinct reservations[3]—of the "Uppsala" approach exceeds the wont of many non-Scandinavian scholars.[4] On the other hand, in the specific matters of traditio-historical research he, like Mowinckel, tries to strike a balance between it and literary criticism—in this case to the irritation of especially Engnell.[5] In the face of the latter's objection, Bentzen reaffirms the viability of his compromise position,[6] recognizing the importance of the oral prehistory of the Old Testament material but refusing to see it as an exclusive alternative to literary criticism: "The slogan 'oral tradition' must not become a sort of smoke-screen blacking out the problems of the text."[7] According to him, all cases of repetition, contradiction, and obscurity cannot simply be attributed to the process of oral transmission, as Engnell pictures it.[8] His agreement with Mowinckel about the continued importance of literary criticism[9] is obvious, as is also

---

2. This has been carried out above all in his *Introduction*, though also in such articles as "Skandinavische Literatur zum Alten Testament 1939-1948," *TRu*, NS 17 (1948/49), 273-328.

3. Cf., e.g., his *Messias—Moses redivivus Menschensohn: Skizzen zum Thema Weissagung und Erfüllung*, ATANT 17, Zurich 1948, 9, 54; and *Det sakrale kongedømme: Bemaerkninger i en löbende diskussion om de gammeltestamentlige Salmer*, Copenhagen 1945. The latter monograph and also his article, "Kan ordet 'messiansk' anvendes om Salmernes kongeforestillinger?," *SEÅ* 12 (1947), 36–50, provide an excellent survey of the Scandinavian debate on, respectively, the sacral-kingship ideology and the understanding of the term "messianic." Cf. also his "King Ideology—'Urmensch'—'Troonsbestijgningsfeest'," *ST* 3 (1949), 143–57.

4. Bentzen's alliance with other Scandinavians at these religio-historical points is criticized by, e.g., Noth ("Gott, König, Volk im Alten Testament," *Ges. Stud.* 3rd ed., 1966, 199, 209, 228).

5. Referring positively to Bentzen's work on Isaiah (*Jesaja* I, Copenhagen 1944; II, Copenhagen 1943), Engnell writes (*SEÅ* 10, 1945, 37): "Bentzen evinces already in his *Indledning til det G.T.* (1941) noticeable influence of the traditio-historical view without realizing the impossibility of uniting it in a compromise with a view fundamentally resting on the literary-critical standpoint."

6. Bentzen, *Introduction*, I, 103ff., and II, 60ff.; *Messias—Moses redivivus—Menschensohn*, 46–47.

7. *Introduction*, II, 63.

8. Cf. above, pp. 203–5; and Bentzen, *Introduction*, II, 25–26.

9. Cf. above, pp. 208–10.

true in his use of Lindblom's argument about the negligible difference between a fixed and firm oral tradition and its written counterpart.[10] He refutes Eissfeldt's contention that oral transmission was employed only at the "preliterary stage" and not also among "literary" people.[11] In Bentzen's eyes literary criticism is especially valuable in the effort to solve problems of composition, to determine how smaller literary units are combined into larger complexes.[12]

1. Hypothesis of Hexateuchal Stratification

On the basis of these general remarks about Bentzen's methodological orientation, we might find some value now in turning our attention briefly to his treatment of three specific Old Testament problems with a traditio-historical dimension. Concerning the Hexateuch,[13] Bentzen admits the difficulties and weaknesses in the Documentary Hypothesis but refuses to jettison it and the literary-critical method entirely, as Engnell and others tend to do. What then is Bentzen's solution to the problems of the Pentateuch? His own words are worth noting: "I think we must stop speaking of 'documents'. I am deliberately more inclined to say 'strata', indicating that I am a little more optimistic concerning the task of getting behind the 'last tradents', back to the story-tellers whose traditions they have taken up in their collections. I think the truth of the documentary hypothesis must be accounted for in this way."[14] To these different "strata" of traditions, which developed primarily in the preredactional period and which are basically identical in content with JE, P, and D, he assigns the various stylistic, material, and theological "constants," somewhat in the same way as did Humbert.[15] Bentzen appeals for only a relative and approximate dating of the strata, that is, of "the main stem" of each stratum, for the strata were reworked and supplemented repeatedly in the circles to which they belonged. Since all the strata contain both earlier and later materials, we must regard them as being "as much parallel as successive."[16] Bentzen thus concurs with Uppsala scholars in maintaining that "the task is now to

---

10. Cf. above, p. 189; and Bentzen, *Introduction*, I, 105.
11. Bentzen, *Introduction*, I, 108.
12. Ibid., I, 252ff.
13. Bentzen prefers this term and viewpoint, although without disapproving too strongly of Noth's and Engnell's "Tetrateuch"; cf. Bentzen, *Introduction*, II. 75–76, and Appendix, 17.
14. Bentzen, *Introduction*, II, 31, also 60ff.; and his "Bermerkungen über neuere Entwicklungen in der Pentateuchfrage," *ArOr* 19 (1951), 226–32.
15. Bentzen, *Introduction*, II, 24ff., with reference to Humbert (1938). Cf. Engnell's response, *GT-I*, 191–209.
16. Bentzen, *Introduction*, II, 64.

grasp the *oral prehistory* of the material,"[17] but with his "hypothesis of stratification" he intends to research deeper into the actual history of tradition than Engnell is inclined to do.

2. Israel and Ancient Near Eastern Motifs

In a study of Amos 1–2, Bentzen makes the point that influence from ancient Near Eastern lands on Israelite material should generally be asserted sparingly and always with extreme care.[18] We have seen above[19] that Engnell advocates the same, although with respect to only the question of oral transmission; Bentzen here applies this principle also to religio-historical motifs. He thus speaks only of *resemblances* between the Amos text and the Egyptian execration texts.[20] When at another point he finds an ancient motif in Dan 6, he admits that he is often reluctant and hesitant to work along these lines, for it cannot always be clearly shown "that the old ideas are still alive in the Israelite-Jewish context, and that perhaps antiquarian interest hinders concrete understanding of the given text in its peculiarity."[21] This is precisely what Bentzen criticizes in some of the religio-historical work of his Scandinavian colleagues—the failure to differentiate sufficiently between the Israelite use of a motif and its original form and meaning in earlier cultures.[22]

3. The Book of Daniel

In his work on the book of Daniel,[23] Bentzen gives the clear impression that, although the actual writing of the book should be dated around 165 B.C.E., the material itself is considerably older and underwent a long period of

---

17. Ibid., 63.
18. "The Ritual Background of Amos i 2—ii 16," *OtSt* 8 (1950), 86–87. Cf. also Bentzen, "Der Hedammu-Mythus, das Judithbuch und ähnliches," *ArOr* 18,3 (1950), 1–2.
19. Above, pp. 218–19, 231 n. 37.
20. Contrary to Engnell's classification of the book of Amos in the *diwān*-category (cf. above, p. 213), Bentzen (*OtSt* 8, 1950, 97, 93) holds that at least the first two chapters are of the liturgy-type, being an imitation of the New Year festival liturgy. At one point he speaks of composers of the book of Amos, at another place he refers to its collectors (ibid., 69–70); no more details about its transmission are given.
21. "Daniel 6: Ein Versuch zur Vorgeschichte der Märtyrerlegende," Bertholet-Festschrift, Tübingen 1950, 62. According to Bentzen, Kapelrud's *Joel Studies* (Uppsala 1948) is often guilty of making this mistake.
22. Cf. below, pp. 296–97. Cf. also Bentzen, "Der Tod des Beters in den Psalmen: Randbemerkungen zur Diskussion zwischen Mowinckel und Widengren," Eissfeldt-Festschrift, Halle an der Saale 1947, 57–60.
23. *Daniel*, HAT 19, 2nd ed., Tübingen 1952.

development prior to its being recorded.[24] He speaks of "a—certainly primarily oral—prehistory of the legends" and refers to "the presence of marks of diverse ages in the individual stories."[25] However he only attempts to isolate and identify these older traditional materials and does not seek to uncover the prehistory of the final form of the tradition. A good example is in Dan 6, behind which legend (and also that of Dan 3) Bentzen is inclined to see the ancient motif of the hero's descent into Hades (in Daniel's case, with his miraculous escape). This schema of the martyr-legend, according to Bentzen, probably has an original, close connection to the psalms of lamentation; and because these legends are "embodiments of striking assertions" (e.g., Pss 57:4–6; 91:13; 66:12), they embody the hope of the complaint psalms. This notion strengthens his hypothesis "that in the synagogal-church interpretation of both legends tones from the stories resonate which once accompanied the music of the martyr legends."[26] He does not give more details about how this dynamic process from early times down to Judeo-Christian interpretations could have occurred.

4. SUMMARY

From this brief presentation of various studies carried out by Bentzen, we can see that in his research method and interests he has been influenced as much by German Old Testament scholars as by his Scandinavian colleagues. This observation is especially true in the use he makes of the traditio-historical method. He recognized the importance of the prehistory of Old Testament traditions, even though he does not always attempt to investigate this developmental stage to the extent possible. The same is true for religio-historical motifs, though he is more reluctant than several at Uppsala to assume the ubiquity of these motifs—at least in their original meanings—throughout the Old Testament. He agrees to the importance of the role played by oral transmission but seeks to be realistic about its extent and reliability in comparison with written means of transmission. Pedersen's and Engnell's claim that the literary-critical method is outmoded and no longer acceptable is rejected by Bentzen, but he does appeal for a more moderate use of literary criticism, one which avoids the extremes and the minutiae of previous works of this type. We thus have a picture of Bentzen as a researcher who cannot be regarded as

---

24. Ibid., 6, 8.
25. Ibid., 9.
26. Bentzen, Bertholet-Festschrift, 62. Cf. also *Daniel*, 53ff.

a pioneer or even a chief proponent of traditio-historical research[27] and yet as *one who was influenced strongly by the growing interest in this field and who then attempted to incorporate those theses and to fulfill those traditio-historical tasks that, after a careful appraisal, he felt to be feasible and important.*

B. Arvid S. Kapelrud

The Norwegian Arvid S. Kapelrud (1912-1994) belongs also to that group of Old Testament scholars in Scandinavia who have been influenced by and who themselves have supported and contributed to the work of the Uppsala Circle. More so than Bentzen, he stands close to the Uppsala Circle and in some sense could almost be regarded as one of its members because of his having studied in Uppsala. Unlike Bentzen he has not gone on record as having serious reservations about some of the Uppsala research into religio-historical motifs and the predominant role of oral transmission; indeed, Kapelrud himself has also been involved in this work.[28] Kapelrud's research interests include the Ras Shamra texts,[29] the importance of the cult in Israel,[30] and the traces in the Old Testament of the sacral-kingship ideology and the fertility cult.[31] But in order for us to gain an idea of how Kapelrud makes use of the traditio-historical method, we should concentrate especially on his studies of Ezra, Joel, and the Pentateuch.[32]

1. The Origin of the Ezra-Narrative

One of Kapelrud's earliest publications, a study of the Ezra-tradi-

---

27. Bentzen is thus quite similar to Lindblom in this; cf. above, pp. 185-89. Note, e.g., the increased attention which Bentzen gives to traditio-historical problems in the second English edition of his *Introduction* (1952) in comparison with the first Danish edition in 1941. These changes reflect his development along these lines, as instigated and influenced by especially Noth, von Rad, Mowinckel, and Engnell. Cf. Bentzen, *TRu*, NS 17 (1948/49), 321.
28. Cf. Bentzen's criticism of Kapelrud, above, p. 258 n. 21.
29. *Baal in the Ras Shamra Texts*, Copenhagen 1952; *The Ras Shamra Discoveries and the Old Testament*, Norman, Oklahoma 1963 (Norwegian edition in 1953); and *The Violent Goddess: Anat in the Ras Shamra Texts*, Oslo 1969.
30. Cf., e.g., his "Cult and Prophetic Words," *ST* 4 (1950), 5-12; and "The Role of the Cult in Old Israel," *The Bible in Modern Scholarship*, ed. J. P. Hyatt, Nashville/New York 1965, 44-56.
31. Cf., e.g., "König David und die Söhne des Saul," *ZAW* 67 (1955), 198-205; "King and Fertility: A Discussion of II Sam. 21:1-14," *NTT* 56 (1955), 113-22.
32. We omit thereby his monograph, *Central Ideas in Amos*, SNVAO, II. Hist.- Filos. Klasse, 1956, No. 4; as well as other diverse publications.

tion,³³ consists primarily of a lexical examination of Ezra 7–10 and Neh 8,³⁴ but his results enable him to draw some noteworthy conclusions about the origin and development of these chapters. He first concludes that there exists no linguistic or stylistic difference between the third-person sections and the first-person sections in the Ezra-narrative, other than the simple fact that some sections are in the third- and others are in the first-person. Both sections, in their present form, come from the Chronicler circles, so this is their "common denominator" and explains their many points of agreement.³⁵ However, this is not to imply that the Ezra-narrative originated with the Chroniclers, only that it can be traced back to them. Regarding its earlier stages, Kapelrud makes two points that demonstrate clearly his proximity to the line of thought at that time becoming popular in Scandinavia. (a) The Ezra-narrative developed at the oral level, probably in several different circles, until the Chronicler circles gathered together the several stories and recorded them. Kapelrud emphasizes that this is thus different from the origin of the Nehemiah memoirs, which existed already in written form but were supplemented by some orally transmitted details at the hands of the Chroniclers. At any rate, Neh 8 most likely circulated in different groups than did Ezra 7–10, and the resultant disorder of the total narrative at the oral stage probably best explains its varied arrangement in the different traditions.³⁶ (b) Having thus affirmed that the Ezra-narrative existed in some form before the Chronicler circles received and reworked it, Kapelrud then goes on to maintain that it is *not possible for us to get behind the present tradition and to determine the details of this earlier form.* The reason for this is simply that the Chronicler circles were too thorough and effective in their work. "The entire tradition was completely changed in these circles. The choice of words, tone of the language and stylistic effects are now those that were natural in Chr circles, and any attempt to peel it down to the 'original' tale, is doomed in advance to failure."³⁷

---

33. *The Question of Authorship in the Ezra-Narrative: A Lexical Investigation*, SNVAO, II. Hist.-Filos. Klasse, 1944, No. 1. Cf. also his earlier article, "Forskningen omkring Ezra og Ezraboken," *NTT* 43 (1942), 148–65.

34. Kapelrud, in agreement with Mowinckel (*Ezra den skriftlærde* and *Statholderen Nehemia*, both Kristiania 1916) but in contrast to Noth (*ÜSt*, 127–28), does not consider that Neh 9 and 10 belong to the Ezra-narrative. Cf. now also Mowinckel, *Studien zu dem Buche Ezra-Nehemia* I–III, SNVAO, N.S. II, Hist.-Phil. Klasse, No. 3, 5, 7, Oslo 1964–65.

35. Kapelrud, *The Question of Authorship*, 95.

36. In 3 Ezra and in Josephus, Neh 8 follows immediately after Ezra 10, rather than being separated from these chapters, as in the MT. Cf. ibid., 96–97, 93–94.

37. Ibid., 96. Kapelrud makes clear, however, that the situation is not so hopeless in other parts of the Old Testament, as e.g., in Nehemiah, in which long sections can be separated that quite certainly belonged to the original "memoirs." Cf. also Engnell, *GT-I*, 251ff.

To answer the question of who the "Chronicler" was, Kapelrud maintains that we must not see in him a single author but rather "a whole circle or more probably groups of circles that have grown up in a definite Levite-influenced milieu in Jerusalem"; they were rigorous in the law, stayed close to the temple, and were influenced also by Nehemiah and Ezra.[38] Kapelrud concludes his treatise with the appeal for a new appraisal of the entire question of the origin and sources of Chronicles—a task that Noth's *ÜSt* fulfilled in part in the year preceding Kapelrud's publication, although the latter apparently did not have the opportunity to consult it before his own study was completed.

2. Pentateuch Miscellanea

Kapelrud has not produced any thoroughgoing, detailed examination of the Pentateuch, but some of his smaller articles dealing with specific problems contain several comments of relevance to traditio-historical research. In one general article on the Pentateuch,[39] he briefly reviews pentateuchal research (primarily that of Noth and of the Scandinavians) and isolates as the four most important results of this research: (a) the significant role played by oral transmission in the formation of the pentateuchal traditions; (b) the division of the historical books into the P-work (Genesis–Numbers) and the D-work (Deuteronomy–2 Kings); (c) the decision that E is not an independent source; and (d) the new view of P not as one of several sources, but as the whole Tetrateuch, a complete work containing traditions of varying age.[40] Kapelrud has also paid special attention to the Priestly Code,[41] concluding that, because Deutero-Isaiah was familiar with and used expressions from P's creation story and the exodus narrative whereas such traces are lacking in Jeremiah and Ezekiel, the P-work should be dated sometime between 585 and 550 B.C.E., having by the latter date reached its final, present form (except for some later additions and minor adjustments). Addressing himself in another connection to the problem of the alternation of divine names in the Tetrateuch, Kapelrud appeals to similar phenomena in the Ras Shamra texts and in the Psalms and maintains that changing the name of the deity is "simply a stylistic device" and "an ancient custom" and thus is not an indication that different sources are involved.[42] Here Kapelrud's opposition to this

---

38. Kapelrud, *The Question of Authorship*, 97.
39. "Pentateuch-problemer," *NTT* 56 (1955), 185–201.
40. Ibid., 196–98.
41. "The Date of the Priestly Code (P)," *ASTI* 3 (1964), 58–64.
42. Kapelrud, *Baal in the Ras Shamra Texts*, 46. Bentzen (*Introduction*, II, 29, and Appendix, 15) sharply criticizes Kapelrud at this point for his failure to distinguish between prose and poetic styles.

literary-critical criterion is quite in accord with the opinions of other Scandinavians, especially Engnell.[43]

3. Origin and Development of the Book of Joel

But more important than Kapelrud's diverse, short articles on the Pentateuch is his *Joel Studies*.[44] This work was submitted as a dissertation at Uppsala and betrays at many points the influence that the various members of the Uppsala Circle had on him. In opposition to the literary-critical work on the book of Joel, typified by Duhm's analyses, Kapelrud advocates the *unity of the book*, refusing to draw a sharp line between the prophetic (Joel 1–2) and the apocalyptic (Joel 3–4) sections: "The many allegedly apocalyptic interpolations are not interpolations at all, but integral to the continuity of thought in the Book of Joel."[45] Whereas Engnell holds the reference to the locusts as probably being only the figurative language (from ancient Tammuz-liturgies) of a cultic description of disaster and misfortune,[46] Kapelrud maintains that an actual disaster wrought by locusts was the point of departure for the prophet's message about the Day of Jahweh. Joel's favorable disposition to the cult has often led scholars to set him in a later period, but Kapelrud feels that the cultic background of the book and especially its allusions to the fertility cult speak far more for a preexilic dating of Joel.[47] This conclusion is supported also by Joel's close relationship to the ideas of Jeremiah and Zephaniah.[48] Kapelrud agrees with Engnell that the book of Joel, form-critically seen, is structured like a liturgy[49]—or more specifically: "the Book is built up in the style of a psalm of lamentation followed by the usual oracle that gives the answer of Yahweh."[50] How does Kapelrud then view the origin and historical development of the book of Joel? According to him, Joel is not the author of the book but the originator of the sayings, dated at ca. 600 B.C.E., which from that time on were preserved and transmitted at the oral level, probably in circles associ-

---

43. Cf. above, e.g., pp. 203–5.
44. UUÅ 1948:4, Uppsala and Leipzig 1948.
45. Ibid., 176, cf. also 121–26.
46. In Engnell's article "Joels bok," *SBU* 1, 1948, cols. 1075–1077; cf. Kapelrud, *Joel Studies*, 14ff., 177., 193–94.
47. *Joel Studies*, 180, 18–24. For Kapelrud's answer to his critics at this point, cf. *ST* 4 (1950), 5–12.
48. *Joel Studies*, 179–81, 189–90.
49. Ibid., 9, 13–14, 120, 193ff. Engnell (*SBU* I, 1948, cols. 1076–77) suggests that the book is originally a liturgy for a day of penitence, or at least a prophetic imitation of such an original cult liturgy.
50. *Joel Studies*, 9.

ated with the temple, and were recorded in writing at the latest in the fourth or third century B.C.E.[51] However, regarding the possibility of describing the history of this tradition more specifically, Kapelrud is skeptical and reluctant: "The originator of the sayings is the temple-prophet Joel ben Petuel, but which portions of the text are due to him or to others, it is of course not possible to ascertain."[52] At this point Kapelrud agrees with Birkeland[53] and is especially in full accord with the traditio-historical principles laid down by his mentor in Uppsala, Ivan Engnell: the researcher should not seek to stratify the tradition but should rather *examine the final form* of the tradition for its historic theological ideas, compositional structure, religio-historical motifs, and the manner in which it originated. *Of all the Old Testament scholars affected by the traditio-historical direction taken by many of the Uppsala scholars, Kapelrud and Nielsen are probably the ones who have been most strongly influenced by this approach.*

C. Eduard Nielsen

Eduard Nielsen of Copenhagen has perhaps been even more affected than Kapelrud by ideas of the Uppsala Circle.[54] This impact is most obvious in the monograph he wrote on oral tradition,[55] whereas some of his later traditio-historical analyses indicate a methodological modification of the approach originally advanced by Engnell. It would be well to look more closely at two of his publications in order to understand better the influence that the position championed by Engnell and others could have on scholars outside of Uppsala.

---

51. Ibid., 176, 181–82, 191–92. Especially Joel 3–4 contain indications of this later period.

52. Ibid., 176. Kapelrud believes (192), though, that only minor changes occurred during the transmittal period because of the firm structure of the cultic-liturgical pattern.

53. Birkeland, *Traditionswesen*, 64, regarding Joel 1–2: "Also in this case we must regard Chaps. 1–2 as a product of tradition, and we must attempt to interpret them in the form in which they were transmitted. If the chapters gained their form through a longer or shorter oral tradition, then we will never succeed in extracting possible so-called 'secondary' elements." Cf. also Gunneweg, *Tradition*, 65.

54. Nielsen has in fact studied in Uppsala and admits readily the inspiration he has received from the views of Nyberg, Engnell, as well as Pedersen; cf. *Oral Tradition*, 9.

55. *Oral Tradition: A Modern Problem in Old Testament Introduction*, SBT 11, London 1954. This book is an English translation of four Danish articles: the first, "Jeremja og Jojakim," in *DTT* 13 (1950), 129–45; and the other three in *DTT* 15 (1952): "Mundtlig tradition: I. Til orientering i et aktuelt indledningsproblem," 19–37; "II. 'Når din søn spørger dig i morgen, da skal du sige...,'" 88–106; and "III. Et par traditionshistoriske analyser," 129–46.

THE INFLUENCE OF AND RESPONSE TO THE UPPSALA CIRCLE

1. The Thesis of a Predominant Oral Tradition

The arguments and the evidence to which Nielsen appeals in stating the case for oral tradition vary only at minor points from those advanced to one extent or another by, for example, Nyberg, Birkeland, Engnell, Mowinckel, Haldar, Ringgren, and Ahlström—and reviewed often enough above. His study is also riddled with phrases and polemical statements reminiscent of the writings of some of these men. At the very outset we should note that, like so many of his compatriots in the North, Nielsen's research is motivated in part by a distaste for *literary criticism*. Indeed he concedes this himself by referring to his monograph as a "work which tries to combat literary criticism" and by stressing that his analyses of Old Testament traditions should indicate that "literary criticism is not the only legitimate scientific approach to the texts of the Old Testament."[56] As did Engnell before him, Nielsen disdains the "book-view" of literary critics, the supposition that we in the Western world can expect the same of ancient Semites as we do of ourselves with regard to literary publication and written transmission.[57] According to Nielsen, the tradition historian, being fully aware of the cultural presuppositions of his time, tends to show more "reverence and respect for tradition"—although this does not mean that one is fundamentally either more or less critical, conservative, religious, or pious than the literary critic.[58] This idea of *reverence for tradition* is not original to Nielsen,[59] but for all of its elusiveness he pushes it to a curious extreme when he tries to explain what he means by it: that the tradition historian "believes the creators of our written Old Testament capable of better things than mere editorial clumsiness," and that the tradition historian thus gives "these men credit for so much human dignity that he attempts with all his might to reach an understanding of the (sensible) motives that asserted themselves in the formation of large complexes of traditions."[60] Nielsen main-

---

56. *Oral Tradition*, 9. An appraisal of Nielsen's work in this regard is made by S. Segert, "Zur Methode der alttestamentlichen Literarkritik (Quellenscheidung und Überlieferungsgeschichte)," *ArOr* 24 (1956), 610–621.
57. *Oral Tradition*, 84, 73.
58. Ibid., 63–64, 37–38, 39.
59. Engnell suggested it before him; cf. e.g., *GT–I*, 183.
60. *Oral Tradition*, 63. Nielsen's use of loaded terms here helps in no way to secure his argument. The issue is not whether an editor was "clumsy" or not, but rather whether an editor existed at all, in other words whether transmission and the joining of traditions occurred at the written or oral level. And for this historical problem, "human dignity" is an immaterial and irrelevant issue. Nielsen's admission that the tradition historian can accept some of the detailed work of the literary critics (ibid., 63) amounts in effect to partial refutation of his broadside attack on literary criticism.

tains that oral transmission as such should be regarded as being reliable, not only because of the widespread emphasis upon memory capabilities among ancient Semites, but also because oral transmission itself was usually subject to control: fellow traditionists as well as all the listeners served to uphold the tradition and to prohibit the individual traditionist from carrying through a corrupt recension.[61]

To establish the predominant role played by oral transmission, Nielsen first appeals to conditions in the ancient Near East and then also to parallel situations in ancient Greece and in Iceland.[62] This question has been treated earlier by Nyberg, Birkeland, Widengren, Læssøe, and others;[63] so one can justly be disappointed to see that *Nielsen fails here to offer precisely that which is needed*: a thoroughgoing, fresh presentation and analysis of all available evidence for the methods of transmission in the ancient Near East, together with a detailed description of these methods and the precise bearing this general Near Eastern situation had on Israelite transmission, supplemented also by a discussion of the problem of oral tradition as a historical source.[64] Approximately the same criticism can be made with regard to Nielsen's treatment of the role of oral tradition in the Old Testament.[65] As his point of departure he subscribes to Nyberg's dictum that the written form of the Old Testament is primarily a creation of the postexilic Jewish community,[66] and from this point Nielsen proceeds to deal with three topics: the subordinate role of writing in preexilic Israel,[67] the

---

61. Ibid., 37. An obvious question needs to be posed: In light of this "control," how then were the various traditions ever able to become expanded and developed in the first place? Would it not also have been equally difficult for an individual traditionalist to get an embellished rendition of a tradition accepted, or a complex of traditions that one had joined together for the first time? Cf. below, pp. 290–91, on the important distinction between oral formation and oral transmission.

62. *Oral Tradition*, 18–38.

63. Widengren's and Læssøe's conclusions are different from Nielsen's; cf. above, pp. 230–37. Cf. most recently J. C. de Moor, *Mondelinge Overlevering in Mesopotamië, Ugarit, en Israël*, Leiden 1965.

64. An exemplary study of this type, done on oral tradition in Africa, can now be seen in the work of Jan Vansina, *De la tradition orale: Essai de methods historique*, Tervuren 1961; English edition: *Oral Tradition: A Study in Historical Methodology*, Chicago 1965. —It should however be noted that Gunneweg (*Tradition*, 19ff.) regards Nielsen's *Oral Tradition* as valuable—and here he is fully right—insofar as it offers to the wider reading public a structured presentation of the main theses, and the evidence for them, of the Scandinavian traditio-historical school. Cf., though, the sharp criticisms directed at Nielsen by Widengren, *AcOr* 23 (1959), 216–18, 224–25.

65. *Oral Tradition*, 39–62.

66. Ibid., 391; cf. above, p. 179.

67. In response to Nielsen's statement (25) that "the art of writing is the business of the specialist and not of the common man," North in reviewing this book asserts pointedly that

positive evidence of the existence of oral transmission in Israel, and the reason for the change from an oral to a written literature.[68] Again here we find considerable duplication—or, at best, a summary—of the ideas and the interpretation of the data that appeared earlier in the studies of Mowinckel, Engnell, Birkeland, and others.[69]

One important item, however, is Nielsen's list of *the possible criteria for identifying oral and written transmission*.[70] For traditions (especially prose) occurring only once, the appearance of the following formal characteristics may indicate that it was handed down orally: "a monotonous style, recurrent expressions, a fluent, paratactic style, a certain rhythm and euphony which are especially noticeable when one hears the account, and finally anacolutha which a literary writer would hardly have let pass, but which may have been accompanied by a gesture in oral delivery or even have come into existence by the incorporation of a 'stage direction' in the text."[71] Nielsen adds to these the "epic laws" formulated by Axel Olrik[72] and others: the law of repetition, the law of the number three, the scenic law of the number two, and the conscious emphasizing of memory words and representative themes which "may also betray an organic connection with oral tradition and composition."[73] For traditions occurring two or more times the criteria have to do with the kind of variations that exist between the two renditions—whether these variations are of the graphic or phonetic type.[74] Admittedly, all of these criteria amount

---

"the writers of the putative 'documents' were presumably such specialists" (*ExpTim* 66, 1954/55, 39).

68. Cf. Gunneweg's thorough critique (*Tradition*, 19–32) of the negative and positive evidence on which Nielsen builds his case. Gunneweg's conclusion (31) is that Nielsen's arguments and pieces of evidence "demonstrate only that both types, oral and written tradition, existed together (which we certainly do not doubt at all) and that thereby the oral method of transmission was normal (which we also cannot doubt, based on all that we know)."

69. Cf., e.g., Nielsen's treatment of the prophetic traditions (52–54), the law materials (42, 45–48, 56–58), and the various "books" referred to by the Deuteronomist (41–42, 48–52).

70. For other significant work done in this area, cf. J. Hempel, "The Forms of Oral Tradition," *Record and Revelation*, ed. Robinson, Oxford 1938, 28–44; C.H. Lohr, "Oral Techniques in the Gospel of Matthew," *CBQ* 23 (1961), 403–35; R.C. Culley, "An Approach to the Problem of Oral Tradition," *VT* 13 (1963), 113–25; and Culley, *Oral Formulaic Language in the Biblical Psalms*, Toronto 1967.

71. *Oral Tradition*, 36. Ahlström (*HTR* 59, 1966, 72) justifiably asks whether a "monotonous style" and a "fluent" one are not contradictory styles. Also Richter is not convinced by Nielsen's criteria; *Exegese als Literaturwissenschaft*, 159 n. 27.

72. Olrik, "Episke love i folkedigtningen," *DS* 1908, 69–89; "Epische Gesetze der Volksdichtung," *ZAL* 51 (1909), 1–12; cf. also M. Moe, "Episke Grundlove," *Edda* 2 (1914), 1–16, 233–249, and *Edda* 4 (1915), 85–126.

73. *Oral Tradition*, 36.

74. Ibid., 36–37; and on Ringgren, above, pp. 238–40.

to only probable, not conclusive, evidence that oral transmission was in play for any given tradition.

As noted above, the major part of Nielsen's *Oral Tradition* amounts essentially to a summary or restatement of certain traditio-historical ideas and arguments which were in currency at the time of his publication. As an introduction to the debate on oral tradition, the book is indeed valuable—despite its one-sidedness. However, of considerably more importance for the furtherance of traditio-historical research are his several studies of specific Old Testament tradition complexes. In his *Oral Tradition* he offers, as illustrations of the traditio-historical method, some cursory remarks about Jer 36, Mic 4–5,[75] and Gen 6–9.[76] But these hardly deserve the attention that do his investigations of the Shechem traditions and of the Decalogue.[77] We will restrict ourselves to the latter because Nielsen's application of the traditio-historical method here is in many ways exemplary and justifies our reviewing it in some detail.

2. Tradition History of the Decalogue

Nielsen takes other studies of the Decalogue, particularly that of Gerstenberger,[78] as his starting point and from there attempts to lead the discussion to a new stage. His procedure is first to reconstruct the original form of the Decalogue and then to trace its development up to its present form in Exod 20 and Deut 5. To be sure, Nielsen deals as well with other problems, such as the question of the actual number of commandments,[79] the different enu-

---

75. On Nielsen's analysis of Micah 4–5, cf. Otzen, *Studien über Deuterosacharja*, 222–27; and Gunneweg, *Tradition*, 60–64. Also Segert (*ArOr* 24, 1956, 614ff.) offers a critique of Nielsen's three analyses.

76. Nielsen, *Oral Tradition*, 63–103. It is interesting to note that these are presented as traditio-historical studies rather than as examples of the workings of oral tradition. This fact demonstrates clearly how closely "oral tradition" is identified with "tradition history" by Nielsen (and other Scandinavians).

77. Nielsen, *Shechem: A Traditio-Historical Investigation*, Copenhagen 1955, 2nd ed. 1959; and *De ti bud: En traditionshistorisk skitse*, Copenhagen 1965 (= *Die Zehn Gebote: Eine traditionsgeschichtliche Skizze*, transl. by H. M. Junghans, ATDan 8, Copenhagen 1965; and *The Ten Commandments in New Perspective: A Traditio-Historical Approach*, transl. by D. J. Bourke, SBT Second Series 7, London 1968. References here are made to the German edition, with the page numbers of the English edition in parentheses.) Another article of interest is Nielsen's "Deuterojesaja: Erwägungen zur Formkritik, Traditions- und Redaktionsgeschichte," *VT* 20 (1970), 190–205.

78. *Wesen und Herkunft des "apodiktischen Rechts,"* WMANT 20, Neukirchen-Vluyn 1965 (in dissertation form in 1961).

79. To this problem and on the whole to the gathering of Old Testament laws in groups of ten, see the article by E. Auerbach, "Das Zehngebot—Allgemeine Gesetzes-Form in der Bibel," *VT* 16 (1966), 255–76.

meration systems employed throughout history, and various text-critical and literary-critical problems present in the two transmitted forms of the "ethical" Decalogue.[80] But traditio-historical matters receive the majority of his attention—not just the analysis of the first form and of the final form, but also of all the stages of development in between.

a. Form-Critical Reconstruction of the Original Decalogue

On the basis of a text-critical and literary-critical analysis, Nielsen first concludes that the "classical Decalogue" does not belong originally to either of its present contexts, Exod 19–34 or Deut 4–11 but that it was inserted into these narrative sections sometime between 622 B.C.E. (Josiah's reform) and 560 B.C.E. (the approximate date of the composition of the Deuteronomistic History).[81] Concerning *form-critical* questions Nielsen aligns himself with Gerstenberger's criticisms both of Alt's ideas about apodictic law,[82] as well as of the hypothesis of a close, original relationship between apodictic precepts and the "covenant formulary" of the ancient Near East.[83] Gerstenberger develops the thesis that the earliest form of the apodictic law, a simple prohibition of a hypothetical crime expressed authoritatively in the second person singular, stems not from the cultic but from the secular sphere of tribal or family ethics and that such prohibitions were at first gathered into short groups of two or three commandments at the secular level before being transformed much later into series of ten or twelve commandments with cultic or covenantal overtones.[84] In agreement with this thesis—except for the late date of the longer series of commandments[85]—and on the basis of a form-critical

---

80. Nielsen, *Die Zehn Gebote*, 13–48 (ET: 6–55).
81. Ibid., 34–48, 93 (ET: 34–55, 119).
82. A. Alt, "Die Ursprünge des israelitischen Rechts" (1934), *Kl. Schr.* I, 278–332.
83. Cf. especially G.F. Mendenhall on the Hittite treaties, *Law and Covenant in Israel and the Ancient Near East*, Pittsburgh 1955; G. Heinemann, *Untersuchungen zum apodiktischen Recht*, Diss. Hamburg 1958; also Kapelrud, "Some Recent Points of View on the Time and Origin of the Decalogue, *ST* 18 (1964), 81–90; and Nielsen, *Die Zehn Gebote*, 57ff. (ET: 68ff.).
84. A lively discussion has focused on our understanding of Israelite law in general and the Decalogue in particular, and in this regard the reader is referred especially to the following publications and to the literature discussed there: J.J. Stamm with M.E. Andrew, *The Ten Commandments in Recent Research*, SBT, Second Series 2, London 1967; H. Graf Reventlow, "Kultisches Recht im Alten Testament," *ZTK* 60 (1963), 267–304; H.J. Boecker, *Redeformen des Rechtslebens im Alten Testament*, WMANT 14, Neukirchen-Vluyn 1964; G. Fohrer, "Das sogenannte apodiktisch formulierte Recht und der Dekalog," *KD* 11 (1965), 49–74; and G.J. Botterweck, "Form- und überlieferungsgeschichtliche Studie zum Dekalog," *Concilium* 1 (1965), 392–401.
85. Cf. Nielsen, *Die Zehn Gebote*, 62–63 (ET: 76–78).

analysis, Nielsen reconstructs an "Urdekalog" ("primitive decalogue")[86] as follows.[87]

(1) לא תשתחוה לאל אחר
(2) לא תעשה לך פסל
(3) לא תשא את־שם יהוה לשוא
(4) לא תעשה מלאכה ביום השבת
(5) לא תקלה את־אביך ואת־אמך
(6) לא תנאף את־אשת רעך
(7) לא תשפך את־דם רעך
(8) לא תגנב איש מרעך

---

86. In this "Urdekalog" Nielsen builds on—and in effect brings to a culmination—the work done previously in this same direction, especially that of E. Meier, H. Schmidt, and K. Rabast; cf. Nielsen, *Die Zehn Gebote*, 64–67, 55n. (ET: 78–83, 66n.); and also H. Haag, "Der Dekalog in der Verkündigung," *Anima* 19,2 (1964), 120–28. The earliest such attempt to reconstruct an "Urdekalog" may have been made in 1795 by Nachtigal, in his article reviewed above, pp. 49–51. Appealing to linguistic reasons, Nachtigal asserted (vol. 4, 1795, 11): "... we must imagine these commandments in another language than that in which we read them now. That language is not different from that of the Davidic period; at the same time, it expresses the commandments much more concisely in many respects, e.g.: 1) Only Jehovah is God! 2) Make no idols for yourselves! 3) Swear not falsely! 4) Celebrate the Sabbath! 5) Honor father and mother! 6) Murder not! 7) Be not an adulterer! 8) Steal not! 9) Be not a false witness! 10) Covet not that which belongs to others! (For most of these sentences the ancient Hebrews probably needed only one word.)"

87. Nielsen, *Die Zehn Gebote*, 68 (ET: 84–85), in transliteration and translation. There is much to be said here both for and against these formulations of the individual commandments, but a critique of this reconstructed "Urdekalog," derived through form-critical means, is beyond the scope of our interests here. Three things, however, may be noted: First, Nielsen's ultimate purpose in this study is not simply to reconstruct a hypothetical "Urdekalog" but rather to *outline the developmental history of our present Decalogue*. In other words, the drawing up of an "Urdekalog" is only a penultimate goal for him; the final purpose is to be able to write a history of the Decalogue tradition, and to this end an "Urdekalog" can be of some assistance, in Nielsen's opinion. Secondly, Nielsen discusses individually each of these formulations listed above, and the reader is referred to the presentation of his reasons for each, ibid., 69–73 (ET: 86–92). Suffice it here to mention that for the reconstructed form of the first commandment Nielsen draws especially on Exod 34:14; for the fifth commandment—Deut 27:16; for the sixth commandment—Lev 20:10; for the seventh—Gen 9:6; Jer 7:6 and 22:3 (he might also have referred to Lev 19:16); and for the eighth commandment—Exod 21:16. Thirdly, he makes transcription errors in five of the commandments, either in the German, in the English, or in both renditions: (2) read *pāsel* instead of *pesel* if it is to be in the pausal form as are the final words in the other commandments; (3) read *laššāw'* instead of *lēšāw'* for which there is no evidence elsewhere in the Old Testament; (6) in the English read *tinăp* instead of *tīn'ap*; (7) in the English read *dam* instead of *dām*; (9) in the English read *ta'ăne* instead of *ta'ane*, and in both English and German read *běrē'ăkā* instead of *běrē'ekā*.

(9) לא תענה ברעך עד שקר
(10) לא תחמד בית רעך

Nielsen readily admits the definite hypothetical character of this list and the problems certain of these formulations have,[88] and he of course is not even able to prove that all ten commandments were in fact present in this original list.[89] However, on the basis of form criticism and traditio-historical examination, Nielsen comes to an important historical conclusion about the origin of the Decalogue. In a climactic section, "Divine Utterance or Collection of Laws?" he argues that the Decalogue at its very beginning was formed and transmitted as a "collection of laws, and that it was only at a later stage in its tradition that its formulation was changed, so that now it appears as an address by Yahweh—and that only in part."[90] This view of the "Urdekalog" as a collection of laws rather than as a covenant document excludes, of course, the possibility of any original connection with the "Hittite treaty formula."[91] Nielsen comes to this conclusion especially by observing that the commandment additions formulated in the first person (in the first and second commandments) can easily be changed back into a hypothetically original formulation in the third person, whereas the additional clauses in the fourth commandment, formulated now in the third person, are not capable of being changed back into a supposedly original first person form.[92] If all of the expansions in these commandments were thus originally in the third person, this tends to indicate that *at the beginning the Decalogue was indeed a "collection of laws" rather than a "divine utterance."*

---

88. One must acknowledge how refreshing it is to see the readiness with which Nielsen concedes the inconclusive character of both form-critical and traditio-historical research; the reason he gives has to do especially with the fragmentary nature of much of our source material from preexilic times; cf. *Die Zehn Gebote*, 69, 93, 75 (ET: 86, 119, 94). However, precisely because of the hypothetical nature of "Urdekaloge" like the one proposed by Nielsen, other scholars have emphasized the uselessness of such reconstructions; cf. especially H. Gese "Der Dekalog als Ganzheit betrachtet," *ZTK* 64 (1967), 125–26; and A. Jepsen, "Beiträge zur Auslegung und Geschichte des Dekalogs, *ZAW* 79 (1967), 282, 298–99. The latter two opt rather, to use Jepsen's term, for a "Grundform," reached by eliminating certain words and clauses, in preference to an "Urform," which is form-critically uniform but historically suspect.

89. For a critique of Nielsen's monograph, cf. especially the review by de Vries in *VT* 16 (1966), 530–34.

90. Nielsen, *Die Zehn Gebote*, 100 (ET: 129).

91. Ibid., 100–101 (ET: 130–31).

92. Also the additions in the fifth commandment fit better in the third person, while the expansions in the third commandment could just as well have been in either first or third person form; ibid., 99–100, 79 (ET: 128–30, 100).

b. Traditio-Historical Analysis

Having thus arrived form-critically at the surmised original form of each of the laws in this collection, what is Nielsen able to conclude about the tradition history of the Decalogue, about the developmental history of the commandments both individually and as a group? His first step is to examine the secondary expansions in five of the commandments (those dealing with images, Jahweh's name, the sabbath, parents, and covetousness), the secondary abbreviations in three of the commandments (adultery, murder, and theft), and the transformation of two of the prohibitions into positive commandments (sabbath and parents).[93] In the case of each alteration to which the commandments were subjected he tries to account for its origin and development, especially by seeking answers—to the extent possible—for the questions of why, how, and when these changes occurred. Nielsen fashions the results of these investigations into a *traditio-historical sketch of the development of the Decalogue* from its original form on down to its present form in Exod 20 and Deut 5,[94] and this sketch can be summarized as follows: The substance of the first four commandments in their short, prohibitive forms stems from the period before the tribal entry into the land, for these commandments are permeated with the conception of Jahweh as אל קנה.[95] For the final six commandments it cannot be decided with the same degree of certainty whether these prohibitions come out of a nomadic or a settled culture,[96] but in all likelihood the systematic codification of these fundamental rules of morality and justice resulted from a "desire for synthesis" during the period which von Rad terms the "free-thinking era" of the early monarchy.[97] In light of its affinity to the Israelite heritage of justice, this early form of the Decalogue should not be regarded as a "mere catechism-like collection of moral precepts."[98] Drawing on the references to the משפט-המלכה (1 Sam 10:25) and to the משפט-המלך (1 Sam 8:11ff.), Nielsen formulates his *thesis* with respect to the origin and the setting of the Decalogue. *The Decalogue was devised in northern Israel not only to serve as a standard of behavior for all Israelites, but especially to function as a "basic law" for the king in his capacity as the*

---

93. Ibid., 76–92 (ET: 95–118).
94. Ibid., 92–99, 102–10 (ET: 118–28, 132–43).
95. Ibid., 93–94, 106–7 (ET: 120–21, 139).
96. Ibid., 94 (ET: 121). Aside from such cursory remarks, Nielsen avoids delving into the possibility that any or all of the individual commandments alone had a prehistory or an earlier form than that in which they appear in his "Urdekalog."
97. Cf. von Rad, *Theologie* I, 5th ed. 1966, 62–70 (ET: I, 48–56); and *Genesis*, ATD 2, 5th ed. 1958, 7–22. Cf. Nielsen, *Die Zehn Gebote*, 95–96 (ET: 123–24).
98. Nielsen, *Die Zehn Gebote*, 103 (ET: 133).

*highest judge in civil disputes.*⁹⁹ The "Sitz im Leben" of the Decalogue as a code of law was thus the secular court of justice in the northern kingdom until 722 B.C.E., and it can perhaps be assumed—although of course not proved—that this basic law was composed at Shechem by the priests and the elders.¹⁰⁰

On the basis of the *secondary additions* to the commandments, considerably more can be said about the history of the Decalogue. Some of these alterations could have arisen during the period of the monarchy since it is quite probable that the Decalogue during that time existed as a more or less "living tradition of law" at the hands of the *elders*, those generally immediately responsible for justice.¹⁰¹ It is also quite possible that the Decalogue, or at least the first commandment (note the expression על־פני), was at some time handed down as "a 'shrine' tradition," i.e. especially in *priestly circles*.¹⁰² After the downfall of the monarchy in Samaria in 722 B.C.E., the Decalogue was probably taken over by *Levitical circles* that remained active at the northern shrines, and thus began the final stage of the Decalogue tradition. In connection with their liturgical activities, preaching, and popular instruction, these Levitical circles¹⁰³ left their imprint on the Decalogue at numerous points and especially were responsible for adding the introduction and thus transforming the Decalogue into a covenant document and giving it the status of sacral tradition,¹⁰⁴ in which form it was inserted into its present contexts in Exod 20 and Deut 5 sometime between 622 and 560 B.C.E.¹⁰⁵

---

99. Quite obviously, the central role of the king, to which Nielsen here appeals in his search for the original function of the Decalogue, is an ever-recurring theme in the writings of many Scandinavian Old Testament scholars. However, *simply* by pointing to this fact one does by no means succeed in refuting Nielsen's thesis, especially since he does not at this point envision the king in any mythic-cultic role but rather as the chief, secular judge. If one is to dispute Nielsen's contention, it is far more necessary to do it on historical grounds or to offer another, more compelling thesis, such as Jepsen tries to do (*ZAW* 79, 1967, 300ff.) in arguing that the Decalogue has "von je" been connected with the Sinai tradition and was transmitted in early times in the same noncultic circles as the Sinai tradition was.

100. Nielsen, *Die Zehn Gebote*, 103–7 (ET: 134–39).

101. Ibid., 96–97 (ET: 124). It is interesting to note that also Jepsen (*ZAW* 79, 1967, 302–4) argues for a noncultic "Sitz im Leben" for the Decalogue and that he assumes that the "Traditionsträger" were first the elders and then the Levites.

102. *Die Zehn Gebote*, 94–95 (ET: 121–22).

103. For a more detailed study of the Levitical circles, cf. Nielsen's *Shechem*, 264–83; and his "The Levites in Ancient Israel," *ASTI* 3 (1964), 16–27.

104. *Die Zehn Gebote*, 107ff., 101 (ET: 140ff., 131). This late date for the association of the Decalogue with the covenant formulary is criticized by de Vries, *VT* 16 (1966), 333–34.

105. In his book on the Shechem tradition, Nielsen puts forth the thesis (*Shechem*, 121–22, 355) that "the account of every decisive phase of the history of the nation by the Deuteronomists begins with the inauguration of a special code of laws," e.g., the wanderings in the desert—Exod 15:25b; the conquest of Palestine—the Deuteronomic law-giving on the plains of Moab; the

Nielsen's investigation of the Decalogue admittedly[106] does not offer a definitive solution; indeed there are a number of points that are not convincing and that require further research, such as the form of the "Urdekalog," its "Sitz im Leben" in the king's court, the late date for its formulation as a "divine utterance." However, one must admit that with his traditio-historical approach Nielsen has developed a new perspective on the Decalogue, which indeed is the purpose of his monograph. If one does not forget the hypothetical character of such conjectures about the earlier stages of a tradition, a traditio-historical examination like this can give the present form of the tradition a historical dimension and depth and thereby improve our understanding of the text.

What can be said in summary about Nielsen's relation to the methodological approaches current among Scandinavian scholars? Whereas he adheres quite strictly to Nyberg's and Engnell's theses about the predominance of oral tradition, he parts paths with Engnell regarding the traditio-historical method and task. We have seen above that Engnell in his earlier writings counsels against probing the depths of a tradition and distinguishing too sharply primary from secondary elements; his reason is the "Schmelzofen" effect of oral transmission. However, in contrast to this Nielsen maintains that the *special task of the tradition historian is to attempt to uncover the whole history of the traditum.* This he does not only in his work on the Decalogue but also in his investigations of the Shechem traditions and in his shorter studies at the end of his monograph *Oral Tradition*. We can also observe a methodological shift in his own work. On the one hand, in his study on oral tradition he regarded traditio-historical research as a necessary alternative to literary criticism, a stance thus similar to Engnell's; but now in his work on the Decalogue he recognizes traditio-historical work as an *individual investigative step to be carried out after text criticism, literary criticism, and form criticism have been completed.* Because of his interpretation and application of the traditio-historical method, Nielsen must be regarded as one of the important representatives of this type of Old Testament research in Scandinavia. His own formulation of the task that he as a researcher (in this case, of the Decalogue) faces deserves to be reproduced in its entirety as a concluding statement:

---

settlement in Canaan—Josh 24:25b; the introduction of the kingship—1 Sam 10:25. However, according to Nielsen, the Deuteronomists regarded these law-givings as something special for a specific period, whereas the legislation inaugurated at Sinai/Horeb was the "everlasting ten words of the covenant" and therefore the basis of all later covenants, in the eyes of the Deuteronomists.

106. Nielsen, *Die Zehn Gebote*, 5–6 (ET: x).

In its original form the material of the tradition under investigation [scil., the Decalogue] was organically connected with a particular time and a particular place. As it now exists it has been separated from these and has become an element in a literary complex. Between these two stages in its development lie the numerous phases and epochs through which it has passed. It is taken that the special task of the traditio-historical approach is to trace the course of the material transmitted through these, examining each stage independently with the aim of determining its special interest, instead of (as happens all too often) concentrating exclusively upon the beginning and the end of the development.[107]

D. Magne Sæbø on Deutero-Zechariah

The investigation of Deutero-Zechariah published by the Norwegian Magne Sæbø[108] is one of the most significant Scandinavian contributions to the traditio-historical research of the Old Testament, and in many respects—especially in terms of its methodological and analytical refinement and transparency—it can rightly be regarded as an exemplary traditio-historical investigation, and this despite some of its weaknesses as will be described below. With respect to the history of traditio-historical research, Sæbø's study occupies a special position in that it does not conform strictly to the pronounced direction taken by most of the Scandinavian scholars reviewed in the above sections,[109] but that it rather constitutes more of an *eclectic combination* of certain features of this direction together with various analytical procedures employed by researchers coming from non-Scandinavian traditions as well. The decisive influence of especially German critical scholarship is certainly to be attributed, as much as anything, to his years of study in Kiel under Hertzberg and in Heidelberg under von Rad. The fact that Sæbø, coming out of one distinct tradition, thus opts to take a moderate stand regarding characteristic features of Scandinavian Old Testament research (e.g., the cultic-mythic importance of the king, the central role played by oral transmission, the antipathy toward literary criticism) while at the same time appropriating analytical procedures and thematic concerns from primarily the German sphere—this all may be an indication of a dwindling influence of the Uppsala Circle, even within Scandinavia. The precise extent to which Sæbø aligns himself with the Scandinavian direction on the one hand and with the German direction on the other will become clearer in the following discussion.

---

107. Nielsen, *The Ten Commandments in New Perspective*, x (GT: 6).
108. Sæbø, *Sacharja 9–14: Untersuchungen von Text und Form*, WMANT 34, Neukirchen-Vluyn, 1969. Cf. also his history of the previous research on Deutero-Zechariah: "Die deuterosacharjanische Frage: Eine forschungsgeschichtliche Studie," *ST* 23 (1969), 115–40.
109. Cf. especially pp. 165–67 above.

1. Analytical Orientation and Procedure

One of the definite strengths of Sæbø's book on Deutero-Zechariah is his conscious, continual effort to describe and clarify the method, presuppositions, and goals of his investigations. As a *working hypothesis, he submits that the material in Zech 9-14 has a long history of formation and transmission that stretches all the way down to the final stabilization of the text by the Masoretes.*[110] His analytical procedure is to take the present form of the text as the starting point and then to seek to "roll back the tradition history of the material step by step—from the final form of the Massoretic text back to its beginnings."[111] Thus Sæbø's conception of the extensive scope and task of traditio-historical research corresponds to that of Noth and Carlson,[112] and his method is to start from the "Endstadium" of the tradition and gradually penetrate back to its very beginnings. He intends to accomplish this analysis in two stages: in the present book through a concentration on the formal problems of text criticism and form criticism, and in a later volume through an examination of the "motivgeschichtliche," "milieugeschichtliche," and "zeitgeschichtliche" aspects of the material itself, concluding then with a detailed "Redaktionsgeschichte" of these chapters.[113] This first study then, by analyzing the smallest literary units and their inner tensions and historical connections, is to determine the "load capacity" ("Tragfähigkeit") of the text as a basis for the material analyses to be performed in the second volume.[114]

---

110. This view that the Deutero-Zecharian textual and formal "stratification" is the result of a gradual growth process can be found also in the works of Mitchell, Jepsen, Horst, and Birkeland; cf. Sæbø, *Sacharja 9-14*, 310, and *ST* 23 (1969), 130-31.

111. Sæbø, *Sacharja 9-14*, 7, 20; cf. also *ST* 23 (1969), 140.

112. This notion that "tradition history" embraces the entire history of a literary piece—from earliest beginnings on down to the last gloss—is in fact very common; cf. above, pp. 18-19. See also pp. 21-23, where we argue that it is better though to restrict "tradition history" to the development of a formally defined tradition prior to its inclusion in a literary composition.

113. *Sacharja 9-14*, 20-21, 134, 318. We should also take note of the importance Sæbø sees in such an investigation of Deutero-Zechariah According to his presentation of the history of the research (*ST* 23, 1969, 115-40), the "Deutero-Zecharian question" actually comprises two parts: (a) the general problem, which deals with the relationship between Zech 1-8 and 9-14; and (b) the *specific* problem, which is restricted to Zech 9-14—its forms, contents, and historical background. Whereas the general question was in the center of the discussion prior to ca. 1880 (i.e., Stade), since then the specific question has received most attention, although with very diverse results. Sæbø is of the opinion that the general problem has not yet been satisfactorily solved and is therefore in need of a thorough investigation, but before he can undertake such a study he maintains that it is necessary for him to concentrate on the specific problems posed by Deutero-Zechariah alone (*ST* 23, 1969, 137ff.; *Sacharja 9-14*, 13ff.)

114. *Sacharja 9-14*, 7, 20. Richter's program (*Exegese als Literaturwissenschaft*, e.g., 41-42, 75-78, 174-78) of examining first the aspects of form and then those of content is thus quite in

An important feature of Sæbø's work is his understanding of *the traditio-historical method*, for he sees it as *a comprehensive concept embracing all the various analytical methods just mentioned and constituting the overriding whole to which each analytical phase contributes.*[115] However, he holds it to be advantageous to keep the various analytical procedures and methods as separate and distinct from each other as possible, "in order to be better able to distinguish critically the components of the traditio-historical mesh-work."[116] To this end he wants to restrict the present text-critical and form-critical studies to the "formal tradition history" (i.e., *the traditio*, dealing with the "act of transmission," with the "transmittal process and the transmittal mode"), leaving then the second volume to concentrate primarily on "*the transmitted entity in the material sense*" (i.e., on the *traditum*, thus an ideological or theological tradition history, or "Motivgeschichte").[117] Sæbø admits readily, though, that it is difficult and not always desirable to carry out a consistent division between form and content like this, and for this reason he reserves the right to introduce occasionally problems of the *traditum* into his text-critical and form-critical analyses at those points where such considerations may contribute to the understanding of text or form.[118] Nonetheless it should be noted that especially in his form criticism Sæbø takes up problems of content more often than he perhaps originally intended, but this is not so much a criticism of his analyses as it is an indication of the fluid, imprecise, if not even imaginary boundary-line between form and content, or between *traditio* and *traditum*—with the consequent difficulty and sometimes even artificiality of distinguishing fully between the two.[119]

2. Text Criticism Understood Traditio-Historically

Following Sæbø's division of his present study into a text-analytical and a form-analytical part, we will examine closer his method in each section in order to see how it contributes to the traditio-historical research of Deutero-Zechariah. Somewhat more attention should be paid to his text criticism because this is seldom treated from such a pronounced traditio-historical

---

alignment with Sæbø's method.

115. *Sacharja 9–14*, 133–34, 310. This comprehensive view of the traditio-historical method is shared by Engnell and Carlson; cf. above, pp. 19, 214–15, 245–46. However, we have argued (above, pp. 21–23) that a delimitation of the traditio-historical method as one of several investigative steps is more advisable.

116. *Sacharja 9–14*, 134.

117. Ibid., 134, 310.

118. Ibid., 133–34, 314, 318.

119. Cf. also Koch, *Was ist Formgeschichte?*, 5, 34, 47–48.

viewpoint as here in Sæbø's study. In what respects does he regard textual criticism as being a part of traditio-historical research? Sæbø indicates clearly that the transmission of the text must be viewed as a historical process and that in his own study he understands and treats "the whole history of the text expressly as history of tradition."[120] What this means for him is that the present text form must be given a traditio-historical dimension by investigating the history of the text "with a view to the *traditio-historical* development of the MT and to its possible primitive form."[121] Here it is made clear that one of his aims is to try to reconstruct the "Urtext" readings when possible, that is, *to work back to the beginning of the transmission of the text*[122]—an objective that, by the way, corresponds to that of, for example, Wellhausen and Kittel but not to the text-critical goal of Nyberg and Engnell.[123] However, it is only seldom possible to deduce the original reading of a particular text, so Sæbø tries to trace the many-layered history of the text as far back as possible, namely, to

---

120. Sæbø, *Sacharja 9–14*, 40; cf. also 24, 17ff. This view of the text as having a long developmental history may at first sight seem to be the obvious one, but as Sæbø shows (ibid., 40) the simple affirmation of this basic fact by any given scholar is no guarantee that it will be given the proper degree of consideration. But is it not a banality for Sæbø (ibid., 20) to insist that the analysis must begin with the text as such, that the text itself must serve as the starting point? He maintains that, although this also may seem to be a self-evident truth, in fact it has not always been carried out. Examples from the literature on Deutero-Zechariah include: B. Otzen, *Studien über Deuterosacharja*, ATDan 6, Copenhagen 1964; and P. Lamarche, *Zacharie IX–XIV. Structure littéraire et messianisme*, Paris 1961. Both Otzen and Lamarche, despite their seeming dependence on the text, do not—according to Sæbø (15–18)—invest their primary interest in the text as such, nor do they reckon seriously with the fact that the text itself could have had a long history, but rather for both of them the text is "in fact only an opening for reaching elements lying behind it" (so Sæbø, 17)—for Otzen (*Studien über Deuterosacharja*, 35ff.), to try to determine the political and historical background of the text and also to clarify the cultic material in the text; and for Lamarche (*Zacharie IX–XIV*, 8, 10–11, 105ff.), to examine the composition of Zech 9–14, which he finds often to be structured artistically according to chiastic principles, presumably the product of only one author. Lamarche in fact notes explicitly (ibid., 105) that he is omitting consideration of "the prehistory of the text." Sæbø, however, regards it as an absolute necessity to begin with a detailed and exact examination of the text so that—as mentioned above—its "Tragfähigkeit" can be established for later questions of form and content.

121. Sæbø, *Sacharja 9–14*, 127.

122. That this is only one of Sæbø's goals becomes clear in his analysis of, e.g., Zech 12:10 (96–102), for which he can conjecture an original form but feels obliged nonetheless to hold to the present, difficult MT form for current text editions.

123. Sæbø, ibid., 39–40; cf. also A. Jepsen, "Von den Aufgaben der alttestamentlichen Textkritik," VTSup 9 (1963), 333–35; and Noth, *Die Welt des Alten Testaments*, 4th ed. 1962, 310–11, 318. Sæbø thereby rejects Nyberg's and Engnell's text-critical goal of establishing the final MT form (cf. above, pp. 179–80, 200–201), as well as Jepsen's objective of reconstructing the text form which became canonized (Jepsen, VTSup 9, 1963, 336–37; cf. Sæbø's valid criticisms of Jepsen's purpose, 40).

follow it from its present form back to the proto-Masoretic stage and, when circumstances permit, to the pre-Masoretic and paleo-Hebraic strata.[124] Sæbø asserts that it should be possible to reach some positive results in this enterprise if the text critic, in his application of the usual methods, views the textual variations not simply as competing alternatives, but as possible indications of earlier text forms which were suppressed by the main Masoretic stream.[125] One must admit that it would be ideal to be able to uncover the historical development of the text in this way, but it is indeed another question whether such an ambitious task can be carried out to any satisfactory degree of certainty so as to make it worthwhile.[126] Quite rightly, Sæbø emphasizes that we must not forget the hypothetical, conjectural character of all such text-critical work that deals with the reconstruction of earlier text forms.[127] On the whole, it should be said that Sæbø's tendency to turn to the often complex history of the text for an explanation of a difficult MT reading—rather than immediately to emend the text—is laudable.[128] *This "respect for the MT" is one characteristic that he has received from Nyberg and Engnell,[129] although he is definitely more interested in investigating the prehistory of the MT readings than are Nyberg and Engnell.*[130] We have thus seen that Sæbø's intention in his text criticism is to attempt in a novel way to investigate traditio-historically the development of the text, working from the MT back to its possible primitive forms.[131] It now remains to be asked: What general results of traditio-historical importance does Sæbø reach through his text-critical analysis of Deutero-Zechariah?

---

124. Cf. Sæbø, *Sacharja 9–14*, 41. According to Sæbø, the *proto-Masoretic* text is the result of the first-century C.E. scribal activity in trying to produce an authoritative, unified text; the *pre-Masoretic* text is then the predecessor of the proto-Masoretic form and is basically in agreement with it; the *paleo-Hebraic* form represents the earliest stratum, thus the "Urtext."

125. Sæbø, *Sacharja 9–14*, 41.

126. However, it should be recognized that, despite his purported interest in the "Urtext," Sæbø generally refrains from conjecturing an *original* reading of a specific text but contents himself with extrapolating readings, especially from the pre-Masoretic stage, which may have preceded the MT form. Taking the tradition complex Zech 12–13 as an example, we find that in his text-critical analyses Sæbø (88–108) succeeds in extrapolating forms for expressly mentioned strata only in the following cases: paleo-Hebraic stratum (or "Urtext")—12:2,5,10; pre-Masoretic stratum—12:7,10; 13:1; proto-Masoretic stratum—none; in addition general reference to possible "Beweglichkeit" in the early history of the text—13:4,6,7,8,9.

127. Sæbø, *Sacharja 9–14*, 41–42.

128. Cf. ibid., e.g., 90, 100.

129. Sæbø, in a conversation with the author in August 1971; cf. also ibid., 41 n. 3.

130. Cf. above, pp. 179–80, 200–201.

131. Sæbø, *Sacharja 9–14*, 127. As Sæbø indicates (23–25, 28–30, 127), this text-critical goal is also shared by Jansma, "Inquiry into the Hebrew Text and the Ancient Versions of Zechariah ix–xiv," *OtSt* 7 (1950), 1–142.

While he maintains that the greatest importance of his verse-by-verse textual criticism lies in the analysis of the individual parts, he draws two general conclusions from these investigations:[132] (a) "the great age and the great stability of the Mass. text form," and (b) "the multiplicity of strands and the fullness of variations in the text tradition." Concerning (a), Sæbø maintains that the Hebraic textual tradition of Deutero-Zechariah underwent a transmission marked at times by conserving interests and at times by actively reforming interests—both at the proto-Masoretic as well as at the later Masoretic stage. This Hebraic text form held priority over all other text forms; there is no indication of any "local recensions" having competed with it.[133]

The versions are for the most dependent on the Hebraic tradition; only occasionally are their divergent readings of any value for the reconstruction of a pre-Masoretic text form.[134] On the whole, the reliability of the MT can be affirmed as a result of the textual analysis.[135] With regard to (b), Sæbø argues that despite the stability of the Masoretic text form it should not be regarded as a "fixed entity," for the text-critical analysis of Deutero-Zechariah has shown also a certain "multiplicity of strands" of the text tradition at the pre-Masoretic stage, so that the intended task of determining the "Urtext" becomes more complex.[136] Possible indications of these pre-Masoretic tradition strands can be seen in certain inner-Hebraic variants (e.g., in Zech 9:13; 10:1, 6; 11:2, 5, 13; 12:10; 13:7; 14:5, 6, 10, 12), especially in varying readings and conflations resulting probably from earlier duplicate traditions (e.g., in Zech 9:8, 13, 15; 10:6; 11:13; 12:2, 10; 14:6, 18), and also in alterations intentionally made by later Hebrew transmitters (e.g., in Zech 9:8; 11:7, 11; 12:2; 14:2, 5, 10).[137] However, this early "multiplicity of strands" should not be overrated, for the Masoretic mainstream tradition exhibits, in Sæbø's words, "already in the oldest (paleo-Hebr. or pre-Mass.) stage a surprisingly great

---

132. Sæbø, *Sacharja 9–14*, 127–28.

133. Ibid., 128. Jansma (*OtSt* 7, 1950, 2–3) is of the opposite opinion, positing the existence of "several Palestinian and one Egyptian recension of the Hebrew text"; cf. Sæbø, *Sacharja 9–14*, 25.

134. Cf., e.g., Sæbø's treatment of Zech 9:8; 11:13; 12:2; 14:5,10.

135. Sæbø, *Sacharja 9–14*, 318.

136. Ibid., 130–31, 36.

137. Ibid., 130–31. One misses here an attempt to see if any possible connecting lines or common points exist among these variants indicative of early text forms. In other words—the readings which Sæbø succeeds in reconstructing from the earlier stages in the history of specific verses are left disconnected with respect to each other. One would have welcomed a discussion of possible relationships among the extrapolated readings in order to see what tradition strands existed during each of the stages, pre-Masoretic and paleo-Hebraic. Or is such a task to be undertaken in his subsequent "Redaktionsgeschichte" of these chapters?

uniformity..., which later is by and large tenaciously retained."[138] Sæbø thus maintains that his text-critical analysis tends to support Goshen-Gottstein's objection to Kahle's excessive emphasis on textual plurality in the pre-Masoretic period.[139]

There is a third conclusion that Sæbø reaches: that *his textual analysis has made probable the presence of oral (in addition to written) means in the transmission of the text,*[140] especially where duplicate traditions exist.[141] He suggests that conflations arose during the transition from primarily oral over to written transmission but emphasizes that these two transmittal means must not be regarded as exclusive of each other and chronologically successive.

3. Form Criticism Understood Traditio-Historically

Turning now from Sæbø's text-critical method and results to his form-critical analysis of Deutero-Zechariah, the first thing that strikes us is his insistence on regarding *text-critical and then form-critical work in a methodological continuum*, and in a word that which connects them is the concept "tradition history." This Sæbø states explicitly: The traditio-historical "aspect connects the [text-critical and form-critical] operations; through it is possible to retrace diachronically not only textual development in its narrower sense but also the gradual formation of form, the growth of the substance."[142] To express it differently: Sæbø's overriding concern is the tracing of the "historical development" of these chapters,[143] and in this he is persuaded that "the narrower history of the text links together with the broader history of form and the development of literature."[144]

---

138. Sæbø, *Sacharja 9–14*, 131 (in italics).
139. Cf. the discussion of this problem in Sæbø, ibid., 31–39, 130–32.
140. Ibid., 132, 41. From our point of view the problem is by no means so clear. What makes this simple assertion by Sæbø so problematic and unfortunate is the fact that throughout his text analysis he is seldom explicit about which variant readings or conjectured forms arose or existed at the oral level. Such phrases as "early duplicate tradition" (62), "plurality of text forms in the paleo-Hebr. and pre-Mass. stage of the history of the text" (80; cf. also 58), "old traditional material" (99), "a living tradition process" (113), "multiplicity of text strands in history" (115), "the transmission has contaminated different traditions" (126) – such phrases could just as well be understood as referring to a literary as to an oral stage. In a word: a careful reading of Sæbø's investigations shows that such a general conclusion does not follow as much from his textual analysis as perhaps from his form analysis.
141. E.g., in Zech 9:13, 15; 10:6; 11:13; 12:10; 14:6, 18.
142. Sæbø, *Sacharja 9–14*, 310 (in italics); cf. also 133–34, 127.
143. Ibid., 318.
144. Ibid., 131.

As with his text criticism, Sæbø seeks to restrict his attention in the form-critical analysis to the *traditio*, that is, to the developmental process and transmission of the *formal* aspects of the tradition.[145] Here literary criticism is important in uncovering unevennesses in the text, as is also the consideration of phraseology, word statistics, formulas, forms, compositional peculiarities, internal oppositions, and so forth.[146] *Sæbø thus does not share the antipathy which other Scandinavian scholars have shown toward literary criticism,*[147] *for it is his opinion that it is a method that must by no means be neglected in the analysis of a pericope.* Whereas his own investigations concur at many points with the results attained by previous literary critics, he emphasizes that his analyses have not been carried out "under a strict *literary* viewpoint."[148] This, in addition to his misgivings about occasional excesses in the literary-critical analyses of others,[149] is indicative of *another methodological compromise* between the direction typical of German scholars on the one hand and that of the Uppsala Circle on the other hand.

Sæbø sees the "Schwerpunkt" of his form-critical section in its "minute analytical work,"[150] which he regards as being of importance and necessity because of the lack of thoroughgoing form-critical work on Deutero-Zechariah in the past.[151] The result of his study is a complex picture of diverse form elements, compositional "seams" ("Nahtstellen"), numerous small sections with independent origins—all in all, a "stratification of the formal structure" which Sæbø thinks can best be understood as the "final result of a lengthy and very complex tradition history and process of gradual growth."[152] Let us make this clearer with the help of an example: Two tradition units, Zech 9:1–8 and 12:2–13:6, proved to be especially interesting and complex, for they developed—according to Sæbø—in a way that he terms a "*compilatory-interpretative* method of formation and transmission," that "around a *core word* ('Kernwort') there were placed thematically related *encasing words* ('Rahmenworte') which occasionally were then encased or expanded by new words, *so*

---

145. Ibid., 134, 310.
146. Ibid., 134, 27, 310.
147. Cf., e.g., Sæbø's criticism (256) of Otzen's adoption of the Engnellian position regarding literary criticism.
148. Sæbø, *Sacharja 9–14*, 310, emphasis original.
149. E.g., that of H.-M. Lutz, *Jahwe, Jerusalem und die Völker: Zur Vorgeschichte von Sach 12,1–8 und 14, 1–5*, WMANT 27, Neukirchen-Vluyn 1968; cf. Sæbø, *Sacharja 9–14*, 258ff.
150. Sæbø, *Sacharja 9–14*, 309.
151. Ibid., 133; *ST* 23 (1969), 134–35.
152. *Sacharja 9–14*, 318, 309.

that the final tradition can look back on a multistage development."¹⁵³ For Zech 12:2–13:6, Sæbø, drawing on the frequent occurrence of the formula ביום ההוא or והיה ביום ההוא as well as on the shifting between prophetic and divine speech, thus posits three, originally independent units—each with its "Kernwort" and consequent development around this kernel.¹⁵⁴ These units with their second and third traditio-historical stages can be schematized as follows:

Unit A: 12:(1b)2–6	Unit B: 12:8–13:1	Unit C: 13:2–6
"Kernwort": 12:3–4a	"Kernwort": 12:9–10	"Kernwort": 13:2
2nd Stage: 12:2, 4bα, 6	2nd Stage: 12:11–14; 13:1	2nd Stage: 13:3–6
3rd Stage: 12:2bα, 4bβ, 5	3rd Stage: 12:8, 7	

How can one then set these three units in a traditio-historical relationship with each other? With certain reservations, Sæbø concluded that "Unit B, especially the 'Kernwort' vss. 9–10 (perhaps also vs. 11), constituted the primitive rock of the present tradition and that the remainder, certainly first of all the divine speeches of Units A and C, can be explained traditio-historically as successive expansions around this germ cell."¹⁵⁵ In addition, Sæbø supposes that in all likelihood this complex process occurred at the stage of *oral* prophetic transmission and that the compositional unity of this tradition complex is thus due to some transmittal circle with an invested hope in

---

153. Ibid., 311, emphasis original. This seems to be a miniature form of Klostermann's "Kristallisationshypothese"; cf. above, pp. 55–56. Cf. also Otzen's structural analyses, *Studien über Deuterosacharja*, 213–29; and Sæbø's response, *Sacharja 9–14*, 214.

154. Sæbø's form-critical analysis of this pericope is, however, somewhat problematic and unconvincing. For one thing, the criteria by which he determines the three units and their "Kernworte" are not entirely transparent—whether he draws only on form-critical aspects or reverts also to the content of the traditions. Regarding his form criticism, his distinction between divine speeches and prophetic speeches is too inconclusive in this section to serve as a basis for the separation of the three units and the subsequent traditio-historical reconstructions. Furthermore, when he regards the lengthier version, והיה ביום ההוא in Zech 12:3, 9 and 13:2 as an introductory formula for a divine speech and thus for a "Kernwort" as well, he fails to provide a satisfactory reason for the occurrence of the same formula in 13:4, where according to Sæbø it introduces neither a divine speech nor a "Kernwort." And finally, a more detailed picture of the connecting lines among the three units and of the way in which they became joined together with each other would have enhanced the plausibility of this form criticism of the complex.

155. Sæbø, *Sacharja 9–14*, 276.

the future.¹⁵⁶ It may at this point be noted that Sæbø's general position with regard to the oral/literary question tends toward that which is usually identified as the Scandinavian opinion but is definitely closer to Mowinckel's than to Engnell's stance. Thus he holds that much of the formation and growth of these traditions is best *conceivable* as a phenomenon from the oral stage, but his carefully expressed suppositions to this effect, as well as his occasional references to additions and changes stemming from the written stage, amount perhaps to a further indication of the influence that German scholarship has had on him.

4. PRELIMINARY CONCLUSIONS ABOUT COMPOSITION AND BACKGROUND

Consistent with his emphasis on the details of his form-critical analysis, Sæbø relegates most remarks dealing with larger connections to a very brief section at the end of his book, where he offers a preliminary "Redaktionsgeschichte" of Deutero-Zechariah and a preview of what is to appear in his subsequent volume on the *traditum* of Deutero-Zechariah. Here he concludes that all the small tradition elements in Deutero-Zechariah can be grouped into *four larger tradition complexes,* namely, Zech 9–10, 11, 12–13, and 14—whereby one must, however, emphasize the special position of Zech 14 over against the previous complexes.¹⁵⁷ On the whole, the traditio-historical perspective of these chapters militates against positing the existence of an individual author for all of these complexes. Likewise assuming an "anthological style"¹⁵⁸ or an artistic literary structure (so, e.g., Lamarche) cannot do justice to the formal complexity of these chapters. Rather, "whatever unity may be present seems much more to be basically a phenomenon of historical development."¹⁵⁹ Sæbø feels to have established in his form-critical analysis that this complex development indeed took place.

Turning then to the *traditum* of Deutero-Zechariah,¹⁶⁰ Sæbø insists upon the necessity of traditio-historically considering the location and function of

---

156. Ibid. Sæbø is quite consistent in withholding details about which group(s) of transmitters could have been responsible for these and the other traditions, but he is of the opinion (311) that they at any rate functioned sometimes as *collectors* of traditional material and sometimes as creative *interpreters* and innovators.

157. Sæbø, *Sacharja 9–14,* 313. Interestingly enough, Otzen (*Studien über Deuterosacharja,* 216ff.) arrives at the same division—though by examining primarily the content rather than only the form, as Sæbø does.

158. Sæbø, *Sacharja 9–14,* 313–14, 19–20; *ST* 23 (1969), 129 n. 68, 135 n. 98.

159. Sæbø, *Sacharja 9–14,* 314.

160. Ibid., 314–17. Cf. also Lutz, *Jahwe, Jerusalem und die Völker;* and O. Plöger, *Theokratie und Eschatologie,* WMANT 2, 2nd ed., Neukirchen Kreis Moers 1962, 97–117.

the various themes, motifs, and concepts; for the dependence on other prophetic words is not one of literary borrowing, but rather the situation is so: "by ascertaining a formative history extending from 'Kernworte' via encasing and expansions onto the larger units, [the analyses done here] have exposed *the connective prophetic tradition as a restless and 'living' entity*, as a conserving, transmitting, occasionally also reactualizing or correcting activity."[161] The present form of the traditions thus contains certain tendencies which betray the activity of various prophetic circles of transmission and which reflect different historical times and situations. Sæbø sees *four such lines connecting Deutero-Zechariah with other traditions.*[162] (a) That a certain similarity exists between the "Kernworte" Zech 9:3ff., 9:9(10) and the "Kernworte" in 12:2–13:6 (note especially the ideas: Zion/Jerusalem, David's house, messianism) seems to point to the imprint of the *Isaianic tradition* (in the widest sense, including "Trito-Isaiah" and the Isaianic disciples). (b) Finding a connection with *Proto-Zechariah* (compare the "Kernwort" 9:9 with 2:14; note also the word of salvation in 9:8, as well as the possible dependency of the basic layer of 9:4ff. and also of 11:4ff. on the prophet Zechariah), Sæbø ventures the suggestion that "a foundation for the tradition in these chapters can be brought into connection with the preaching of the prophet Zechariah and with the 'messianic movement around 520.'"[163] (c) However, the present form of Zech 9–13 is no longer dominated by such a Zecharianic-Isaianic tradition but rather more by "a diction characteristic of Jeremiah and Ezekiel and a Dtr impress on the material."[164] The older materials thus seem to have been framed and expanded by a *Deuteronomistic group* of transmitters similar to the one which left its mark on the books of Jeremiah and Ezekiel. Traces of the material having been preached (e.g., 10:1–2; 9:11ff.) as well as an influence from wisdom traditions (e.g., in 9:1–2; 10:1; 11:1–3, 17; 12:1b) can yet be seen in the additions stemming from the Deuteronomistic circle. And finally, (d) the reference to the "house of David" and the "house of Levi" in the secondary section 12:11–14 induces Sæbø to speculate carefully that *"the Dtr final form passed gradually over to a Chr. form."*[165] This does not apply, however, to

---

161. Sæbø, *Sacharja 9–14*, 314–15, emphasis original.
162. Ibid., 315ff. One is disposed to suspect that Sæbø is too rash here in drawing these lines of relationship before having analyzed the material and motifs more thoroughly. A further objection may be that he does not adequately respect the distinction between "similarity" on the one hand and "dependency" on the other. At least prior to the appearance of Sæbø's more detailed treatment of these matters in his second volume on Deutero-Zechariah, the reader can well be expected to be somewhat skeptical at this point.
163. Sæbø, *Sacharja 9–14*, 316.
164. Ibid.
165. Ibid., 317, emphasis original.

Zech 14, which does not appear to have been submitted to a Deuteronomistic redaction and which must on the whole be reckoned as being separate from the other chapters in its development.

5. Summary

In this review and critique of Sæbø's study of Deutero-Zechariah we have thus seen that Sæbø envisions the traditio-historical method as a comprehensive investigative approach embracing all techniques that can help uncover the prehistory of the present state of the pericope. His position departs decidedly from the Engnellian principle of restricting the investigation to an analysis of primarily the final form of the text. We have also observed that Sæbø has been influenced strongly from both the Scandinavian and the German research traditions. From Scandinavian researchers he has received an appreciation (though by no means extreme) for the role played by oral transmission in Israel, a "respect" for the reliability of the MT, and the view of traditio-historical research as a comprehensive whole; but beyond these matters the points of contact and commonality with other Scandinavian researchers are difficult to ascertain. The influence from German research is especially noticeable in his drive to penetrate behind the final state of the tradition and of the text itself, and also in his form-critical and traditio-historical methods of investigation. The results of his examination of Deutero-Zechariah constitute a complex picture of the prehistory and developmental stages of both text and form. In connection with his subsequent study of the contents of the Deutero-Zecharian traditions, this present investigation can indeed be considered as being methodologically exemplary and traditio-historically instructive—even though at times he conjectures too audaciously and without the requisite restraint.

15
Critique

One aspect of the Scandinavian direction in Old Testament scholarship should have become clear as a result of the above history of the research: *resolute divergence and disagreement despite extensive similarity of method and interests*. Certain issues have recurred again and again: oral versus written transmission, the value of the literary-critical method, the reliability of tradition, transmitters, tradition complexes, religio-historical problems (divine kingship, the myth-and-ritual pattern, the role of king and prophet in the cult, "antievolutionism"), the traditio-historical method and task. At all of these points and more, a pronounced diversity of opinion among the Scandinavian scholars themselves has yielded a lively debate within their ranks. This has been true even among members of the Uppsala Circle, for despite the usual characterization of these scholars as constituents of a "school" we have seen that some of the sharpest criticisms of, e.g., the oral-transmission thesis have come from their own midst (viz., Widengren). Nonetheless, despite this lack of uniformity there is some justification in our speaking of a "Scandinavian direction" in Old Testament research. Inasmuch as the debate has centered on certain key issues and has been marked by a conscious effort among some of the scholars to distinguish their work and methods from that of especially German literary criticism—to this degree our use of the terms "Scandinavian direction" and "Uppsala Circle" is certainly justifiable. But in this we must not lose sight of the extent to which internal heterogeneity has existed. It is perhaps just as proper (or as improper) to try to typify the Scandinavian research as it is to do so for, e.g., German or British research.

The importance of taking the Scandinavian work seriously into account and the need to engage in a critical analysis and discussion of the main theses have not been lost on researchers from other scholarly traditions.[1] However, that there have not been more non-Scandinavians who have entered the debate

---

1. Cf. Bentzen, *TRu*, NS 17 (1948/49), 318–19.

is perhaps due on the one hand to the inability of most to read the literature published in the Scandinavian languages, and on the other hand to certain disinterest in new ideas that appear to be extreme and that have too often been propagated polemically. Any such lack of interest is indeed regrettable, for an interchange of research methods and results can only serve to benefit the total enterprise of reaching a better historical and theological understanding of the Old Testament. Be this as it may, various aspects of the Scandinavian work have indeed aroused attention and interest, and a number of appraisals of Scandinavian research have consequently appeared. In addition to the more general surveys and descriptions of this work,[2] special attention should be drawn to those articles which concentrate on specific aspects of the Scandinavian research direction: the question of oral transmission,[3] the religio-historical theses,[4] and the general understanding of the traditio-historical task and method.[5] Throughout the above presentation of the work of the Scandinavian scholars we have had opportunity to comment critically on numerous details and to refer frequently to these articles just mentioned. Consequently, what remains to be done now is to seek to evaluate—in general

---

2. Cf. especially: G. W. Anderson, "Some Aspects of the Uppsala School of Old Testament Study," *HTR* 43 (1950), 239–56; H.-H. Schrey, "Die alttestamentliche Forschung der sogenannten Uppsala-Schule," *TZ* 7 (1951), 321–41; the articles by C. R. North, O. Eissfeldt, A. R. Johnson, and G. W. Anderson, in *The Old Testament and Modern Study: A Generation of Discovery and Research*, ed. H. H. Rowley, London 1951; J. Scharbert, "Das Traditionsproblem im Alten Testament," *TTZ* 66 (1957), 321–35; as well as Aa. Bentzen, "Skandinavische Literatur zum Alten Testament 1939–1948," *TRu*, NS 17 (1948/49), 273–328; G. Fohrer, "Neuere Literatur zur alttestamentlichen Prophetie. 2. Teil: Literatur vom 1940–1950," *TRu*, NS 20 (1952), 199–205; Kraus, *Geschichte*, passim; and Nyberg, "Die schwedischen Beiträge zur alttestamentlichen Forschung in diesem Jahrhundert," VTSup 22 (1972), 1–10.

3. J. van der Ploeg, "Le rôle de la tradition orale dans la transmission du texte de l'Ancien Testament," *RB* 54 (1947), 5–41; C. R. North, "Living Issues in Biblical Scholarship: The Place of Oral Tradition in the Growth of the Old Testament," *ExpTim* 61 (1949/50), 292–96; A. H. J. Gunneweg, *Mündliche und schriftliche Tradition der vorexilischen Prophetenbücher als Problem der neueren Prophetenforschung*, FRLANT 73, Göttingen 1959; K. Koch, *Was ist Formgeschichte?*, Neukirchen-Vluyn 1967, 97ff.

4. Cf. especially: M. Noth, "Gott, König, Volk im Alten Testament: Eine methodologische Auseinandersetzung mit einer gegenwärtigen Forschungsrichtung," *ZTK* 47 (1950), 157–91 (=*Ges. Stud.*, 188–229; and K.-H. Bernhardt, *Das Problem der altorientalischen Königsideologie im Alten Testament, unter besonderer Berücksichtigung der Geschichte der Psalmenexegese dargestellt und kritisch gewürdigt*, VTSup 8, Leiden 1961.

5. R. Rendtorff, "Literarkritik und Traditionsgeschichte," *EvT* 27 (1967), 138–53 (in Swedish translation in *SEÅ* 31, 1966, 5–20); also H. Ringgren, "Literarkritik, Formgeschichte, Überlieferungsgeschichte. Erwägungen zur Methodenfrage der alttestamentlichen Exegese," *TLZ* 91 (1966), cols. 641–650 (in somewhat altered form and in Swedish in *RoB* 25, 1966, 45–56).

terms—a few primary issues, not only for the purpose of criticism but also in order to determine the contributions of these Scandinavians to our understanding of the tradition history of the Old Testament.

A. Oral Composition and Transmission

We turn first to the topic most commonly associated with the Scandinavian scholars: the decisive role putatively played by oral transmission in the development and handing down of Old Testament traditions. Indeed the fervor with which this problem is treated and the frequency of its occurrence in the Scandinavian publications render appropriate North's analogy: "One gets the impression that 'oral' and 'written' are like Demetrius and Lysander in 'A Midsummer-Night's Dream', chasing one another in the dark wood."[6] However, the importance of this issue is not to be underestimated, and it certainly deserves the thorough, searching critique it has received at the hands of van der Ploeg,[7] North, and Gunneweg.[8] We will restrict our comments to the following.

---

6. North, "Oral Tradition and Written Documents," *ExpTim* 66 (1954/55), 39.

7. *RB* 54 (1947), 5-41. The essence of van der Ploeg's critique is an admission that oral transmission was certainly employed among the Israelites especially in the early period of nomadic and tribal life and then primarily for legal, lyrical, and sacro-historical materials. However, with the monarchy writing began to increase in importance and superseded oral means still in the preexilic period. So Nyberg's thesis of the postexilic recording of the Old Testament is unjustifiable. Van der Ploeg's handling of this issue unfortunately leaves the impression that he from the outset was intent on defending his own critical (and orthodox? cf., e.g., 35, 41, on the prophecies as "paroles de Jahvé," with the implication that this necessitated the certainty of written preservation; cf. however North, *ExpTim* 61, 1949/50, 292) view against a new hypothesis. He apparently did not familiarize himself with Engnell's work on the subject, nor with Mowinckel's *Prophecy and Tradition*. Indeed, the Scandinavian debate was just in its beginning stages when van der Ploeg published his critique.

8. Gunneweg's monograph (*Tradition*, 1959) is the most intensive examination that has yet been published on the Scandinavian direction in oral-tradition studies. Restricting his attention primarily to the preexilic prophetic traditions, he first reviews and responds to the positive and the negative evidence to which Engnell, Nielsen, and the others appeal for support for their thesis that the prophetic books are the deposit of oral tradition. As a result of his own investigation, especially into the position of the preexilic prophets in the cult and at the sanctuaries, Gunneweg comes to the conclusion that oral transmission was in fact the *normal* way to transmit traditions in the ancient Orient and thus also in Israel but that Nyberg, Engnell, and Nielsen have not proved their case for its being "maßgebend" and "bestimmend" for the prophetic books in their present form (31-32, 40-41, 70ff.). Gunneweg seeks then to establish his own view that oral tradition had its "Sitz im Leben" in the *private* sphere (cf. Gunkel on the *pater familias*) whereas the written transmission was carried out at the sanctuaries, to which the prophets, the נביאים, were officially connected (77ff.). Oral tradition, common outside the

1. The Question of Reliability

The reliability of oral transmission is a debatable question and one for which a general answer for the Israelite period can hardly be expected.[9] While Nyberg, Engnell, Nielsen, and others have predicated its constancy and ability to keep the tradition basically uncorrupted, van der Ploeg, Gunneweg, as well as many others before them[10] tend to be more skeptical, supposing that an oral tradition was more susceptible to change and that once it was recorded the written form must have gained some recognition as being normative.[11] To this we can add that if the oral transmission was supposed to have been a "living" and dynamic process[12] during which traditions were developed, often restructured and even joined with other traditions into a larger complex, precisely this "liveliness" undermines, in effect, its reliability at the stage of tradition formation.[13] Therefore, it becomes necessary for us to distinguish roughly between, on the one hand, *the oral stage of formation and composition* and, on the other, *the oral period of transmitting traditions already basically fixed.*[14] For the former stage it is not so much a question of reliability as it is of

---

circles attached to the sanctuaries and courts, duplicated much of what was also preserved in writing; but it was clearly subordinate to the official, authentic written form of the traditions (119ff.). Gunneweg concludes therefore that "our prophetic books must derive from sources that reach back to the oldest period. But not everything now in our prophetic books flowed out of these sources, for alongside the written tradition continued the oral tradition, with the latter enriching the former" (121). This side-by-side existence of oral and written means has been suggested often enough (cf. Gunneweg, 74; also above, pp. 209, 213–14), but with regard to the secondary importance of oral tradition this much is clear: Gunneweg is as unable to prove his case as have been the Scandinavians. That written transmission had its primary "Sitz im Leben" at the sanctuaries and courts is probably correct, but it does not follow from this that oral tradition had its primary domain in the private life of the people. That Gunneweg's argument here is *e silentio* has been adequately demonstrated by Gerhardsson (*SEÅ* 25, 1960, 175–81; German translation in: *TZ* 17, 1961, 216–20), although the latter's contention that specialists in oral tradition could as well have been attached to the sanctuaries is no less *e silentio*. The result of this debate amounts to a stalemate in which both sides admit the presence and even importance of oral tradition but neither one is able to define conclusively its actual place and role in the history of traditions.

9. Precisely this same point is made by Ahlström; cf. above, p. 243.
10. Van der Ploeg, *RB* 54 (1947), 23–24; Gunneweg, *Tradition*, 69–70, 72; cf. also above, pp. 69–72.
11. Cf. here also A. Bertholet, *Die Macht der Schrift in Glauben und Aberglauben*, AAB, Phil.-hist. Kl. 1948, 1, Berlin 1949.
12. Cf. above, e.g., pp. 179–80, 200, 217–18.
13. Cf. Gunneweg, *Tradition*, 69–70, 72–73.
14. A similar distinction is also made by Mowinckel, *Prophecy and Tradition*, 26ff. Cf. also Ahlström, *HTR* 59 (1966), 69–70.

plausibility and likelihood with respect to the tradition in question.[15] For the latter, however, it is a question of reliability.

2. COMPARATIVE EVIDENCE

It is precisely at this point that the issue of recourse to other cultures can be relevant. Whereas we do not have sufficient, direct information about the oral formation of composite, complex traditions among other peoples, we can assume that it has occurred often enough, perhaps especially among the analphabetic.[16] However, the capacity of the human mind to memorize exceedingly long bodies of material is an indisputable phenomenon of the present-day Near East and thus by inference can be assumed for early Arabic, Judaic, and Israelite times as well. Arguments from analogy can indeed too often be arbitrary and contrived; no better example for this can be found than the controversy between Engnell and Widengren, each appealing to Arabic and Near Eastern parallels and arriving at contrary conclusions. It is indeed highly questionable whether any more can be derived from analogic sources than that the Israelites *could* have employed oral and/or written means for the formation as well as for the further transmission of their traditions.[17] *The ultimate decision for each case should be made on the basis of internal criteria.*[18] But inasmuch as these are not always available, analogic investigations of the kind executed by Widengren on the one hand or Culley[19] on the other are necessary, instructive, and often quite profitable.[20]

3. THE CRITICAL ANALYSIS OF "ORAL LITERATURE"

Engnell's concept of an "oral literature" in an already virtually fixed form[21] has been accepted by several critics with the observation that such a body of col-

---

15. So, e.g., for Sæbø's form analysis of Zech 12–13; cf. above, pp. 283–84.
16. Cf., e.g., J. Vansina, *Oral Tradition: A Study in Historical Methodology*, Chicago 1965.
17. Cf. also Ahlström, *HTR* 59 (1966), 70–71 n. 7.
18. This point is also made by Engnell, cf. above, p. 231 n. 37. An example of this type of examination is Ringgren, *ST* 3 (1949), 34–59. Engnell has also emphasized that the sacral character of Old Testament traditions influenced positively the reliability of the transmission, and this is surely a factor not to be forgotten; cf. above, p. 218 n. 103; and Carlson, *David, the Chosen King*, 18–19. The question remains, though: At what point did the traditions become considered sacral so that the transmitters felt less "free" with them? Are we again here to distinguish roughly between the formative and the transmittal stages?
19. R. C. Culley, "An Approach to the Problem of Oral Tradition," *VT* 13 (1963), 113–25.
20. Cf. also van der Ploeg, *RB* 54 (1947), 8–9.
21. Cf. above, p. 202, also p. 189 on Lindblom.

lected traditions, if indeed as rigid as Engnell claims, should be as liable to some type of "source-critical" examination as is a written literature.[22] Engnell had assumed, though, that the transmission process transformed the tradition to such an extent (like in Birkeland's "Schmelzofen") that attempts to analyze the development of the *traditum* are doomed to frustration and failure from the outset. Yet in the debate that centered on this point, it became obvious that *one must not exclude all possibility of determining some of the strata and component parts of the traditions during their developmental stage.* The work done by Sæbø is one example of an attempt by a Scandinavian scholar to get behind the delivered traditions.[23] As North states it, "we are not necessarily dealing with a welter of unco-ordinated and unco-ordinable oral tradition."[24] However, it is wrong to suppose that it is only of antiquarian interest whether oral or written means were predominant or involved in any given case, for compositional structure and formation as well as the types of variations and changes in already fixed traditions can often be directly dependent on the way in which they were transmitted, that is, whether oral or written.[25] This then constitutes the justification for the importance which Scandinavian scholars have vested in the factor of oral transmission.

4. The Stage of Literary Fixation

Engnell had furthermore postulated that the traditions (of almost all literary genres) had developed and gained such a fixity at the oral level that their recording brought no essential change to them. But a divergent opinion was later rendered by Lord[26] on the basis of field-study of Balkan narrators. His point is that a tradition may indeed have been fixed at the oral stage but that, when some scribe attempted to record it, the tradition was removed from its normal situation and transformed appreciably as it became written literature. *There is obviously a direct conflict between these two estimations of the recording process, and a closer examination of the problem is now overdue.*[27] This is all the more important because the obvious consequence of Lord's thesis is that tra-

---

22. E.g., Mowinckel, cf. above, pp. 210–11; North, *ExpTim* 61 (1949/50), 294, *ExpTim* 66 (1954/55), 39, and in *OTMS* (ed. Rowley, 1951), 78–79; Scharbert, *TTZ* 66 (1957), 330; Rendtorff, *EvT* 27 (1967), 144; cf. also Ringgren, *RoB* 25 (1966), 52.
23. Cf. above, pp. 275–86.
24. *ExpTim* 61 (1949/50), 294.
25. This has been demonstrated by, e.g., Ringgren, *ST* 3 (1949), 34–59; and R. C. Culley, *Oral Formulaic Language in the Biblical Psalms*, Toronto 1967.
26. *The Singer of Tales*, Cambridge, Mass. 1960, 124ff.
27. An attempt has been made for the New Testament situation by E. Güttgemanns, *Offene Fragen zur Formgeschichte des Evangeliums*, BEvT 54, Munich 1970.

CRITIQUE

ditio-historical research becomes basically invalid. How can one reconstruct the history of a tradition if the recording stage itself becomes an impenetrable barrier? The problem is perhaps not so crucial for Old Testament traditions since the cultic use and preservation of so many of them could have ensured a certain constancy. Yet the popular legends may be affected to a certain degree by this aspect, as Lord would maintain.

5. The Scandinavian Contributions

It is by now generally recognized—both within and without Scandinavia—that Nyberg's initial thesis[28] is basically untenable.[29] That the written stage cannot be virtually restricted to exilic and postexilic times, that both oral and written means were important and in use throughout the preexilic centuries, sometimes existing side by side, sometimes the one or the other more predominant depending upon the literary type or the tradition in question,[30] and that we must consequently reckon with both written and oral sources in the prehistory of our Old Testament literature—these points are hardly contested any longer. But it should be just as clear that the Scandinavian scholars have here made an essential contribution: Their theses about and their research into the important role played by oral tradition have thrust this issue into the consciousness of Old Testament scholars as a factor of which one must take careful consideration.[31] Similarly significant, it may be mentioned, has been their recognition of the activity of circles of transmitters (e.g., prophetic communities) in preserving and expanding the traditions, although it is again a moot point here whether and in which cases these circles worked with written and when with oral sources.[32] It is, though, highly unfortunate that the Scandinavian researchers have not produced more studies in detail of specific Old Testament texts, analyzing them for traces or signs of oral activity and

---

28. *Studien zum Hoseabuche*, Uppsala 1930, 8: "The written Old Testament is a creation of the Jewish community after the Exile; what preceded it was surely only in smaller part fixed in writing.... The prehistory of the Old Testament material was thus predominantly oral."

29. Cf. above, pp. 247-48, on Carlson's position with regard to this. Cf. also A. Murtonen, "The Fixation in Writing of Various Parts of the Pentateuch," *VT* 3 (1953), 46-53.

30. This last point is even admitted by Engnell; cf. above, pp. 213-14.

31. We have seen above, pp. 69-72, that earlier researchers were also aware of the oral stage in tradition development. However, the Scandinavians were responsible for establishing and emphasizing its importance; cf. also Scharbert, *TTZ* 66 (1957), 331ff.

32. Note again the disagreement between Gunneweg and Gerhardsson, above, pp. 289-90 n. 8. Mowinckel's work in this area was decisive; cf. above, pp. 170-71. Cf., however, van der Ploeg, *RB* 54 (1947), 35, 38-39; and Scharbert, *TTZ* 66 (1957), 29-30; but then also Mowinckel, *NTT* 43 (1942), 82.

determining the effect which oral transmission has had on the traditions in their earlier as well as their final forms. Precisely such intensive work on all types of pericopes and tradition complexes is what is now needed. Also necessary are more systematic, thorough investigations of the phenomenon and techniques of oral transmission in ancient times and of the criteria by which we can tell when oral composition or transmission were in play.[33]

B. The Importance of Religio-Historical Studies

This preoccupation with the problem of oral transmission is not the only characteristic of the direction taken by Scandinavian Old Testament scholars, and we must be careful not to give it disproportionate importance in our discussion. Equally significant is their work in the area of comparative religions, which as a part of the *traditum* is also relevant for traditio-historical research. Here such scholars as Engnell, Mowinckel, Widengren, Bentzen, Riesenfeld, Kapelrud, and Ringgren have been engaged in investigations on sacral (or divine) kingship, myth-and-ritual patternism, the importance of the cult, the messiah-motif, and the high-god theory. Their work has been paralleled and supplemented by their British colleagues of the "Myth-and-Ritual School." Indeed the amount of literature produced in these areas by European and American scholars is voluminous.[34] We shall not in this connection deal any further with these religio-historical questions other than to make two things clear.

1. On the Divine-Kingship Ideology

A decisive, if not final, response to these issues, primarily to that of divine kingship, has been given in Noth's extraordinarily perceptive article: "Gott, König, Volk im Alten Testament."[35] In this tightly argued treatise Noth concedes the presence of the divine kingship ideology in ancient Egypt, in

---

33. The works of Olrik, Moe, Lohr, Culley, and others would provide the foundation for such further work.

34. As an example, cf. the volume: *The Sacral Kingship / La regalità sacra*, Studies in the History of Religions (Supplements to *Numen*) IV, Leiden 1959.

35. Subtitled: "Eine methodologische Auseinandersetzung mit einer gegenwärtigen Forschungsrichtung," *ZTK* 47 (1950), 157–91 (= *Ges. Stud.*, 188–229). A more thorough critique of the sacral-kingship ideology is to be found in Bernhardt, *Königsideologie*. Cf. however Ahlström's response, "Die Königsideologie in Israel: Ein Diskussionsbeitrag," *TZ* 18 (1962), 205–10; also Zimmerli, in: *Probleme biblischer Theologie*, 636–37, 640.

Mesopotamia,³⁶ and probably also in the Syro-Palestinian world of the fourteenth century B.C.E., although its actual extent and character is somewhat nebulous.³⁷ Noth doubts that premonarchical Israel knew of this ideology³⁸ but admits that "the possibility of Israel having taken over elements of an 'agricultural' ideology bound up with the establishment of the monarchy cannot *a priori* be ruled out. We merely need to prove the existence of one such adoption."³⁹ But, asserts Noth, this evidence has not been produced convincingly enough by the Scandinavians.⁴⁰ Especially the tendency of these scholars to be so historically and temporally indiscriminate in their search for Old Testament and Eastern evidence arouses suspicion.⁴¹ Noth's final conclusion turns the tables on the proponents of the divine-kingship hypothesis: "The fact that we appear to have deviations from conceptions of a divine king ideology, applied in the Old Testament to the Jerusalem monarchy, is stronger evidence that this ideology itself was not accepted on the basis of the Old

---

36. As Noth (*Ges. Stud.*, 202) points out, H. Frankfort (*Kingship and the Gods: A Study of Ancient Near Eastern Religion as the Integration of Society and Nature*, Chicago 1948) shows that one must distinguish between, on the one hand, the Egyptian conception of the Pharaoh as incarnated god and, on the other hand, the Mesopotamian view of the king as the chosen servant of the god. That Frankfort however has differentiated too sharply between the two conceptions is shown by Bentzen, "King Ideology—'Urmensch'—'Troonsbestijgingsfeest,'" *ST* 3 (1949), 143–57.

37. Noth, *Ges. Stud.*, 2015.

38. Ibid., 207, 211. Schrey (*TZ* 7, 1951, 338) correctly counters that this had not even been maintained by the Uppsala scholars.

39. Noth, *Ges. Stud.*, 216 [ET: 167]. To be sure, there has been a lack of clarity surrounding these issues, not least among their proponents themselves; cf. Holm-Nielsen, *DTT* 18 (1955), 137–39. However, as correct as Noth is in laying the burden of proof on the shoulders of the advocates of the divine-kingship ideology, his own case is weakened by three factors: (a) He does not recognize the difference between *divine* and *sacral* kingship, the latter of which comes most in question for Israel (cf. Ringgren, *Israelitische Religion*, Stuttgart 1963, 213). (b) He does not sufficiently consider the argument that the sacral ideas "disintegrated" and were "democratized" early in Israel's history. And (c) to a large extent Noth bases his critique on the four-page summary (actually only a preview) in Engnell's dissertation, which is too small a basis to refute the whole question of sacral kingship.

40. According to Noth (*Ges. Stud.*, 222ff.), Pss 2:7; 110:3; and 2 Sam 7:14 depict the *adoption* of the king as God's son, and this differs significantly from the conception of the king as incarnated god or as a divine being; cf. also Kraus, *Psalmen* I, 14ff. To Ps. 45:7, the key passage for divine-kingship arguments, Noth—despite his problematic interpretation of this verse—observes accurately that "in no case can the phrase in Ps. XLV.7a bear the whole burden of the thesis of a *divine* kingship in Israel" (*Ges. Stud.*, 226 [ET: 175]; cf. also Kraus, *Psalmen* I, 331ff.).

41. This is a criticism made also by Bentzen, *Messias—Moses redivivus—Menschensohn*, 9, 54; cf. also Bentzen, "Der Tod des Beters in den Psalmen," *Festschrift Otto Eissfeldt*, Halle/S. 1947, 57–60.

Testament belief."[42] The minimum consequence of this total rebuttal by Noth is that the thesis of divine or sacral kingship in the ancient Near East and in Israel in particular can no longer be treated as a self-evident presupposition in the interpretation of Old Testament texts.

2. Constitutive Elements of the *Traditum*

Whether or not this issue is resolved, one matter should by now have become clear: *religio-historical considerations can and should be an integral part of the work of the tradition historian.* Even Engnell, who otherwise rebukes efforts to research the prehistory of the final form of the traditions, could not resist plunging "valiantly and resolutely into the depth"[43] of religio-historical motifs. Indeed religio-historical research as a whole is not to be subsumed methodologically under traditio-historical research, but in the proper sense of the term a "history of traditions" must also deal with the content, the *traditum*, and this includes examining comparative-religious motifs. As Rendtorff writes with regard to the Canaanite elements in the Psalms: "Here the history of tradition becomes the history of religion, in that it pursues the path of certain religious notions from the Canaanite religion (and in some cases also its transformations in the latter itself) onto the Israelite religion."[44] The fluid boundary between the two fields of study can be observed also in Gunkel's work.[45] Ascertaining the cultic and religious elements, the background, and the function of a tradition in society or religion will contribute to our understanding of how the tradition was formed. But we also must not lose sight of the fact that it is not the origin of a motif that is most important for the interpretation of an Old Testament text, but rather the way in which the motif is used and the reason for its presence in the Old Testament tradition.[46]

---

42. *Ges. Stud.*, 226 [ET: 175].
43. Ringgren, *TLZ* 91 (1966), col. 646.
44. Rendtorff, *EvT* 27 (1967), 146; cf. also Ringgren, *TLZ* 91 (1966), cols. 646, 648.
45. Cf. above, pp. 60–62, 65–66.
46. Wellhausen, reviewing Gunkel's *Schöpfung und Chaos* (1895), emphasized also the primary importance of understanding mythological elements in their *present* Old Testament context, i.e. in the way that the writers of the Old Testament meant them or used them. Wellhausen thus depreciated the search for the origins of religio-historical motifs as being only of "antiquarian interest" for theologians and exegetes; cf. Bentzen, Eissfeldt-Festschrift (1947), 59–60. In our opinion, however, the problem is not so simple. Indeed for Old Testament investigations the chief question is: What is the meaning of the motif in its present context? Nonetheless, just as an Old Testament tradition has a prehistory which must be studied if we are to improve our understanding of its final form, so also must a motif be examined for its origin and historical development—especially since the tradition in question could very well have used the motif more in its original meaning at an earlier stage of the history of the tradition, before

Although the importance of the study of comparative religions for the Old Testament has been advocated since A. Eichhorn, Gunkel, and Gressmann, *Scandinavian scholars have ensured its place within the context of traditio-historical research.*

C. General Contributions and the Present State of the Research

It has been stated that one result of Scandinavian traditio-historical studies of the Old Testament is that scholars became more inclined to talk about traditions, tradition streams and complexes, and transmitters—instead of sources, documents, and authors.[47] There is perhaps a real advantage in this tendency because it recognizes clearly that the present form of most Old Testament pericopes is the result of a historical development in which often many persons or groups have participated and that this growth process is a valid object of investigation. The earlier Wellhausenian concept of, for example, the origin of the Pentateuch also included the idea that an oral tradition existed prior to the written documents, but it was felt that this oral stage was too nebulous and diffused (and even unimportant?) to deserve the attention that must be paid to the individual authors of the documentary sources. *The Scandinavian researchers have helped establish the importance of the preliterary period* and have maintained not only that it was at this stage that individual traditions and tradition streams developed, but also that the joining of traditions into complexes and even their editing began already in the preliterary and semiliterary periods as well. Of course, the various literary genres cannot all be treated according to one general traditio-historical scheme, and the necessity of examining each type individually has been stressed often enough above.

There is another general, positive consequence of the Scandinavian research that we must not overlook—the importance they lay on seeing the tradition as a whole, on understanding its final form and its function in the life of the Israelites. We often have the tendency to fragmentize a text, to separate secondary elements from primary ones as if the secondary parts are in some way inferior or less important. From Scandinavian scholars we can learn that a prime factor in the history of a tradition was its function in life and that new elements could be added only when the function of the tradition

---

it became "demythologized." (For an example of this, cf. above, pp. 240–41 n. 80, on Ringgren's study of the creation narrative.) This is the traditio-historical importance of religious motifs in Old Testament texts; cf. also Carlson, *David, the Chosen King*, 21.

47. Cf. Scharbert, *TTZ* 66 (1957), 333–34; Ahlström, *HTR* 59 (1966), 69; and Noth's "Appreciation," in Engnell's *Studies in Divine Kingship*, 2nd ed., Oxford 1967, xxi; also above, p. 183.

changed and thereby permitted it. The new elements could be introduced and retained only if the community accepted them, and for this reason the final cumulative state of the tradition, as well as each of its earlier stages, is of great historical and theological importance for us. Basic to all is the Israelite respect for tradition. When this factor is combined with the fact that so many traditions had their "Sitz im Leben" in the cult, we can assume with Engnell and others that despite the historically necessary alterations and adaptations many traditions were in essence preserved faithfully—or at least can still contain very old elements. That this central interest in the final form of the tradition does not, however, relieve the researcher of carrying out critical investigations should be obvious.[48]

What then do Scandinavian scholars understand as traditio-historical work? In its breadth, it seems that it is regarded by many of the Old Testament researchers from the North (e.g., Engnell, Carlson, and Sæbø) as being all-inclusive and comprehensive, that is, as embracing most other investigative methods. However, Mowinckel and especially Ringgren tend, like most scholars elsewhere, to have a narrower view of the traditio-historical method—as complementing, not including, the other analytical procedures. Thus uniformity does not exist among the Scandinavian scholars at this point—perhaps no more than it does elsewhere.[49]

Regarding the method, we have seen that one characteristic of the earlier writings of Nyberg, Birkeland, Engnell, Kapelrud, Carlson, and others was the restriction of their analyses to the final state of the traditions. They argued that because the formative period was a "living" one, the narrated or transmitted goods were so thoroughly altered, expanded, and restructured—like a melting process in an oven—that it is now impossible for us to describe this process or to identify the original elements (e.g., the *ipsissima verba* of the prophets). Even in their attempts to illuminate religio-historical motifs, they treated them primarily as the distant background of the tradition and did not attempt to trace their history down to the present form. In a word: they examined the beginnings and the final stage and neglected the developmental period that lay in between. Thus these researchers restricted their investigations primarily to compositional questions and to the *traditio*, thereby leaving the complex history of the *traditum* virtually outside the range of their method. This methodological principle, however, was challenged by Mowinckel,[50] and by now it appears that most Scandinavian researchers have

---

48. Cf. Gunneweg, *Tradition*, 66; Eissfeldt, *Kl. Schr.* III. 56, 58; Richter, *Exegese als Literaturwissenschaft*, 154.

49. Cf. our introduction above, ch. 2.

50. Cf. above, pp. 208-12.

abandoned it in favor of an interest in recovering the *history* of the traditions, i.e., the prehistory of the final form and the stage-by-stage development of the traditions. Engnell's later emphasis on the two tasks of *analysis* (breaking the traditions down into their various units) and *synthesis* (examining their import in their present contexts)[51] perhaps opened the way for this methodological shift. Thus Nielsen seeks to reconstruct an "Urdekalog" and to trace its development down to its present form, and Sæbø strives where possible to stratify and describe the formation of the Deutero-Zecharian text and content. This understanding of the task and possibilities of traditio-historical research is therefore a primary point at which Scandinavian work has undergone an essential change, and the result is that their methods and their research results are no longer as distinctive from non-Scandinavian work as was at first the case.

---

51. Cf. above, pp. 214–15, 219; also Ringgren, *TLZ* 91 (1966), cols. 647–48.

Epilogue:
Does Tradition History Have a Future?*

In 1968 I undertook a project to write a history and critique of the traditio-historical study of the Hebrew Bible.[1] The same year witnessed the beginning of deep political changes in universities and in the society at large. At that time, however, one could hardly have imagined that the following decades would also bring with them thoroughgoing changes, both philosophical and critical as well as social—changes that would exert an almost revolutionary effect on our academic methods and processes. Circumstances today are substantially different from what they were in 1968, and now one commences—or better: should commence—a traditio-historical study with greater reserve than was commonly practiced in times past. What has changed since roughly 1970, and how should this research method now be applied?

One should not forget that, when the traditio-historical method was first introduced and applied, it represented a radical break from previous research methods. Gerhard von Rad wrote in 1938 of "a stalemate which many view

---

* Translation, with slight modifications, of "Har gammeltestamentlig tradisjonshistorie en fremtid?", *Tidsskrift for Teologi og Kirke* 4 (1998) 263–77; used with permission. The publication in *TTK* was a slightly revised version of a lecture presented at the meeting of the Norwegian Old Testament Society, held at the Norwegian School of Theology, Oslo, on 4 November 1995. Arvid Tångberg (1946–2000) kindly invited me to deliver the lecture. Thanks also to Kåre Berge for correcting the final form of the Norwegian manuscript and to Magne Sæbø, who as editor of *TTK* arranged for its publication.

1. *Rediscovering the Traditions of Israel: The Development of the Traditio-Historical Research of the Old Testament, with Special Consideration of Scandinavian Contributions* was first published in 1973 by the Society of Biblical Literature (Missoula, Montana) in its Dissertation Series (no. 9). The revised version in 1975 and the reprinting in 1979 were published by Scholars Press. The book is based on a dissertation written under Professor Hans-Joachim Kraus at Georg-August-Universität, Göttingen. The second half is devoted to positions and contributions within Scandinavian circles, and interviews with several scholars helped to explicate various details: Arvid Kapelrud, Magne Sæbø, Helmer Ringgren, Gösta Ahlström, Geo Widengren, R. A. Carlson, and Ilmari Soisalon-Soininen.

with considerable anxiety,"² and he sought to develop an alternative that could revitalize both the subject and the field of biblical studies. Ten years later Martin Noth, writing in the preface to *A History of Pentateuchal Traditions*, which became a highpoint in the development of this new method, noted: "I was especially concerned here to raise questions which must be asked and whose answers must be attempted, even though the answers may sometimes appear purely hypothetical. The concern of this work would be realized in large measure if the manner of raising the questions proved itself to be proper."³ In Scandinavia Ivan Engnell, expressing dissatisfaction and no little frustration, wrote in 1945 of the reigning viewpoint: "the logicism and rationalism of the literary-critical epoch, together with its often naïve historicism, marked by an evolutionistic orientation in the writing of history and the history of religion." He was of the opinion that the "new traditio-historical insight" could introduce a thorough reform, even if "it must as yet remain to a great extent a question of proper directions, not of definitive results."⁴ These three pronouncements all occurred in the years during or shortly after World War II, a critical period also followed by new social, political, and philosophical conditions. Some thirty years of active biblical research ensued, during which time scholars renewed their efforts to uncover the gradual growth of traditions among the people of ancient Israel. The text was considered the "Endstadium" (as von Rad called it), and significant theological meanings were attributed to its prior stages.

One might have expected that such research efforts would lead to increasing certainty and improved results, and it has probably done so for certain circles of scholars. If one considers all the advances since the 1940s in archaeological, sociological, anthropological, historical, and other areas, is it not reasonable to assume that things should look much better in the area of historical-critical studies of the text as well? Precisely the opposite has occurred, however. Many today, if not the majority, are fundamentally more skeptical than previously with respect to certain traditional exegetical and historical methods of research. Some, such as Rolf Rendtorff, even speak of a paradigm

---

2. Von Rad, *The Problem of the Hexateuch and Other Essays*, transl. E. W. Trueman Dicken (Edinburgh: Oliver & Boyd, 1966), 1 = *Das formgeschichtliche Problem des Hexateuch*, BWANT IV/26 (Stuttgart: Kohlhammer, 1938), 1 = *Gesammelte Studien zum Alten Testament*, 3rd ed., TB 8 (Munich: Kaiser, 1965), 9.

3. Noth, *A History of Pentateuchal Traditions*, transl. Bernhard W. Anderson (Englewood Cliffs: Prentice-Hall, 1972) xxxv = *Überlieferungsgeschichte des Pentateuch* (Stuttgart: Kohlhammer, 1948), v.

4. Engnell, *Gamla Testamentet: En traditionshistorisk inledning*, vol. 1 (Stockholm: Svenska Kyrkans Diakonistyrelses Bokförlag, 1945), 10–11.

shift.⁵ It seems almost as if a dissolution of scholarly confidence has occurred, not the least regarding the traditio-historical work on the Hebrew Bible. Has the method itself been faulty, and have its practitioners been naïve? One could almost suspect as much in light of the critique coming from various angles.

I will address five areas—historiography, social history, ideological criticism, tradents, and exegetes—that raise problems for the ways in which tradition history has so far been understood and conducted. For my part, I should note at the outset that I take the criticisms very seriously. Each argument must be assessed with respect to the question of the extent to which traditio-historical exegesis is still conceivable and useful. If the objections raised seem to be too radical, negative, or superfluous, I can only say that our current period represents a turning-point for biblical studies, and we can hardly avoid scrutinizing the problems that go to our very presuppositions and methods. While these problems are wide-reaching and touch many aspects of our overall field of study, my comments here will focus on their significance for the traditio-historical study of the Hebrew Bible. And in this methodological discussion one must not forget Martin Noth's principle—that the answers we provide in our work are often not as important as the questions we seek to answer.

A. Historiography

The first, most obvious problem has been raised by historians, namely, that, historiographically considered, it is not at all as easy to find or confirm historical details in ancient Israel as one often thinks. In other words, to the extent that traditio-historical research understands itself to be a historical enterprise—and it does so fundamentally—one must not engage in excessive historical speculation. Restraint is necessary whenever we are dealing with something about which we do not possess assured information, rather than developing a scenario filled with details thought to be possible for a given stage in Israel's history. The multiplication of hypotheses in an almost boundless manner can be as dangerous for tradition historians as it is for historians.

The categories of "certainty" and "proof" are of course subject to discussion, and we are all familiar with disagreements among historians in almost every area. But regarding the historiographical problem of sources, we can perhaps take a lesson from an analogy with journalism today. If a report

---

5. Rendtorff, "The Paradigm Is Changing: Hopes—and Fears," *Biblical Interpretation* 1 (1992) 34-55.

could be legally sensitive, or so vital that one cannot risk making an error of fact, it is commonplace for the editor to require at least two independent sources to confirm the truth or accuracy of the report before it is published. It is not seldom for the investigative journalist to encounter special difficulties in securing additional support for a tip or a message from an informant. Of course this journalistic situation is not identical to the historical tasks we face. First, we can hardly interview someone with direct knowledge of what transpired in ancient Israel. Moreover, we are fortunate that no party to those events can initiate legal action against us because of something we say or write about events or persons in ancient Israel. Nonetheless, "sources" and "proofs" remain problems that historians must constantly resolve. If we were expected to work under the same expectations as journalists face, requiring us always to produce supportive evidence for whatever the Bible maintains or assumes, a book on the history of ancient Israel would be extremely thin—precisely because independent, contemporary epigraphic or textual witnesses are seldom available for occurrences and actors in literature.[6] If archaeological findings are considered as supporting evidence—as should be the case—then we are better equipped in certain areas.

However, an archaeological discovery, whether of a writing or another object, means extremely little without interpretation, and therein lies the rub. Perhaps no better example exists, especially from recent years, than the inscription found on 21 July 1993 at Tel Dan, which contains six letters reported widely in the press, following the first academic publication,[7] to be the absolutely earliest extrabiblical reference to King David. While specialists are still debating the reading and interpretation of the inscription,[8] we can here simply note that its meaning is not self-evident. Several divergent interpretations can be, and have been, reasonably advocated. At any rate, the

---

6. Philip R. Davies (*In Search of "Ancient Israel"* [2nd ed.; JSOTSup 148; Sheffield: Sheffield Academic Press, 1995]) presents the historiographical situation by identifying three different ways to think of ancient "Israel": the "Israel" of modern scholarship, the "Israel" of the Bible, and the "Israel" that existed in reality. The latter, he notes, must not be facilely equated with the first or the second. Among the many efforts to work in the new historiographical situation is Thomas L. Thompson, *Early History of the Israelite People: From the Written and Archaeological Sources* (SHANE 4; Leiden: Brill, 1992).

7. Avraham Biran and Joseph Naveh, "An Aramaic Stele Fragment from Tel Dan," *IEJ* 43 (1993): 81–98.

8. Among the many studies that followed Biran and Naveh's article are Frederick H. Cryer, "On the Recently-Discovered 'House of David' Inscription," *SJOT* 8 (1994): 3–19; E. A. Knauf, A. de Pury, and T. Römer, "*BaytDawid ou *BaytDod? Une relecture de la nouvelle inscription de Tel Dan," *BN* 72 (1994): 60–69; and Hans Barstad and Bob Becking, "Does the Stele from Tel-Dan Refer to a Deity Dôd?" *BN* 77 (1995): 5–12.

point is that the inscription is not as clear as it initially seemed to be, and once again we learn that one often errs in drawing quick conclusions before carefully considering a range of possibilities. Whether the inscription is referring to *bet-david*, to *bet-dod*, to a toponym, or to something else remains uncertain. Even though an additional inscribed piece has now appeared,[9] we still lack sufficient information for the majority of researchers to concur on a single or primary interpretation. Nevertheless, we can at least try to be clearer about our own presuppositions, which have a decisive effect on our historical work.[10] Does one assume that proof of a historical David is conceivable or not? What constitutes "positive proof"? Is it in principle possible to document a historical negative, that is, to prove that a certain person did not exist or that a certain event did not occur? How should we write a history when we can basically find footing only in possibilities, probabilities, fragments, and traditions? And finally, why is it important or unimportant for us—for each one of us—that, for example, an Israelite king named David existed and performed the actions the Hebrew Bible ascribes to him?

There are thus two significant aspects in the convergence between historiography and tradition history. First, even though the traditio-historical method understands itself to be an investigation internal to the text, or at least an analysis that begins with the text, it is fundamentally historical-critical in orientation and must necessarily attend to the same criteria that apply to other historiographical fields, especially with respect to verification and plausibility. Tradition historians must apply the critical methods expected of historical work in general. In other words, they must maneuver just as carefully as historians should in developing hypotheses. For example, in 1938, simultaneously with von Rad's *Das formgeschichtliche Problem des Hexateuch*, the Norwegian Harris Birkeland maintained that the tradition process within prophetic circles was analogous to a "smelting-furnace of the community."[11] If this is true, is it then surprising that historians and others should doubt whether tradition historians can separate traditions thus fused?[12] Exegetes do not help the situation by producing results that are so precise, detailed, and definitive as to throw in question their plausibility. One recalls the excessively

---

9. Biran and Naveh, "The Tel Dan Inscription: A New Fragment," *IEJ* 45 (1995): 1–18.

10. In this connection, see Niels Peter Lemche and Thomas L. Thompson, "Did Biran Kill David? The Bible in the Light of Archaeology," *JSOT* 64 (1994): 3–22.

11. Birkeland, *Zum hebräischen Traditionswesen: Die Komposition der prophetischen Bücher des Alten Testaments* (ANVAO, II. Hist.-filos. kl.; Oslo: Dybwad, 1938), 23–24; see p. 184 above.

12. See, among others, John Van Seters's critique in *Abraham in History and Tradition* (New Haven: Yale University Press, 1975).

detailed source criticism conducted by some during the early decades of the twentieth century, which inadvertently led to a premature discrediting of this research direction. When tradition historians try to reconstruct early traditions and their historical and ideological contexts, they must keep in mind the question of how much weight this method can bear. And they should also remain aware that history is much more extensive than the Bible tends to acknowledge. Several new efforts to produce a regional history without privileging the Bible as the main source or the biblical period as the main object of study are now available.[13]

The second aspect concerns the historian's own presuppositions. A primary problem focuses—now as before—on the extent to which the biblical text is useful as a historical source for the various times it describes. Opinions vary considerably about the extent to which tradition historians are able to uncover early literary stages that historians would then find acceptable to use as sources. Within each of the groups of historians commonly labeled either "maximalists" or "minimalists" there is no unity about this question, which applies to both periods in which these labels have been used, both in the 1950s–1960s and in the 1990s. Among the so-called "maximalists" are historians who advocate the traditio-historical method because it can strengthen the case for a tradition's antiquity, while others associated with this group are less enthusiastic about this exegetical method because its results often contravene conventional historical and theological interpretations. On the other side, those associated with the "minimalist" position also seem to follow various paths with regard to the usefulness of tradition history. Martin Noth, for example, based his historical studies heavily on traditio-historical analyses, while more recent historians often find such results to be entirely too speculative and hypothetical to use as a historical basis—or at most, only as possible support for what other historical indicators suggest. Such dissent or variance within each of these groups, in both their more recent forms as also their forms from the mid-twentieth century, underscores once again why we should avoid the problematic caricaturing of "maximalists" and "minimalists." Such facile classifications and generalizations must not take the place of the historian's careful and critical discussion of the problem of sources, which has direct implications for traditio-historical exegesis—and vice versa.

---

13. For example, Mario Liverani, *Antico Oriente: Storia, società, economia* (Rome: Laterza, 1988); idem, *Israel's History and the History of Israel* (trans. Chiara Peri and Philip R. Davies; London: Equinox, 2005); Helga Weippert, *Palästina in vorhellenistischer Zeit* (Munich: Beck, 1988); and Gösta W. Ahlström, *The History of Ancient Palestine* (Sheffield: JSOT Press; Minneapolis: Fortress, 1993).

B. Social History

One may well wonder whether developments in the study of the Hebrew Bible since roughly 1970 now compel us to adopt a new orientation in exegesis, in historiography in general, and in traditio-historical research specifically. I am thinking here of social history and ideological criticism, which are now being conducted in a variety of areas. While each method has its own analytical steps and subject matter, they also share common ground: an expansion of the field of vision and a certain suspicion that the social and political aspects of the texts were in fact not what they present themselves to be.

The special field of *social history* is undertaken by modern historians who maintain that much of interest and significance in society does not even occur among those who possess power and wealth. To the contrary, one limits the horizon by attending only to the upper-classes and their affairs, that is, to political history. The effects of these groups can, of course, be traced throughout much of society, but many other elements belong also to the history of a culture. Ferdinand Braudel, for example, attempts to extend the concept of history by giving attention not only to great individuals and events but also to physical conditions (the milieu), economy, social systems, political structures, and civilizations. All such domains must be studied, brought in relation to each other, and viewed in "la longue durée."[14] Social history takes into careful consideration the everyday life of the people: guilds or unions of laborers, religious sects, political factions, residential arrangements, family conditions, status of various groups (e.g., women, children, the elderly), diet and eating customs, health, and much more. Social history differs from sociology and historical sociology, which are more theoretically interested in social structures and empirically attentive to various social facts. Social historians are not blind to structural aspects, but they primarily try to follow social phenomena longitudinally in an effort to understand alterations and stability within a society's history. The extensive studies of diverse social topics in modern times are now being developed in a new direction under the influence of Critical Theory and deconstruction, with the result that one now inquires also after the political advantages and special interests at play.

Several recent efforts to use this method in biblical studies have underscored its usefulness and its insights. Niels Peter Lemche presented a sociohistorical overview, Rainer Albertz investigated Israelite religion sociohistorically, Frank Crüsemann conducted a similar study of laws, and several

---

14. Braudel, *Civilization and Capitalism, 15th-18th Century* (3 vols; London: Collins; New York: Harper & Row, 1981, 1982, 1984); and *The Mediterranean and the Mediterranean World in the Age of Philip II* (2 vols.; New York: Harper & Row, 1972, 1976).

similar efforts have appeared.[15] In addition, there are two new series oriented to social history, one organized chronologically and the other thematically.[16] There have also been advances in archaeology since the 1960s, when the so-called "new archaeology" was introduced, with its efforts to discover all that could be relevant to daily life among the ancient Israelites.[17] It can, in fact, be argued that without this redirection in archaeology our sociohistorical investigations would have had little chance of moving beyond Max Weber's time. In principle, the developments in our culture since the 1960s fostered the new directions in both archaeology and history-writing since that time, with archaeologists taking the first steps in delivering materials for the social historians' innovations.

A useful context for viewing the social history of ancient Israel lies in the model of the agrarian society. Macro-sociologist Gerhard Lenski has developed a detailed description of this social type with reference to numerous cultures from various periods and places in human history.[18] Several features are characteristic of an agrarian society: technological progress, wars and internal conflicts, cities dominating the society, diverse professions, commerce, and a religious institution connected to the centralized state but also often subject to conflicts. A conspicuous inequality in social power, privileges, and prestige marks advanced agrarian societies, and the state itself functions as the source of this disparity. Kings regard the state as their own property to use however they wish, and their archives tell mainly of them, their wars, and their projects—and virtually nothing about life among the commoners. The agrarian society also has a governing or ruling class, a small minority usually not larger than 2 percent of the total population and often

---

15. Lemche, *Ancient Israel: A New History of Israelite Society* (trans. Fred Cryer; Sheffield: JSOT Press, 1988); Albertz, *A History of Israelite Religion in the Old Testament Period* (trans. John Bowden; 2 vols.; London: SCM; Louisville: Westminster John Knox, 1994); and Crüsemann, *The Torah: Theology and Social History of Old Testament Law* (trans. Allan W. Mahnke; Minneapolis: Fortress, 1996).

16. Biblische Enzyklopädie (ed. Walter Dietrich and Wolfgang Stegemann; Stuttgart: Kohlhammer); and Library of Ancient Israel (ed. Douglas A. Knight; Louisville: Westminster John Knox).

17. See Thomas E. Levy, ed., *The Archaeology of Society in the Holy Land* (New York: Facts on File, 1995); and recently, Philip J. King and Lawrence E. Stager, *Life in Biblical Israel* (Library of Ancient Israel; Louisville: Westminster John Knox, 2001).

18. Lenski, *Power and Privilege: A Theory of Social Stratification* (Chapel Hill: University of North Carolina Press, 1984). See also my "Herrens bud—elitens interesser? Lov, makt, og rettferdighet i Det gamle testamente," *NTT* 97 (1996), especially 237ff. = "Whose Agony? Whose Ecstasy? The Politics of Deuteronomic Law," in *Shall Not the Judge of All the Earth Do What Is Right? Studies on the Nature of God in Tribute to James L. Crenshaw* (ed. David Penchansky and Paul L. Redditt; Winona Lake, Ind: Eisenbrauns, 2000), 97–112.

much smaller. This governing class exercises political and economic power on the national level and includes such persons as officials, high military officers, the wealthy, and others to whom the king grants lands, offices, or special rights. These two groups—the royal house and its political apparatus on the one hand and the governing class on the other—become aligned to hold the populace in check, both the farmers in the villages and the artisans in the cities, and to extract from them any economic surplus. As a result, less than 2 percent of the population usually possesses up to 50 percent of the nation's income. But the balance of power between the king and the governing class can be unstable. Either party can dominate the other and thus obtain primary control over the country. In addition, other specialists exist who, while dependent on the political elite, are privileged in comparison to the exploited masses: functionaries, retainers, merchants, and priests. Israel corresponds quite well to this societal model, though one must adjust the pattern in light of the different situations presented in the premonarchic, monarchic, and colonial periods.

Further investigations along sociohistorical lines are now needed. The relations among population groups and institutions require more nuanced description. It is also important to recognize the pluralism and diversity within Israel—not the least the difference between the so-called "official" and the "popular" positions. The latter represents, in all likelihood, the vast number of Israelites and requires attention for their contributions to the culture. The method of social history affirms a more inclusive perspective on historical realities, and it is vital that traditio-historical exegesis now operates in this context in trying to reconstruct the growth of biblical texts.

C. Ideological Criticism

In a clear and crucial respect social history and ideological criticism converge. The phenomenon of ideology has received much more attention in philosophical, sociological, and political circles in the past century than one might conclude from the relative silence about the subject in biblical studies until recent years. The reason probably lies in the fact that we, with our own religious interests and traditions, are often tied closely to the text's own ideologies. Nonetheless, scholarly inquiry is obliged to analyze this aspect of literature, and thereby to scrutinize our own presuppositions as well. A many-sided concept, ideology is most useful for historians in presenting how a group, especially the ruling group, advances and legitimizes its special interests vis-à-vis others in the society. Ideology also entails power—not so much power in general, but the conditions of power that are central for the social system in its entirety or in its principal parts. The ideology of a text often lies in what Terry Eagleton calls the "measurable absences,"[19] elements that in all likelihood were politically or economically most effective if they were not explicitly stated. Such information is relevant for historians since the ideology is tied to the power-structure, the social power that those in control seek to reinforce and renew.[20] To carry out ideological criticism involves, then, a measuring of the absences in the text, points where we should be able to obtain a fleeting glimpse of the historical circumstances in which the authors, redactors, or tradents were especially interested—politically, economically, socially, and religiously. On the one hand, this step appears to be quite problematic—a historiographical maneuvering among possibilities, a process that has now become less accepted by historians than it may have been previously. But on the other hand, such information is precisely what the text may try to conceal from its readers and hearers. Consequently, our exegetical task should endeavor to search for such traces.

Ideological criticism has received little attention until recent years. There has, of course, been a long-standing interest in identifying a text's *Tendenz*, its intention or leaning, and there is no lack of perceptive descriptions of the theological perspectives behind specific texts. In recent years we have learned caution in trying to describe an author's intention, which literary critics maintain has little relevance for today's interpretation. But with this we have not reached the text's ideology, which is masked because of its special political and economic interests. Efforts in the area of ideological criticism include Giovanni Garbini's *History and Ideology in Ancient Israel*,[21] the collection of essays in *Semeia* 59,[22] as well as numerous feminist, materialist, and other analyses. Norman Gottwald's "Social Class and Ideology in Isaiah 40–55"[23] is a good example of ideological criticism, especially in the Eagletonian mode. Basing his work on previous form-critical and traditio-historical studies of Deutero-Isaiah, Gottwald focuses on the text's social and ideological dimensions. The author's ideology, Gottwald proposes, is evident in the belief in a sovereign God, the hope for a restoration with the help of the Persians, and the expectation that the people must suffer before the restoration can be fulfilled. Two "measurable absences" are discernible in the text: that nothing

---

19. Eagleton, *Criticism and Ideology: A Study in Marxist Literary Theory* (London: Verso, 1976), 72.

20. Eagleton, *Literary Theory: An Introduction* (Minneapolis: University of Minnesota Press, 1983), 14–15.

21. Translated by John Bowden. London: SCM, 1988; Italian original in 1986.

22. *Ideological Criticism of Biblical Texts*, ed. David Jobling and Tina Pippin, *Semeia* 59 (1992).

23. In *Semeia* 59 (1992): 43–57.

explicit is said about the Judeans who remained in Judah during the exilic period, and that the text is completely silent about societal organization after the exiles' return from Babylon. Gottwald argues that both absences point to a political and economic ideology presupposing that the exilic generation has been punished enough in Babylon and now will return to the land and again take up the same leading positions their aristocratic parents had. Also in *Semeia* 59 is an article by Robert Carroll on "The Myth of the Empty Land,"[24] in which he proposes that the myth that the land of Judah was vacant during the seventy years of exile (2 Chr 36:17–21), just like the myth that the land prior to Joshua was defiled by the Canaanites and needed to be cleansed, is an ideological history designed to control membership in the new society. Both of these ideological-critical insights could well have been reached with a traditio-historical exegesis. So far, tradition historians have primarily tried to uncover theological ideas and religious tendencies in their exegeses, and now it is important for us to attempt to widen the investigation by attending also to the political and economic dimensions of the traditions. And with that we come to the question of the tradents.

D. The Tradents: Who and Who Not?

Tradition criticism begins with the text, where one hopes to find traces of stages in the growth of the traditions that, *ex hypothesi*, preceded the text in its present form. The critical steps one takes and the textual indications one looks for will, in my view, continue in the future along lines quite similar to what has been practiced until now. But no tradition is simply suspended in the air. It requires, of course, transmitters or traditionists, that is, tradents, to preserve it, to receive it from predecessors, to revise it as they wish—and here is where we find the creative, noteworthy stage—and then to deliver it to the next tradents in the line of transmission. The process itself is much more complicated than this schematization suggests, but tradition historians tend in general to imagine it along these lines. And assuming that a given text was not created by just one author, it is reasonable—considering the nature of folk-literature among preindustrial peoples—to presuppose such a developmental process.[25] Who, then, played the role of tradents, and what motivated them? Tradition historians identify groups such as priests, prophets, temple-singers, archivists, storytellers, teachers, sages, and others, though often these

---

24. In *Semeia* 59 (1992): 79–93.
25. The intricate relationship between oral traditions and a writing culture is also relevant. See Susan Niditch, *Oral World and Written Word: Ancient Israelite Literature* (LAI; Louisville: Westminster John Knox, 1996; London: SPCK, 1997).

groups are merely mentioned and their theological viewpoints described. Discussions since roughly 1970, however, have emphasized that we must also consider their societal milieu, their social profile, and their primary interests within political and economic spheres.

Feminist research constitutes perhaps the most unexpected, though probably also one of the richest fields of study developed since roughly 1970. It serves as a supreme example of how generations can disregard, if not even disdain, a central dimension of human life—until someone exposes its significance and makes it clear that a comprehensive analysis must necessarily attend to it. While such research contributes especially to social history and ideological criticism, it also obliges us to reassess the question of tradents. Carol Meyers, for example, asserts that the Hebrew Bible stems largely from males and not females, from the elites and not the commoners, from urban rather than rural populations, and from those working in public affairs and not only in private life.[26] If this depiction is correct, we need to reckon with only about 1–2 percent of the whole population having had anything directly to do with the production of the Bible, at least during its later stages when it became written, reworked into a literary whole, and copied and preserved. This is not a large segment of the whole people, and one can thus hardly speak of "Israel's" literature when the texts stemmed in the main from a tiny minority connected with the upper classes. Meyers's model appears somewhat broad-brush, and one probably needs to differentiate among specific literary forms and their likely tradents. Yet she has set the problem in good relief. Even if we regard the Hebrew Bible as a type of folk-literature, we must not imagine that it is the product of the whole people or that the commoners stand behind it.

We thus can justifiably pose ideological questions: Whose text or tradition was it in fact? To whom did it belong? Whose interests were being advanced? The socioeconomic class of the tradents has until now received entirely too little attention in traditio-historical studies. Not long ago Norman Gottwald underscored this lack in more general terms—that we have not shown much interest in the class levels of the Israelites—and he lays the fault at the feet of our own class interests: that we who are occupied with this research belong primarily to the upper or upper-middle classes and therefore attend first and foremost to those who belonged to the same or higher social classes in ancient Israel.[27] In other words: our own ideology determines our scholarship. We

---

26. Meyers, *Discovering Eve: Ancient Israelite Women in Context* (New York: Oxford University Press, 1988) 11ff.

27. Gottwald, *Semeia* 59 (1992): 43–57; idem, "Social Class as an Analytic and Hermeneutical Category in Biblical Studies," *JBL* 112 (1993): 3–22.

need to train ourselves to remain attentive to this fact, not in the hopes of escaping it but in order to take it into better consideration in our work. Otherwise, our historical, and thus also our traditio-historical, investigations will remain limited in scope. I will return to this issue in the next section.

We are well aware that various factions existed side by side in Israel. Tradition historians have identified these groups in general and have clarified the theological differences among them—Deuteronomists, prophets, priests, Yahwists, and many others. But one tends to describe the groups only in comparison with each other, and with good grounds, since each had its own institutional orientation and interests, if not polemic, which becomes most evident when one compares them with each other. Odil Hannes Steck[28] identified four broad, dominant "streams of tradition" ("Traditionsströme") that developed and transmitted nearly everything that fills the Hebrew Bible: the cultic stream and the sapiential stream, both based primarily in Jerusalem, the diverse prophetic stream and the Deuteronomic/Deuteronomistic stream prominent more in the Judean countryside. Walter Brueggemann[29] has distinguished between two "trajectories": a Davidic or royal tradition with its seat in the cities, politically oriented toward those who possessed power and expressed theologically in the picture of God as the preserver and protector of the status quo; and, on the other hand, a Mosaic or liberating tradition supported primarily by villagers and promulgated politically and theologically as a revolutionary idea. Several other efforts exist to describe groups that were perhaps responsible for producing the biblical literature. At the moment, it is important for us to underscore three social aspects that we all too seldom keep in mind as we consider such groups of tradents.

(1) I am not certain that we have any idea of the animosity that probably prevailed among many such groups in ancient Israel. We hear of occasional conflicts in the Hebrew Bible, especially prophets against priests and prophets against kings, but also prophets against prophets. Otto Plöger, Morton Smith, Paul Hanson, and others made efforts some decades ago to describe several factions in the postexilic context, and more recent research has extended the controversies to social, political, and economic domains.[30] If the situation was

---

28. Steck, "Theological Streams of Tradition," in *Tradition and Theology in the Old Testament* (ed. Douglas A. Knight; Philadelphia: Fortress; London: SPCK, 1977; repr., Sheffield: JSOT Press, 1990), 183–214.

29. Brueggemann, "Trajectories in Old Testament Literature and the Sociology of Ancient Israel," *JBL* 98 (1979): 161–85.

30. Plöger, *Theokratie und Eschatologie* (2nd ed.; WMANT 2; Neukirchen Kreis Moers: Neukirchener Verlag, 1962) = *Theocracy and Eschatology* (trans. S. Rudman; Richmond: John Knox, 1968); Smith, *Palestinian Parties and Politics That Shaped the Old Testament* (New York: Columbia University, 1971); Hanson, *The Dawn of Apocalyptic: The Historical and Sociological*

this tense and heterogeneous in the Persian period, we have little grounds to imagine that the situation was more harmonious in other periods, especially under kings when an institution's health and continued existence revolved around its success vis-à-vis other groups. If two or more religious factions represented distinct political or economic alternatives, their rivalry would have been all the more intense as each party had so much at stake. Instead of concentrating on only their theological orientation, we also ought to weigh the tradents' own special interests and the political history of the institutions to which they belonged.

(2) In addition to the relationship between one circle of tradents and another, the relationship between the tradents on the one hand and the larger population on the other also takes on substantial significance. We exegetes consider entirely too seldom how leadership groups, including those transmitting the traditions, tried to improve their own position among the people, a step that can hardly be regarded as anything other than a power-move. It happens often enough among us today, and in principle we should not expect it to be otherwise in ancient Israel. We may, indeed, find it somewhat uncomfortable if it appears that certain groups, especially those publicly in charge of the people's religious life, colluded with the king or with the economic elite to manipulate or profit from the people. But should it surprise us? If the picture of the agrarian society is correct, the tradents belonged mainly to the privileged groups used by the political elite to improve the latter's position and reputation and to keep control of the masses. The tradents, for their part, preserved and modified the traditions in a manner that would bring them benefits from their benefactors and patrons.[31] Those who were literate were to be found primarily among the priests and among the class in service to the elites—or bureaucrats in the state system. Their loyalty, especially that of the retainer class, was directed toward those who had the power to secure or threaten their position. The priests were similarly clear about who could give or remove favors and privileges for the cult. Sometimes, but probably not

---

Roots of Jewish Apocalyptic Eschatology (rev. ed.; Philadelphia: Fortress, 1979). See now also Joel Weinberg, *The Citizen–Temple Community* (trans. Daniel L. Smith-Christopher; JSOTSup 151; Sheffield: JSOT Press, 1992); the volumes of *Second Temple Studies*, published by Sheffield Academic Press, Sheffield; Jon L. Berquist, *Judaism in Persia's Shadow: A Social and Historical Approach* (Minneapolis: Fortress, 1995), 131ff.; Lester L. Grabbe, *The Persian and Greek Periods* (vol. 1 of *Judaism from Cyrus to Hadrian*; Minneapolis: Fortress, 1992), 103–19; and Pierre Briant, *Histoire de l'empire perse de Cyrus à Alexandre* (Paris: Arthème Fayard, 1996), 53–59 and passim = *From Cyrus to Alexander: A History of the Persian Empire* (trans. Peter T. Daniels; Winona Lake, Ind.: Eisenbrauns, 2002).

31. Niels Peter Lemche, "Kings and Clients: On Loyalty between the Ruler and the Ruled in Ancient 'Israel,'" *Semeia* 66 (1994): 119–32.

very often, a powerless person from among the people could find a defender in the privileged classes. It is too cynical of us to interpret the situation in this manner? Are we naïve if we do not consider what might have benefited the tradents economically and politically?

(3) One other critical problem deserves attention. How many of the people's traditions circulating in ancient Israel became preserved in the Hebrew Bible? We can only guess that a rich and comprehensive corpus, including stories, customary laws, songs, proverbs, and more, emerged and were orally transmitted among the farmers, pastoralists, and artisans. While much became lost to history, it is reasonable to assume that some survived and became incorporated in the literature we now call the Hebrew Bible. The tradents, many of them skilled servants and priests, were also affected by the popular traditions and could use them to gain acceptance among the commoners. Several of the reformist prophets were likely supported and sheltered by those who did not belong to the central powers.[32] Our traditio-historical research in the future should include, in other words, a clear expectation that popular culture and nonelite viewpoints will be considered in our search for the prehistory of a given text.

E. Modern Exegetes

One more factor should be emphasized, a necessary but all too neglected aspect of our critical work. Postmodernism has made it clear that we need to analyze anew not only the text but also ourselves as exegetes. To what extent are we reflected in the very methods we employ and in the conclusions we draw?

Out of curiosity I counted the names in the index of authors in the first two editions of the present book.[33] Not surprisingly, of 317 names only three were women and—as far as I could determine—no one stemmed from outside Europe, North America, or Israel. One might try to explain this distribution by referring to the demographic situation in the field of biblical studies up to the time of 1970, but there were specialists in other countries who simply were not referenced or included in discussions in the so-called "First World." The low number of women active in scholarly work indicates in itself a problem with deep and fundamental causes in society. To be sure, an overview focusing on recent decades would show a broader distribution. But the question remains unavoidable: Is traditio-historical exegesis in the main an androcentric and Euro-American method?

---

32. Robert R. Wilson, *Prophecy and Society in Ancient Israel* (Philadelphia: Fortress, 1980). Regarding the legal traditions, see my article mention in n. 18 above.

33. See n. 1 above.

Almost sixty years ago Engnell referred to an "*interpretatio europeica moderna*," which in his view was closely connected with source-critical and evolutionary perspectives.[34] The *interpretatio euroamericanica moderna* that we face today goes much deeper because it concerns not just ideas but our very social identity. White males from the "First World" cannot and must not deny they belong to that world, but they—that is, all of us—need to learn that our viewpoints are limited and idiosyncratic. And that means that our critical questions and analytic methods are also limited and idiosyncratic.

(1) We who were trained in the notion of objectivity in scholarly research must learn anew that such an illusory idea, a chimera, deceives us into expecting something that cannot be accomplished. One cannot distinguish fully between what the text meant and what it now means for us—because *we* are the ones trying to decide what the text meant in its original context. We exegetes bring more to the text than we are aware of, and for this reason it is wholly impossible to interpret the text in an objective manner. One need only remind oneself of Edward Said's thesis regarding the thoroughgoing effect our peculiar perception of the "Orient" has had on scholarship and other areas of activity.[35] For a method such as tradition history it means we need to show restraint in maintaining that we can reconstruct the growth of a text: if the text's meaning and especially its intents are so uncertain, then its preceding tradition's meaning and intents are equally uncertain—and probably even more so. The problem lies as much with us, not just with the subject matter we study.

(2) Poststructuralism and postmodernism go even further in "de-privileging" the position of author/tradent and interpreter, emphasizing instead the dynamic and heterogeneity in the stages of creation and interpretation. Ideological criticism belongs as well to this direction in philosophy and literary theory. Regarding biblical exegesis, it may be enough simply to mention the book by Daniel Patte, *Ethics of Biblical Interpretation*.[36] Patte argues that a postmodern exegesis should be critical without being arrogant. The text itself is polysemic, and therefore it must be interpreted with a multidimensional exegesis. A legitimate interpretation, he maintains, is based on the text, but at the same time it also recognizes the legitimacy of other interpretations. This paradigm-shift implies a new recognition of the roles of a method and its

---

34. Engnell, "Profetia och tradition: Några synpunkter på ett gammaltestamentligt centralproblem," *SEÅ* 12 (1947): 114; see also above, p. 215.

35. Said, *Orientalism* (New York: Vintage Books, 1979).

36. Patte, *Ethics of Biblical Interpretation: A Reevaluation* (Louisville: Westminster John Knox, 1995). See also Elisabeth Schüssler Fiorenza, "The Ethics of Biblical Interpretation: Decentering Biblical Scholarship," *JBL* 107 (1988): 3–17.

opposing methods. It also means that we need to accept that every interpretation is an "advocacy interpretation," which stems from our own social location and which possibly can be oppressive of those from other social locations.[37] Patte calls the method he uses an "androcritical multidimensional" exegesis because it pointedly attempts to analyze critically the extant interpretations or to offer new ones—always with a view toward the plurality of the text and of its interpretations.

The specific implications of postmodernism for a critical method such as tradition history can be difficult to calculate, but clearly research cannot henceforth simply continue along old, conventional paths. If we exegetes do not participate in discussions underway within philosophical and cultural-critical circles, we stand in danger of failing to learn from our colleagues in other fields, with the result that we may remain stuck in the previous critical epoch.

F. Conclusion

We have covered considerable terrain—historiographical methodology, social history, ideological criticism, and finally the question of our own roles as exegetes. Yet today's biblical criticism is precisely of this nature: thorny methodological problems and few simple solutions. It should not surprise us that the traditio-historical study of the Hebrew Bible is especially affected as its method extends more broadly than do many other exegetical methods. The question pressing us concerns whether or not tradition history can continue on the same course it has until now followed. Perhaps it may help to recall Martin Noth's thesis that the questions are more important than are the answers. To conduct traditio-historical exegesis in the future requires exegetes to expand the social context of the traditions, include more perspectives, and apply ideological criticism to the traditions as well as to the interpreters, all the while testing how much we can in fact know regarding all that happened during ancient Israel's history—that is, submitting our hypotheses to a "reality test." In a word, a new orientation is needed. If we manage to achieve the needed discussion with our colleagues within and outside of the biblical field, then in my view the traditio-historical study of the Hebrew Bible does in fact have a future.

---

37. See also Fernando F. Segovia and Mary Ann Tolbert, eds., *Reading from This Place*, vol. 1: *Social Location and Biblical Interpretation in the United States*; vol. 2: *Social Location and Biblical Interpretation in Global Perspective* (Minneapolis: Fortress, 1995).

Bibliography

Ackroyd, Peter R. *Continuity: A Contribution to the Study of the Old Testament Religious Tradition.* Oxford: Basil Blackwell, 1962.
———. "The Temple Vessels—A Continuity Theme." *Studies in the Religion of Ancient Israel,* VTSup 23 (1972) 166–81.
———. "The Theology of Tradition: An Approach to Old Testament Theological Problems." *BTF* 3 (1971) 49–64.
Ahlström, Gösta W. *Aspects of Syncretism in Israelite Religion.* HS 5. Lund: Gleerup, 1963.
———. "Die Königsideologie in Israel: Ein Diskussionsbeitrag." *TZ* 18 (1962) 205–10.
———. "Oral and Written Transmission: Some Considerations." *HTR* 59 (1966) 69–81.
———. "Der Prophet Nathan und der Tempelbau." *VT* 11 (1961) 113–27.
———. *Psalm 89: Eine Liturgie aus dem Ritual des leidenden Königs.* Lund: Gleerup, 1959.
Albright, William Foxwell. "Abram the Hebrew: A New Archaeological Interpretation." *BASOR* 163 (1961) 36–54.
———. *The Archaeology of Palestine and the Bible.* 2nd ed. New York: Revell, 1933.
———. *From the Stone Age to Christianity: Monotheism and the Historical Process.* 2nd ed. with a new introduction. Garden City, N.Y.: Doubleday, 1957.
———. "The Israelite Conquest of Canaan in the Light of Archaeology." *BASOR* 74 (1939) 11–23.
———. *Yahweh and the Gods of Canaan: A Historical Analysis of Two Contrasting Faiths.* London: Athlone, 1968.
Alt, Albrecht. "Erwägungen über die Landnahme der Israeliten in Palästina." *PJ* 35 (1939) 8–63. Also in *Kleine Schriften zur Geschichte des Volkes Israel,* I:126–75. Munich: Beck, 1953.
———. "Der Gott der Väter." BWANT 3/12. Stuttgart: Kohlhammer, 1929. Also in *Kl. Schr.,* I:1–78. ET: "The God of the Fathers." *Essays on Old Tes-*

tament History and Religion, 1–77. Translated by R. A. Wilson. Oxford: Basil Blackwell, 1966.

———. "Josua." *Werden und Wesen des Alten Testaments*, 13–29. Edited by P. Volz, F. Stummer, and J. Hempel. BZAW 66. Berlin: Töpelmann, 1936. Also in *Kl. Schr.*, I:176–92.

———. "Die Landnahme der Israeliten in Palästina." Reformationsprogramm der Universität Leipzig 1925. Also in *Kl. Schr.*, I:89–125. ET: "The Settlement of the Israelites in Palestine." *Essays on Old Testament History and Religion*, 133–69. Translated by R. A. Wilson. Oxford: Basil Blackwell, 1966.

———. "Die Staatenbildung der Israeliten in Palästina." Reformationsprogramm der Universität Leipzig 1930. Also in *Kl. Schr.*, II:1–65. ET: "The Formation of the Israelite State in Palestine." *Essays on Old Testament History and Religion*, 171–237. Translated by R. A. Wilson. Oxford: Basil Blackwell, 1966.

———. "Das System der Stammesgrenzen im Buche Josua." *Sellin-Festschrift: Beiträge zur Religionsgeschichte und Archäologie Palästinas*, 13–24. Leipzig: Deichert, 1927. Also in *Kl. Schr.*, I:193–202.

———. *Die Ursprünge des israelitischen Rechts*. BAL, Phil.-hist. Klasse, 86/1. Leipzig: Hirzel, 1934. Also in *Kl. Schr.*, I:278–332. ET: "The Origins of Israelite Law." *Essays on Old Testament History and Religion*, 79–132. Translated by R. A. Wilson. Oxford: Basil Blackwell, 1966.

Altmann, Alexander, ed. *Biblical Motifs: Origins and Transformations*. Cambridge, Mass.: Harvard University Press, 1966.

Alver, Brynjulf. "Category and Function." *Fabula (Zeitschrift für Erzählforschung)* 9 (1967) 63–69.

Anderson, Bernhard W. *Creation Versus Chaos: The Reinterpretation of Mythical Symbolism in the Bible*. New York: Association Press, 1967.

———. "Martin Noth's Traditio-Historical Approach in the Context of Twentieth-Century Biblical Research." *A History of Pentateuchal Traditions*, by Martin Noth, xiii–xxxii. Translated by B. W. Anderson. Englewood Cliffs, N.J.: Prentice-Hall, 1972.

Anderson, George W. "Johannes Lindblom's Contribution to Biblical Studies." *ASTI* 6 (1968) 4–19.

———. "Some Aspects of the Uppsala School of Old Testament Study." *HTR* 43 (1950) 239–56.

Astruc, Jean. *Conjectures sur les mémoires originaux dont il paroit que Moyse s'est servi pour composer le Livre de la Genèse*. Bruxelles: Fricx, 1753.

Auerbach, Elias. "Das Zehngebot—Allgemeine Gesetzes-Form in der Bibel." *VT* 16 (1966) 255–76.

Bardtke, Hans. "Henning Bernhard Witter (Zur 250. Wiederkehr seinen Promotion zum Philosophiae Doctor am 6. November 1704 zu Helmstedt)." *ZAW* 66 (1954) 153–81.

Barr, James. *Comparative Philology and the Text of the Old Testament*. Oxford: Clarendon, 1968.

———. *Old and New in Interpretation: A Study of the Two Testaments*. London: SCM, 1966.

———. *The Semantics of Biblical Language*. London: Oxford University Press, 1961.

———. "Tradition and Expectation in Ancient Israel." *SJT* 10 (1957) 24–34.

Barth, Christoph. "Grundprobleme einer Theologie des Alten Testaments." *EvT* 23 (1963) 342–72.

Barth, Hermann, and Odil Hannes Steck. *Exegese des Alten Testaments: Leitfaden der Methodik: Ein Arbeitsbuch für Proseminare, Seminare und Vorlesungen*. 2nd ed. Neukirchen-Vluyn: Neukirchener Verlag, 1971. ET: Odil Hannes Steck, *Old Testament Exegesis: A Guide to the Methodology*. Translated by James D. Nogalski. 2nd ed. Atlanta: Scholars Press, 1998.

Baumgärtel, Friedrich. "Gerhard von Rad's 'Theologie des Alten Testaments.'" *TLZ* 86 (1961) cols. 801–16, 895–908.

———. *Verheissung: Zur Frage des evangelischen Verstandnisses des Alten Testaments*. Gütersloh: Bertelsmann, 1952.

Becker, Joachim. *Israel deutet seine Psalmen: Urform und Neuinterpretation in den Psalmen*. SBS 18. Stuttgart: Verlag Katholisches Bibelwerk, 1966.

Begrich, Joachim. "Die Paradieserzählung: Eine literargeschichtliche Studie." *ZAW* 50 (1932) 93–116. Also in *Gesammelte Studien zum Alten Testament*, 11–38. Edited by W. Zimmerli. TB 21. Munich: Kaiser, 1964.

———. "Zur Frage der alttestamentlichen Textkritik." *OLZ* 42 (1939) cols. 473–83.

Bentzen, Aage. "Bemerkungen über neuere Entwicklungen in der Pentateuchfrage." *ArOr* 19 (1951) 226–232.

———. *Daniel*. 2nd ed. HAT 19. Tübingen: Mohr Siebeck, 1952.

———. "Daniel 6: Ein Versuch zur Vorgeschichte der Märtyrerlegende." *Festschrift für Alfred Bertholet*, 58–64. Tübingen: Mohr Siebeck, 1950.

———. "Der Hedammu-Mythus, das Judithbuch und ähnliches." *ArOr* 18,3 (1950) 1–2.

———. *Introduction to the Old Testament*. 2 vols. 2nd ed. Copenhagen: Gad, 1952.

———. *Jesaja, fortolket*. Vol. I, *Jes. 1–39*; Vol. II, *Jes. 40–66*. Copenhagen: Gad, 1944 and 1943.

———. "Kan ordet 'messiansk' anvendes om Salmernes kongeforestillinger?" *SEÅ* 12 (1947) 36–50.

———. "King Ideology—'Urmensch'—'Troonsbestijgingsfeest.'" *ST* 3 (1949) 143–57.

———. *Messias—Moses redivivus—Menschensohn: Skizzen zum Thema Weissagung und Erfullung*. ATANT 17. Zürich: Zwingli-Verlag, 1948.

———. "The Ritual Background of Amos i 2 - ii 16." *OtSt* 8 (1950) 85–99.

———. *Det sakrale kongedømme: Bemærkninger i en løbende diskussion om de gammeltestamentlige Salmer.* In *Festskrift Københavns Universitet, November 1945*. Copenhagen: Bianco Lunos Bogtrykkeri, 1945.

———. "Skandinavische Literatur zum Alten Testament 1939–1948." *TRu* NS 17 (1948/49) 273–328.

———. "Der Tod des Beters in den Psalmen: Randbemerkungen zur Diskussion zwischen Mowinckel und Widengren." *Festschrift Otto Eissfeldt*, 57–60. Edited by Johann Fück. Halle an der Saale: M. Niemeyer, 1947.

Bernhardt, Karl-Heinz. *Das Problem der altorientalischen Königsideologie im Alten Testament, unter besonderer Berücksichtigung der Geschichte der Psalmenexegese dargestellt und kritisch gewürdigt.* VTSup 8. Leiden: Brill, 1961.

Bernus, A. *Richard Simon et son Histoire critique du Vieux Testament: La critique biblique au siècle de Louis XIV*. Lausanne: Bridel, 1869.

Bertholet, A. *Die Macht der Schrift in Glauben und Aberglauben*. AAB, Phil.-hist. Kl. 1948,1. Berlin: Akademie-Verlag, 1949.

Bevan, Anthony Ashley. "Historical Methods in the Old Testament." *Essays on Some Biblical Questions of the Day by Members of the University of Cambridge*, 1–19. Edited by H. B. Swete. London: Macmillan, 1909.

Beyerlin, Walter. "Gattung und Herkunft des Rahmens im Richterbuch." *Tradition und Situation: Studien zur alttestamentlichen Prophetie (A. Weiser-Festschrift)*, 1–29. Göttingen: Vandenhoeck & Ruprecht, 1963.

———. *Herkunft und Geschichte der ältesten Sinaitraditionen*. Tübingen: Mohr Siebeck, 1961. ET: *Origins and History of the Oldest Sinaitic Traditions*. Translated by S. Rudman. Oxford: Basil Blackwell, 1965.

Birkeland, Harris. *The Lord Guideth: Studies on Primitive Islam*. SNVAO, II. Hist.-Filos. Kl., 1956, No. 2. Oslo: Aschehoug, 1956.

———. "Profeten Hoseas forkynnelse." *NTT* 38 (1937) 277–316.

———. *Zum hebräischen Traditionswesen: Die Komposition der prophetischen Bücher des Alten Testaments.* ANVAO, II. Hist.-Filos. Kl., 1938, No. 1. Oslo: Dybwad, 1938.

———. "Zur Kompositionsfrage des Buches Jeremia." *MO* 31 (1937) 49–62.

Boecker, Hans Jochen. *Redeformen des Rechtslebens im Alten Testament*. WMANT 14. Neukirchen-Vluyn: Neukirchener Verlag, 1964.

Boer, P. A. H. de. *Gedenken und Gedächtnis in der Welt des Alten Testaments*. Stuttgart: Kohlhammer, 1962.

Bonfrère, Jacques. *Pentateuchus Moysis commentario illustratus.* Antwerp, 1625.
Bossuet, Jacques Benigne. *Discours sur l'Histoire universelle, à Monseigneur le Dauphin: Pour expliquer la suite de la Religion et les changemens des Empires.* Paris: Sebastien Mabre-Cramoisy, 1681.
Botterweck, G. J. "Form- und überlieferungsgeschichtliche Studie zum Dekalog." *Concilium* 1 (1965), 392–401.
Bright, John. *Early Israel in Recent History Writing: A Study in Method.* SBT 19. London: SCM, 1956.
———. "Modern Study of Old Testament Literature." *The Bible and the Ancient Near East: Essays in Honor of William Foxwell Albright,* 13–31. Edited by G. Ernest Wright. Garden City, N.Y.: Doubleday, 1961.
Brueggemann, Walter. *Tradition for Crisis: A Study in Hosea.* Richmond: John Knox, 1969.
Buber, Martin. *Moses.* Zürich: G. Müller, 1948. ET: *Moses.* Oxford: East & West Library, 1946.
Buhl, Frants. "Zur Vorgeschichte des Buches Hiob." BZAW 41 (Giessen 1925) 52–61.
Burrows, M. "Variant Readings in the Isaiah Manuscript." *BASOR* 111 (1948) 16–24.
Calvin, John. *Commentaries on the First Book of Moses, called Genesis.* (1550) Translated by John King. Edinburgh, 1847.
Cancik, Hubert. *Mythische und historische Wahrheit: Interpretationen zu Texten der hethitischen, biblischen und griechischen Historiographie.* SBS 48. Stuttgart: Verlag Katholisches Bibelwerk, 1970.
Carlson, R. A. *David, the Chosen King. A Traditio-Historical Approach to the Second Book of Samuel.* Translated by Eric J. Sharpe and Stanley Rudman. Stockholm: Almqvist & Wiksell, 1964.
———. "David, the Chosen King." *SEÅ* 31 (1966) 122–32.
———. "Deuteronomisk." *SBU,* I (2nd ed., 1962) cols. 413–18.
———. "Élie à l'Horeb." *VT* 19 (1969) 416–39.
———. "Élisée—le successeur d'Élie." *VT* 20 (1970) 385–405.
Carlstadt, Andreas Bodenstein von. *De canonicis Scripturis libellus.* Wittenberg: apud Joannen Viridi Montanum, 1520.
Cassuto, Umberto. *La Questione della Genesi.* Florence: F. Le Monnier, 1934.
Chadwick, H. Munro, and N. Kershaw Chadwick. *The Growth of Literature.* 3 vols. Cambridge: Cambridge University Press, 1932, 1936, 1940.
Chemnitz, Martin. *Examen Consilii Tridentini.* Frankfurt, 1578.
Childs, Brevard S. *Memory and Tradition in Israel.* SBT 37. London: SCM, 1962.
———. "A Study of the Formula 'Until this Day.'" *JBL* 82 (1963) 279–92.

Clark, Warren Malcolm. *The Origin and Development of the Land Promise Theme in the Old Testament.* Diss. Yale 1964.

Clericus, Johannes [Jean Le Clerc]. *Genesis sive Mosis prophetae liber primus.* Amsterdam, 1694.

———. *Sentimens de quelques théologiens de Hollonde sur l'Histoire critique du Vieux Testament, composée par le P. Richard Simon de l'Oratoire.* Amsterdam: Henri Desbordes, 1685.

Coats, George W. *Rebellion in the Wilderness: The Murmuring Motif in the Wilderness Traditions of the Old Testament.* Nashville: Abingdon, 1968.

Conzelmann, Hans. "Fragen an Gerhard von Rad." *EvT* 24 (1964) 113–25.

Cross, Frank Moore, Jr. "The Divine Warrior in Israel's Early Cult." *Biblical Motifs: Origins and Transformations,* 11–30. Edited by A. Altmann. Cambridge, Mass.: Harvard University Press, 1966.

Culley, Robert C. "An Approach to the Problem of Oral Tradition." *VT* 13 (1963) 113–25.

———. *Oral Formulaic Language in the Biblical Psalms.* Near and Middle East Series 4. Toronto: University of Toronto Press, 1967.

Danell, G. A. *Studies in the Name Israel in the Old Testament.* Diss. Uppsala 1946.

Diepold, Peter. *Israels Land.* BWANT 95. Stuttgart: Kohlhammer, 1972.

Diestel, Ludwig. *Geschichte des Alten Testamentes in der christlichen Kirche.* Jena: Mauke, 1869.

Dietrich, Walter. *Prophetie und Geschichte: Eine redaktionsgeschichtliche Untersuchung zum deuteronomistischen Geschichtswerk.* FRLANT 108. Göttingen: Vandenhoeck & Ruprecht, 1972.

Eichrodt, Walther. *Theologie des Alten Testaments,* Teile II und III. 4th ed. Stuttgart: Klotz; Göttingen: Vandenhoeck & Ruprecht, 1961. ET: *Theology of the Old Testament.* Vol. II. Translated by J. A. Baker. Philadelphia: Westminster, 1967.

Eising, Hermann. *Formgeschichtliche Untersuchung zur Jakobserzählung der Genesis.* Emsdetten: Lechte, 1940.

Eissfeldt, Otto. *Einleitung in das Alte Testament: Entstehungsgeschichte des Alten Testaments.* 3rd ed. Tübingen: Mohr Siebeck, 1964. ET: *The Old Testament: An Introduction. The History of the Formation of the Old Testament.* Translated by Peter R. Ackroyd. New York: Harper & Row, 1965.

———. "Zur Überlieferungsgeschichte der Prophetenbücher des Alten Testaments." *TLZ* 73 (1948) cols. 529–34. Also in *Kleine Schriften,* III:55-60. Tübingen: Mohr Siebeck, 1966.

Engnell, Ivan. *The Call of Isaiah: An Exegetical and Comparative Study.* UUÅ 1949:4. Uppsala: Lundequistska; Leipzig: Harrassowitz, 1949.

———. *Critical Essays on the Old Testament.* Translated by John T. Willis, with the collaboration of Helmer Ringgren. London: SPCK, 1970. (= *A Rigid Scrutiny: Critical Essays on the Old Testament.* Nashville: Vanderbilt University Press, 1969.)

———. "The 'Ebed Yahweh Songs and the Suffering Messiah in 'Deutero-Isaiah.'" *BJRL* 31 (1948) 54–93.

———. *Gamla Testamentet: En traditionshistorisk inledning, I.* Stockholm: Svenska Kyrkans Diakonistyrelses Bokförlag, 1945.

———. *Israel and the Law.* SymBU 7. Lund: Gleerup, 1946; 2nd ed., 1954.

———. "Joels bok." *SBU*, I (1st ed., 1948) cols. 1075–77.

———. "'Knowledge' and 'Life' in the Creation Story." VTSup 3 (1955) 103–19.

———. "Methodological Aspects of Old Testament Study." *Congress Volume, Oxford 1959*, VTSup 7 (1960) 13–30.

———. "Profetia och tradition: Några synpunkter på ett gammaltestamentligt centralproblem." *SEÅ* 12 [1947] 110–39. (Also in *SEÅ* 12 [1948] 94–123.)

———. "Samuelsböckerna." *SBU*, II (1st ed., 1952) cols. 1043–49; II (2nd ed., 1963) cols. 867–71.

———. *Studies in Divine Kingship in the Ancient Near East.* Uppsala: Almqvist & Wiksell, 1943. (2nd ed. Oxford: Basil Blackwell, 1967.)

———. "Till frågan om Ebed Jahve-sångerna och den lidande Messias hos 'Deuterojesaja.'" *SEÅ* 10 (1945) 31–65.

———. "Traditionshistorisk metod." *SBU*, II (1st ed., 1952) cols. 1429–37.

Fohrer, Georg. "Altes Testament—'Amphiktyonie' und 'Bund'?" *TLZ* 91 (1966) cols. 801–16, 893–904. Revised and reprinted as pages 84–119 in *Studien zur alttestamentlichen Theologie und Geschichte (1949–1966)*. BZAW 115. Berlin: de Gruyter, 1969.

———. "Neuere Literatur zur alttestamentlichen Prophetie. 2. Teil: Literatur von 1940–1950." *TRu*, NF 20 (1952) 193–271.

———. "Das sogenannte apodiktisch formulierte Recht und der Dekalog." *KD* 11 (1965) 49–74. Revised and reprinted as pages 120–48 in BZAW 115.

———. "Tradition und Interpretation im Alten Testament." *ZAW* 73 (1961) 1–30. Revised and reprinted as pages 54–83 in BZAW 115.

Frankfort, Henri. *Kingship and the Gods: A Study of Ancient Near Eastern Religion as the Integration of Society and Nature.* Chicago: University of Chicago Press, 1948.

Freedman, David Noel. "The Interpretation of Scripture III. On Method in Biblical Studies: The Old Testament." *Int* 17 (1963) 308–18.

Frenzel, Elisabeth. *Stoff-, Motiv- und Symbolforschung.* 3rd ed. Stuttgart: Metzlersche Verlagsbuchhandlung, 1970.

———. *Stoff- und Motivgeschichte*. Grundlagen der Germanistik 3. Berlin: Schmidt, 1966.

Fritz, Volkmar. *Israel in der Wüste: Traditionsgeschichtliche Untersuchung der Wüstenüberlieferungen des Jahwisten*. Marburger Theologische Studien 7. Marburg: Elwert, 1970.

Fuss, Werner. *Die deuteronomistische Pentateuchredaktion in Exodus 3–17*. BZAW 126. Berlin: de Gruyter, 1972.

Gadamer, Hans-Georg. "Tradition. I. Phänomenologisch." *RGG*, VI (3rd ed., 1962) cols. 966–67.

———. *Wahrheit und Methode: Grundzüge einer philosophischen Hermeneutik*. 2nd ed. Tübingen: Mohr Siebeck, 1965.

Gandz, Solomon. "The Dawn of Literature: Prolegomena to a History of Unwritten Literature." *Osiris* 7 (1939) 261–522.

———. "Oral Tradition in the Bible." *Jewish Studies in Memory of George A. Kohut*, 248–69. Edited by S. W. Baron and A. Marx. New York: The Alexander Kohut Memorial Foundation, 1935.

Gelin, A. "La question des 'relectures' bibliques à l'intérieur d'une tradition vivante." *Sacra Pagina*, I:303–315. Edited by J. Coppens, A. Descamps, E. Massaux. BETL 12. Gembloux: J. Duculot, 1959.

Gerhardsson, Birger. *Memory and Manuscript: Oral Tradition and Written Transmission in Rabbinic Judaism and Early Christianity*. Translated by Eric J. Sharpe. ASNU 22. Lund: Gleerup; Copenhagen: Mundsgaard, 1961.

———. "Mündliche und schriftliche Tradition der Prophetenbücher." *TZ* 17 (1961) 216–20. (In Swedish: *SEÅ* 25 [1961] 175–81.)

———. "Tradition." *SBU*, II (2nd ed., 1962) col. 1254.

———. *Tradition and Transmission in Early Christianity*. CN 20. Lund: Gleerup; Copenhagen: Munksgaard, 1964.

Gerstenberger, Erhard. *Wesen und Herkunft des "apodiktischen Rechts."* WMANT 20. Neukirchen: Neukirchener Verlag, 1965.

Gese, Hartmut. "Bemerkungen zur Sinaitradition." *ZAW* 79 (1967) 137–54.

———. "Der Dekalog als Ganzheit betrachtet." *ZTK* 64 (1967) 121–38.

———. "Erwägungen zur Einheit der biblischen Theologie." *ZTK* 67 (1970) 417–36.

———. "Geschichtliches Denken im Alten Orient und im Alten Testament." *ZTK* 55 (1958) 127–45.

———. *Der Verfassungsentwurf des Ezechiel (Kap. 40–48) traditionsgeschichtlich untersucht*. BHT 25. Tübingen: Mohr Siebeck, 1957.

Geyer, Hans-Georg. "Geschichte als theologisches Problem." *EvT* 22 (1962) 92–104.

Gispen, W. H. *Mondelinge Overlevering in het Oude Testament*. Meppel: B. Ten Brink en M. Stenvert & Zoon, 1932.

Gloege, Gerhard. *Offenbarung und Überlieferung: Ein dogmatischer Entwurf.* TF 6. Hamburg-Volksdorf: Herbert Reich, Evangelischer Verlag, 1954.

Golka, Friedemann. "Zur Erforschung der Ätiologien im Alten Testament." *VT* 20 (1970) 90-98.

Gottlieb, Hans. "Die Tradition von David als Hirten." *VT* 17 (1967) 190-200.

Graf, Karl Heinrich. "Richard Simon." *Beiträge zu den theologischen Wissenschaften, in Verbindung mit der theologischen Gesellschaft zu Strassburg,* I, 158-242. Edited by E. Reuss and R. Cunitz. Jena, 1847.

Gray, Edward McQueen. *Old Testament Criticism: Its Rise and Progress from the Second Century to the End of the Eighteenth: A Historical Sketch.* New York: Harper & Brothers, 1923.

Grelot, Pierre. "Tradition as Source and Environment of Scripture." Translated by Theodore L. Westow. *The Dynamism of Biblical Tradition,* 7-28. Concilium 20. New York: Paulist, 1967.

Gressmann, Hugo. *Albert Eichhorn und die Religionsgeschichtliche Schule.* Göttingen: Vandenhoeck & Ruprecht, 1914.

———. *Die Anfänge Israels (von 2. Mose bis Richter und Ruth).* SAT I/2. 2nd ed. Göttingen: Vandenhoeck & Ruprecht, 1922.

———. "Die Aufgaben der alttestamentlichen Forschung." *ZAW* 42 (1924) 1-33.

———. *Mose und seine Zeit: Ein Kommentar zu den Mose-Sagen.* FRLANT 18. Göttingen: Vandenhoeck & Ruprecht, 1913.

———. "Ursprung und Entwicklung der Joseph-Sage." *ΕΥΧΑΡΙΣΤΗΡΙΟΝ (Hermann Gunkel Festschrift),* I, 1-55. Edited by H. Schmidt. FRLANT 36. Göttingen: Vandenhoeck & Ruprecht, 1923.

Grønbæk, Jakob H. "David og Goliat: Et bidrag til forståelsen af legenden i 1 Sam. 17 og dennes placering." *DTT* 28 (1965) 65-79.

———. *Die Geschichte vom Aufstieg Davids (1. Sam. 15 - 2. Sam. 5): Tradition und Komposition.* ATDan 10. Copenhagen: Munksgaard, 1971.

Gross, H. "Motivtransposition als Form- und Traditionsprinzip im Alten Testament." *Exegese und Dogmatik,* 134-52. Edited by H. Vorgrimler. Mainz: Matthias-Grünswald-Verlag, 1962.

———. "'Motivtransposition' als Überlieferungsgeschichtliches Prinzip im Alten Testament." *Sacra Pagina,* I:325-34. Edited by J. Coppens, A. Descamps, and É. Massaux. BETL 12. Gembloux: Duculot, 1959.

Gunkel, Hermann. "Aus Wellhausens neuesten apokalyptischen Forschungen: Einige principielle Erörterungen." *ZWT* 42 (1899) 581-611.

———. "Einleitung." *Die grossen Propheten,* xi-lxxii. By Hans Schmidt. SAT II/2. Göttingen: Vandenhoeck & Ruprecht, 1915.

———. *Genesis, übersetzt und erklärt.* HK I/1. 3rd ed. Göttingen: Vandenhoeck & Ruprecht, 1910. ET of "Einleitung": *The Legends of Genesis: The Bibli-*

cal Saga and History. Translated by W. H. Carruth. New York: Schocken, (1901) 1964.

———. Schöpfung und Chaos in Urzeit und Endzeit: Eine religionsgeschichtliche Untersuchung über Gen 1 und Ap Joh 12. Mit Beiträgen von Heinrich Zimmern. Göttingen: Vandenhoeck & Ruprecht, 1895.

———.Die Urgeschichte und die Patriarchen. SAT I/1. 2nd ed. Göttingen: Vandenhoeck & Ruprecht, 1921.

———. Review of Max Reischle's *Theologie und Religionsgeschichte* (Tübingen 1904), *DLZ* 1904, cols. 1100–1110.

Gunneweg, Antonius H. J. *Mündliche und schriftliche Tradition der vorexilischen Prophetenbücher als Problem der neueren Prophetenforschung.* FRLANT 73. Göttingen: Vandenhoeck & Ruprecht, 1959.

———. "Traditionsgeschichtliche Forschung." *BHH*, III (1966) cols. 2018–20.

Güterbock, Hans Gustav. "Die historischen Traditionen und ihre literarische Gestaltung bei Babyloniern und Hethitern bis 1200." *ZA* 42 (1934) 1–91; 44 (1938) 45–149.

Guthrie, H. H., Jr. *Israel's Sacred Songs: A Study of Dominant Themes.* New York: Seabury, 1966.

Güttgemanns, Erhardt. *Offene Fragen zur Formgeschichte des Evangeliums: Eine methodologische Skizze der Grundlagenproblematik der Form- und Redaktionsgeschichte.* BEvT 54. Munich: Kaiser, 1970.

Haag, Herbert. "Der Dekalog in der Verkündigung." *Anima* 19,2 (1964) 120–28.

Haldar, Alfred. *Associations of Cult Prophets among the Ancient Semites.* Uppsala: Almqvist & Wiksell, 1945.

———. *The Notion of the Desert in Sumero-Accadian and West-Semitic Religions.* UUÅ 1950:3. Uppsala: Lundequistska bokhandeln, 1950.

———. "On the Problem of Tradition in Ancient Semitic Religious Literature." *MO* 34 (1946) 1–17.

———.*Studies in the Book of Nahum.* UUÅ 1946:7. Uppsala: Lundequistska bokhandeln, 1947.

Hasel, Gerhard F. *The Remnant: The History and Theology of the Remnant Idea from Genesis to Isaiah.* Andrews University Monographs, 5. Berrien Springs, Mich.: Andrews University Press, 1972.

Heinemann, Günter. *Untersuchungen zum apodiktischen Recht.* Diss. Hamburg 1958.

Hempel, Johannes. "Alttestamentliche Theologie in protestantischer Sicht heute." *BO* 15 (1958) 206–14.

———. "The Contents of the Literature." *Record and Revelation: Essays on the Old Testament by Members of the Society for Old Testament Study,* 45–73. Edited by H. Wheeler Robinson. Oxford: Clarendon, 1938.

———. "The Forms of Oral Tradition." in *Record and Revelation. Essays on the Old Testament by Members of the Society for Old Testament Study*, 28–44 Edited by H. Wheeler Robinson. Oxford: Clarendon, 1938.
Henry, Marie-Louise. *Prophet und Tradition: Versuch einer Problemstellung.* BZAW 116. Berlin: de Gruyter, 1969.
Herberg, Will. "Five Meanings of the Word 'Historical.'" *The Christian Scholar* 47 (1964) 327–30.
Herrmann, Siegfried. "Mose." *EvT* 28 (1968) 301–28.
———. "Das Werden Israels." *TLZ* 87 (1962) cols. 561–74.
Hertzberg, Hans Wilhelm. "Die Nachgeschichte alttestamentlicher Texte innerhalb des Alten Testaments." *Werden und Wesen des Alten Testaments*, 110–21. Edited by P. Volz, F. Stummer, and J. Hempel. BZAW 66. Berlin: Töpelmann, 1936. Also in *Beiträge zur Traditionsgeschichte und Theologie des Alten Testaments*, 69–80. Göttingen: Vandenhoeck & Ruprecht, 1962.
Hesse, Franz. "Bewährt sich eine 'Theologie der Heilstatsachen' am Alten Testament? Zum Verhältnis von Faktum und Deutung." *ZAW* 81 (1969) 1–18.
———. "Die Erforschung der Geschichte Israels als theologische Aufgabe." *KD* 4 (1958) 1–19.
———. "Kerygma oder geschichtliche Wirklichkeit? Kritische Fragen zu Gerhard von Rads 'Theologie des Alten Testaments, I. Teil.'" *ZTK* 57 (1960) 17–26.
Hobbes, Thomas. *Leviathan, or the Matter, Forme, and Power of a Commonwealth Ecclesiastical and Civil.* London, 1651.
Holm-Nielsen, Svend. "Den gammeltestamentlige salmetradition." *DTT* 18 (1955) 135–48, 193–215.
Honecker, Martin. "Zum Verständnis der Geschichte in Gerhard von Rads Theologie des Alten Testaments." *EvT* 23 (1963) 143–68.
Honko, Lauri. *Geisterglaube in Ingermanland.* Helsinki: Suomalainen Tiedeakatemia, 1962.
Hornig, Gottfried. *Die Anfänge der historisch-kritischen Theologie: Johann Salomo Semlers Schriftverständnis und seine Stellung zu Luther.* FSTR 8. Göttingen: Vandenhoeck & Ruprecht, 1961.
Humbert, P. "Le problème du livre de Nahoum." *RHPR* 12 (1932) 1–15.
Hvidberg, Flemming. "The Canaanite Background of Gen. I–III." *VT* 10 (1960) 285–94.
Hylander, Ivar. "Den gammaltestamentlige litterärkritikens kris: Ett bidrag till traditionsproblemet i nyare religionsvetenskaplig forskning." *SEÅ* 2 (1937) 16–64.
———. *Der literarische Samuel-Saul-Komplex (I. Sam. 1–15) traditionsgeschichtlich untersucht.* Uppsala: Almqvist & Wiksell; Leipzig: Harrassowitz, 1932.

———. "Det profetiska ordet." *SEÅ* 4 (1939) 5–12.
———. "Tradition och tolkning." *SEÅ* 5 (1940) 9–19.
Hylmö, Gunnar. *Gamla Testamentets Litteraturhistoria*. Lund: Gleerup, 1938.
Ilgen, Karl David. *Die Urkunden des Jerusalemischen Tempelarchivs in ihrer Urgestalt, als Beitrag zur Berichtigung der Geschichte der Religion und Politik: Erster Theil. Die Urkunden des ersten Buchs von Moses*. Halle: Hemmerde & Schwetschte, 1798.
Jansma, Taeke. "Inquiry into the Hebrew Text and the Ancient Versions of Zechariah ix–xiv." *OtSt* 7 (1950) 1–142.
Jensen, Kjeld. "Om de mosaiske Lovskrifters Alder." *DTT* 5 (1942) 1–14.
Jepsen, Alfred. "Beiträge zur Auslegung und Geschichte des Dekalogs." *ZAW* 79 (1967) 277–304.
———. *Die Quellen des Königsbuches*. Halle an der Saale: VEB Max Niemeyer Verlag, 1953.
———. "Von den Aufgaben der alttestamentlichen Textkritik." *VTSup* 9 (1963) 332–41.
———. "Zur Überlieferungsgeschichte der Vätergestalten." *Alt-Festschrift*, 139–55. WZ Leipzig 3, Gesellschafts- und sprachwiss. Reihe (1953/54).
Jirku, Anton. *Die älteste Geschichte Israels im Rahmen lehrhafter Darstellungen*. Leipzig: Deichert'sche Verlagsbuchhandlung Werner Scholl, 1917.
Johnson, Aubrey Rodway. *The Cultic Prophet in Ancient Israel*. Cardiff: University of Wales Press Board, 1944.
Jones, Douglas. "The Traditio of the Oracles of Isaiah of Jerusalem." *ZAW* 67 (1955) 226–46.
Jousse, Marcel. *Études de psychologie linguistique: Le Style oral rythmique et mnémotechnique chez les Verbo-moteurs*. Archives de philosophie, Volume II, Cahier IV. Paris: Beauchesne, 1925.
Kaiser, Otto. "Die alttestamentliche Exegese." *Einführung in die exegetischen Methoden*, 9–37. By O. Kaiser, W. G. Kümmel, and G. Adam. 4th ed. Munich: Kaiser, 1969.
———. *Einleitung in das Alte Testament: Eine Einführung in ihre Ergebnisse und Probleme*. Gütersloh: Gütersloher Verlagshaus Gerd Mohn, 1969.
Kapelrud, Arvid S. *Baal in the Ras Shamra Texts*. Copenhagen: Gad, 1952.
———. *Central Ideas in Amos*. SNVAO, II. Hist.-Filos. Kl., 1956, No. 4. Oslo: Aschehoug, 1956.
———. "Cult and Prophetic Words." *ST* 4 (1950) 5–12.
———. "The Date of the Priestly Code (P)." *ASTI* 3 (1964) 58–64.
———. "Forskningen omkring Ezra og Ezra-boken." *NTT* 43 (1942) 148–65.
———. *Joel Studies*. UUÅ 1948:4. Uppsala: Lundequistska Bokhandeln, 1948.
———. "King and Fertility: A Discussion of II Sam. 21:1–14." *NTT* 56 (1955) 113–22.

———. "König David und die Söhne des Saul." *ZAW* 67 (1955) 198–205.
———. "Pentateuch-problemer." *NTT* 56 (1955) 185–201.
———. *The Question of Authorship in the Ezra-Narrative: A Lexical Investigation*. SNVAO, II. Hist.-Filos. Kl., 1944, No. 1. Oslo: Dybwad, 1944.
———. *The Ras Shamra Discoveries and the Old Testament*. Translated by G. W. Anderson. Oxford: Blackwell, 1965.
———. "The Role of the Cult in Old Israel." *The Bible in Modern Scholarship*, 44–56. Edited by J. Philip Hyatt. Nashville: Abingdon, 1965.
———. "Some Recent Points of View on the Time and Origin of the Decalogue." *ST* 18 (1964) 81–90.
———. *The Violent Goddess: Anat in the Ras Shamra Texts*. Oslo: Universitetsforlaget, 1969.
Kaufmann, Yehezkel. *The Biblical Account of the Conquest of Palestine*. Translated by M. Dagut. Jerusalem: Magnes Press, Hebrew University, 1953.
———. "Probleme der israelitisch-jüdischen Religionsgeschichte." *ZAW* 48 (1930) 23–43.
Kellermann, Ulrich. *Nehemia: Quellen, Überlieferung und Geschichte*. BZAW 102. Berlin: Töpelmann, 1967.
Kent, Charles Foster. *Narratives of the Beginnings of Hebrew History, from the Creation to the Establishment of the Hebrew Kingdom*. New York: Charles Scribner's Sons, 1904.
Klatt, Werner, ed. "Ein Brief von Hermann Gunkel über Albert Eichhorn an Hugo Gressmann." *ZTK* 66 (1969) 1–6.
———. "Die 'Eigentümlichkeit' der israelitischen Religion in der Sicht von Hermann Gunkel." *EvT* 28 (1968) 153–60.
———. *Hermann Gunkel: Zu seiner Theologie der Religionsgeschichte und zur Entstehung der formgeschichtlichen Methode*. FRLANT 100. Göttingen: Vandenhoeck & Ruprecht, 1969.
Klostermann, August. *Der Pentateuch: Beiträge zu seinem Verständnis und seiner Entstehungsgeschichte*. Leipzig: Deichert, 1893; Neue Folge, 1907.
Knierim, Rolf. *Die Hauptbegriffe für Sünde im Alten Testament*. 2nd ed. Gütersloh: Gütersloher Verlagshaus Gerd Mohn, 1967.
Koch, Klaus. *Was ist Formgeschichte? Neue Wege der Bibelexegese*. 2nd ed. Neukirchen: Neukirchener Verlag, 1967. ET: *The Growth of the Biblical Tradition: The Form-Critical Method*. Translated by S. M. Cupitt. New York: Charles Scribner's Sons, 1969.
Kraus, Hans-Joachim. *Die Biblische Theologie: Ihre Geschichte und Problematik*. Neukirchen: Neukirchener Verlag, 1970.
———. "Der gegenwärtige Stand der Forschung am Alten Testament." *Die Freiheit des Evangeliums und die Ordnung der Gesellschaft*, 103–132. BEvT 15. Munich: Kaiser, 1952.

———. *Geschichte der historisch-kritischen Erforschung des Alten Testaments.* 2nd ed. Neukirchen-Vluyn: Neukirchener Verlag, 1969.
———. "Gespräch mit Martin Buber: Zur jüdischen und christlichen Auslegung des Alten Testaments." *EvT* 12 (1952/53) 59–77.
———. "Gilgal: Ein Beitrag zur Kultusgeschichte Israels." *VT* 1 (1951) 181–99.
———. *Gottesdienst in Israel: Grundriss einer Geschichte des alttestamentlichen Gottesdienstes.* 2nd ed. Munich: Chr. Kaiser Verlag, 1962. ET: *Worship in Israel: A Cultic History of the Old Testament.* Translated by Geoffrey Buswell. Richmond: John Knox, 1965.
———. *Psalmen.* 2 vols. BKAT 15. 3rd ed. Neukirchen-Vluyn: Neukirchener Verlag, 1966.
———. "Zur Geschichte des Überlieferungsbegriffs in der alttestamentlichen Wissenschaft." *EvT* 16 (1956) 371–387. Also in *Biblisch-theologische Aufsätze*, 278–295. Neukirchen-Vluyn: Neukirchener Verlag, 1972.
Kuhl, Curt. "Überlieferungsgeschichtliche Forschung." *EKL*, III (1959) cols. 1525–30.
Læssøe, J. "Literacy and Oral Tradition in Ancient Mesopotamia." *Studia Orientalia Ioanni Pedersen ... dictata*, 205–218. Copenhagen: Munksgaard, 1953.
Lamarche, Paul. *Zacharie IX–XIV: Structure littéraire et messianisme.* Études bibliques. Paris: Gabalda, 1961.
Lande, Irene. *Formelhafte Wendungen der Umgangssprache im Alten Testament.* Leiden: Brill, 1949.
Lapide, Cornelius a [van der Steen]. *Commentaria in Pentateuchum Mosis.* Antwerp: apud Iacobum Meursium, 1681. (First published in 1616.)
Lindblom, Johannes. *Boken om Job och hans lidande.* Lund: Gleerup, 1940; 2nd ed., 1966.
———. "La composition du livre de Job." *Kungliga humanistiska vetenskapssamfundet i Lund: Årsberättelse 1944–1945*, III:111–205. Lund: Gleerup, 1945.
———. "Einige Grundfragen der alttestamentlichen Wissenschaft." *Festschrift für Alfred Bertholet*, 325–37. Tübingen: Mohr Siebeck, 1950.
———. *Gamla testamentets skrifter.* Stockholm: Hugo Gebers Förlag, 1910.
———. *Hosea literarisch untersucht.* AAAbo 1927: Humaniora, V:2. Åbo: Åbo Akademi, 1928.
———. "Joblegenden traditionshistoriskt undersökt." *SEÅ* 5 (1940) 29–42.
———. *Die literarische Gattung der prophetischen Literatur: Eine literargeschichtliche Untersuchung zum Alten Testament.* UUÅ 1924, Teologi 1. Uppsala: Lundequist, 1924.
———. *Micha literarisch untersucht.* AAAbo 1929: Humaniora, VI:2. Åbo: Åbo Akademi, 1929.

———. *Profetismen i Israel*. Stockholm: Svenska Kyrkans Diakonistyrelses Bokförlag, 1934.
———. *Prophecy in Ancient Israel*. Oxford: Basil Blackwell, 1962.
———. *A Study on the Immanuel Section in Isaiah: Is. VII,1–IX, 6*. Lund: Gleerup, 1958.
Lindhagen, Curt. *The Servant Motif in the Old Testament: A Preliminary Study to the 'Ebed-Yahweh Problem' in Deutero-Isaiah*. Uppsala: Lundequist, 1950.
Lods, Adolphe. *Jean Astruc et la critique biblique au XVIIIe siècle. Avec une notice biographique par Paul Alphandéry*. RHPR, Cahiers, No. 11. Strasbourg and Paris: Librairie Istra, 1924.
———. "Un précurseur allemand de Jean Astruc: Henning Bernhard Witter." *ZAW* 43 (1925) 134–35.
———. "Le rôle de la tradition orale dans la formation des récits de l'Ancien Testament." *RHR* 88 (1923) 51–64.
Lohr, C. H. "Oral Techniques in the Gospel of Matthew." *CBQ* 23 (1961) 403–35.
Long, Burke O. *The Problem of Etiological Narrative in the Old Testament*. BZAW 108. Berlin: Töpelmann, 1968.
Lord, Albert Bates. *The Singer of Tales*. Harvard Studies in Comparative Literature, 24. Cambridge, Mass.: Harvard University Press, 1960.
Lubsczyk, Hans. *Der Auszug Israels aus Ägypten: Seine theologische Bedeutung in prophetischer und priesterlicher Überlieferung*. ETS 11. Leipzig: St. Benno-Verlag, 1963.
Lutz, Hanns-Martin. *Jahwe, Jerusalem und die Völker: Zur Vorgeschichte von Sach 12,1–8 und 14,1–5*. WMANT 27. Neukirchen-Vluyn: Neukirchener Verlag, 1968.
Maag, V. "Historische oder ausserhistorische Begründung alttestamentlicher Theologie." *SThU* 29 (1959) 6–18.
Margival, H. *Essai sur Richard Simon et la critique biblique au XVIIe siècle*. Repr., Genève, 1970. (First appeared as articles in *Révue d'histoire et de littérature religieuses*, 1–5 [Paris 1896–1900].)
Masius, Andreas. *Josuae imperatoris historia illustrata atque explicata*. Antwerp, 1574.
Mendenhall, George E. *Law and Covenant in Israel and the Ancient Near East*. Pittsburg: The Biblical Colloquium, 1955.
Merendino, Rosario Pius. *Das deuteronomische Gesetz: Eine literarkritische, gattungs- und überlieferungsgeschichtliche Untersuchung zu Dt 12–26*. BBB 31. Bonn: Hanstein, 1969.
Metzger, Martin. *Die Paradieseserzählung: Die Geschichte ihrer Auslegung von J. Clericus bis W. M. L. de Wette*. Abhandlungen zur Philosophie, Psychologie und Pädagogik, 16. Bonn: Bouvier, 1959.

Michelet, S., S. Mowinckel, and N. Messel. *Det Gamle Testamente: II, De tidligere profeter (d. e. de historiske böker)*. Translated by S. Michelet and S. Mowinckel. Oslo: Aschehoug, 1935.

———. *Det Gamle Testamente: III, De senere profeter*. Translated by S. Mowinckel and N. Messel. Oslo: Aschehoug, 1944.

Mildenberger, Friedrich. *Gottes Tat im Wort: Erwägungen zur alttestamentlichen Hermeneutik als Frage nach der Einheit der Testamente*. Gütersloh: Gütersloher Verlagshaus Gerd Mohn, 1964.

———. *Die vordeuteronomistische Saul-Davidüberlieferung*. Diss. Tübingen 1962.

Moe, Moltke. "Episke Grundlove." *Edda* 2 (1914) 1–16, 233–49; 4 (1915) 85–126.

Möhlenbrink, Kurt. "Die Landnahmesagen des Buches Josua." *ZAW* 56 (1938) 238–68.

Moor, J. C. de. *Mondelinge Overlevering in Mesopotamië, Ugarit, en Israël*. Leiden: Brill, 1965.

Mowinckel, Sigmund. *Le Décalogue*. Paris: Alean, 1927.

———. *Ezra den skriftlærde: Studier til den jödiske menighets historie og litteratur*. Kristiania (Oslo) 1916.

———. "Hellighet og guddommelighet i det gamle Israel: Js. Pedersens Israel III–IV." *NTT* 38 (1937) 1–72.

———. *Hvordan Det gamle testament er blitt til (Israelittiskjödisk litteraturhistorie)*. Oslo: Universitetsforlaget, 1934; 2nd ed., 1968.

———. *Jesaja-disiplene: Profetien fra Jesaja til Jeremia*. Oslo: Aschehoug, 1926.

———. "Kan forholdet mellem Det Gamle og Det Nye Testamente uttrykkes som profeti og oppfyllelse?" *NTT* 62 (1961) 223–37.

———. "Komposisjonen av Jesajaboken kap. 1–39." *NTT* 44 (1943) 159–71.

———. "Om tilblivelsen av profetbøkene." *NTT* 39 (1938) 318–20. (Review of H. Birkeland's *Zum hebräischen Traditionswesen*. Oslo 1938.)

———. "Oppkomsten av profetlitteraturen." *NTT* 43 (1942) 65–111.

———. "Oral Tradition." *IDB*: IV (1962) 683–85.

———. *Profeten Jesaja*. Oslo: Aschehoug, 1925.

———. *Prophecy and Tradition: The Prophetic Books in the Light of the Study of the Growth and History of the Tradition*. ANVAO, II. Hist.-Filos. Kl., 1946, No. 3. Oslo: Dybwad, 1946.

———. *Psalmenstudien III: Kultprophetie und prophetische Psalmen*. SNVAO, II. Hist.-Filos. Kl., 1922, No. 1. Kristiania (Oslo): Dybwad, 1923.

———. *Statholderen Nehemia: Studier til den jödiske menighets historie og litteratur*. Kristiania (Oslo): Norlis, 1916.

———. *Studien zu dem Buche Ezra-Nehemia*. 3 vols. SNVAO, N.S. II. Hist.-Phil. Kl., No. 3, 5, 7. Oslo: Universitetsforlaget, 1964–1965.

———. *Tetrateuch—Pentateuch—Hexateuch: Die Berichte über die Landnahme in den drei altisraelitischen Geschichtswerken.* BZAW 90. Berlin: Töpelmann, 1964.

———. *Zur Frage nach dokumentarischen Quellen in Josua 13-19.* ANVAO, II. Hist.-Filos. Kl., 1946, No. 1. Oslo: Dybwad, 1946.

Muilenburg, James. "Form Criticism and Beyond." *JBL* 88 (1969) 1-18.

Murtonen, A. "The Fixation in Writing of Various Parts of the Pentateuch." *VT* 3 (1953) 46-53.

Nachtigal, Johann Christoph [pseudonym: Otmar]. "Fragmente über die allmählige Bildung der den Israeliten heiligen Schriften, besonders der sogenannten historischen." *Magazin für Religionsphilosophie, Exegese und Kirchengeschichte.* Edited by Henke. vol. 2:433-523 (Helmstädt, 1794); vol. 4:1-36, 329-370 (Helmstädt, 1795).

Nicholson, E. W. *Deuteronomy and Tradition.* Philadelphia: Fortress, 1967.

Nielsen, Eduard. "Deuterojesaja: Erwägungen zur Formkritik, Traditions- und Redaktionsgeschichte." *VT* 20 (1970) 190-205.

———. "The Levites in Ancient Israel." *ASTI* 3 (1964) 16-27.

———. *Oral Tradition: A Modern Problem in Old Testament Introduction.* Translated by Asta Lange. SBT 11. London: SCM, 1954. (Danish in *DTT* 13 [1950] 129-45; 15 [1952] 19-37, 88-106, 129-46.)

———. *Shechem: A Traditio-Historical Investigation.* 2nd ed. Copenhagen: Gad, 1959.

———. *Die Zehn Gebote: Eine traditionsgeschichtliche Skizze.* Translated by H.-M. Junghans. ATDan 8. Copenhagen: Munksgaard, 1965. ET: *The Ten Commandments in New Perspective: A Traditio-Historical Approach.* Translated by D. J. Bourke. SBT 2/7. London: SCM, 1968.

North, C. R. "Living Issues in Biblical Scholarship: The Place of Oral Tradition in the Growth of the Old Testament." *ExpTim* 61(1949/50) 292-96.

———. "Oral Tradition and Written Documents." *ExpTim* 66 (1954/55) 39.

Noth, Martin. "As One Historian to Another." *Int* 15 (1961) 61-66.

———. "Der Beitrag der Archäologie zur Geschichte Israels." *VTSup* 7 (1960) 262-82. Also in *Aufsätze zur biblischen Landes- und Altertumskunde*, 34-51. Edited by H. W. Wolff. I. Neukirchen-Vluyn: Neukirchener Verlag, 1971.

———. *Das Buch Josua.* HAT I,7. Tübingen: Mohr, 1938; 2nd ed., 1953.

———. *Geschichte Israels.* 2nd ed., Göttingen: Vandenhoeck & Ruprecht, 1954. ET: *The History of Israel.* Translated by Stanley Godman. London: Adam & Charles Black, 1958.

———. "Die Gesetze im Pentateuch: Ihre Voraussetzungen und ihr Sinn." SGK, Geisteswiss. Kl. 17. Halle: Niemeyer, 1940. Also in *Gesammelte Studien zum Alten Testament*, 3rd ed., 9-141. TB 6. Munich: Kaiser, 1966.

ET: "The Laws in the Pentateuch: Their Assumptions and Meaning." *The Laws in the Pentateuch and Other Studies*, 1–107. Translated by D. R. Ap-Thomas. Edinburgh: Oliver & Boyd, 1966.

———. "Gott, König, Volk im Alten Testament: Eine methodologische Auseinandersetzung mit einer gegenwärtigen Forschungsrichtung." *ZTK* 47 (1950) 157–91. Also in *Ges. Stud.*, 188–229. ET: "God, King, and Nation in the Old Testament." *The Laws in the Pentateuch and Other Studies*, 145–78. Translated by D. R. Ap-Thomas. Edinburgh: Oliver & Boyd, 1966.

———. "Grundsätzliches zur geschichtlichen Deutung archäologischer Befunde auf dem Boden Palästinas." *PJ* 34 (1938) 7–22. Also in *Aufsätze*, I:3–16.

———. "Hat die Bibel doch recht?" *Festschrift für Günther Dehn*, 7–22. Edited by W. Schneemelcher. Neukirchen Kreis Moers: Neukirchener Verlag, 1957. Also in *Aufsätze*, I:17–33.

———. *Das System der zwölf Stämme Israels*. BWANT IV/1. Stuttgart: Kohlhammer, 1930. 2nd ed., Darmstadt: Wissenschaftliche Buchgesellschaft, 1966.

———. *Überlieferungsgeschichte des Pentateuch*. 1st ed. Stuttgart: Kohlhammer, 1948; 3rd ed., 1966. ET: *A History of Pentateuchal Traditions*. Translated by with an introduction by B. W. Anderson. Englewood Cliffs, N.J.: Prentice-Hall, 1972.

———. *Überlieferungsgeschichtliche Studien: Die sammelnden und bearbeitenden Geschichtswerke im Alten Testament*. 3rd ed. Tübingen: Niemeyer, 1967. (1st ed., 1943.)

———. "Überlieferungsgeschichtliches zur zweiten Hälfte des Josuabuches." *Alttestamentliche Studien, Friedrich Nötscher zum 60: Geburtstag gewidmet*, 152–67. BBB 1. Bonn: Hanstein, 1950.

———. "Die Vergegenwärtigung des Alten Testaments in der Verkündigung." *EvT* 12 (1952/53) 6–17. Also in *Probleme alttestamentlicher Hermeneutik*, 54–68. Edited by C. Westermann. TB 11. Munich: Kaiser, 1960. ET: "The 'Re-presentation' of the Old Testament in Proclamation." Translated by James L. Mays, *Essays on Old Testament Hermeneutics*, 76–88. Edited by C. Westermann and James L. Mays. Richmond,: John Knox, 1963.

———. *Die Welt des Alten Testaments: Einführung in die Grenzgebiete der alttestamentlichen Wissenschaft*. SamT, II/3. 4th ed. Berlin: Töpelmann, 1962. ET: *The Old Testament World*. Translated by Victor I. Gruhn. London: Adam & Charles Black, 1966.

Nübel, Hans-Ulrich. *Davids Aufstieg in der Frühe israelitischer Geschichtsschreibung*. Diss. Bonn 1959.

Nyberg, Henrik Samuel. *Irans forntida religioner.* Stockholm: Svenska Kyrkans Diakonistyrelses Bokförlag, 1937. (German: *Die Religionen des alten Iran.* Translated by H. H. Schaeder. MVAG 43. Leipzig: Hinrichs, 1938.)

———. "Koraḥ's uppror (Num. 16f.): Ett bidrag till frågan om traditionshistorisk metod." *SEÅ* 12 (1947) 230–52. (Also in *SEÅ* 12 [1948] 214–36.)

———. "Die schwedischen Beiträge zur alttestamentlichen Forschung in diesem Jahrhundert." *Congress Volume, Uppsala 1971,* VTSup 22 (1972) 1–10.

———. *Studien zum Hoseabuche: Zugleich ein Beitrag zur Klärung des Problems der alttestamentlichen Textkritik.* UUÅ 1935:6. Uppsala: Lundequistska Bokhandeln, 1935.

———. "Das textkritische Problem des Alten Testaments, am Hoseabuche demonstriert." *ZAW* 52 (1934) 241–54.

Olrik, Axel. "Episke love i folkedigtningen." *DS* 1908, pp. 69–89. GT: "Epische Gesetze der Volksdichtung." *ZAL* 51 (1909) 1–12. ET: "Epic Laws of Folk Narrative." *The Study of Folklore,* 129–41. Edited by Alan Dundes. Englewood Cliffs, N.J.: Prentice-Hall, 1965.

Orlinsky, H. M. "The Tribal System of Israel and Related Groups in the Period of the Judges." *OrAnt* 1 (1962) 11–20.

Östborn, Gunnar. *Cult and Canon: A Study in the Canonization of the Old Testament.* UUÅ 1950:10. Uppsala: Lundequist; Leipzig: Harrassowitz, 1950.

———. *Tōrā in the Old Testament: A Semantic Study.* Lund: Ohlssons, 1945.

———. *Yahweh's Words and Deeds: A Preliminary Study into the Old Testament Presentation of History.* UUÅ 1951:7. Uppsala: Lundequist; Wiesbaden: Harrassowitz, 1951.

Ottosson, Magnus. *Gilead: Tradition and History.* ConBOT 3. Lund: Gleerup, 1969.

Otzen, Benedikt. *Studien über Deuterosacharja.* Copenhagen: Munksgaard, 1964.

Pannenberg, Wolfhart. "Heilsgeschehen und Geschichte." *KD* 5 (1959) 218–37 and 259–88. (Shortened version of first part in *Probleme alttestamentlicher Hermeneutik,* 295–318. Edited by C. Westermann. TB 11. Munich: Kaiser, 1960. ET: "Redemptive Event and History." Translated by Shirley Guthrie, *Essays on Old Testament Hermeneutics,* 314–35. Edited by C. Westermann and James L. Mays. Richmond: John Knox, 1963.)

———. "Historieteologi og overleveringshistorie." *NTT* 66 (1965) 137–51.

———. "Kerygma und Geschichte." *Studien zur Theologie der alttestamentlichen Überlieferungen,* 129–40. Edited by R. Rendtorff and K. Koch. Neukirchen Kreis Moers: Neukirchener Verlag, 1961.

Pannenberg, Wolfhart, H. Rendtorff, U. Wilckens, and T. Rendtorff. *Offenbarung als Geschichte*. KD Beiheft 1. 3rd ed. Göttingen: Vandenhoeck & Ruprecht, 1965. ET: *Revelation as History*. Translated by David Granskou. New York: Macmillan, 1968.

Pascal, Blaise. *Pensées*. Port-Royal, 1670.

Pedersen, Johannes. *Den arabiske bog*. Copenhagen: Fischers, 1946.

———. "Die Auffassung vom Alten Testament." *ZAW* 49 (1931) 161–81. (Also as: "Opfattelsen af det gamle testamente." *NTT* 32 [1931] 137–62.)

———.*Israel: Its Life and Culture*. London: Geoffrey Cumberlege, Oxford University Press; Copenhagen: Povl Branner, I–II, 1926 (in Danish: 1920); III–IV, 1940 (in Danish: 1934).

———. "Passahfest und Passahlegende." *ZAW* 52 (1934) 161–75.

Pereira, Bento. *Tomus I–IV commentariorum et disputationum in Genesim*. Lugduni (Lyons), 1594–1600.

Perlitt, Lothar. *Vatke und Wellhausen: Geschichtsphilosophische Voraussetzungen und historiographische Motive für die Darstellung der Religion und Geschichte Israels durch Wilhelm Vatke und Julius Wellhausen*. BZAW 94. Berlin: Töpelmann, 1965.

Peyrère, Isaak de la. *Systema Theologicum, ex Praeadamitarum Hypothesi*. Pars prima. 1655; repr., Hildesheim: Olms. ET: *Man before Adam*. London 1656; repr., Hildesheim: Olms.

Pfeiffer, Robert H. Review of Mowinckel's *Prophecy and Tradition*, *JBL* 66 (1947) 480–81.

Ploeg, J. van der. "Le rôle de la tradition orale dans la transmission du texte de l'Ancien Testament." *RB* 54 (1947) 5–41.

Plöger, Otto. *Theokratie und Eschatologie*. WMANT 2. 2nd ed. Neukirchen Kreis Moers: Neukirchener Verlag, 1962. ET: *Theocracy and Eschatology*. Translated by S. Rudman. Richmond: John Knox, 1968.

Porteous, Norman W. "The Prophets and the Problem of Continuity." *Israel's Prophetic Heritage: Essays in Honor of James Muilenburg*, 11–25. Edited by Bernhard W. Anderson and Walter Harrelson. New York: Harper, 1962.

Porter, J. R. "Pre-Islamic Arabic Historical Traditions and the Early Historical Narratives of the Old Testament." *JBL* 87 (1968) 17–26.

Procksch, Otto. *Die Genesis übersetzt und erklärt*. KAT 1. 3rd ed. Leipzig: Deichert, 1924.

Quell, Gottfried. "Der Kultprophet." *TLZ* 81 (1956) cols. 401–4.

Rad, Gerhard von. "Antwort auf Conzelmanns Fragen." *EvT* 24 (1964) 388–94.

———. *Deuteronomium-Studien*. FRLANT 58. 2nd ed. Göttingen: Vandenhoeck & Ruprecht, 1948. ET: *Studies in Deuteronomy*. SBT 9. Translated by David Stalker. London: SCM, 1953.

———. *Das erste Buch Mose: Genesis, übersetzt und erklärt.* ATD 2–4. 5th ed. Göttingen: Vandenhoeck & Ruprecht, 1958; 9th ed., 1972. ET: *Genesis: A Commentary.* Rev. ed. Translated by John H. Marks. Philadelphia: Westminster, 1972.

———. "Das formgeschichtliche Problem des Hexateuch." BWANT IV/26. Stuttgart: Kohlhammer, 1938. Also in *Gesammelte Studien zum Alten Testament*, 9–86. 3rd ed. Munich: Kaiser, 1965. ET: "The Form-Critical Problem of the Hexateuch." *The Problem of the Hexateuch and Other Essays*, 1–78. Translated by E. W. Trueman Dicken. Edinburgh: Oliver & Boyd, 1966.

———. "Das hermeneutische Problem im Buche Genesis." *VF* 1942/46 (1946/47) 43–51.

———. "Hexateuch oder Pentateuch?" *VF* 1947/48 (1949/50) 52–56.

———. "Literarkritische und überlieferungsgeschichtliche Forschung im Alten Testament." *VF* 1947/48 (1949/50) 172–94.

———. "Offene Fragen im Umkreis einer Theologie des Alten Testaments." *TLZ* 88 (1963) cols. 401–16. ET: *Old Testament Theology*, II:410–29. Translated by D. M. G. Stalker. Edinburgh: Oliver and Boyd, 1966.

———. Review of Martin Noth's *Geschichte Israels*, 2nd ed., 1953. *VF* 1953/55 (1956) 129–34.

———. *Theologie des Alten Testaments. I: Die Theologie der geschichtlichen Überlieferungen Israels.* (1st ed., 1957.) 5th ed. Munich: Kaiser, 1966. ET: *Old Testament Theology. I: The Theology of Israel's Historical Traditions.* Translated by D. M. G. Stalker. Edinburgh: Oliver & Boyd, 1962.

———. *Theologie des Alten Testaments. II: Die Theologie der prophetischen Überlieferungen Israels.* (1st ed., 1960.) 5th ed. Munich: Kaiser, 1968. ET: *Old Testament Theology. II: The Theology of Israel's Prophetic Traditions.* Translated by D. M. G. Stalker. Edinburgh: Oliver & Boyd, 1965.

———. "Verheissenes Land und Jahwes Land im Hexateuch." *ZDPV* 66 (1943) 191–204. Also in *Ges. Stud.*, 87–100. ET: "The Promised Land and Yahweh's Land in the Hexateuch." *The Problem of the Hexateuch and Other Essays*, 79–93. Translated by E. W. Trueman Dicken. Edinburgh: Oliver & Boyd, 1966.

———. *Weisheit in Israel.* Neukirchen-Vluyn: Neukirchener Verlag, 1970. ET: *Wisdom in Israel.* Translated by J. D. Martin. Nashville: Abingdon, 1973.

Rast, Walter E. *Tradition History and the Old Testament.* Guides to Biblical Scholarship, Old Testament Series. Edited by J. C. Rylaarsdam. Philadelphia: Fortress, 1972.

Rendtorff, Rolf. "Geschichte und Überlieferung." *Studien zur Theologie der alttestamentlichen Überlieferungen*, 81–94. Edited by R. Rendtorff and K. Koch. Neukirchen Kreis Moers: Neukirchener Verlag, 1961.

———. "Hermeneutik des Alten Testaments als Frage nach der Geschichte." *ZTK* 57 (1960) 27–40.

———."Literärkritik und Traditionsgeschichte." *EvT* 27 (1967) 138–53. (In Swedish: *SEÅ* 31 [1966] 5–20.)

Reuss, Eduard. "Richard Simon." *RE*, XIV (1st ed., Gotha 1861) 399–408.

Reventlow, Henning Graf. "Kultisches Recht im Alten Testament." *ZTK* 60 (1963) 267–304.

Richardson, Ernest Cushing. "Oral Tradition, Libraries and the Hexateuch." *PTR* 3 (1905) 191–215.

Richter, Wolfgang. *Die Bearbeitungen des "Retterbuches" in der deuteronomischen Epoche*. BBB 21. Bonn: Hanstein, 1964.

———. "Beobachtungen zur theologischen Systembildung in der alttestamentlichen Literatur anhand des 'kleinen geschichtlichen Credo.'" *Wahrheit und Verkündigung: Festschrift M. Schmaus*, I:175–212. Edited by L. Scheffczyk. Munich: Schöningh, 1967.

———.*Exegese als Literaturwissenschaft: Entwurf einer alttestamentlichen Literaturtheorie und Methodologie*. Göttingen: Vandenhoeck & Ruprecht, 1971.

———. *Die sogenannten vorprophetischen Berufungsberichte: Eine literaturwissenschaftliche Studie zu 1 Sam 9,1–10,16, Ex 3f. und Ri 6,11b–17*. FRLANT 101. Göttingen: Vandenhoeck & Ruprecht, 1970.

———. *Traditionsgeschichtliche Untersuchungen zum Richterbuch*. 2nd ed. BBB 18. Bonn: Hanstein, 1966.

Riesenfeld, Harald. *Jésus transfiguré: L'arrière-plan du récit évangélique de la transfiguration de Notre Seigneur*. ASNU 16. Copenhagen: Munksgaard, 1947.

Rignell, Lars Gösta. *Die Nachtgesichte des Sacharja: Eine exegetische Studie*. Translated by Christa-Maria Lyckhage. Lund: Gleerup, 1950.

Ringgren, Helmer. "Är den bibliska skapelseberättelsen en kulttext?" *SEÅ* 13 (1948) 9–21.

———. *Israelitische Religion*. Die Religionen der Menschheit, 26. Stuttgart: Kohlhammer, 1963. ET: *Israelite Religion*. Translated by David E. Green. Philadelphia: Fortress, 1966.

———."Literärkritik, Formgeschichte, Überlieferungsgeschichte: Erwägungen zur Methodenfrage der alttestamentlichen Exegese." *TLZ* 91 (1966) cols. 641–50.

———. "Litterärkritik, formhistoria, traditionshistoria—eller vad?" *RoB* 25 (1966) 45–56.

———. "Oral and Written Transmission in the O.T.: Some Observations." *ST* 3 (1949) 34–59.

———. *Religionens form och funktion*. Lund: Gleerup, 1968.

Robertson, Edward. *The Old Testament Problem: A Re-investigation, Together with Two Other Essays.* Manchester: Manchester University Press, 1950.

Rohland, E. *Die Bedeutung der Erwählungstraditionen Israels für die Eschatologie der alttestamentlichen Propheten.* Diss. Heidelberg, 1956.

Rost, Leonard. *Das kleine Credo und andere Studien zum Alten Testament.* Heidelberg: Quelle & Meyer, 1965.

———. "Sinaibund und Davidsbund." *TLZ* 72 (1947) cols. 129–34.

———. "Tradition, III: Im AT." *RGG*, VI (3rd ed., 1962) cols. 968–69.

Rowley, H. H. (ed.). *The Old Testament and Modern Study: A Generation of Discovery and Research.* Oxford: Clarendon, 1951.

———. "Ritual and the Hebrew Prophets." *JSS* 1 (1956) 338–60.

Rubow, Paul V. *Reflexioner over dansk og fremmed Litteratur: Nye kritiske Studier.* Copenhagen: Munksgaard, 1942.

———. "De tre Fortællere i Pentateuchen." *DTT* 3 (1940) 101–8.

The Sacral Kingship/La regalità sacra. (Contributions to the Central Theme of the VIIth International Congress for the History of Religions, Rome, April 1955). Studies in the History of Religions (Supplements to NUMEN) 4. Leiden: Brill, 1959.

Sæbø, Magne. "Die deuterosacharjanische Frage: Eine forschungsgeschichtliche Studie." *ST* 23 (1969) 115–40.

———. *Sacharja 9–14: Untersuchungen von Text und Form.* WMANT 34. Neukirchen-Vluyn: Neukirchener Verlag, 1969.

Sauer, Georg. "Die chronologischen Angaben in den Büchern Deut. bis 2. Kön." *TZ* 24 (1968) 1–14.

———. "Überlieferung." *BHH*, III (1966) cols. 2035–38.

Scharbert, J. "Die prophetische Literatur: Der Stand der Forschung." *ETL* 44 (1968) 346–06.

———. "Das Traditionsproblem im Alten Testament." *TTZ* 66 (1957) 321–35.

Schille, Gottfried. "Literarische Quellenhypothesen im Licht der Wahrscheinlichkeitsfrage." *TLZ* 97 (1972) cols. 331–40.

Schmid, Herbert. *Mose: Überlieferung und Geschichte.* BZAW 110. Berlin: Töpelmann, 1968.

———. "Der Stand der Moseforschung." *Judaica* 21 (1965) 194–221.

Schmidt, Johann Michael. "Erwägungen zum Verhältnis von Auszugs- und Sinaitradition." *ZAW* 82 (1970) 1–31.

———. "Vergegenwärtigung und Überlieferung: Bemerkungen zu ihren Verständnis im dtn.-dtr. Überlieferungsbereich." *EvT* 30 (1970) 169–200.

Scholder, Klaus. *Ursprünge und Probleme der Bibelkritik im 17. Jahrhundert: Ein Beitrag zur Entstehung der historischkritischen Theologie.* FGLP, X/33. Munich: Kaiser, 1966.

Schottroff, Willy. *'Gedenken' im alten Orient und im Alten Testament: Die Wurzel zākar im semitischen Sprachkreis.* WMANT 15. 2nd ed. Neukirchen-Vluyn: Neukirchener Verlag, 1967.

Schrey, Heinz-Horst. "Die alttestamentliche Forschung der sogenannten Uppsala-Schule." *TZ* 7 (1951) 321–341.

Schwarzwäller, Klaus. "Das Verhältnis Altes Testament—Neues Testament im Lichte der gegenwärtigen Bestimmungen." *EvT* 29 (1969) 281–307.

Schwertner, Siegfried. "Erwägungen zu Moses Tod und Grab in Dtn 34,5.6." *ZAW* 84 (1972) 25–46.

Seebass, Horst. *Mose und Aaron, Sinai und Gottesberg.* Abhandlungen zur Evangelischen Theologie, 2. Bonn: Bouvier, 1962.

Segert, Stanislav. "Zur Methode der alttestamentlichen Literarkritik (Quellenscheidung und Überlieferungsgeschichte)." *ArOr* 24 (1956) 610–21.

Seitz, Gottfried. *Redaktionsgeschichtliche Studien zum Deuteronomium.* BWANT V/13. Stuttgart: Kohlhammer, 1971.

Sellin, Ernst. *Einleitung in das Alte Testament*, bearbeitet von Georg Fohrer. 10th ed. Heidelberg: Quelle & Meyer, 1965. ET: Fohrer, *Introduction to the Old Testament.* Translated by D. E. Green. Nashville: Abingdon, 1968.

Simon, Richard. *Histoire critique du Vieux Testament.* (1st ed., 1678) 5th ed. Rotterdam: Reinier Leers, 1685.

———. [pseudonym: Le Prieur de Bolleville]. *Réponse au Livre intitulé Sentimens de quelques Theologiens de Hollande sur l'Histoire Critique du Vieux Testament.* Rotterdam: Reinier Leers, 1686.

Smend, Rudolf. *Elemente alttestamentlichen Geschichtsdenkens.* ThSt 95. Zürich: EVZ-Verlag, 1968.

———. "Das Gesetz und die Völker: Ein Beitrag zur deuteronomistischen Redaktionsgeschichte." *Probleme biblischer Theologie: Gerhard von Rad zum 70. Geburtstag,* 494–509. Edited by H. W. Wolff. Munich: Kaiser, 1971.

———. *Jahwekrieg und Stämmebund: Erwägungen zur ältesten Geschichte Israels.* FRLANT 84. 2nd ed. Göttingen: Vandenhoeck & Ruprecht, 1966. ET: *Yahweh War and Tribal Confederation: Reflections upon Israel's Earliest History.* Translated by Max Gray Rogers. Nashville: Abingdon, 1970.

———. *Das Mosebild von Heinrich Ewald bis Martin Noth.* BGBE 3. Tübingen: Mohr Siebeck, 1959.

———. "Nachruf auf Martin Noth." *Gesammelte Studien zum Alten Testament,* II:139–165. By Martin Noth. TB 39. Munich: Kaiser, 1969.

———. "Überlieferungsgeschichtliche Forschung." *VF* 1960/62 (1963/65) 35–42.

———. "Zur Frage der altisraelitischen Amphiktyonie." *EvT* 31 (1971) 623–30.

Smith, Morton. "A Comparison of Early Christian and Early Rabbinic Tradition." *JBL* 82 (1963) 169–76.
———. "The Present State of Old Testament Studies." *JBL* 88 (1969) 19–35.
Soggin, J. Alberto. "Alttestamentliche Glaubenszeugnisse und geschichtliche Wirklichkeit." *TZ* 17 (1961) 385–98.
———. "Geschichte, Historie und Heilsgeschichte im Alten Testament: Ein Beitrag zur heutigen theologisch-hermeneutischen Diskussion." *TLZ* 89 (1964) cols. 721–36.
Soisalon-Soininen, Ilmari. *Aabrahamista Joosefiin*. Helsinki: Kirjayhtymä, 1965.
———."Begreppet funktion i gammaltestamentlig traditionsforskning." *SEÅ* 33 (1968) 55–67.
———. "Der Charakter der ältesten alttestamentlichen Erzähltraditionen." *Temenos* 4 (Turku 1969) 128–39.
———. "Die Urgeschichte im Geschichtswerk des Jahwisten." *Temenos* 6 (Turku 1970) 130–41.
Spinoza, Benedict de. *Tractatus theologico-politicus*. Hamburg (actually Amsterdam), 1670.
Staerk, W. "Zur alttestamentlichen Literarkritik: Grundsätzliches und Methodisches." *ZAW* 42 (1924) 34–74.
Stamm, J. J., with M. E. Andrew. *The Ten Commandments in Recent Research*. SBT 2/2. London: SCM, 1967. (Translated with additions by M. E. Andrew, from: Stamm, *Der Dekalog im Lichte der neueren Forschung*. 2nd ed. Bern: Haupt, 1962.)
Steck, Odil Hannes. "Genesis 12,1–3 und die Urgeschichte des Jahwisten." *Probleme biblischer Theologie: Gerhard von Rad zum 70. Geburtstag*, 525–54. Edited by H. W. Wolff. Munich: Kaiser, 1971.
———. *Israel und das gewaltsame Geschick der Propheten: Untersuchungen zur Überlieferung des deuteronomistischen Geschichtsbildes im Alten Testament, Spätjudentum und Urchristentum*. WMANT 23. Neukirchen-Vluyn: Neukirchener Verlag, 1967.
———. "Das Problem theologischer Strömungen in nachexilischer Zeit." *EvT* 28 (1968) 445–58.
———. *Überlieferung und Zeitgeschichte in den Elia-Erzählungen*. WMANT 26. Neukirchen-Vluyn: Neukirchener Verlag, 1968.
Steffen, Uwe. *Das Mysterium von Tod und Auferstehung: Formen und Wandlungen des Jona-Motivs*. Göttingen: Vandenhoeck & Ruprecht, 1963.
Steiger, Lothar. "Offenbarungsgeschichte und theologische Vernunft: Zur Theologie W. Pannenbergs." *ZTK* 59 (1962) 88–113.
Steinmann, Jean. *Richard Simon et les origines de l'exégèse biblique*. Paris: Brouwer, 1960.

Stummer, Friedrich. *Die Bedeutung Richard Simons für die Pentateuchkritik.* Alttestamentliche Abhandlungen, III/4. Münster: Aschendorff, 1912.

Tournay, R. J. "Les anciens manuscrits hébreux récemment découverts." *RB* 56 (1949) 204-33.

Unger, Rudolf. *Literaturgeschichte als Problemgeschichte: Zur Frage geistesgeschichtlicher Synthese, mit besonderer Beziehung auf Wilhelm Dilthey.* SGK, Geisteswiss. Klasse 1. Berlin: Deutsche Verlagsgesellschaft für Politik und Geschichte, 1924.

Vansina, Jan. *Oral Tradition: A Study in Historical Methodology.* Translated by H. M. Wright. Chicago: Aldine, 1965.

Vollmer, Jochen. *Geschichtliche Rückblicke und Motive in der Prophetie des Amos, Hosea und Jesaja.* BZAW 119. Berlin: de Gruyter, 1971.

Volz, Paul, and Wilhelm Rudolph. *Der Elohist als Erzähler: Ein Irrweg der Pentateuchkritik?* BZAW 63. Giessen: Töpelmann, 1933.

Vries, S. J. de. Review of E. Nielsen's *Die Zehn Gebote, VT* 16 (1966) 530-34.

Wallis, Gerhard. *Geschichte und Überlieferung: Gedanken über alttestamentliche Darstellungen der Frühgeschichte Israels und der Anfänge seines Königtums.* Arbeiten zur Theologie, II/13. Stuttgart: Calwer, 1968.

Ward, Roger Lemuel. *The Story of David's Rise: A Traditio-Historical Study of I Samuel xvi 14 - II Samuel v.* Diss. Nashville, 1967.

Weidmann, Helmut. *Die Patriarchen und ihre Religion im Licht der Forschung seit Julius Wellhausen.* FRLANT 94. Göttingen: Vandenhoeck & Ruprecht, 1968.

Weippert, Manfred. *Die Landnahme der israelitischen Stämme in der neueren wissenschaftlichen Diskussion: Ein kritischer Bericht.* FRLANT 92. Göttingen: Vandenhoeck & Ruprecht, 1967. ET: *The Settlement of the Israelite Tribes in Palestine.* SBT 2/21. London: SCM, 1971.

Weiser, Artur. "Die Legitimation des Königs David: Zur Eigenart und Entstehung der sogen. Geschichte von Davids Aufstieg." *VT* 16 (1966) 325-54.

Wellhausen, Julius. *Die Composition des Hexateuchs und der historischen Bücher des Alten Testaments.* 4th ed. (= 3rd ed.). Berlin: de Gruyter, 1963.

———. *Grundrisse zum Alten Testament.* Edited by Rudolf Smend. TB 27. Munich: Kaiser, 1965.

———. *Israelitische und jüdische Geschichte.* 7th ed. Berlin: Reimer, 1914. (9th ed. Berlin: de Gruyter, 1958.)

———. *Prolegomena zur Geschichte Israels.* 6th ed. Berlin: de Gruyter, 1927. ET: *Prolegomena to the History of Ancient Israel.* (With a reprint of the article "Israel" from the Encyclopædia Britannica.) Translated by J. Sutherland Black and Allan Menzies. New York: Meridian, 1957.

———. "Zur apokalyptischen Literatur." *Skizzen und Vorarbeiten* 6 (1899) 215-49.

Westermann, Claus. "Arten der Erzählung in der Genesis." *Forschung am Alten Testament: Gesammelte Studien*, 9-91. TB 24. Munich: Kaiser, 1964.

———. "Zur Auslegung des Alten Testaments." *Die hermeneutische Frage in der Theologie*, 181-239. Edited by O. Loretz and W. Strolz. Schriften zum Weltgespräch 3. Freiburg: Herder, 1968.

———, ed. *Probleme alttestamentlicher Hermeneutik: Aufsätze zum Verstehen des Alten Testaments*. TB 11. 3rd ed. Munich: Kaiser, 1968. ET: *Essays on Old Testament Hermeneutics*. Edited by Claus Westermann and James L. Mays. Richmond: John Knox, 1963.

Westphal, Alexandre. *Les Sources du Pentateuque, étude de critique et d'histoire. I: Le problème littéraire*. Paris: Librairie Fischbacher, 1888.

Whybray, Roger Norman. *The Succession Narrative: A Study of II Samuel 9-20; I Kings 1 and 2*. SBT 2/9. London: SCM, 1968.

Widengren, Geo. *The Ascension of the Apostle and the Heavenly Book*. (King and Saviour III) UUÅ 1950:7. Uppsala: Lundequist, 1950.

———. *Hochgottglaube im alten Iran: Eine religionsphänomenologische Untersuchung*. UUÅ 1938:6. Uppsala: Lundequist, 1938.

———. "King and Covenant." *JSS* 2 (1957) 1-32.

———. *The King and the Tree of Life in Ancient Near Eastern Religion*. (King and Saviour IV.) UUÅ 1951:4. Uppsala: Lundequist, 1951.

———. *Literary and Psychological Aspects of the Hebrew Prophets*. UUÅ 1948:10. Uppsala: Lundequist, 1948.

———. "Oral Tradition and Written Literature among the Hebrews in the Light of Arabic Evidence, with Special Regard to Prose Narratives." *AcOr* 23 (1959) 201-62.

———. *Psalm 110 och det sakrala kungadömet i Israel*. UUÅ 1941:7,1 Uppsala: Lundequist, 1941.

———. *Religionsphänomenologie*. Berlin: de Gruyter, 1969.

———. "Det sakrala kungadömet bland öst- och västsemiter." *RoB* 2 (1943) 49-75.

———. *Sakrales Königtum im Alten Testament und im Judentum*. Stuttgart: Kohlhammer, 1955.

———. *Till det sakrala kungadömets historia i Israel*. HS, I/3. Stockholm: Diakonistyr., 1947.

———. "Tradition and Literature in Early Judaism and in the Early Church." *Numen* 10 (1963) 42-83.

Wikander, Stig. "Indoeuropeisk religion." *RoB* 20 (1961) 3-13.

Willi, Thomas. *Herders Beitrag zum Verstehen des Alten Testaments*. BGH 8. Tübingen: Mohr Siebeck, 1971.

Willis, John T. "I. Engnell's Contributions to Old Testament Scholarship." *TZ* 26 (1970) 385–94.
Wilpert, Gero von. *Sachwörterbuch der Literatur*. 5th ed. Stuttgart: Kröner, 1969.
Witter, Henning Bernhard. *Jura Israelitarum in Palaestinam*. Hildesiae, 1711.
Wolff, Hans Walter. *Amos' geistige Heimat*. WMANT 18. Neukirchen-Vluyn: Neukirchener Verlag, 1964. ET: *Amos the Prophet: The Man and His Background*. Translated by Foster R. McCurley. Philadelphia: Fortress, 1973.
———. *Bibel: Das Alte Testament: Eine Einführung in seine Schriften und in die Methoden ihrer Erforschung*. Themen der Theologie, 7. Stuttgart: Kreuz-Verlag, 1970.
———. "Gespräch mit Gerhard von Rad." *Probleme biblischer Theologie: Gerhard von Rad zum 70. Geburtstag*, 648–58. Edited by H. W. Wolff. Munich: Kaiser, 1971.
———. "Hoseas geistige Heimat." *TLZ* 81 (1956) cols. 83–94. Also in *Gesammelte Studien zum Alten Testament*, 232–50. TB 22. Munich: Kaiser, 1964.
———. "Das Kerygma des deuteronomistischen Geschichtswerks." *ZAW* 73 (1961) 171–86. Also in *Ges. Stud.*, 308–24.
———. "Das Kerygma des Jahwisten." *EvT* 24 (1964) 73–98.
———. "Das Thema 'Umkehr' in der alttestamentlichen Prophetie." *ZTK* 48 (1951) 129–48. Also in *Ges. Stud.*, 130–50.
Woude, Adam Simon van der. *Uittocht en Sinai*. Nijkerk: Callenbach, 1960.
Woudstra, M. H. "Prophecy, Magic, and the Written Word." *CTJ* 2 (1967) 53–56.
Wright, G. Ernest. "Archeology and Old Testament Studies." *JBL* 77 (1958) 39–51.
———. *The Old Testament and Theology*. New York: Harper & Row, 1969.
Zimmerli, Walther. "Alttestamentliche Traditionsgeschichte und Theologie." *Probleme biblischer Theologie: Gerhard von Rad zum 70. Geburtstag*, 632–47. Edited by H. W. Wolff. Munich: Kaiser, 1971.
———. *Ezechiel*. 2 vols. BKAT 13. Neukirchen-Vluyn: Neukirchener Verlag, 1969 (1955ff.).
———. "Form- und Traditionsgeschichte im Dienst der Verkündigung." *ZKT* 92 (1970) 72–81.
———. "Die historisch-kritische Bibelwissenschaft und die Verkündigungsaufgabe der Kirche." *EvT* 23 (1963) 17–31.
———. "In Memoriam Martin Noth." *VT* 18 (1968) 409–13.
———. Review of G. von Rad's *Theologie des Alten Testaments*, *VT* 13 (1963) 100–111.
———. Review of M. Noth's *Geschichte Israels*, GGA 207 (1953) 1–13.

Zimmermann, H. *Neutestamentliche Methodenlehre: Darstellung der historisch-kritischen Methode.* 2nd ed. Stuttgart: Katholisches Bibelwerk, 1968.

Index of Authors

Page numbers in bold indicate sections devoted exclusively to the traditio-historical work of the particular scholar.

Ackroyd, Peter R. 15
Adam, Gottfried 19
Ahlström, Gösta W. 231, **241–44**, 265, 267, 290–91, 294, 297, 301, 306
Albertz, Rainer 307–8
Albright, William Foxwell 70–72, 127, 129–30, 148–50, 152–55, 159
Alt, Albrecht 7, 67, **73–76**, 77, 86, 117, 123, 126, 128–29, 149, 152–53, 269
Altmann, Alexander 12, 114, 159
Alver, Brynjulf 240
Anderson, Berhard W. 15, 62, 110, 115–16, 126, 129–30, 149, 151, 155, 302
Anderson, George W. 185, 203, 222, 228, 288
Andrew, Maurice E. 269
Astruc, Jean 35, 45–47, 49, 70
Auerbach, Elias 268
Bardtke, Hans 45
Barr, James 10, 13, 79, 91, 99–101, 103, 105, 107, 109
Barstad, Hans 304
Barth, Christoph 96, 101
Barth, Hermann 10–11, 13–15, 17–20, 23–25, 28, 140, 142, 144, 147
Baumgärtel, Friedrich 102, 106
Becker, Joachim 16, 241
Becking, Bob 304
Begrich, Joachim 68, 179
Bentzen, Aage 11, 165, 181, 198, 221, 224, 228, 235, **255–60**, 262, 287–88, 294–96

Bernhardt, Karl-Heinz 288, 294
Bernus, A. 37, 42–43
Berquist, Jon L. 314
Bertholet, A. 187, 236, 258–59, 290
Bevan, Anthony Ashley 71, 234
Beyerlin, Walter 82
Biram, Avraham 304–5
Birkeland, Harris 8, 18, 64, 70, 156, 177, 179, **182–85**, 187, 189–92, 196, 198, 201, 202, 205, 217, 225–26, 228–29, 231, 233–34, 237, 255, 264–67, 276, 292, 298, 305
Bleek, F. 52
Boecker, Hans Jochen 269
Boer, P. A. H. de 8
Bonfrère, Jacques 34, 39
Bossuet, Jacques Benigne 38, 40, 70
Botterweck, G. J. 269
Bourke, David J. 268
Bousset, Wilhelm 57, 143
Bowden, John 308, 310
Braudel, Ferdinand 307
Briant, Pierre 314
Bright, John 82, 127, 130, 148–53, 155, 157–60
Brueggemann, Walter 104, 313
Buber, Martin 93, 94
Budde, Karl 202
Buhl, Frants 188
Bultmann, Rudolf 106
Burrows, Millar 239

INDEX OF AUTHORS

Calvin, John 33–36, 40, 46, 70
Carlson, R. A. 9, 18–19, 22, 28, 54, 121–22, 124, 165, 167, **245–53**, 276–77, 291, 293, 297–98, 301
Carlstadt, Andreas B. von 34, 39
Carroll, Robert 311
Caspari, Wilhelm 120
Cassuto, Umberto 172, 204
Causse, A. 242
Chadwick, H. Munro 71, 84
Chadwick, N. Kershaw 71, 84
Chemnitz, Martin 33, 35–36, 40, 70
Childs, Brevard S. 8, 102, 153–54
Clark, Warren Malcolm 86
Clericus, Johannes 43, 46
Coats, George W. 115
Conzelmann, Hans 96, 105
Cross, Frank Moore, Jr. 114, 159–60
Crüsemann, Frank 307–8
Cryer, Frederick H. 304, 308
Culley, Robert C. 267, 291–92, 294
Dagut, Menachem B. 123
Dahse, J. 204
Danell, G. A. 223
Daniels, Peter T. 314
Davies, Philip R. 304, 306
Dibelius, Martin 143
Diepold, Peter 14, 121, 122
Diestel, Ludwig 33, 37, 43
Dietrich, Walter 122, 308
Duhm, Bernhard 263
Eagleton, Terry 310
Eichhorn, Albert 47, **57–58**, 67, 143, 297
Eichrodt, Walther 96, 101
Eising, Hermann 117
Eissfeldt, Otto 47, 179, 210, 224, 257–58, 288, 295–96, 298
Engnell, Ivan 7–9, 18–20, 22–23, 28–29, 54, 64–65, 70, 83–84, 93, 112, 119, 121, 124, 148, 156, 160–61, 165–67, 169, 174, 177, 180, 184–85, 189–91, 195–96, **197–220**, 221–34, 237–38, 240–43, 245–50, 253, 256–61, 263–65, 267, 274, 277–79, 284, 289–99, 302, 316
Ewald, Heinrich 52–53, 68
Fohrer, Georg 5, 18–19, 23, 80, 104, 120, 128, 269, 288
Frankfort, Henri 295
Frazer, James 71
Freedman, David Noel 148, 159–60
Frenzel, Elisabeth 11–12
Fridrichsen, Anton 197
Fritz, Volkmar 117
Fuss, Werner 121
Gadamer, Hans-Georg 1, 107
Gandz, Solomon 1, 70–71, 84
Garbini, Giovanni 310
Geddes, A. 52
Gelin, A. 16
Gerhard, Johann 33
Gerhardsson, Birger 1, 229, 290, 293
Gerstenberger, Erhard 74, 268–69
Gese, Hartmut 100, 106, **135–39**, 142, 271
Geyer, Hans-Georg 101
Gispen, W. H. 70, 72
Gloege, Gerhard 99
Golka, Friedemann 153
Gordon, Cyrus H. 127
Goshen-Gottstein, Moshe 281
Gottlieb, Hans 249
Gottwald, Norman 310–12
Grabbe, Lester L. 314
Graf, Karl Heinrich 37, 43, 52
Gray, Edward McQueen 34, 42–43, 47
Green, W. H. 204
Grelot, Pierre 107
Gressmann, Hugo 19, 57, 59, **67–69**, 70, 75, 77, 87, 111, 119–20, 123, 126, 131–32, 152, 172, 174, 203, 208, 297
Grønbæk, Jakob H. 24, 249
Grønbech, Vilhelm 166
Gross, H. 12
Gunkel, Hermann 2, 7, 9, 12, 17, 22, 28, 46, 48, 51–53, 55, **57–66**, 67–72, 74, 77, 79, 84, 87–94, 96, 111, 113, 115, 126, 129, 131–32, 143, 152, 160, 166–67, 169, 172, 175, 186, 199, 202–4, 208, 242–43, 289, 296–97

INDEX OF AUTHORS

Gunneweg, Antonius H. J.   18, 64, 178, 198–99, 202, 213, 225, 232, 235–37, 240, 264, 266–68, 288–90, 293, 298
Güterbock, Hans Gustav   232
Guthrie, H. H., Jr.   13
Güttgemanns, Erhardt   48, 65, 292
Haag, Herbert   270
Haldar, Alfred   64, 213, **223–28**, 229, 237, 265
Halévy, J.   204
Hanson, Paul   313
Harrelson, Walter   15
Hasel, Gerhard F.   15
Heinemann, Günter   269
Hempel, Johannes   9, 13, 70–72, 101, 202, 267
Henke, Heinrich P. C.   49
Henry, Marie-Louise   15, 104
Herberg, Will   100
Herder, Johann Gottfried   **47–49**, 51, 58
Herrmann, Siegfried   19, 54, 116, 129–30, 148, 152, 155–57, 159–60
Hertzberg, Hans Wilhelm   107, 249–50, 275
Hesse, Franz   96, 101–2, 154
Hobbes, Thomas   34, 39
Holm-Nielsen, Svend   241–42, 295
Hölscher, Gustav   120
Honecker, Martin   99, 101–2
Honko, Lauri   240
Hornig, Gottfried   42, 47
Horst, Friedrich   276
Humbert, P.   227, 257
Hupfeld, Hermann   52
Hvidberg, Flemming   241
Hyatt, J. Philip   260
Hylander, Ivar   69, 119, **174–77**, 190–91, 194
Hylmö, Gunnar   202
Ibn Ezra, A. b. M.   34, 39
Ilgen, Karl David   47, 70
Jacob, B.   204
Jacob, Edmond   96
Jansma, Taeke   279–80
Jensen, Kjeld   206
Jepsen, Alfred   18, 117, 120, 123, 271, 273, 276, 278
Jirku, Anton   70–71, 127
Jobling, David   310
Johnson, Aubrey Rodway   224–25, 288
Jones, Douglas   192
Jousse, Marcel   71, 84
Junghans, Hans-Martin   268
Kahle, Paul   281
Kaiser, Otto   19–20, 252
Kapelrud, Arvid S.   121, 165, 207, 222–23, 245, 255, 258, **260–64**, 269, 294, 298, 301
Kaufmann, Yehezkel   123, 127, 206
Kellermann, Ulrich   125
Kent, Charles Foster   70–71
King, Philip J.   308
Kittel, G.   13
Kittel, R.   126, 204, 278
Klatt, Werner   17, 57–59, 61–63, 65–66, 90
Klostermann, August   **55–56**, 117, 131, 204, 206, 283
Knauf, Ernest Axel   304
Knierim, Rolf   13
Knight, Douglas A.   308
Koch, Klaus   12, 17–20, 23–25, 29, 99, 147, 277, 288
Köhler, Ludwig   96
König, E.   204
Kraus, Hans-Joachim   7, 28, 34–37, 39–43, 47–48, 57, 65, 69, 79, 83, 90, 93, 98–99, 102–3, 107, 109, 117, 119–20, 124, 132, 156, 241–42, 288, 295, 301
Kuenen, Abraham   52
Kümmel, W.   19
Læssøe, J.   232, 236, 266
Lamarche, Paul   278, 284
Lande, Irene   11
Lapide, Cornelis   34, 36, 39, 40
Le Clerc, Jean. *See* Clericus, Johannes
Lemche, Niels Peter   305, 307–8, 314
Lenski, Gerhard   308
Levy, Thomas E.   308

Lindblom, Johannes **185-89**, 212, 224, 229, 257, 260, 291
Lindhagen, Curt 224
Liverani, Mario 306
Lods, Adolphe 45-46, 70, 72, 127
Lohr, C. H. 267, 294
Long, Burke O. 153
Lord, Albert Bates 8, 65, 84, 292-93
Loretz, Oswald 11
Luther, Martin 33
Lutz, Hanns-Martin 282, 284
Maag, V. 101, 109
Mahnke, Allan W. 308
Majus, Johann Heinrich 37
Margival, H. 37, 43, 44
Masius, Andreas 34, 36, 39, 40
Meier, E. 270
Mendenhall, George E. 269
Merendino, Rosario Pius 122
Metzger, Martin 35, 46, 127
Meyers, Carol 312
Michelet, S. 191
Mildenberger, Friedrich 99, 102, 106, 249
Mitchell, Hinckley G. T. 276
Moe, Moltke 71, 115, 267, 294
Möhlenbrink, Kurt 123
Moor, Johannes C. de 266
Mowinckel, Sigmund 8, 18, 28, 52, 59, 64-65, 70, 77, 82, 106, 121, 123, 125, 127, 131, 152, 165-67, **169-71**, 172-73, 180, 182-83, 188, **190-96**, 198-99, 201-2, **208-12**, 213-18, 222, 224-25, 229, 234, 237, 242, 245, 247, 255-56, 258, 260-61, 265, 267, 284, 289-90, 292-94, 298
Murtonen, A. 293
Nachtigal, Johann Christoph **49-51**, 64, 70, 169, 270
Naveh, Joseph 304-5
Neher, André 127
Nicholson, E. W. 122
Niditch, Susan 311
Nielsen, Eduard 8, 10, 18-20, 28, 52, 54-55, 59, 63-64, 165, 167, 172, 222-23, 234, 241-43, 245, 247, 250, 255, **264-75**, 289-90, 295, 299
North, C. R. 222, 266, 288-89, 292
Noth, Martin 2, 5-7, 13, 17-19, 22, 25, 28, 49, 52-54, 66, 68, 70, 73-75, 77-78, 81, 84, 92, 94, 108, **109-30**, 131-33, 135-36, 138-39, 148-60, 167, 174, 198-99, 205-7, 229, 246, 248-50, 252-53, 256-57, 260-62, 276, 278, 288, 294-97, 302-3, 306, 317
Nübel, Hans-Ulrich 249
Nyberg, Henrik Samuel 8-9, 18, 64-65, 70, 72, 165-67, 169, 173, 175, **177-82**, 184-85, 189-90, 192-93, 196-204, 210, 217, 221-23, 225-26, 228-29, 231, 237, 239, 242, 245, 247-48, 264-66, 274, 278-79, 288-90, 293, 298
Oesterley, William O. E. 127
Olmstead, Albert T. 127
Olrik, Axel 71, 115, 267, 294
Orlinsky, Harry M. 127-28
Östborn, Gunnar 223
Ottosson, Magnus 245, 250
Otzen, Benedikt 24, 268, 278, 282-84
Pannenberg, Wolfhart 99-102, 106
Pascal, Blaise 35, 40, 70
Patte, Daniel 316
Pedersen, Johannes 7, 54, 84, 131, 160, 166, **171-73**, 183, 190-91, 201, 204-6, 222, 224, 229, 232, 236, 255, 259, 264
Penchansky, David 308
Pereira, Bento 34, 39
Peri, Chiara 306
Perlitt, Lothar 53, 172
Peyrère, Isaak de la 34, 36, 39, 40
Pfeiffer, Robert H. 218
Pippin, Tina 310
Ploeg, J. van der 178, 213, 217, 235, 237, 240, 288-91, 293
Plöger, Otto 15, 284, 313
Porteous, Norman W. 15
Porter, J. R. 233
Procksch, Otto 90, 112
Pury, Albert de 304
Quell, Gottfried 224

INDEX OF AUTHORS

Rabast, Karlheinz 270
Rad, Gerhard von 2, 6, 9-10, 15, 18-19, 22, 28, 49, 52-55, 65-66, 68-70, 74, 76, **77-109,** 110-14, 116, 118, 121-22, 124, 126, **128-33,** 135, 139, 148, 154-55, 159-60, 167, 174-75, 192, 196, 201, 204, 248-49, 260, 272, 275, 302, 305
Rast, Walter E. 19, 24-25, 29, 160
Redditt, Paul L. 308
Reischle, Max 61
Rendtorff, Rolf 19-20, 29, 99-102, 129, 220, 245, 247, 288, 292, 296, 302-3
Reuss, Eduard 38
Reventlow, Henning Graf 269
Ricciotti, Giuseppe 127
Richardson, Ernest Cushing 36, 72
Richter, Wolfgang 10-13, 17-21, 23-24, 28, 54, 80, 123, **139-42,** 143, 147, 153, 157, 243, 247, 267, 276, 298
Riesenfeld, Harald 229, 294
Rignell, Lars Gösta 179
Ringgren, Helmer 18-20, 23, 165, 197-98, 200, 218, 222-23, 232, **238-41,** 244, 247-48, 265, 267, 288, 291-92, 294-99, 301
Robertson, Edward 55
Robinson, H. Wheeler 9, 13, 70, 267
Robinson, Theodore H. 127
Rohland, E. 15, 97
Römer, Thomas 304
Rost, Leonhard 80-81, 97, 249
Rowley, H. H. 28, 224, 288, 292
Rubow, Paul V. 172
Rudolph, Wilhelm 172
Rupprecht, E. 204
Sæbø, Magne 19, 28, 107, 139, 157, 165, 167, 201, 246, 255, **275-86,** 291-92, 298-99, 301
Said, Edward 316
Sauer, Georg 123
Scharbert, J. 18, 288, 292-93, 297
Schille, Gottfried 22
Schmid, Herbert 116
Schmidt, Johann Michael 6, 82, 132, 270

Schneemelcher, Wilhelm 150
Scholder, Klaus 33
Schottroff, Willy 8
Schrey, Heinz-Horst 198, 228, 288, 295
Schüssler Fiorenza, Elisabeth 316
Schwarzwäller, Klaus 105
Schwertner, Siegfried 116
Seebass, Horst 117
Segert, Stanislav 265, 268
Segovia, Fernando F. 317
Seitz, Gottfried 123
Sellin, Ernst 18, 19, 23, 127
Semler, Johann Salomo 42, 47
Simon, Richard 2, 28, **33-44,** 45-47, 51, 130
Smend, Rudolf 54-55, 68, 122, 126, 128, 149, 153-54, 158
Smith, Morton 150-51, 153, 229, 313
Smith-Christopher, Daniel L. 314
Söderblom, Nathan 166
Soggin, J. Alberto 100, 102
Soisalon-Soininen, Ilmari 240, 245, 301
Spinoza, Benedict de 34, 36-37, 39, 40
Stade, Bernhard 276
Staerk, W. 69, 172
Stager, Lawrence E. 308
Stalker, David M. G. 10, 95
Stamm, J. J. 269
Steck, Odil Hannes 10-11, 13-15, 17-20, 23-25, 29, 62, 86, 140, **142-46,** 147, 313
Steffen, Uwe 12
Steggemann, Wolfgang 308
Steiger, Lothar 101
Steinmann, Jean 37, 38, 43
Strolz, Walter 11
Stummer, Friedrich 33, 37, 43, 46-47
Swete, Henry Barclay 71, 235
Thompson, Thomas L. 304-5
Tolbert, Mary Ann 317
Tournay, R. J. 239
Troeltsch, Ernst 57
Unger, Rudolf 13
Van Seters, John 305
Vansina, Jan 266, 291

INDEX OF AUTHORS

Vater, Johann Severin — 52
Vatke, Wilhelm — 172
Vollmer, Jochen — 15, 104
Volz, Paul — 172
Vries, Simon J. de — 271, 273
Vriezen, Theodorus — 96
Wallis, Gerhard — 98, 102, 130
Ward, Roger Lemuel — 249
Weber, Max — 308
Weidmann, Helmut — 74, 117, 151
Weinberg, Joel — 314
Weippert, Helga — 306
Weippert, Manfred — 129, 149, 151, 153, 306
Weiser, Artur — 249
Wellhausen, Julius — 2, 17, **51-55**, 59, 64, 68, 74-75, 81, 84, 89, 93, 112, 117, 120, 126-27, 129, 151, 160, 172, 175, 191, 199-200, 203-4, 206, 209, 278, 296
Westermann, Claus — 5, 11, 19, 23, 25, 100, 106, 153
Westphal, Alexandre — 37, 43
Wette, Wilhelm M. L. de — 52
Whybray, Roger Norman — 249
Widengren, Geo — 28, 165, 167, 183, 190, 198-99, 208, 217, 222, **228-37**, 238, 240, 244, 247, 258, 266, 287, 291, 294, 301
Wiener, H. M. — 204
Wikander, Stig — 230
Willi, Thomas — 48-49
Willis, John T. — 197-98, 218
Wilpert, Gero von — 12, 23
Wilson, Robert R. — 315
Witter, Henning Bernhard — 45-47, 49
Wolff, Hans Walter — 13, 15, 18, 80, 85-86, 88, 91, 97, 103, 122, 124
Woude, Adam Simon van der — 81-82
Woudstra, M. H. — 236
Wrede, William — 57
Wright, G. Ernest — 96, 99, 148, 150-52, 154-55
Yahuda, A. S. — 204
Zimmerli, Walther — 10, 25, 68, 74, 80-81, 91, 97, 101, 104, 106-7, 116, 126, 137-39, 201, 294
Zimmermann, Heinrich — 19
Zimmern, Heinrich — 60

Index of Subjects

Aaron 116, 180, 206
Abraham 6, 35–36, 48, 74, 78, 86, 97, 114, 116–17, 151, 305
actualization/reactualization 5, 8, 10, 15, 20, 25, 29, 42, 62, 105–7, 133–34, 193, 196, 285
agglomeration 9–10, 21, 51–52, 98, 116–20, 131–33
Albright School 129, 148, 159
Amos 170, 187, 193, 213, 235, 258
amphictyony 73, 82, 84, 90, 113–14, 118, 127–29, 133, 181
Arab(ic) 35, 106, 183, 224–25, 229, 231–35, 238, 291
archaeology 68, 73, 127, 148–49, 151, 158, 219, 232

Balaam 84, 116
Bathsheba 248, 251
Begriff. *See* concept
Bethel 7, 94, 115
bruta facta 93, 102, 154

Canaan(ite) 78, 82, 100, 127, 159, 171, 203, 216, 241–42, 274, 296
canonization 9, 15, 107, 194, 195
charismatic-ecclectic interpretation 104–6
Christian interpretation and tradition 6, 20, 90, 105–8, 143–44, 259
Chronicler's History (Chr) 97, 103, 120–21, 124, 126, 205, 207, 247, 261, 285
composition 8–9, 18, 22–24, 29, 41, 45, 51–53, 64–66, 75, 78–79, 83–85, 88–89, 91–92, 108, 122, 124–26, 138, 140–41, 173, 179, 183–85, 188–89, 195–96, 200, 205, 207, 232, 243, 248, 250, 252–53, 257, 267, 269, 276, 278, 290, 294, 298
composition, oral. *See* oral composition
concept 11, 13, 15, 21, 23, 25, 96, 285
conquest/settlement and tradition 54, 78, 81–83, 85–86, 103, 114–16, 121, 123, 148–51, 159, 235, 273
continuity 15, 25, 132–33, 135, 154, 225–26, 263
covenant 35, 81–82, 97–98, 104, 115, 129, 159, 174, 269, 271, 273–74
credo, credenda 9, 79–83, 85, 87–88, 91, 95, 111–12, 118, 132–33
crystallization 13, 55, 83, 93–94, 97, 117, 131, 206
cult 7, 25, 29, 45, 55, 63, 68, 74–75, 78–80, 82–85, 91–92, 94, 97, 112, 115, 118, 124, 126, 129, 131–33, 156, 159, 166, 170–71, 177, 179, 190, 200, 202–4, 206, 216, 221, 224–25, 227, 230, 241–42, 260, 263, 287, 289, 294, 298, 314
cultural presuppositions, anachronistic 29, 53–54, 160–61, 212, 215–16, 219, 316

Daniel 195, 258
David 50, 73, 97–98, 103, 123, 125, 141, 203, 248–53, 285
Decalogue 50, 268–75, 299
deeds (acts) of Jahweh 36, 99, 100–105, 123

INDEX OF SUBJECTS

demythologizing   62, 240, 297
Deutero-Isaiah   104, 213, 262, 268, 310
Deutero-Zechariah   276–81, 284, 286, 299
Deuteronomist(ic)   51–52, 80, 103, 120–26, 141, 144, 145, 172, 204–5, 207, 242, 248, 250–52, 257, 262, 267, 273, 285
Deuteronomistic History (Dtr)   6, 22, 97, 103, 111, 120–26, 141, 205, 207, 269, 285
disciple, prophetic   7, 10, 170, 183, 187, 190, 193, 194, 195, 201, 210, 213, 214, 215, 216, 218, 230, 236, 244, 285
divine kingship. See sacral kingship
diwān-type   213, 216, 227, 258
documentary-literary method   22, 247

Endstadium 68, 87, 89, 98, 106, 111, 248, 276
elders   7, 273
election traditions   97
Elijah   10, 192–93, 216, 226
Elisha   192–93, 216
Elohist (E)   8, 51–53, 55, 64, 68, 88–91, 112, 118, 120–21, 141, 172, 180, 183, 204–5, 207, 257, 262
Endstadium   68, 87, 89, 98, 107, 112, 248, 276
epic techniques and laws   71, 115, 267
etiology   7, 67, 75, 82, 86, 90, 92, 115, 152–53, 171
evolutionism   54, 166, 172, 199–200, 203, 212, 215, 225, 287, 302, 316
exile   7–8, 50, 72, 81, 86, 103, 120, 137, 178–79, 182, 203, 217, 230, 241, 243, 247, 251–52, 293, 311
exodus and tradition   49, 81–85, 97–98, 114, 123, 127–28, 159, 262
external evidence 148–53, 172, 217, 224, 230–34, 238, 246, 266–68, 291, 295, 304
Ezekiel   104, 135–38, 235–36, 262, 285
Ezra   36, 40, 43, 125, 260–61

fable   7, 140
faith   9, 15, 25, 93–95, 100, 102, 111, 128–29, 159
fertility cult   260, 263
fixation, process of   8, 43, 62, 107, 116, 118, 143, 177, 195, 200, 236
flood story   94, 235
folklore   59, 71, 240
form   10–11, 21, 63, 67, 92, 149, 152, 173, 175, 189, 202, 211, 249, 252, 277, 281, 285–86, 297
form criticism (Formgeschichte)   9, 11, 19, 24, 58, 92, 95–97, 108–9, 120–21, 131–32, 137, 144, 147, 152, 155, 162, 190–91, 199, 203, 209, 240–41, 246, 263, 269, 271, 274, 276–77, 281, 286
formula   11, 67, 216
function   8, 10, 12, 83, 90, 92, 240, 251–52, 284, 296–97

Gattung   10–12, 14, 19, 21, 24, 59, 62–63, 80, 140, 149, 186
Gattungsgeschichte   2, 11, 58, 60, 62–66, 69, 140
genealogy   40, 48, 117, 125, 204
Gilead   245
Gilgal   7, 75, 83–84
Gilgamesh Epic   232
Greek(s)   71, 99, 230, 266

Haftpunkt   75, 115–16
Habakkuk   170, 194, 213
Heavenly Book   236
Heilsgeschichte   2–3, 54, 79–81, 84, 91, 95, 102–5, 108–9, 119, 124
Hexateuch   77–80, 83–84, 86–88, 95, 97, 100, 103, 108, 110–11, 118, 120–21, 131–34, 149, 257
"high-god" theory   166, 203, 221, 229, 294
historicity 39, 92, 140, 151–54, 159, 171, 176
history, picture of   54, 68, 75, 96, 100–101, 125, 133, 145, 149, 160
Hittite   232, 269, 271

INDEX OF SUBJECTS

Homeric studies 176
Hosea 170, 187, 193, 213, 235

Icelandic traditions 55, 176, 266
inspiration 33, 38–40, 42, 44, 70, 193, 201
interpretation/reinterpretation 5–6, 8, 10, 15–16, 20–21, 25, 29, 38, 42, 49, 51, 57, 62, 90, 97, 99, 103–7, 133, 154, 156, 160, 184–85, 194–96, 230, 244, 250, 284, 306, 310, 316
ipsissima verba 10, 180, 184, 195, 201, 208–9, 211, 214, 218, 298
Isaac 74, 115, 117
Isaiah 170, 190, 193, 201, 213, 226, 235, 239, 256, 285
Israel (northern kingdom) 7, 14, 94, 141, 145, 272
Itture sopherim 10

Jacob 10, 35–26, 65, 74, 114, 116–17
Jahwist (J) 8–9, 52–53, 55, 59, 64, 68, 79, 83–85, 87–92, 94–95, 112, 118, 120, 126, 132–33, 141, 172, 180, 183, 204–7, 257
Jeremiah 50, 104, 171, 213, 226, 235, 244, 262, 263, 285
Jerusalem 7, 14, 82, 97, 125, 129, 204, 212, 242–43, 262, 285, 295, 313
Job 39, 188–89
Joel 213, 260, 263
Joseph 65, 68, 117
Joshua 35–36, 39–40, 50, 67, 75, 78, 80, 83, 86, 97, 116, 311
Judah 7–8, 14
Judaism 6, 72, 107–8, 143–44, 179, 195, 201, 203, 206, 229, 258–59, 266, 291, 293
judge 113, 123, 129, 225, 273

Keret epic 248, 252
kerygma 85, 87, 92, 94–96, 101–2, 118, 124, 155
Kethib/Qere 10
king 123, 125, 224, 229, 242, 256, 260, 272, 275, 287
Korah 180
Koran 144, 178, 182–83, 233

land, promised 78–82, 86, 97
language 10, 23, 149, 167, 192, 195, 199, 239, 261, 263, 288
law 7, 21, 36, 40, 50, 55, 73, 82, 121–22, 145, 170–71, 178–79, 202, 204, 206, 226, 243, 262, 267, 269, 271, 273
Leah-tribes 129
Levites 6, 14, 138, 145, 226, 262, 273
linguistics 140, 142, 144, 148, 151, 204, 219, 246
literary criticism 9, 19, 24, 45, 51, 54, 57–59, 62, 65, 67, 69–70, 72, 108, 112, 121, 125, 131–32, 136–37, 139–40, 143, 147, 155, 160, 162, 166, 169, 171–75, 177, 180, 183, 185, 190–91, 195, 203–5, 207–9, 212, 214–16, 219, 221, 223, 227, 235, 240–41, 247, 249, 256, 259, 263, 265, 269, 274–75, 282, 287
literature, oral. *See* oral: literature
Literaturgeschichte 2, 22, 48, 62, 69, 171
liturgy-type 213, 216, 227, 258
"living tradition." *See* tradition: living
Lot 116

Masoretic text and tradition 166, 179, 200, 276, 278–81, 286
memory 8, 35, 114, 154, 159, 170, 180, 189, 192–93, 211, 236, 238–39, 242, 266–67
Mesopotamia 60–62, 231–32, 295
messianic 49, 212, 215–16, 218, 236, 251, 256, 285, 294
Micah 170, 187, 194
Moses 34, 36, 38, 40, 42–46, 50, 54, 68, 70, 78, 116–17, 122, 155, 158, 170, 180, 206, 224
motif 6, 11–12, 15, 19, 23, 27, 59, 67, 106, 135, 145, 147, 166, 174–75, 177, 188, 191, 203, 215, 219, 221, 223,

INDEX OF SUBJECTS

motif (continued) 228, 241–42, 248, 258–59, 264, 285, 296, 298
Motivgeschichte   11–12, 21, 276–77
Muhammed   182, 233, 236, 237
myth   57, 60–62, 87, 100, 159, 178, 182, 200, 224, 227, 232, 240, 242, 244, 248, 252, 256, 273, 275, 296–97, 311
myth-and-ritual   166, 287, 294

Nahum   170, 194, 213, 227
Nathan   243, 251
Nehemiah   125, 261
New Testament   22, 42, 57, 105–8, 216
nomads/seminomads   73, 235, 272, 289
notion   11, 13, 15, 19, 23, 28, 60, 62, 135, 142–44, 146–47, 296

oral
  composition   24, 29, 52, 64, 83, 196, 243, 267, 294
  literature   7, 83, 171, 202, 267, 291
  "oral/written" debate   7, 139, 169, 178–83, 186–87, 189, 192–93, 195, 200–205, 209–10, 213, 219, 222, 227, 229–34, 237–38, 243–44, 289–94
  transmission/tradition   7–8, 17–18, 20, 23, 29, 34, 45–46, 48–49, 60–62, 68–69, 71, 83, 110, 116, 118, 126, 139, 160–61, 166–67, 169, 171, 173, 176–83, 187, 189–92, 194–95, 197, 200, 203–10, 213–14, 216, 218–19, 221, 225, 228–33, 235–40, 242–44, 247, 250, 253, 256, 258–67, 274–75, 281, 283, 286–94, 297
Ortsgebundenheit   7, 75, 117, 152–53

Palestine   50, 63, 73–74, 86, 113–14, 116, 127–28, 145, 151, 179, 225, 232, 235, 273, 295
parenesis   80
patriarchal period and traditions   34–35, 59, 70, 74–75, 86, 93, 103, 114, 117, 127, 129, 149–51, 153, 158, 235, 240

Pentateuch   6, 13, 34, 39–40, 43–45, 47–48, 50–53, 55, 87, 109–12, 115, 119–21, 125–26, 129, 131–32, 148, 172, 191, 203, 209, 217, 237, 257, 260, 262, 297
plot   11, 12
politics   7, 127, 141, 156, 180, 225–27, 278, 301–2, 307, 309–15
post-history   15–16, 61
precompositional stage   51–54, 59, 200
prehistory   2, 11, 16, 18–19, 23, 45, 47, 53, 58, 62, 67, 78, 92, 113, 124–25, 128–31, 133, 139, 143, 147, 161, 252–53, 256, 258–59, 272, 278–79, 286, 293, 296, 299
preliterary stage   57, 62, 67, 89, 111–12, 132, 136, 143, 257, 297
Priestly document (P)   51–52, 55, 59–60, 89–90, 112, 118, 120, 138, 172, 180, 205, 206–7, 257, 262
priests   6, 14, 36, 44, 123, 138, 202, 206, 224–26, 230, 242, 273, 309, 311, 313–15
primeval history   86, 119
Problemgeschichte   11, 13, 21
promise and fulfillment   78, 85, 106, 108
prophetic speech   22, 40, 70, 96–98, 170, 186, 283
prophets   14, 43, 50, 105, 143–44, 166, 170, 179–80, 183, 186–87, 192–95, 201, 208–12, 214–16, 218, 224, 226–27, 235–36, 243, 298
Psalms   22, 49, 67, 170, 190, 202, 238, 241, 259, 262, 296

Qumran   106

Rachel   114, 116
rawi   202, 233
reactualization. *See* actualization/reactualization
redaction   9, 18–19, 22–23, 45, 49, 65, 70, 90, 110, 120, 122, 126, 136, 138, 141, 144, 180, 202, 205, 245, 247–48, 250, 252–53, 286

INDEX OF SUBJECTS

Religionsgeschichte 2, 57–58, 60, 62, 66, 67, 206, 294–97
respect for tradition. *See* tradition: respect for
revelation 74, 79, 82, 102, 103, 186, 194, 201

sacral/divine kingship 166, 197, 218, 221–22, 229, 256, 260, 287, 294–96
saga 6–7, 11, 48, 50, 53, 62, 64–65, 68, 75, 87, 90–94, 111, 177, 235
Samaria 44, 273
Samuel 50, 174, 249
Saul 73, 123, 174, 249
Schmelzofen der Gemeinschaft 56, 184–85, 217, 226, 228, 274, 292
Scripture 15, 33, 35, 37–38, 41, 70, 107–8
Shechem 7, 82, 84, 115, 268, 273, 274
Sinai events and tradition 51, 54, 81–87, 97–98, 103, 114, 116–17, 129, 159, 206, 273
Sitz im Leben 2, 7–8, 63, 65, 74, 79, 87, 140, 144–45, 166, 176, 240–42, 273–74, 289–90, 298
Solomon 123, 141, 249
source criticism 8, 22, 36, 38, 45–47, 49–54, 58–59, 62, 67–72, 90, 112, 119–23, 155–56, 159, 161, 172–73, 183, 191, 199, 202–4, 210–11, 214, 292, 297, 306
Stoff 11–12, 19, 21, 68, 111, 177
stratum 68–70, 83, 137–38, 257, 279
structural analysis 9, 91, 105, 140, 283
succession narrative 123, 249
Synoptic Gospels 144, 176
synthesis 14, 20, 24, 219, 299

Tammuz 263
Tetrateuch 120, 205–7, 257, 262
text criticism 19, 24, 72, 136, 143, 147, 175, 178, 200–201, 269, 274, 276–77, 279, 282
theme 6, 11–13, 15, 19, 23, 84, 111–20, 132, 133, 135, 285

theology and tradition. *See* tradition: theology and
Tiqqune sopherim 10
traditio 6–9, 18, 20, 24, 27, 36, 41, 43, 49, 51, 62–63, 66, 87, 98, 105–7, 118, 130, 133, 138, 143, 219, 223, 229, 231, 277, 282, 298
tradition
   definition of 5, 20–21, 132, 190, 201, 210, 246
   historical 97, 99–100, 103, 105, 121, 139, 160–61, 179, 226
   history and 51, 53, 54, 65, 75, 92, 98, 100–102, 108, 128, 130–31, 141, 144, 152, 155, 157, 160, 174–75, 211, 266
   living 9, 21, 49, 79, 87, 145, 179, 200, 216, 273, 281, 285, 290, 298
   prophetic 6, 7, 15, 50, 64, 69, 96, 103, 104, 105, 135, 143, 148, 156, 160, 161, 167, 169, 171, 187, 190, 192, 194, 208, 216, 225, 226, 228, 230, 235, 238, 243–44, 267, 283, 285, 289
   respect for 20, 124, 159, 176, 214, 250, 265, 279, 286, 298
   stratification of 41, 83, 139, 142, 156–57, 177, 209, 217–18, 228, 246, 248, 253, 257–58, 264, 276, 282, 292, 299
   streams of 14–15, 19, 23, 29, 135, 143, 147, 158, 181, 216, 297
   theology and 6, 95, 96, 97, 98, 108, 131, 158
tradition criticism 19, 65, 68, 87, 131–32, 139–40, 143, 156, 174
tradition history
   definition of 12, 17, 19, 21–24, 27, 108, 110, 122, 136, 139, 142–43, 147, 156, 174–75, 200, 209–10, 212, 214–15, 219, 245–46, 248, 274, 276, 286, 296, 298
   methodology 19–20, 23, 27, 72, 87, 95, 103–5, 107–8, 115, 119, 126, 131–32, 135–36, 139, 144, 147,

tradition history: methodology (continued)
  154–55, 157, 159, 162, 166, 174, 176, 180, 183, 185, 190–91, 195, 209–12, 214, 216, 218–19, 238, 245–47, 264–65, 272, 274, 276–77, 281, 286, 296, 298
traditum   6, 10–14, 16, 18, 24, 27, 41, 51, 58, 62, 66, 87, 91, 98, 104, 111, 118, 130, 132–33, 143, 214, 219, 223, 274, 277, 284, 292, 294, 296, 298
transmission/tradition
  ancient Near Eastern   7, 72, 178–79, 181–82, 217, 230–31, 237, 242, 266, 289
  oral. *See* oral: transmission/tradition
  reliability of   8, 20, 34, 36, 41, 46, 65, 70–71, 166, 178, 182, 199, 210, 217, 219, 243–44, 247, 266, 287, 290–91
transmitters/traditionists   6, 14, 19, 22, 72, 140, 143–45, 187, 193, 201–2, 206, 213, 228, 230, 234, 237, 239, 248, 266, 280, 284–85, 287, 293, 297
Trent, Council of   37, 41
Trito-Isaiah   285
typology   105

Ugarit(ic) (Ras Shamra)   232, 248, 260, 262, 266
Uppsala Circle   20, 28, 112, 197, 199, 208, 221–22, 228, 237, 240, 245, 255–56, 260, 263–64, 275, 282, 287

Vorstellung. *See* notion

Wilderness traditions   50, 54, 114–15, 117, 121–22, 127, 203
wisdom literature   97, 171, 202, 233, 285
writing
  literacy   71, 230, 232, 236
  magical power of   234, 236
  stage of committing to   16, 22, 24, 48, 64, 71, 83, 95, 110, 118, 171, 173, 189, 193, 195, 202, 204, 206, 230, 233, 235, 236, 237, 240, 290, 292
  tranmission/tradition, written   239
  transmission/tradition, written 7, 8, 16, 36, 40, 41, 42, 43, 49, 72, 122, 139, 179, 192, 195, 209, 210, 213, 214, 219, 229, 231, 232, 235, 236, 237, 238, 242, 244, 247, 257, 259, 267, 281, 287, 290, 291, 292, 293

Zakokites   138
Zechariah   104, 158, 285
Zephaniah   170, 194, 263